MEN OF LETTERS

IN COLONIAL MARYLAND

Men of Letters

IN COLONIAL MARYLAND

J. A. LEO LEMAY

THE UNIVERSITY OF TENNESSEE PRESS

KNOXVILLE

Library of Congress Catalog Card No. 79–177357
International Standard Book No. 0–87049–137–7

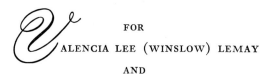
FOR
VALENCIA LEE (WINSLOW) LEMAY
AND
JOSEPH ALBERT LEMAY
WITH FILIAL LOVE

*O*UR FIRES ARE WOOD, OUR HOUSES AS GOOD;

OUR DIET IS SAWNEY & HOMINE.

DRINK, JUICE OF THE APPLE, TOBACCOE'S OUR STAPLE,

GLORIA TIBI DOMINE.

—from "an old Maryland song," quoted by Henry
Callister in a letter of August 1, 1743

PREFACE

The literature of colonial America continues to be neglected. Moses Coit Tyler wrote the best literary history of colonial America nearly a century ago—before the great collections of America had been made and before the major bibliographies had appeared. Tyler did an amazingly good job, but in 1878 the canon of colonial writers had not been established. For example, take the Maryland authors: Tyler knew of only one of Andrew White's three major promotion tracts—and that was a nineteenth-century English translation of a Latin text. Tyler never heard of Maryland's two dominant literary men, Richard Lewis and Dr. Alexander Hamilton, nor of the Reverend James Sterling, who had established a reputation as poet and playwright before emigrating to America. The literature of colonial Maryland is inadequately dealt with by Tyler, yet no one since has attempted to treat it in as much depth. The standard surveys, like the *Cambridge History of American Literature* (1917), *The Literary History of the United States* (1948), and *The Literature of the American People* (1951), all fire fleeting shots at the early writers as they chronologically safari on to the big game of the nineteenth and twentieth centuries.

Although there have been many political, economic, and institutional histories of the various American colonies, there has not previously appeared a thorough literary study. The major objection to a study of the literature of a colony is its narrow, even solipsistic, focus. Obviously early Maryland literature is a part of early American literature, which in turn is part of the literature written in the

English language in the seventeenth and eighteenth centuries. But just as each colony had its own political, economic, and institutional characteristics, so each had its distinctive literary history. Each colony focused on a main town, had its own socially and intellectually dominant individuals, and fostered its own literary circles. To be sure, Marylanders read the Pennsylvania or Virginia newspapers (as well as London periodicals) and corresponded with friends, relations, and business contacts in other colonies; but for the most part, they read the *Maryland Gazette*; they went to Annapolis to see plays, to have their pamphlets printed, or to convene with the other members of the legislature; and they wrote primarily for a circle of Maryland friends. Moreover, each colony went through several stages in its literary history: the period of promotion tracts, written to attract settlers to the new land; the literature of exploration, recounting the early explorations of the unknown land and describing the native Indians, wildlife, and terrain; the reports of wars with the savages—and with one another; the poems and essays that a few people found time and opportunity to write despite the frontier conditions; and, after the introduction of the printing presses, the gradual flourishing of literature, often associated with a newspaper, a club, a tavern, or simply an individual whose genius and interests made him the center of a literary circle. The stages in colonial literature came to various colonies at different times. Virginia and Massachusetts had nearly stopped producing promotion literature by the time that Maryland began. In Pennsylvania promotion literature did not begin for fifty more years, and in Georgia, not for a century.

At the conclusion of his magisterial *A History of American Literature, 1607–1763*, Moses Coit Tyler wrote that "the study of American Literature in the colonial time, is the study of a literature produced, in isolated portions, at the several local seats of English civilization in America." He observed that "the isolation of each colony or of each small group of colonies, reflects itself both in the form and in the spirit of our early literature,—giving to each colony or to each group its own literary accent." Although Tyler may overemphasize the unique characteristics peculiar to each colony, he is, I believe, basically correct in characterizing early American literature as local. The distinguishing qualities of the literature of each colony result, in part, from the personality and writings of a dominant literary individual, whether a Joseph Green of Boston, a Benjamin Franklin of Philadelphia, an Alexander Hamilton of Maryland, or a Robert Bolling of Virginia.

One might object that this book is primarily a series of biographies, that biography forces a pattern of organic life on literature and emphasizes matters largely irrelevant to literary history. Obviously I think that biography is an aspect of literary history, that the writer's parents, date and place of birth, education, associates, friends, politics, religion, philosophy, occupation, and general milieu—all may have something to do with a particular literary work. They may not, too, but if these facts are unknown, their possible influence cannot be determined. Secondly, the organic pattern (a beginning, early attempts, mastery, falling–off, and end) need not be imposed by a biographical approach, either on an author, a literary work, or a literary history. A writer may, like George Alsop, write only one work, or he may, like Ebenezer Cook, write his best effort first. Furthermore, the biographical approach seems particularly suitable where so little is known of the author or of his writings. Biography has enabled me to make some attributions that would otherwise have been impossible. Although I cannot claim with Dr. Johnson that "The biographical part of literature . . . is what I love most," yet I am interested in men as well as in literature, and I hope that these interests are not ill–married in the following chapters.

Some readers may expect and want a neat conceptual framework, a ruling principle or thesis to form a basis for a conceptualization of the literature. But such theses are obvious or highly selective. I have chosen to present the authors and the literature in depth and to allow the material to speak for itself. Of course, certain ideas recur and I point out what I consider to be their significance. In the following chapters one may trace the development of a number of motifs and themes generally regarded as characteristic of American literature. The view of the American wilderness as cornucopia—an inexhaustible fount of food, raw materials, and *lebensraum*; America as the new Eden; the tall tale; the American Dream; the barbarism of frontier life; the initiation of the tenderfoot; the application of the (anthropologists') comparative method and stage theory to American literature; the lament for the passing Edenic wilderness; the loss of former innocence; the *translatio* theme (i. e., the ancient but flourishing idea of the westward movement of arts [*translatio studii*] or of empire [*translatio impereii*], an idea which had its best-known American manifestation in poems of the Early National Period on the "Future Glory of America"), etc. These themes and motifs are usually said to begin in the late eighteenth or early nineteenth centuries, but as we will see, they are present in colonial American literature. And the reasons for their origin and repeated appearance are, to a degree, evident when these characteristic themes and motifs are examined in their early appearances in American literature. Although I find colonial literature interesting for the light that it sheds upon the appearance of such themes and motifs in later American writers, I primarily find this literature interesting in itself.

How much literature of intrinsic interest was written in colonial America? To date, colonial American literature has been examined in the most perfunctory fashion. No one, for example, has previously made extensive use of an obvious source for colonial American literature—the newspaper. Assuming that colonial newspapers are like today's newspapers, students ignore a fertile combination of literary, scientific, political, and scholarly journals, as well as today's newspapers. If Maryland is representative of other colonies, the following study indicates that they too have writers of merit whose names are as yet unknown and whose writings are available only in widely dispersed manuscripts and rare (often unique) printed works. I believe that Richard Lewis and Dr. Alexander Hamilton are interesting and important writers, but no previous scholar has treated either of them in detail. I urge the reader to judge for himself, not only by reading the chapters which follow, but also by reading the works of these writers in the editions that are to come.

What is needed is a series of studies which ask the basic questions about early American literary activity. What literature existed? Who wrote it? Why was it written? How does it compare with similar works? What are its sources and influences? Is it significant in American literary or cultural history? Such questions have not been asked. Maryland was a small colony with a modest population. The literature of Virginia, Pennsylvania, or New York is much more voluminous—and the amount of writing from colonial Massachusetts is staggering. Similar studies of the authors and the literature are needed for all the other colonies.

A word about the dates. I have retained the old–style dating (i. e., the Julian calendar, used by Great Britain and her colonies until 1752), but to avoid possible confusion for the period between January 1 and March 25 (under the Julian calendar, the new year began on March 25), I have adopted the common practice of giving both years: thus Benjamin Franklin's birthday, January 6, 1705 (Julian calendar; which would be January 17, 1706, new-style or Gregorian calendar) is given as January 6, 1705/6.

J. A. LEO LEMAY

The Huntington Library
San Marino, California
December 18, 1971

$\mathcal{A}$CKNOWLEDGMENTS

A grant from the Research Department of Colonial Williamsburg, Inc., provided the opportunity to do the basic research on John Hammond and William Parks. An earlier version of this book was read by Professors Theodore Hornberger, Richard Dunn, and Arthur H. Scouten, all of the University of Pennsylvania, where it was presented as a Ph. D. dissertation. A version of the chapter on Richard Lewis was published in *PMLA* in 1968.

The research and writing of the book have been aided by the cooperation of many libraries and librarians, mainly in Maryland and California. In Annapolis, at the Maryland State Library, I read the complete file of Jonas Green's *Maryland Gazette*; at the Maryland Hall of Records, with the help of Dr. Morris Radoff and Mrs. Lois Green Carr, I pursued the factual records of the various writers. In Baltimore, at the Maryland Room of the Enoch Pratt Free Library, at Evergreen House of the Johns Hopkins University Library, and especially at the Maryland Historical Society, I read the relevant books, manuscripts, and secondary sources of my various authors—and of other Maryland litterateurs, who were finally regretfully excluded. During the period that I worked on this manuscript, Mr. Garner Ranney arranged and indexed the manuscript collections of the Maryland Diocesan Society Library, now housed at the Maryland Historical Society. I frequently used the Library of Congress, where Tracy (the guard in the Rare Book Division) always made me feel welcome. In California, I have repeatedly used the UCLA Research Library, and, on nearly every Saturday, the collections of rare books, manuscripts, and reference materials of the Huntington Library. To all of these institutions, and to their helpful, underpaid, and devoted staffs, I am grateful.

A number of friends have been generous. Professors Theodore Hornberger and Richard Beale Davis have given me many suggestions. My colleague at UCLA, Richard A. Lanham, has read the entire manuscript and made several suggestions. Professors Lewis Leary and Carl Dolmetsch have given me thoughtful comments. Dr. Whitfield J. Bell, Jr., librarian of the American Philosophical Society, and Mr. Manfred J. Waserman, of the History Division of the National Library of Medicine, have given assistance. Finally, my parents, and my friend Charles H. F. Conner, and my dearest wife, Ann, all helped in material ways while I spent my spare time in the study of early Maryland writers and writings.

L. L.

CONTENTS

SEVENTEENTH-CENTURY LITERATURE

THE WILDERNESS

I

In the beginning, there was the inviolate and fertile land—a wilderness of superabounding plenty, but lurking within it strange wild beasts and savages. The fruitfulness and beauty of the primeval American continent amazed and delighted the early writers, who saw the New World as a latter-day Eden, a new chance for man to found a new and more perfect civilization and to create a new kind of man. Judged especially deserving of comment were the plentiful wild grapes covering the tree-tops of the virgin forests; the great forests themselves, stretching from the water's edge as far as the eye could see into the unknown continent; the new kind of colorful bee-like bird, the hummingbird; a strange and fearful but polite snake, which gave warning before striking; a bird that imitated the sounds of other birds, the mockingbird; an enormous and delicious game bird that weighed up to sixty pounds, the turkey; a curious animal that hung by its tail, kept its young in a pouch in its stomach, and could play dead, the opossum; a squirrel that glided in the air like a bird; a noisome weed that people could smoke, enjoy, and become addicted to; and a new and delicious staple, Indian corn. More amazing than even the strangeness of the birds and animals was their abundance: deer and turkeys, ducks and geese, muskrats, beavers and foxes, bears, wolves and buffalo—all were common. And the Chesapeake Bay seemed an inexhaustible supply of fish, crabs, and oysters. Even in the late seventeenth century, the game seemed to have no end. Jasper Danckaerts wrote of

the great number of wild geese we saw here on the river. They rose not in flocks of ten or twelve, or twenty or thirty, but continuously, wherever we pushed our way; and as they made room for us, there was such an incessant clattering made with their wings upon the water where they rose, and such a noise of those flying higher up, that it was as if we were all the time surrounded by a whirlwind or a storm. This proceeded not only from geese, but from ducks and other waterfowl; and it is not peculiar to this place alone, but it occurred on all the creeks and rivers we crossed.

Descriptions of the abundance and fertility of the New World characterized that early important genre of American literature, the promotion tract, which also included reports of exploration and travel, geography, climate, and frequently a chapter on the Indians. The tracts were written for the purpose of promoting America, that is, of luring emigrants to the New World. All the best seventeenth-century Maryland publications were promotion tracts. Since there was no printing press in Maryland when the major promotion tracts were written (and even if there had been, the audience for promotion tracts was prospective emigrants), seventeenth-century Maryland writings (whether written in England or in the colony) were printed and sold in London.

The colony began with an active advertising program. Andrew White, an English Jesuit and friend of the Calverts, wrote *A Declaration of the Lord Baltimore's Plantation in Maryland* (London, 1633) to stir up interest in the proposed colony. He stressed the opportunities for wealth and prestige that awaited the prospective colonists and urged Englishmen to sail with Lord Baltimore and his company for Maryland on September 8, 1633. White sailed with the first expedition and sent back to London a description of the earliest explorations and settlement. This account, with some additions, was promptly published by Lord Baltimore as *A Relation of the Successful Beginnings* (London, 1634). During the next year, White began learning the Indian language. When he sent a revised and expanded version of his *Successful Beginnings* to Lord Baltimore, he included a section on the Maryland Indians. Calvert promptly published the enlarged pamphlet under the title *A Relation of Maryland* (London, 1635). White's three pamphlets constituted the opening advertising campaign, but several private accounts dealing with this new area of America circulated in manuscript. Captain Robert Wintour, who evidently sailed with the first colonists, wrote a "Discourse of Maryland" (1636) urging prospective planters, particularly Captain John Reade, to emigrate. Wintour's "Discourse" contains only general arguments for

4

colonization—a type of promotion tract made familiar by Richard Hakluyt, Francis Bacon, and Samuel Purchas, but now superseded and outdated by the experience of colonization itself as well as by the writings of Captain John Smith, Edward Winslow, and, among others, Andrew White. The several extant descriptions by Cyprian Thorowgood, Henry Fleet, and Thomas Yo[u]ng of small exploring parties which opened new areas of the Chesapeake country—manuscripts of value to the contemporary colonists—are all, unfortunately, devoid of intrinsic literary interest.

After the initial settlement of the colony, no propaganda appeared for over a decade. But in the 1640s and 1650s, as the Civil War raged between the Puritans and Royalists in England, a series of conflicts broke out in America over control of the various colonies. The parties fighting in the colonies attempted to win their cause in that final court, the English Parliament, by presenting their case to the English public. Most of these pamphlets are of little merit, though Lord Baltimore's *A Moderate and Safe Expedient* (London, 1646) contains an early plea for religious toleration. The pamphlet war of the 1650s did, however, uncover one enterprising Maryland planter with a flair for words, a vigorous style, an exactness of close observation, and some ideas important in the growth of American nationalism. John Hammond, who managed to escape his Puritan enemies in Maryland, told the story of his supposed crimes and pled for his life in *Hammond versus Heamans* (London, 1655). After Lord Baltimore, the booksellers, and Hammond himself discovered that he had so able a pen, he wrote and published a promotion tract for his adopted country, *Leah and Rachel, or, the Two Fruitful Sisters Virginia and Maryland* (London, 1656). In addition to creating the most detailed seventeenth-century formulation of the American Dream, Hammond delightfully depicts some archetypal Americans.

An indentured servant with the abilities of a London literary wit made the next notable contribution to the literature of seventeenth-century Maryland. His Menippean satire *A Character of the Province of Maryland* (London, 1666) attempted to erase the ugly memory of Maryland's civil wars and to attract settlers. George Alsop's tall tales and burlesque tone, his lively combination of prose and verse, his satire of English society and of some Americans, and his praise of life in the woods, foreshadow a direction in American literature that culminates in the writings of Henry David Thoreau.

Although other troubles were to beset the colony in the seventeenth century (particularly a miniature Glorious Revolution in 1689), and although a printer, William Nuthead, published in Maryland in 1686–1694, nothing of literary value is extant from these pygmy revolutions. In 1695, the Reverend Thomas Bray began issuing pamphlets relating to Maryland. The minister had been asked to accept the position of commissary to the Maryland clergy. He consented, on the condition that the bishop of London encourage the establishment of colonial libraries for clergymen and their parishioners. Bray's writings about the libraries are interesting for what they reveal about the literary culture. His sermons preached in Maryland in 1700 are of interest, but because Bray was important in importing books and libraries to colonial America, he has been the subject of several books and scores of articles. He is not, however, an important writer and spent little time in Maryland; therefore he is not discussed separately.

Seventeenth-century Maryland literature is thus essentially the product of three men, a Jesuit, a planter, and an indentured servant. All were writing for an immediate purpose, all wrote in the same genre, all wrote for the same audience, all published in the same place, and all were evidently commissioned or encouraged by Lord Baltimore. The three demonstrate familiarity with previous promotion literature—and undoubtedly Hammond knew White's writings, and Alsop knew both White's and Hammond's. Their common purpose was to lure people to America. For this end, reality was slanted, twisted, and sometimes misrepresented. America was simultaneously portrayed as a virgin and a fruitful mother. The animals almost begged to be eaten and three harvests could be gathered yearly with little work. As early as Hammond's *Leah and Rachel* (1656) and Alsop's *Character* (1666), the promotion writers thought (or pretended) that Americans were somehow different from the English. Such propaganda coming from every colony deluged the English at home. The promotion writers also created the American Dream, i. e., the possibility and even the promise that an individual could, by emigrating to America, become whatever he wanted; most frequently, the promotion tracts said that by honest hard work an emigrant could rise from poverty and from social and political impotence to a position of wealth and power in America. The advertisers promised that crossing the Atlantic (like switching to a new brand of cigarettes or buying a new automobile) would create in the adventurer a new personality. The promotion tract characterization of Americans was an important step toward the creation of a national identity. Although promotion tract writers reflected their own personalities, as well as popular English ideals and previous promotion tracts, they all wanted to inculcate an aura of greatness about the American. The number of people who believed the tracts, emigrated to America, and, in some cases, fulfilled their own fond hopes, testifies to the success of the early promotion writers.

ANDREW WHITE

APOSTLE OF MARYLAND

Linguist, explorer, priest, theologian, anthropologist, fanatic, and writer—Father Andrew White, S. J., was an Elizabethan of zeal and ability, and a master of the promotion tract. White was intimately associated with the Calverts and the earliest years of Maryland. Andrew White met George Calvert, first Baron Baltimore, sometime before 1629. When Maryland was granted to Cecil Calvert, second Baron Baltimore, Andrew White became his chief writer. White wrote the prospectus advertising the colony in 1633 and accompanied the first group of planters to Maryland, describing the exploring forays, the climate, resources, and Indians in a promotion tract published in 1634. Although it has previously not been attributed to him, White also wrote the major part of the most elaborate colonization pamphlet of Maryland, the *Relation* of 1635. Subsequently, he became a missionary among the Indians, made a grammar and dictionary of their language, and translated a catechism into it.[1] His baptism of Emperor Chitomachon, the greatest Indian chief of early Maryland, at Piscataway on the Potomac on July 5, 1640, was among the most celebrated Indian conversions in the American colonies.

The biographical facts of Andrew White's life are fragmentary, scattered, and sometimes contradictory. Nothing is known of White's family or early years. Evidently he was born in 1579. Since he often appears as "Londinens" in the Jesuit records, he was probably born

---

[1] See the discussion in the bibliographical notes on White, p. 352.

in London.[2] Like many other Catholics, White was sent to the Continent for his education. He matriculated at Douai College in April, 1593, and later entered St. Alban's College, Valladolid, on November 1, 1593.[3] About 1600, White went to Seville, "and on his way addressed the King, and his son the Prince Royal, returning thanks for the benefits conferred upon St. Omer's College."[4] At St. Hermenegild's College, Seville, he met Father Richard Green, whom he later recommended as a Jesuit.[5] After study at St. Hermenegild's, White returned to Douai College. He arrived on June 4, 1604, and took vows as a priest at Douai in 1605.[6]

White's first mission was dangerous. The new priest arrived in England at the time of the Gunpowder Plot. In the panic, White was promptly arrested and imprisoned. Although some priests were executed, he, fortunately, was only banished from England on pain of death.[7]

The earliest surviving manuscripts by White are two letters dated October 27, 1606. Both letters recommended Richard Green as a Jesuit; one is addressed to Father Robert Parsons, and the other to Father John Gerard.[8] White himself was evidently thinking of becoming a Jesuit, and on February 1, 1607, "F. Andrew White, Londoner, of the age of 28 years" was admitted as a novitiate at the Jesuit college of St. John's, Louvain.[9] In 1612, White, now a Jesuit, ignored the death sentence awaiting him in England and returned to London as a missioner.[10]

[2] Thomas A. Hughes, *History of the Society of Jesus in North America* (London and New York, 1907-10), 1:156. (This work is in four volumes, two of text and two of documents; unless otherwise noted, references are to the volumes of text.) Henry J. Foley, "The Nationality of Father White," *Woodstock Letters* 15 (1886):80-81, refuted William P. Treacy's suggestion that White was born in Ireland: Treacy, "What was Father Andrew White's Nationality?" ibid. 14 (1885):384-86.

[3] Thomas Francis Knox, ed., *The First and Second Diaries of the English College, Douay* (London, 1878), 281. Edwin Henson, ed., *Registers of the English College at Valladolid 1589-1862* (London, 1930), 35.

[4] Henry J. Foley, *Records of the English Province of the Society of Jesus* (London, 1875-83), vol. 7, pt. 2, 1458; Hughes, 1:168.

[5] Hughes, *Documents*, 1:6.

[6] Edwin H. Burton and Thomas L. Williams, eds., *The Douay College Diaries, 1598-1654* (London, 1911), 1:57-58.

[7] Ibid., 1:74; Hughes, 1:159.

[8] Hughes, 1:157. White's letter to Gerard is printed in facsimile in Hughes, facing 1:157.

[9] Ibid., 1:159-60.

[10] Foley, vol. 7, pt. 2, 834-35.

White was an able scholar, teaching at several of the Jesuit colleges in his thirties and forties. From 1615 to 1619, at Louvain, he manifested a tendency to follow the doctrines of St. Thomas Aquinas more closely than the Jesuits found practical or desirable.[11] But his heart was in missionary work, not teaching: the Jesuits, in accordance with his desire, sent him back to England, after he again professed the order's four vows on June 15, 1619. From 1619 to 1622, he held a variety of missionary posts in England. White probably met George Calvert and became interested in Lord Baltimore's colonization plans sometime during this period.[12]

By 1623, White had returned to teaching in the Jesuit colleges on the Continent. On August 3, 1623, as Professor of Sacred Theology at Louvain, White formally delivered his opinion on a matter of theology.[13] In 1624, he was at Liège, where, in 1625, he became prefect of studies. His strict interpretation of the Jesuit's program of studies and his close adherence to the teachings of Aquinas caused a difference of opinion between him and the rector of Liège, Father Robert Parsons. White wrote a number of letters to the general of the Society of Jesus, Father Mutius Vitelleschi, complaining about the lax conditions at Liège. Actually, the Apostle of Maryland seems to have been too strict a Thomist even in the opinion of the general. But White remained at Liège until the spring of 1629, when he "crossed over to England."[14]

While at Liège, White corresponded with his friend George Calvert. From Newfoundland, Calvert wrote him in 1627 or 1628, saying that he would "divide even every and the very last bit" with his Jesuit friend.[15] White wanted to emigrate to America with Calvert. On March 3, 1629, the general of the order wrote him: "as to that holy readiness of soul that has made you offer yourself to Father Provincial for the mission of instructing the American colonies of the

---

[11] Hughes, 1:170 n. 6.

[12] Ibid. Foley, vol. 7, pt. 2, 834–35. Since George Calvert wrote to Andrew White from Newfoundland in 1627 or 1628, and since White had not been in England since 1622, it is probable that White and Calvert met before 1623. Although John Gee, *The Foot Out of the Snare* (London, 1624), lists "F. White" on the penultimate page of "The Names of the Romish Priests and Iesuites now resident about the City of London, March 26. 1624," it appears that Gee was listing every priest he had ever heard of who had recently been in London.

[13] Hughes, 1:169 and n. 3.

[14] Ibid., 169–76.

[15] Maryland Historical Society. *The Calvert Papers* (Baltimore, 1889–99), 1:205.

English in Catholic doctrine, I do not doubt but he is as much pleased with it as I am."[16] White returned to London before June, 1629, when he made profession of the vows before Richard Blount, superior of the Society of Jesus for England.[17] He spent at least part of the next few years at the Mission of St. Thomas, Hampshire County.[18] Meanwhile, Lord Baltimore's plans to start a colony near Virginia were receiving favorable attention at the English Court.

The advertising of Baltimore's colony was done mainly by word of mouth—but one tract appeared early in 1633 calling for settlers to sail with Lord Baltimore for Maryland. This eight-page pamphlet, dated at the end, "February 10, anno 1633," was the first Maryland colonization tract: *A Declaration of the Lord Baltimore's Plantation in Mary-land, nigh upon Virginia: manifesting the Nature, Quality, Condition and rich Utilities it contayneth* (London, 1633).[19] White wrote two versions of the *Declaration*. When Father Richard Blount asked for authorization to send a Jesuit mission with Calvert's expedition to Maryland, the general replied that he would like to "receive fuller particulars about the project." White wrote one version for Lord Baltimore as a colonization tract and wrote a slightly different version for the general.[20] Additional evidence of White's authorship exists: some years later, referring to the conditions of plantation in the *Declaration*, White wrote Cecil Calvert, "I remember when your Lordship corrected the written copie which I made."[21] Evidently White drafted the tract and Calvert revised it.

In the opening of the *Declaration*, Andrew White explains that Lord Baltimore has been granted a province "neare unto the English Plantation in Virginia" named "Mary-land, in honour of our most

---

[16] Hughes, 1:174.
[17] Facsimile of MS, Maryland Historical Society.
[18] Foley, vol. 7, pt. 2, 834–35.
[19] No. 20 in Elizabeth Baer, *Seventeenth Century Maryland; A Bibliography* (Baltimore, 1949). The unique extant copy of the printed prospectus of Maryland is in the Archives of the Roman Catholic Archdiocese of Westminster. A facsimile edition by Lawrence C. Wroth was published in Baltimore in 1929. Wroth has also discussed it in his "The Maryland Colonization Tracts, 1632–1646," in *Essays Offered to Herbert Putnam . . .* (New Haven, 1929), 539–55.
[20] White's letter to the general of the Jesuit order was first printed in Edwin A. Dalrymple, ed., *Relatio Itineris in Marylandiam*, Maryland Historical Society *Fund Publication, No. 7* (Baltimore, 1874), 44–53, and is more accurately printed in Hughes, *Documents*, 1:145–49.
[21] *The Calvert Papers*, 1:209.

gracious Queene." Lord Baltimore's reasons for settling the colony are to bring Christianity to the savages, "To enlarge his Majesties Empire and Dominions," and to gain honor and profit for himself and for those, "both Adventurers and others," who voyage with him. White tells how Baltimore is painstakingly planning the trip, taking the "advice of grave and experienced persons," and benefiting "not only by the papers his noble Father, an eye-witness left him, of the Excellency of the land; but by others also, who daily come from that, and the places nigh upon it, as also by the true printed Historie of Captaine Smith." Baltimore plans to leave for Maryland "about the middle of September" and will give especially generous conditions of plantation to the earliest settlers. He will grant 2,000 acres of land to every person who sets out, properly equipped, with five able men.

White shows both religious enthusiasm and credulity in his account of the Indian's spiritual needs. According to him, the conversion of savages is "an intendment so full of Christian honor, making men Angels who undertake it." (Incidentally, the Latin pun on the words *English* and *angel* suggests that White wrote the Latin version first.) He tells a story that the modern reader cannot help but think an exaggerated rumor: "The Indians themselves sending farre and nigh for Teachers, to instruct and Baptize them; and at this present, some are in Towne, who as Eye-witnesses affirme, they saw Messengers sent to *James-Towne* in *Virginia* from their Kings to the same purpose: as also, Children sent to be baptized into New-England on the other side." But for all his personal enthusiasm, White knew that "all men are not so noble-minded, as to hold their levell purely at this end . . . but commonly Pleasure, wealth and honour" are the lures that draw them. The Jesuit may here reveal the influence of Captain John Smith's *Description of New England* (1616), where the adventurer wrote: "For, I am not so simple to thinke, that ever any other motive then wealth, will ever erect there a commonweale." [22] White assures his readers that "Gods deerely-good Providence hath wrapped also all these together in this one Action, that neither higher nor lower inducements might be wanting."

Describing the area's geography, White says that both the Chesapeake and Delaware bays are "rich bosomes of Fish." Trying to give a reason for the abundance, White indulges a pseudo-scientific flight of fancy:

[22] Edward Arber and A. G. Bradley, *The Travels and Works of Captain John Smith* 1 (Edinburgh, 1910):212.

The reason of this great fishing is, for that the Northeast Wind blowing ever constant from the *Canary* Isles, rolles the Ocean and the fish with it into *Mexico*-Bay, where finding no passage South or West, is forced up North with a strong current, and sweepeth along with it great shoales of Fish, by the Coast of *Florida, Mary-land, New England*, and *New-foundland*, which fleeing the Whales, who feed upon them, make to the Land and take the Protection of shallower Water, and inlets thereof, where they are easily taken.

White claims that a flourishing trade in beaver skins exists with the natives; that last year some merchants brought back furs worth ten thousand pounds, "and the returne of these commodities with which they traded for these Beavers with the Natives yeelded them thirty for one." He lists the kind of trees found in Maryland—oak, walnut, cypress, mulberry, pine, elm, cedar, ash, and chestnut—saying that "the Oakes are so tall and straight, as many of them yeeld beames 60. foot long, and two foot and a half every way square." He further claims, "But yet these Woods are sheere and of free passage for horse and man, there beeing few or none undershrubs, which one thing makes them no lesse pleasant, then usefull for food of all kinde of Beasts." He writes that the trees can be used for "building Houses, and ships, for Wanescot, Pipe-staves, Pitch, Rozen, Tarre, Turpentine, Soape-Ash, Perfumes, and Salves, as Merchants can tell." He itemizes the native fruits: cherries ("as bigge as Damascens"), gooseberries, three sorts of plums, mulberries, chestnuts, walnuts, strawberries, and "raspices." The catalogue includes fish, wildlife, domestic animals, and farmer's produce. Like other writers of the promotion tract, White claims that the land is a veritable cornucopia. Corn "is very plentiful in each of three Harvests in the same yeare, yeelding in greatest penurie two hundred for one, in ordinary yeares five or sixe hundred; and in the better, fifteen or sixteen hundred for one." This prodigious harvest easily enables the planter "to keepe all manner of Poultrie and Fowle for the Table all the yeare long." White lists tobacco as one of the drugs found in the country; and among the minerals, he includes copper, gold, and iron. He concludes the tract by claiming that there are "many other Commodities, which time, industry, and Art will discover; The fruits whereof may be easier tasted, then beleeved."

In a postscript to the *Declaration*, White promises further information and advice for "any man that desireth to adventure in this Plantation" from Lord Baltimore, "whose house is in Bloomesbery, at the upper end of Halborne, in London." He adds that Baltimore's ship, "called the Arke of Mary-land, being about 400 Tunne" will weigh anchor from London about August 20 and leave from "Poresmouth" for the new colony about September 8, 1633.

Written primarily for the industrious middle class and for the younger sons of noblemen, the *Declaration* stresses the economic advantages and honor of colonizing. White implies that everyone who goes to America will make a fortune and become a hero. Although the author is religiously fervent and zealous, he knows that "Pleasure, wealth, and honour" attract the generality of men and emphasizes these lures. Written plainly and simply, yet with verve and knowledge, the *Declaration* reveals a thoroughness and understanding of the problems of colonization that augur well for the proposed province.

Andrew White assisted Lord Baltimore throughout the summer of 1633. Between June 29 and July 3, 1633, he wrote an argument in favor of allowing Catholics to emigrate to Maryland. This argument, "Objections Answered touching Mariland," was later (1646) printed as part of a colonization pamphlet (which will be considered in the next chapter). On August 30, 1633, the general of the Jesuit order replied to White's plea to go to America. The general wrote to the superior of the English mission, "If you consider Father Andrew White to be well fitted for that mission, and if he himself desires it so ardently, I see no reason why I should object to his being sent thither."[23]

On November 22, 1633, White sailed with the first colonists for the new province. His next promotion tract tells of the exploration and first settlement of Maryland. Entitled *A Relation of the Successefull Beginnings of the Lord Baltemore's Plantation in Mary-land. Being an extract of certaine Letters written from thence, by some of the Aduenturers, to their friends in England. To which is added, The Conditions of plantation propounded by his Lordship for the second voyage intended this present yeere, 1634*, it was probably published in London in the latter part of July, 1634. There are two other versions of *Successful Beginnings*. The first, *Relatio Itineris in Marylandiam*, is White's report, as superior of the Maryland mission, to the Society of Jesus.[24] The second, "A Brief Relation of the voyage unto

---

23 Hughes, 1:247.
24 The best text (Latin only) of the *Relatio Itineris in Marylandiam* is in Hughes, *Documents* 1:94–107. A translation appeared in (1) Peter Force, comp., *Collection of Historical Tracts* (Washington, D.C., 1846), 4, no. 12; in (2) *A*

Maryland," was enclosed in Governor Leonard Calvert's letter, dated Point Comfort, May 30, 1634, to Sir Richard Lechford.[25] The latter versions are similar, but differ in several important respects from the published account. These differences can be explained by the propagandizing purpose and the audience of the published tract. *Successful Beginnings* was written to attract settlers and investors to Maryland. Therefore, the long, arduous voyage to Maryland is described in a single sentence—although related in detail in the other versions. (An account of dangerous storms and deaths at sea, of the plants of Barbados, and of the wonders of the exotic pineapple were not likely to attract settlers to Maryland.) Detailed references to Catholic practices and indirect aspersions on Protestants are found in the private accounts—but omitted or glossed over in *Successful Beginnings*. The published account also serves a political end, for it praises the kind treatment that the Marylanders received from Governor John Harvey of Virginia and describes in detail the visit of Governor Harvey and the Indian "King of Patuxent" to Governor Leonard Calvert. Finally, *Successful Beginnings* was composed with more care than either the "Brief Relation" or the *Relatio*. *Successful Beginnings* has greater detail and is more exact. The date of the company's arrival at Point Comfort, Virginia (February 24) is given only in the pamphlet. Similarly, the date of composition, an account of domestic animals and commodities, and a direct appeal for colonists are found only in the version that White wrote for publication, the *Successful Beginnings*, 1634.

White opens *Successful Beginnings* with a fast-moving sentence describing the trip to Maryland:

> On *Friday* the 22. of *Nouember* 1633. a small gale of winde comming gently from the Northwest, we weighed from the *Cowes* in the Ile of *Wight*, about ten in the morning; and (hauing stayed by the way

Relation of the Colony of the Lord Baron of Baltimore, in Maryland, near Virginia; a Narrative of the First Voyage to Maryland (Baltimore, 1847); in (3) *Woodstock Letters* 1 (1872):12-24, 71-80, 145-55; 2 (1873):1-13; and (4) in Dalrymple, *Relatio Itineris in Marylandiam*, 10-43. Moses Coit Tyler only knew of this one tract (and only the Latin version) and yet he wrote: "The Jesuit priest, Father Andrew White, an accomplished man and a devout servant of his order, wrote in Latin an elegant account of the voyage of the first colonists to Maryland...." *A History of American Literature, 1607-1765* (Ithaca, 1949), 53.
25 First published in *The Calvert Papers*, 3:26-45. Reprinted in Clayton Colman Hall, *Narratives of Early Maryland, 1633-1684* (New York, 1910), 25-45.

twenty dayes at the *Barbada's* and fourteene dayes at *St. Christophers*, upon some necessary occasions) wee arriued at *Point-Comfort* in *Virginia* on the 24. of *February* following, *the Lord be praised for it*. (p. 1)

The first person that Lord Baltimore's company met was Captain William Claiborne, who was coming "from the parts where wee intended to plant." Claiborne told them that all the natives of the country were preparing for war, "by reason of a rumour some had raised amongst them, of sixe ships that were to come with a power of *Spanyards*, whose meaning was to driue all the inhabitants out of the countrey." Virginia's Governor Harvey received them cordially, at Jamestown, promising that "his Lordship [i. e., Lord Baltimore] should not want any thing that Colony [Virginia] had."

The colonists entered the Chesapeake on March 3, 1633/4, and sailed to the Potomac River, which elicited an enthusiastic description:

> This riuer, of all I know, is the greatest and sweetest, much broader than the *Thames*; so pleasant, as I for my part, was neuer satisfied in beholding it. Few Marshes, or Swamps, but the greatest part sollid good earth, with great curiosity of woods, which are not choaked vp with vnder-shrubbs, but set commonly one from the other, in such distance, as a Coach and foure horses may easily trauell through them. (p. 2)

William Bullock echoed this description in his *Virginia Impartially Examined* (London, 1649), p. 3, when he wrote that the forests in America were "not like ours in England, for they are so clear from Under-woods, that one may be seen above a mile and a half in the Wood, and the trees stand at that distance, that you may drive Carts or Coaches between the thickest of them." White reports that "At the first looming of the ship vpon the riuer, wee found (as was foretold us) all the Country in Armes." The chief of the "*Paschattowayes*" had gathered 1,500 bowmen, and the savages' beacon fires burned in the forest all night. The *Ark* was the largest ship that the Maryland Indians had ever seen, the Indian scouts reporting that the colonists "came in a Canow, as bigge as an Island, and had as many men as there bee trees in the woods."

The colonists sailed up the Potomac until they came to St. Clement's (now Blackistone) Island, where White, in a solemn ceremony, said Mass, "taking possession of this Countrey for our Sauior, and for our soueraigne Lord the King of *England*." White also tells of a domestic mishap at St. Clement's: while the women were washing clothes, "by the ouerturning of the Shallop, the maids . . . were almost drowned, beside the losse of much linnen, and among the rest I lost the best of mine, which is a very maine losse in these parts." When Baltimore's people met Captain Henry Fleet,[26] the latter advised Governor Leonard Calvert "not to land for good and all, before hee had beene with the Emperour of *Paschattoway*, and had declared unto him the cause of our comming: which was, first to learne them a diuine Doctrine, which would lead their soules to a place of happinesse after this life were ended: And also to enrich them with such ornaments of a ciuill life, wherewith our Countrey doth abound." The governor therefore took "two Pinnaces, his owne [the *Dove*], and another hired at *Virginia*" and sailed up the Potomac River to "*Patoemeck* Towne, where the King being a child, *Archihau* his Uncle governed." Archihau welcomed Calvert and his party. One of the explorers (the *Relatio* identifies him as Father John Altham, adding that White stayed at the island) entered into "a little discourse with him touching the errours of their religion, hee seemed well pleased therewith; and at his going away desired him to return vnto him againe, telling him hee should liue at his Table, his men should hunt for him, and hee would diuide all with him." From "Patoemeck Towne, the Governor and his party sailed to *Paschattoway*:"

All were heere armed: 500 Bow-men came to the Water-side. The Emperour himselfe more fearlesse than the rest, came priuately a boord, where hee was courteously entertained; and vnderstanding wee came in a peaceable manner, bade vs welcome, and gaue vs leave to sit downe in what place of his kingdome wee pleased. While this King was aboard, all the *Indians* came to the Water-side, fearing treason, whereupon two of the King's men, that attended him in our shippe were appointed to row on shoare to quit them of this feare: but they refusing to goe for feare of the popular fury; the interpretours standing on the Deck shewd the King to them that hee was in safety, where-with they were satisfied. (pp. 3-4)

White notes that while the governor and his party were away, the Indians near St. Clement's Island began to lose their suspicion and to visit the fortified camp. He writes that "it was worth the hearing, for those who vnderstood them, to heare what admiration they made at our ship; calling it a Canow, and wondering where so great a tree grew that made it, conceiving it to bee made of one piece, as their Canow's are" (p. 4).

[26] The best sketch of Henry Fleet is in Annie Lash Jester and Martha Woodruff Hiden, *Adventurers of Purse and Person, Virginia 1607-1625* (Princeton, 1956), 172-74.

After the governor returned, the company sailed "some nine leagues lower to a riuer on the North-side of that land, as bigg as the *Thames*: Which we called Saint *George's* river." Since the king of Yaocomico lived on the left side, the colonists took up a place on the right, "one mile within the land." White said that the land was as good as England's best. They bought it from the king for "Hatchetts, Axes, Howes, and Cloathes" and named it St. Mary's. The natives were happy to sell the land, for the ferocious Susquehanna Indians often came down from the head of the Chesapeake Bay and attacked the village on this site.

After the colonists had begun building their town, Sir John Harvey, governor of Virginia, sailed up the bay for a visit, and the king of Patuxent, hearing that both governors were there, also came. Captain Henry Fleet and Master Golding interpreted. White records a picturesque speech that the king of the Patuxent made when he heard the firing of the *Ark's* great guns: "*When wee shoote, our Bow-strings giue a twang that's heard but a little way off: But doe you not heare what cracks their Bow-strings giue?*" The Jesuit recounts the explorations and describes the Indians, saying that they are "swarthy by nature, but much more by Art: Painting themselves with colours in oyle, like a darke Red, which they doe to keep the *Gnatts* off: wherein I confesse, there is more ease than comlinesse." He depicts their appearance and dress, and tells of their prowess with bow and arrow. After praising their manners and their "calme and quiet reason," White tells what he knows of their religion, commenting that "they seeme to haue knowledge by tradition, of a flood wherein the World was drowned for sinne" (p. 9). He carefully notes that he has not yet been able to learn enough of the language of the Indians to inquire into their religious beliefs, and that what he knows, he has learned from "Master Throughgood." [27]

Describing St. Mary's, the place "chosen for our plantation," White says that "Wee have beene vpon it but one month, and therefore can make no large relation of it." The colonists built a "good strong Fort"

[27] This must have been Cyprian Thorowgood, author of "A relation of A voyage made by Me Cyprian Thorogood to the head of the Baye" (Hugh Henry Young MSS, Pratt Library, Baltimore). Leonard Calvert in his letter of May 30, 1634, *The Calvert Papers*, 3:23, tells the number of furs that Thorowgood collected. Thorowgood traded with the Indians for at least four more years. *Maryland Historical Magazine* 48 (1952):210. See also the short biographical sketch in Harry Wrigert Newman, *The Flowering of the Maryland Palatinate* (Washington, D.C., 1961), 263–65.

and mounted cannons on it. They planted crops and hope for wine from the "quantitie of Vines, and Grapes." They already have hogs, cows, goats, and chickens, but will have to bring horses and sheep from England, "for wee can haue none in *Virginia*."

Of natural resources, White can say little so far, but he has sent back "a good quantitie of Iron-stone, for a tryall, which if it prooue well, the place is likely to yeeld infinite store of it." He also praises the rich, fertile soil. The last paragraph is devoted mainly to a list of the fauna of Maryland. White concludes: "By all which it appeareth, the Countrie aboundeth, not onely with profit but with pleasure. And to say trueth, there wanteth nothing for the perfecting of this hope-full plantation, but greater numbers of our countrey-men to enjoy it" (p. 10). The precise date and place of composition is given at the end of the work, "From St. *Maries* in *Mary-land*, 27. May, 1634." The next page contains a testimonial by "Adventurers in this first voyage," who had returned in the *Ark* to England and, supposedly, meant to go back to Maryland: Captain Edward Wintour, Captain William Humber, Robert Smithson, and Robert Sympson.

There is no doubt of the *Successful Beginnings'* truthfulness, not because of the testimonials or because the pamphlet pretended to be a compilation of "certaine Letters written from thence, by some of the Adventurers, to their friends in England" (both the testimonial and the compilation of letters were usual devices in promotion litera-ture), but because of the exactness and reasonableness of the entire document. If any authority other than internal evidence is needed, perhaps the judgment of Governor Leonard Calvert will suffice. He calls the "Brief Relation" version an "exact journal of all our voyage" and affirms that it was written "by a most honest and discreet gentle-man, wherefore you may be confident of the truth of it." [28]

Pages twelve to fourteen of the *Successful Beginnings* contain the all-important "Conditions of plantation." Whoever will transport ten able men, well-equipped, will receive a manor of 3,000 acres "with all such Royalties and Priviledges, as are vsually belonging to Man-nors in *England*" (p. 12). The quit-rent to Calvert will be 600 pounds of good wheat. The skilled laborer ("Carpenter, Ioyner, Brick-layer, Brick-maker, Mason, Wheele-wright, Cooper, or Ship-wright") would be granted 100 acres at the expiration of a term of three years and "a whole yeeres provision of all necessaries according to the

[28] *The Calvert Papers*, 3:23–24.

vsual custome of other plantations." The untrained husbandman or laboring man had to bind himself for a term of five years and would only receive 50 acres at the expiration of his contract. Whoever wants to sail on the second voyage must come or notify William Peaseley, "His lordsh. brother in-law, at his house on the back-side of *Drury-lane*, over against the Cock-pit on the fieldside" before October 20, 1634. The pamphlet is dated "15. Iuly 1634."

White's narrative of the colonization of Maryland holds the reader's interest to the end. Benjamin Franklin, one of America's greatest prose stylists, wrote that combining dialogue with narration was "a Method of Writing very engaging to the Reader, who in the most interesting Parts finds himself as it were brought into the Company, and present at the Discourse"; and Franklin said that the first writers he knew who practiced this method were Defoe and Bunyan.[29] Had Franklin read the *Successful Beginnings*, he would have known that Andrew White, although certainly a lesser artist than Franklin, Bunyan, or Defoe, also knew how to create a living scene. When Governor Calvert, Governor Harvey, and the king of Patuxent were all together, White described the solemn ceremony of carrying the colors to shore and gave the king of Patuxent's words upon hearing "the Arke's great guns." Written plainly, yet with apt images (the trees in the virgin forests of Maryland were so far apart that a coach and four horses could drive through them) and humor (the loss of his underclothes and the remarks of the Indians), Andrew White's *Successful Beginnings* (1634) is a promising opening for literature written in Maryland.

And the *Relation* of 1635 is better. Maryland's third colonization tract, *A Relation of Maryland* (London, 1635) was supposedly written by Cecil Calvert from letters sent to him by the colonists.[30] But the first five chapters of the *Relation* (the majority of the book, and

[29] Leonard W. Labaree et al., eds., *The Autobiography of Benjamin Franklin* (New Haven, 1964), 72.
[30] Clayton Colman Hall, *Narratives*, 65. The most recent consideration of the authorship says, "The Parts of this Tract not taken from Father White or some other indicated source were doubtless derived from the reports which the governing commissioners, Leonard Calvert, Jerome Hawley, and Thomas Cornwallis, were required to make to the proprietor"; Jarvis M. Morse, *American Beginnings* (Washington, D. C., 1952), 83. As I have pointed out in the text, it was a common promotional gimmick to claim that a tract was compiled from a series of letters.

all of it that concerns Maryland) are also the work of the Jesuit father Andrew White. As others have pointed out, the first chapter of the *Relation* of 1635 recapitulates *Successful Beginnings* (1634).[31] No one, however, seems to have noticed that in certain details, the *Relation* of 1635 gives more particulars than *Successful Beginnings*. In the *Relation*, the circumstances concerning the choice of the site of St. Mary's are more exact. Leonard Calvert stopped his exploring trip up the Potomac because he didn't, "for many reasons," want to erect his town "as yet so high in the River," and turned back "to take a more exact view of the lower parts" of the bay. He left the *Ark* and pinnaces at Blackistone Island and "tooke his Barge (as most fit to search the Creekes, and small rivers) and was conducted by a Captaine *Fleete* (who knew well the Countrey) to a River on the North-side of *Patomeck* river, within 4. or 5. leagues from the mouth thereof, which they called Saint *Georges* River [now St. Mary's River]" (p. 5). "Three days after their coming to Yoacomaco [now St. Mary's] the *Arke* with the two Pinnaces arrived there" (p. 7). Information such as this could only have been added by someone who was present, and the logical author is White.

The second chapter of the 1635 *Relation* is "A description of the Countrey." The material in this and the following two chapters, "The Commodities which this Countrey affords naturally" and (Chapter Four) "The commodities that may be procured in Maryland by Industry" was also, for the most part, in White's *Successful Beginnings*; however, the information is now better organized and expanded. The highlight of the 1635 *Relation* is Chapter Five: "Of the Naturall disposition of the *Indians* which inhabit the parts of *Maryland* where the *English* are seated: And their manner of living." This chapter pleads for humane treatment of the Indians and could hardly have been written by anyone other than Andrew White. "The Werowance of Patuxent," writes the author, "goes frequently in English Attire, so doth he of Portoback . . . . " These are places where White went on missions to the Indians.[32] Furthermore, the author of the *Relation* is outraged by the callous attitude toward the Indians displayed by William Wood in *New England's Prospect* (London, 1634) and Captain John Smith in *General History of Virginia* (London, 1624):

[31] Wroth, "Maryland Colonization Tracts," 549.
[32] Hughes, 1:554, attributes activities mentioning these places or Indians to Andrew White.

21

By Captaine *Smith's*, and many other Relations you may be informed, that the People are War-licke, and have done much harme to the *English*; and thereby are made very terrible. Others say that they are a base and cowardly People, and to be contemned: and it is thought by some who would be esteemed States-men, that the only point of pollicie that the *English* can use, is, to destroy the Indians, or to drive them out of the Countrey, without which, it is not to be hoped that they can be secure. The truth is, if they be injured, they may well be feared, they being People that have able bodies, and generally, taller, and bigger limbed then the *English*, and want not courage . . . . Experience hath taught us, that by kind and faire usage, the Natives are not onely become peaceable, but also friendly, and have upon all occasions performed as many friendly Offices to the *English* in *Maryland*, and New-England, as any neighbour or friend uses to doe in the most Civill parts of Christendome: Therefore any wise man will hold it a far more just and reasonable way to treat the People of the Countrey well, thereby to induce them to civility, and to teach them the use of husbandry, and Mechanick trades, whereof they are capable, which may in time be very useful to the *English*; and the Planters to keepe themselves strong, and united in Townes, at least for a competent number, and then noe man can reasonably doubt, either surprise or any other ill dealing from them. (pp. 25–26)

These are the sentiments of a man who has lived with the Indians and has come to respect them. Upon the authority of experience, he tells us that the Indians are as friendly "as any neighbour . . . in the most Civill parts of Christendome." And we note that a similar realistic attitude is found in this author (the colonists must be prepared for trouble, must "keepe themselves strong, and united in townes") as in the Andrew White who wrote that not all men were attracted to plantations by motives of piety, but rather by "Pleasure, wealth, and honour."

Chapter five opens with a paragraph pleading for humane treatment of the Indians, describes their government, customs, habits, dress, and agriculture, and attempts to explain their financial system. But the author's primary concern is moral. He praises the behavior of the Indians: "They have some things amongst them which may well become Christians to imitate, as their temperance in eating and drinking,[33] their Justice each to other . . . . " The writer's narrative

---

[33] We recall here that White was famous for his temperance, that he thought he recovered from his various attacks of fever in Maryland because of his abstinence, and that he blamed the death of several of the adventurers on intemperance.

art (especially his apt illustrations, images, and individualized scenes
—often enlivened by dialogue) also suggest White's authorhip:

> In the most grave assembly [of the Indians], no man can expect to
> find so much time past with more silence and gravitie: Some *Indians*
> coming on a time to *James Towne* in *Virginia*, it happened, that there
> then sate the Councell to heare causes, and the *Indians* seeing such an
> assembly, asked what it meant? Answer was made, there was held a
> *Match-comaco* (which the Indians call their place of Councell) the
> *Indian* replyed, that they all talke at once, but we doe not so in our
> *Match-comaco*. (pp. 31–32)

Near the end of this chapter, the author tells a story illustrating
(with modern anthropological perception) the different values and
customs of the Indians and the whites. It seems that some Susquehannahs and Wicommesses (traditional enemy tribes) met on Kent
Island, where they both had come to trade with Captain Claiborne.
One of the Susquehannahs "did an Injury" to a Wicommess, and some
of Claiborne's people, witnessing it, laughed. The Wicommesses, considering themselves humiliated and despised, ambushed a party of
seven Susquehannahs, killing five of them. They also attacked a group
of Claiborne's men, killing three. About two months later, the Wicommesses sent a messenger to Governor Leonard Calvert "to excuse
the fact, and to offer satisfaction for the harme that was done to the
English." Calvert responded: "I expect that those men, who have
done this out-rage, should be delivered unto me, to do with them as
I shall thinke fit." The "*Wicomese* after a little pause, replyed; It is
the manner amongst us *Indians*, that if any such like accident happen,
wee doe redeeme the life of a man that is so slaine, with a 100. armes
length of *Roanoke* (which is a sort of Beades that they make, and use
for money) and since that you are heere strangers, and come into our
Countrey, you should rather conforme yourselves to the Customes
of our Countrey, then impose yours upon us" (pp. 35–36). Andrew
White concluded the chapter with a short paragraph urging humane
treatment of the Indians: "It is much more Prudence, and Charity, to
Civilize, and make them Christians, then to kill, robbe, and hunt them
from place to place, as you would doe a wolfe."

The rest of the *Relation* of 1635 was undoubtedly put together in
England by Cecil Calvert or an agent (perhaps William Peaseley).
Chapter Six gives the new conditions of the plantation; Chapter
Seven, instructions and advertisements, including a list of necessary

provisions (a modification of the list given by Captain John Smith in his *General History of Virginia*), the form of binding a servant, and the form of a bill of lading. The book closes with a list of the names of "Gentlemen adventurers" that had already gone to Maryland, and with the first publication of "The Charter of Maryland."[34]

Andrew White was head of the Maryland mission of the Jesuit order until Father John Brooke (*alias* Ferdinand Poulton) arrived in 1639.[35] White devoted his time to learning the language of the Indians and to converting them to Christianity. On February 20, 1638/9, White wrote to Lord Baltimore about the conditions in Maryland, advising him what was most needed and which crops could be raised there. He reported that he had already had two grave sicknesses:

> The reliques thereof I carry still about mee not in weakness of body which I never had less; butt in a decay of my hearing when people speake low and I feare in tyme I may loose alltogether: yett as itt is now itt is a hindrance as well in an office I have as your Lordship knows[36] as allso in lerning the Indian language which hath many darke gutterals, and drowneth often the last syllable or letteth it so softely fall as it is even by a good eare harde to bee understood. I am told of one in London who is excellent for such cures: and therefore I write to our Great man there for leave to return for one yeare for helpe: who knows whether itt may proove to wait upon your Lordship hither the yeare following.[37]

But White did not return to England then. On June 2, 1639, he performed the first Maryland marriage, joining John Hollis and Restituta Tue.[38] Until this time, White had devoted most of his time and energy to the conversion of the Patuxent king, the Indian chief who gave the Jesuits a plantation at Mattapany;[39] however, the king fell away from the Christian faith, and Governor Leonard Calvert, fearing for White's safety, asked him to leave the Patuxent king. White next went to Piscataway on the Potomac, a place not far south of the

[34] Baer, No. 18, *The Charter of Maryland* (n.d., n.p.) had been considered by Wroth and Baer the first Maryland colonization tract, but recent research has shown that this assumption was an error. John Cook Wyllie, "The First Maryland Tract: A Reconsideration of the Date of Printing of the Maryland Charter," in *Essays Honoring Lawrence C. Wroth* (Portland, Me., 1951), 475–83.

[35] Hughes, 1:343, and *Documents*, 112–17.

[36] White's reference is undoubtedly to confession.

[37] *The Calvert Papers*, 1:202–203.

[38] *Archives of Maryland*, 1:52.

[39] Hughes, 1:343, and *Documents*, 112–14.

present city of Washington, where he soon won the friendship of the greatest Indian chief of the area, Chitomachon, called the *tayac* or "emperor." Shortly after Father White arrived at "Pascattoway," Chitomachon fell ill, and White was able to use his medical knowledge to good effect on the chief. This, coupled with two dreams the *tayac* had, insured White's welcome at the emperor's home.[40]

Chitomachon soon wanted to be baptized, but the ceremony was deferred until the following summer, when, on July 5, 1640, Andrew White baptized Chitomachon (giving him the Christian name Charles), his wife (Mary), and his infant daughter (Ann). Mosorcoques, the emperor's chief counselor, was baptized John, and the counselor's son, Robert.[41] The Annual Letter to the general of the Jesuit order reported:

> The governor was present at the ceremony, together with his secretary and many others; nor was anything wanting in display which our means could supply . . . . In the afternoon, the king and queen were united in matrimony in the christian manner; then the great holy cross was erected, in carrying which to its destined place the king, governor, secretary, and others, lent their shoulders and hands; two of us [i. e., Jesuits] in the meantime chanting before them the litany in honor of the Blessed Virgin.

Soon after the ceremony, White fell ill and remained sick until the end of the winter. By this time, his work (and that of the other Jesuits) among the Indians was well known in England and America. Roger Williams, in 1643, wrote that "some . . . boast of the Jesuits in *Canada* and *Maryland*" converting the Indians.[42]

While Father White was converting and healing Indians in Maryland, the political upheavals of the Interregnum began in England. Virginia and Maryland obtained information about the turmoil on January 30, 1642, when the Court of Northampton County, Virginia, seized two letters from William Webb to Thomas Noke and Andrew White on the grounds that the letters contained information of the state of England. The letters were sent on to their addressees, after

[40] Hughes, *Documents*, 114–16.
[41] Hughes, 1:344, and Dalrymple, *Relatio Itineris in Marylandiam*, 128.
[42] Quoted from the translation by J. Holmes Converse in *Relatio Itineris in Marylandiam*, 74–75. This baptism was celebrated in seventeenth-century Jesuit literature: see the imaginary picture of the baptism in Mathias Tanner, *Societas Jesu Apostolorum Imitatrix sive gesta praeclara* (Prague, 1694), 803. Roger Williams, *A Key into the Language of America* (London, 1643), in *The Complete Writings of Roger Williams* 1 (New York, 1963):87.

the authorities read Webb's report that the English were in "great fear of turmoils and convulsions" and that he wished he were in Maryland.[43]

When Sir Edmund Plowden sailed for America in the summer of 1642, he carried two letters of introduction from William Webb of London, one to Father Thomas Copley and one to White.[44] White spent most of 1642 at Potupaco (an Indian name, corrupted by popular etymology to the present Port Tobacco) converting and helping the Indians.[45] He also stayed seven weeks at Potomac town, where he succeeded in converting the principal Indians. An incident that occurred in the winter of 1642/3 well illustrates the origins of the prejudice between New England and the South (New England was primarily Puritan; Virginia, Royalist). White had taken passage up the river in the ship of a "hard hearted and troublesome captain of New England" but soon came to feare that "he would either be cast into the sea, or be carried with his property to New England, which is full of puritan calvinists."[46] But nature intervened. The river froze and the ship sank at Potomac town.

Andrew White remained in Maryland until 1644 or 1645, when he and Father Thomas Copley (*alias* Philip Fisher) were captured by Virginia Puritans and sent in chains to England.[47] Tried for high treason under the statute of 27 Eliz. c.ii (for being a priest in England), the Jesuit was acquitted upon the plea that he had been carried to England by force and against his will.[48] Nevertheless, he languished in English jails for over three years. Finally, on January 7, 1647/8, White was released from Newgate and ordered "forthwith discharged of his imprisonment; and he do depart the kingdom within fifteen days after his discharge from his imprisonment."[49] He sailed for Belgium, arriving at Antwerp on March 1, 1647/8.[50] Since the Jesuits wanted detailed reports on their overseas projects, the Annual

---

[43] "Court Records of Northampton County," *Virginia Magazine of History and Biography* 4 (1896–97):405.
[44] Edward Duffield Neill, "Additional Facts concerning Sir Edmund Plowden," *Pennsylvania Magazine of History and Biography* 10 (1886):180–81.
[45] Foley, 3:381; Hughes, 1:554.
[46] Dalrymple, 80–81.
[47] Hughes, 1:562.
[48] Foley, vol. 7, pt. 2, 834–35.
[49] Leo Francis Stock, ed., *Proceedings and Debates of the British Parliaments Respecting North America, 1542–1688* (Washington, D.C., 1924), 203.
[50] Hughes, *Documents*, 128.

Letter to the general of the order for 1649 promised a "general and exact" ("perfecta et exacta") history of the Maryland mission by its founder, Andrew White. Unfortunately, this history, like one later proposed by Governor Benedict Leonard Calvert, seems never to have been written.[51]

Although White repeatedly begged the Jesuit superior to send him back to Maryland, he was refused, probably because of his age and poor health. He remained for several years at Antwerp where he influenced the famous Teresian nun, Margaret Mostyn, who speaks glowingly of him in her autobiography.[52] He returned to England about 1650 and became chaplain to a noble family in the Hampshire District. He was a missionary priest in the College of St. Thomas, Hamphire, in 1655, and reportedly died in Hampshire, on December 27, 1656.[53] Among his fellow Jesuits he had always been noted for his intellectual prowess, piety, and asceticism.[54]

Andrew White, S. J., wrote all or part of the four earliest colonization tracts of Maryland. He was a competent, though not a major, writer. He is not as vigorous, interesting, or appealing as Captain John Smith, whose works are full of high adventure, memorable pleas for the value of colonization, and vivid scenes. Occasionally, a bit of lively dialogue, an apt simile, or a flash of humor enliven White's writings. He is important not for the greatness of his writing, but because he recorded the earliest explorations in Maryland. Like the astronauts, he voyaged to distant places and experienced new conditions which fascinated his contemporaries. Early American literature is rich in accounts by men of action, like White, whom chance made writers.

[51] Ibid., 127. For Benedict Leonard Calvert's proposed history, see Aubrey C. Land, "An Unwritten History of Maryland," *Maryland Historical Magazine* 61 (1966):77–80.
[52] Edmund Bedingfield, *The Life of Margaret Mostyn* (London, 1878), 53 and 152.
[53] These are the most frequently cited date and place, but some sources list the place as London or near London, and some sources give the date as Jan. 6, and others as June 6, 1656. Carlos Sommervogel's edition of Augustine de Backer, *Bibliothèque de la Compaynie de Jésus*, vol. 8 (Brussels, 1898), cols. 1091–93, gives both dates, and Foley prints the different dates at different places (vol. 7, pt. 2, 834–35; cf. 3:338). Francis X. Curran, in a discussion of some cruxes in White's biography, "The Mystery of Andrew White," *Woodstock Letters* 85 (1956):375–80, summarizes the conflicting reports on pp. 379–80. I suspect that Jan. 6, 1656, represents a New Style date for his death and that June 6, 1656, was simply an error for Jan. 6.
[54] Hughes, 1:423.

JOHN HAMMOND

PARTISAN IN MARYLAND'S CIVIL WAR

Several American colonies fought miniature versions of the English Civil War. In Maryland, Lord Baltimore's supporters (mainly Royalists) and William Claiborne's forces (primarily Puritans) warred for control of the province. One weapon in the struggle was the propaganda which attempted to win the support of the English government. During the pamphlet war, John Hammond appeared as a partisan of Lord Baltimore and became one of the ablest promoters of seventeenth-century America. The other tracts discussed below are noteworthy because they provide the background for Hammond, whose full formulation of the American Dream was an important advance in the national identity and in American literature.

Lord Baltimore fired the opening salvo in the literary battle for control of Maryland. *A Moderate and Safe Expedient* (London, 1646) presented the proprietor's account of Maryland's war. Richard Ingle, a Puritan leader, had captured St. Mary's, the capital of Maryland, and forced Governor Leonard Calvert to flee into exile. At the crucial time while a measure was pending before the House of Lords for the repeal of Lord Baltimore's charter, and before Cecil Calvert learned that his brother Leonard had recovered control of the colony, Lord Baltimore published his defense.

A Moderate and Safe Expedient is a promotion tract aimed particularly at English Catholics. The author asks Parliament to give Catholics freedom of religion in England or else to allow them to sell their property and emigrate to Maryland. The pamphlet is of unusual bibliographical interest because a section, "Objections Answered touching Mariland," evidently was written some thirteen years before. Consisting of full answers to five objections concerning the emigration of Catholics, "Objections Answered" is addressed, "as its phraseology shows, to the Royal government." Lathrop C. Harper believed that "Objections Answered" had been "intended originally for the private instruction of Lord Baltimore in defending the Charter in its passage of the Great Seal," in 1632.[1] It seems more likely, however, that "Objections Answered" was written over a year later.

After Lord Baltimore was granted the colony of Maryland, Claiborne and the Virginia adventurers petitioned His Majesty against the plantation. On May 12, 1633, Charles I referred the petition to the Privy Council, which heard the case on June 28. The Council ordered Lord Baltimore and the Virginia adventurers to meet before July 3 to settle their differences "in a friendly manner if it might be and likewise Set down in writing the propositions made by Either party with their severall answers and reasons, to be presented to the board this day [July 3], which was likewise accordingly done."[2] "Objections Answered" was probably part of Lord Baltimore's "severall answers and reasons" presented (in reply to the Virginia adventurers' objections) in the Star Chamber on July 3, 1633. If so, "Objections Answered" was written between June 29 and July 3, 1633. It answers five arguments against Lord Baltimore's colonization of Maryland. The replies are in the logical and vigorous style typical of Andrew White. Although the author cannot now be definitely ascertained, he was evidently a priest working in 1633 for Cecil Calvert and the colonization of Maryland. Father White is the logical author.[3]

The Claiborne forces objected that if the Catholics should "go into Mariland, or any Country where they may have free liberty of their Religion," there will be no hope of making them good Protestants. In reply, Lord Baltimore's party argues that the laws against the Roman

---

[1] Lathrop C. Harper, "A Maryland Tract of 1646," *Bibliographical Essays; a Tribute to Wilberforce Eames* (Cambridge, Mass., 1924), 146.

[2] *Archives of Maryland*, 3:21–22.

[3] Thomas A. Hughes, in his *History of the Society of Jesus* 1:257, wrote, "we do not discover any intrinsic evidence of its being Father White's production." Bradley Tyler Johnson, *The Foundation of Maryland and the Origin of the Act Concerning Religion of April 21, 1649* (Baltimore, 1883), 24, thought that "Objections Answered" was the work of the English provincial of the Society of Jesus, Richard Blount. Harper, 47, and Lawrence C. Wroth, "Maryland Colonization Tracts," 13, follow Johnson in this opinion.

Catholics were not made in order to force them to become good Anglicans (for dissenters are as far from the Established Church as the Catholics): the laws were enacted for "the safety of King and Kingdom."[4]

The second objection maintains that a license for Catholics to go to Maryland "will seem to be a kind of tolleration" of Catholicism. This is beautifully answered. In a long and well-balanced sentence, the author crushes his opponent's argument by a sarcastic portrayal of just what this "tolleration" really amounts to:

> Such scrupulous persons may as well have a scruple to let the Roman Catholics live here, though it bee under persecution, as to give way to such a License, because banishment from a pleasant, plentiful, and ones owne native Country, into a Wilderness, among Savages and wild Beasts, although it proceed (in a manner from ones owne election) yet, in this case, where it is provoked by other wayes of persecution, is but an exchange rather than a freedom of punishment, and perhaps, in some mens opinions, from one persecution to a worse, For divers Malefactors in this Kingdome, have chosen rather to be hanged then goe into Virginia. (p. 10)

The sentence continues on through several more arguments, White finally asking sarcastically if it does not seem to be a toleration of paganism to allow Indians to live in Maryland.

The next objection is economic. Claiborne's party pointed out that revenues from the estates of Catholics will be lost if they are allowed to leave England. White replies that the purpose of the laws was not to gain revenue, but to rid the country of Catholics. Then he ridicules the opposing point with an apt simile: "if there were no Crimes at all committed in *England*, the King would loose many Fines, and confiscations, whereby his Revenue would also be impaired . . . and yet, without question the King and State would both desire it: the same reason holds in this" (p. 12).

The fourth objection claims that England would be weakened by the loss of people and wealth if Catholics emigrated to Maryland. But the author reasons that there are only a few Catholics in England, and the loss of population would be negligible. England will lose little wealth, for the colonists will take: "only usefull things for a Plantation, as Provisions for Cloathing, and Building, and Planting Tools,

---

[4] *A Moderate and Safe Expedient to remove Jealousies and Fears, of any danger, or prejudice to this State, by the Roman Catholicks of this Kingdom, and to mitigate the censure of too much severity towards them . . . Printed in . . . 1646* (London, 1646), 9. Hereafter, page citations will be given in the text.

&c. which will advantage this Kingdome by increase of Trade, and vent of its native Commodities, and transferre the rest of their Estates, by Bills of Exchange, into Bankes beyond Sea, which tend also to the advantage of the Trade of England, for more stock by this means will be employed in it" (p. 13).

It may prove dangerous, says the last objection, to Virginia and New England to have Roman Catholics near them, for the Catholics may suppress the Protestants or shake off any dependence on England. The author replies that "there are already at least three times as many protestants there, as there are Roman Catholiques in all England." And he reasons that even if the Roman Catholics grew strong enough in Maryland to suppress the Protestants, "it were notwithstanding more for the Honour of the English Nation, that English men, although Roman Catholiques, and although not dependent on the Crowne of England, should possesse that Country than Forraigners, who, otherwise, are like to doe it." Then the author introduces the current fears about the empire and gives the probable reason[5] why Lord Baltimore received an extensive grant rather than the piece of the Delmarva Peninsula that he had requested: "for the Swedes and Dutch have two severall Plantations already in New England, and upon the Confines of Mariland, (between the English Colonies in *New-England* and *Mariland*) and doe incroach every day more and more upon that continent, where there is much more Land then all the Kings Protestant subjects in all his Dominions, (were they there) would be able to possesse" (p. 15).

White predicts that the settlement of Maryland, by creating a market for "cattle and many other commodities," will benefit the merchants and settlers of Virginia—and he ends with a dig at the real enemies of Cecil Calvert, the London merchants trading to Virginia: "though perhaps some petty Merchants heere, traders to Virginia, may conceive it prejudicial to them, and therefore may make religion, and other vaine pretences of danger to Virginia, or this state, the cloake of their avarice, to hinder this designe; whereas, in truth, it can bee nothing else, but feare of increase of the Commodities, they deale in, and consequently of an abatement of the prices, that may incline them to oppose it" (p. 16).

The method of the arguments is notable. White usually meets his opponent's objections on several levels. For instance, in answering the

[5] This is the speculation of Charles M. Andrews, *The Colonial Period of American History* (New Haven, 1934-37), 2:281.

third objection, that the loss of people and wealth would hurt the kingdom, he first says that not many Catholics emigrate; he then argues that if they did, England would be better off without them; he says that little wealth would leave England and adds that what wealth does leave would advance England's fortunes by trade. If the author was not Father Andrew White, Cecil Calvert was doubly fortunate in having two Catholics, both able writers, actively promoting his colony in 1633.

A Moderate and Safe Expedient achieved its goal. The motion for repeal of Lord Baltimore's charter was not brought up again in Parliament. But Cecil Calvert had seen that it was necessary both to refute the common notion that Maryland was a hotbed of popery and to change the official policy whereby only Catholics could hold public offices in the colony. He therefore appointed William Stone (a well-known Protestant with powerful allies in the Puritan Parliament) lieutenant governor and reorganized the Council of Maryland, making one-half of its members Protestants. After Leonard Calvert's death in 1647, William Stone was appointed governor. But when Stone visited Virginia in 1651, Thomas Green, a Royalist and acting governor of Maryland, proclaimed Charles II king.

Although Stone rushed back and rescinded the proclamation, Claiborne and the Virginia forces (hoping to get the colony for themselves) seized the opportunity to blacken Lord Baltimore's reputation with Parliament. And when Charles II, on the island of Jersey, heard that Lord Baltimore had rescinded the proclamation, he appointed the poet Sir William Davenant as royal governor of Maryland. With both parties, Puritan and Royal, angry at him, Calvert published *The Lord Baltimore's Case, Concerning the Province of Maryland . . . With full and clear Answers to all material Objections . . .* (London, 1653). The pamphlet narrates Lord Baltimore's efforts in Maryland, describes the conflict with Claiborne's men, and summarizes the dispute between the Virginia merchants and Lord Baltimore. Claiborne's party argued: First, that Maryland was formerly part of Virginia; so was New England, goes the answer, but the king saw fit to grant that land, like Maryland, to others. Second, that Captain William Claiborne was deprived of his plantation, the Isle of Kent; but this was hashed out fourteen years ago, "upon a full hearing of both parties," by the Lords Commissioners for Foreign Plantations, "and the sayd Capt. Cleyborn hath himself, also by divers Letters of his to the Lord

Baltimore, acknowledged the great wrong he did him therein; which Letters were proved at the Committee of the Navy, and are now remaining with that Committee." The most serious argument is the third—that the Patent for Maryland "constitutes an hereditary Monarchy in Maryland which is . . . inconsistent with this Commonwealth." Lord Baltimore's writer answers that Maryland is subordinate to and dependent upon the "Supreme Authority of England." Lord Baltimore's power of veto and his other large powers are essential because "such necessitous factious people as usually new plantations consist of" would otherwise take away his estate in the New World. The author further claims that "such chargeable and hazardous things as Plantations are, will not be undertaken by any, whether it be a Company or a single man, without as great incouragements of priviledges as are in the Lo. Baltemore's patent of Maryland."[6] After a few further minor objections are refuted, there follows a list of "Reasons of State, concerning Maryland in America": in effect, a list of reasons why Maryland should remain a separate colony under Lord Baltimore. Finally, Lord Baltimore printed a copy of the commission "from the late Kings eldest Sonne, to Mr. William Davenant" making him governor of Maryland.

This pamphlet, like the reply to it, is a plain product. The answer of Claiborne and the Puritan forces was *Virginia and Maryland, or the Lord Baltimore's printed Case, uncased and answered* (London, 1655). After a historical survey (from the Virginia merchants' point of view) of the dispute between Maryland and Virginia, the pamphlet rehearses the Maryland wars and concludes with a number of supporting documents.

The chief military action during Maryland's civil war was the Battle of the Severn. Several people were killed, and the battle provoked four pamphlets.[7] Leonard Strong, a Puritan leader, wrote *Babylon's Fall in Maryland: a Fair Warning to Lord Baltimore; or a Relation of an Assault made by divers Papists, and Popish Officers*

---

[6] Clayton Colman Hall, ed., *Narratives*, 174.

[7] There is a brief discussion of these pamphlets (although it confuses, I believe, their chronology) in Jarvis M. Morse, *American Beginnings*, 130–32. For an examination of the Battle of the Severn, see B. Bernard Browne, "The Battle of the Severn," *Maryland Historical Magazine* 14 (1919):154–71. The most recent discussion of the feud is Manfred Jonas, "The Claiborne-Calvert Controversy: An Episode in the Colonization of North America," *Jahrbuch für Amerikastudien* 11 (1966):241–50.

of the Lord Baltimore (London, 1655). Strong enlivened his pamphlet with vigorous dialogue. The archetypal Western gunfighter's reliance on his six-shooter is prefigured by Strong's description of the action of Lord Baltimore's men: "And when they were desired to show by what power or Commission they so acted, they would in a proud bravado clap their hands on their swords, and say, Here is a Commission" (Hall, p. 240).

A Lord Baltimore partisan replied with *A Just and Cleere Refutation of a False and Scandalous Pamphlet Entitled Babylons Fall in Maryland . . . By John Langford, Gentlemen servant to Lord Baltimore.* In the first paragraph of his *Refutation,* he wrote that he had "beene acquainted with and imployed by my Lord *Baltemore* in his affairs relating to that Province, both heere and there, for above twenty years last past" (p. 3).[8] (In 1641 he had been appointed surveyor-general of the colony of Maryland for life.[9]) Langford retells the story of the Battle of the Severn, making the Puritans under William Fuller the villains and damning Roger Heaman, captain of an armed merchant ship, *The Golden Lion,* for his role in the battle. Langford includes in his tract (pp. 15–18) a supporting letter by Dr. Luke Barber, who had served in Cromwell's army and as Cromwell's personal physician. Now a planter in Maryland and a favorite of Cecil Calvert, Barber was highly regarded during the Interregnum. Langford also printed (pp. 27–32) "An Act concerning Religion," which guaranteed freedom of religion in Maryland to all Christians who believed in the Trinity.[10] At approximately the same time that Langford's *Refutation* appeared, Roger Heaman (whose decisive role at the Battle of the Severn gave the victory to the Puritan faction) published *An Additional Brief Narrative of a late bloody design against the Protestants in Ann Arundel County Severn in Maryland . . .* (London, 1655).[11] Heaman claimed that Governor Stone had behaved

[8] Langford had conducted the inventory of George Calvert's estate, Feb. 1, 1632/3. *The Calvert Papers* 1:50.

[9] Donnell MacClure Owings, *His Lordship's Patronage: Offices of Profit in Colonial Maryland* (Baltimore, 1953), 48.

[10] Cecil Calvert's policy from the first had been one of toleration. His first directive to the governor and commissioners for the plantation began by instructing them to "suffer no scandall nor offence to be given to any of the Protestants, whereby any just complaint may heereafter be made." "Instructions 13 Novem: 1633 . . .," in Hall, 16.

[11] Heaman's *Additional Brief Narrative* is dated July 24. Since Heaman's pamphlet supplements Strong's *Babylon's Fall,* and since it contains no reference to Langford's *Refutation* (nor does Langford refer to Heaman's work), it seems

treacherously. *An Additional Brief Narrative* is without literary or—
if one may believe John Hammond—historical value. But Heaman
provoked John Hammond, who entered the lists with *Hammond vs.
Heamans or an answer to an audacious pamphlet, published by an impudent and ridiculous fellow, named Roger Heamans, Calling himself
Commander of the Ship Golden Lion, wherein he endeavours by lies
and holy expressions, to colour over his murthers and treacheries committed in the Province of Maryland* (London, 1655).

Nothing is known of John Hammond's English background.[12]
Since he wrote that he had spent nineteen years in Virginia and two
years in Maryland, he probably emigrated to Virginia in 1633 or
1634. He witnessed a deed in Isle of Wight County, Virginia, on
April 15, 1646. Although he was elected a burgess from Isle of Wight
in 1652, the Assembly of Virginia would have none of him. In the
"Resolutions of the Grand Assembly beginning the 25th of November, 1652" appeared the following dismissal:

> We find Mr. John Hammond returned a Burgesse for the lower
> parish of the Isle of Wight, to be notoriously knowne a scandalous
> person, and a frequent disturber of the peace of the country, by libell
> and other illegall practices, and conceive it fitt he be expelled the
> house, and that a warrant issue to the sherriffe of the said county, for
> the election of another Burgesse in his roome.[13]

Immediately after this rebuff by the Virginia Puritans, Hammond,
with his wife Ann and children (Mordecai, Bernard, Ann, and Daniel) moved to Maryland, where he purchased a plantation from Walter Pake[s] in Newtown, St. Mary's County.[14] By early March,
1652/3, he was living in Newtown and took a case as an attorney be-

---

that Heaman's *Additional Brief Narrative* appeared at approximately the same
time as Langford's *Refutation.*

[12] Harry Wright Newman, *Anne Arundel Gentry* (Baltimore, 1933), 189,
believes that he was a son of Dr. John Hammond (d. 1617), physician to Henry,
Prince of Wales, and brother to the Rev. Henry Hammond (1605-60), chaplain
to Charles I. But G. C. Moore Smith, "Temple and Hammond Families," *Notes
and Queries* 151 (Oct. 2 and Dec. 25, 1926):237-39, 452-53, provides notes on
Dr. John Hammond's descendants—none of whom was named John. For a
genealogical chart of Dr. John Hammond's descendants, see Smith's edition of
The Letters of Dorothy Osborne to William Temple (Oxford, 1928), 323.

[13] Herbert Read McIlwaine, ed., *Journal of the House of Burgesses of Virginia, 1619-1658/9* (Richmond, 1915), 84.

[14] *Archives of Maryland*, 10, 344-45, 385-86. Hammond's wife and children
are named on 291.

fore the Provincial Court of Maryland in June, 1653.[15] On December 5, 1654, the Provincial Court granted him a license "for retayling of wine and Strong Liquors" and also awarded him responsibility for providing "a ferry for the Convenient passage of people over the New-towne River." These licenses were given because Hammond allowed the Court of St. Mary's County to meet at his house, "the most Convenient place," and because he had "undertaken to build forthwith a Sufficient Court house at his own Cost and charges." The St. Mary's County Court continued to meet at his Inn until after his death.[16]

Hammond was active in the Maryland wars, siding with Lord Baltimore's forces against the Puritans. When the Puritan forces won the Battle of the Severn on Sunday, March 25, 1655, they immediately tired to capture Hammond, who was forced to disguise himself. He made his "beloved wife Ann Hamond my true and Lawfull Attorney" together with Walter Pake and fled to England aboard Captain Thomas Thoroughgood's ship *Crescent.* He later wrote from England, November 18, 1656, a "Second Letter of Attorney" making his wife Ann his sole attorney.[17]

In the first paragraph of *Hammond vs. Heamans,* John Hammond shows that he is more than a match for all the Puritan writers. He begins with this *apologia*:

> I was very opposite to publish my self to the world a fool in print, resolving rather to wait the determination of the Supreme Authority of *England,* by who (and not by railing invectives) we must be tryed, than to have expressed so much indifference as to have carped unseasonably at the proceeding of these inhuman, ingrateful, and bloodsucking Sectaries, which mention God in their lips, but their hearts are farre from him; but that I see daily a broaching of lyes, one confederating and in the neck of another, which begets belief amongst many, and carries a vulgar applause along with their action, the only way these people ever pitched on to effect their designs, and the rather are they credited by our silence. (p. 1)

Hammond claims that Lord Baltimore's party desires "to satisfye every man" and that he himself is especially vexed by the Puritans' lying reports, for he knows "more of their deceits and proceedings

---

[15] Ibid., 321. Hammond may have settled in Newtown as early as November, 1652. See also 272, 339, 366.

[16] Ibid., 410. See also Edwin W. Beitzell, "Newtown Hundred," *Maryland Historical Magazine* 51 (1956):125–39; and ibid., "William Bretton of Newtown Neck, St. Mary's County," ibid. 50 (1955):28 and n. 55.

[17] *Archives of Maryland,* 10:471–72.

than any man living" (p. 1). He says that he has written "an Histori-
call relation of the transactions of *Virginia* and *Maryland*, under the
Government and Tyranny of *Richard Bennet* and Colonel *Claiborn*,
with many remarkable passages of such State-policies as they and
their creatures used." He will "forbeare to publish" the tract, because
he desires that this "pen-jarring may cease," but

> if any of this rout shall any more disturbe the world (for us they can-
> not do) with their seeming-sanctified lies, I will then not spare to
> acquaint the world what they are, and how they live, and give each of
> their Characters to open view, which now lyes masked under the
> hood of holinesse and good disposition, in which I shall somewhat
> more largely answer *Leonard Strongs Babylons fall*, the book of *Vir-
> ginia and Maryland*, and other objections and allegations of theirs,
> being all full of impudence and ignorance. (pp. 1–2)

Hammond's wit and liveliness characterize the entire pamphlet. He
is amazed, he says, that Heaman (whose "imbecillity" and "villainy"
he knows) dared to write at all. Hammond is now forced to "anato-
mize and lay him open to the world a fool, to the State a Knave, to
God a notorious offender, whose unfeigned repentance I cordially
wish, and that his future portion of Grace may over-ballance his
former talents of wit and honesty, in the want of which the poor man
hath been too unhappy" (p. 2). According to Hammond, the sailors
on board Captain Heaman's ship were insolent inebriates, a "rude un-
governed Ships Company" (p. 2). When he recapitulates Heaman's
story, the outraged Hammond exclaims "Hear this O ye Heavens!"
(p. 4). Finally, when he tells of his own actions at the Battle of the
Severn, the pamphlet contains swift narrative and scathing invective:

> Governor *Stone* sent me, not knowing of the compact of *Heamans*
> and the rest, to Patuxent to fetch the Records; I went unarmed
> amongst these Sons of Thunder, onely three or four to row me, and
> despite of all their braves of raising the Country, calling in his Ser-
> vants to aprehend me, threatened me with the severity of their new-
> made Law; my selfe alone seized and carried away the Records in
> defiance; at which time, whatever *Heamans* pretends of compacts
> with Heathens and Papists to destroy them, *Richard Preston* their
> great but then quaking-Commander, shewed me a letter from *Hea-
> mans*, wherein he promised the Ship, Ammunition and Men, should
> be at their service if occasion were, and incouraged them not to think
> of yealding to Governor *Stone*, nor any power from the Lord *Balte-
> more*, and this was the first discovery that ever was made by Gover-
> nor *Stone*, and not a man in armes, nor intended to be at that time,
> and yet before this, meerly upon Captaine *Tilmans* words, and their
> own jealousies, had *Heamans* confederated with, and hired himself

37

to them, and yet this fellow must not only justifie his *Judas*-like dealings, but as it were, challenge applause and merit. (p. 5)

Hammond takes Heaman to task time and again, breaking in on the narrative of Maryland events to attack him:

> But how comes it that their little Agent *Strong*, nor the impudent Author of Virginia and Maryland, in either of their whisking Treatises mention these so specious propositions inserted in *Heamans* his works? *Heamans* you do it scurvily, and we shall yet further discover you. The joyning with Heathens, the plundering of houses, the intent to fire your Ship, the firing of *Abraham Hely* and the horrid treacheries you load us with, will more particularly be questioned and answered in another place than here; we have your Book for evidence of your charge, we only fear you will turn *Jack Lilborn*, and put us to prove it to be yours, which if you do, we have other reckonings to put on your score. (p. 6)

Hammond finally introduces the sworn testimony of three witnesses and affirms that "Heamans hath abused the World with his Pamphlet, not a sillable whereof is truth" (p. 15). He concludes with an apt biblical quotation.

Although *Hammond vs. Heamans* ranks with the finest vitriolic tracts of seventeenth-century America, it would not insure a place for Hammond in America's literary history. But this spate of warring tracts, from 1646 to 1655, gave Maryland and Virginia a bad reputation. Partially to refute this unsavory fame, John Hammond wrote *Leah and Rachel, or the Two Fruitful Sisters Virginia and Maryland* (London, 1656).

Hammond dedicated *Leah and Rachel* to his former comrade-in-arms, William Stone, and to his former neighbor in Isle of Wight County, Virginia, James Wilkinson. A second dedication celebrates the ship captains who trade to Maryland, especially John Whittie, captain of the *Freeman*, and Captain Samuel Tilghman, of the *Golden Fortune*, "now bound for the Province of Mary-land." *Leah and Rachel* opens with a justification of colonization:

> It is the glory of every Nation to enlarge themselves, to encourage their own forraign attempts, and to be able to have of their own, within their own territories, as many several commodities as they can attain to, that so others may rather be beholding to them, then they to others; and to this purpose have Encouragements, Privileges and Emunities been given to any Discoveries or Adventurers into remote Colonies, by all politique Common Wealths in the world.
>
> But alas, we Englishmen (in all things else famous, and to other

Countries terrible) do not onely faile in this, but vilifie, scandalize and cry down such parts of the unknown world, as have been found out, setled and made flourishing, by the charge, hazzard and diligence of their own brethren, as if because removed from us, we either account them people of another world or enemies. (p. 1)

An early expression of love for the Chesapeake area is found in Hammond's pamphlet: "It is not long since I came from thence (God knows sore against my will) having lived there upward of one and twenty years; nor do I intend (by Gods assistance) to be long out of it again" (p. 2). Because Hammond has lived in Virginia and Maryland, he writes with the authority of experience and assures the reader that he will give a true picture of life in America. He ridicules those who write from "hearsay (as Bullock[18] and other lying Writters have done, who at randome or for their own private lucre have rendred their Books rediculous and themselves infamous lyars, nor will I like them, over extoll the places, as if they were rather Paradices than earthly habitations; but truly let ye know, what they are, and how the people there live)"; but in fact, life in America is, for the common people, superior. The impartial truth "will undoubtedly clear up those Foggy Mists, that hath to their own ruine blinded and kept off many from going thither, whose miseries and misfortunes by staying in *England* are much to be lamented, and much to be pittied" (p. 2). Hammond briefly sketches the history of the country and lampoons Anglican ministers: "But *Virginia* savouring not handsomely in England, very few of good conversation would adventure thither, (as thinking it a place wherein surely the fear of God was not), yet many came, such as wore Black Coats, and could babble in a Pulpit, roare in a Tavern, exact from their Parishoners, and rather by their dissolutenesse destroy than feed their Flocks" (p. 5).

According to Hammond, the Chesapeake area is "wholesome, healthy and fruitful," and anyone who works hard will surely get ahead there. But it is not paradise, "not such a Lubberland as the Fiction of the land of Ease, is reported to be, nor such a *Utopian* as *Sr. Thomas Moore* hath related to be found out" (p. 6).[19] Hammond

---

[18] William Bullock, *Virginia Impartially Examined, and Left to Public View* (London, 1649).

[19] Benjamin Franklin in his promotion tract "Information to Those Who Would Remove to America" made the same point and may have been echoing Hammond: "In short, America is The Land of Labour, and by no means what the English call Lubberland, and the French *Pays de Cocagne*." See Albert H. Smyth, ed., *The Writings of Benjamin Franklin*, 8 (New York, 1907):607.

says that his style is blunt, suitable to his purpose: "I shall abhor to spirit [kidnap] over any; but go along with such as are voluntarily desirous to go thither, and lead them with my blunt relation (for truth knows little of eloquence) aboard the Ships thither bound, and carrying you into the Country, shew you the courtesie of the place, the disposition of the Inhabitants, the commodities, and give all sorts of people advice how and where to set down for their present benefit and future accomodation" (pp. 6–7). But in the very next paragraph, Hammond's couplings, alliterations, and colloquialisms shows that he writes with constant care for literary effect:

> If any are minded to repair thither, if they are not in a capacity to defray their own charges (if they are I wish they might and so be at their own disposing) let them not be seduced by those mercinary spirits that know little of the place, nor aime at any good of theirs, but onely by foysting and flattering them to gain a reward of those they procure them for; beware them, for it is not only hab nab whether ye go to a good service or a bad, but scandalous to your selves to be so seduced, and it were good and very just that such vagabond people were severely punished, as great betrayers of their own Nation, for ye cannot imagine but there are as well bad services as good; but I shall shew ye if any happen into the hands of such crooked dispositions, how to order them and ease your selves . . . .
> (p. 7)

After a section dealing with the arrangements for emigrating, Hammond describes the bound servant's ordinary labor, comparing it favorably with the labor of a farmer or draftsman in England. He catalogues the ways that bound servants can improve their conditions. When he describes the legal system of Maryland and Virginia, Hammond assures readers that there is practically no stealing, "for as the Proverb is, where there are no receivers, there are no thieves" (p. 13). He concludes his discussion of the morals of Virginia and Maryland with an affirmation "that since my being in *England*, which is not yet four months, I have been an eye and ear witnesse of more deceits and villanies (and such as modesty forbirds me to utter) than I either ever saw or heard mention made of in *Virginia*, in my one and twenty years abroad in those parts" (p. 15).

Hammond praises the superior opportunities in the New World with a striking simile: "And therefore those that shall blemish *Virginia* any more, do but like the Dog bark against the Moon, untill they be blind and weary; and *Virginia* is now in that secure growing condition, that like the Moon so barked at, she will passe on her course, maugre all detractors, and a few years will bring it to that glorious happinesse, that many of her calumniators, will intercede to procure admittance thither, when it will be hard to be attained to" (p. 15). Thus we come to the most frequently quoted part of his pamphlet: Hammond is amazed that people live impoverished and miserable lives in England when they could emigrate to America and become rich and happy. He brings his pamphlet vividly to life with an unforgettable, concrete picture of English poverty. For nearly a century and a half (until Franklin wrote of walking the unpaved streets of Philadelphia with a roll of bread under each arm, munching on the third), Hammond's was the classic portrayal of the American Dream:

> And therefore I cannot but admire, and indeed much pitty the dull stupidity of people necessitated in *England*, who rather then they will remove themselves, live here a base, slavish, penurious life; as if there were a necessity to live and to live so, choosing rather then they will forsake *England* to stuff *New-Gate, Bridewell,* and other Jayles with their carkessies, nay cleave to tyburne it selfe, and so bring confusion to their souls horror and infamiye to their kindred or posteritie, others itch out their wearisom lives in reliance of other mens charities, an uncertaine and unmanly expectation; some more abhorring such courses betake themselves to almost perpetuall and restlease toyle and druggeries out of which (whilst their strength lasteth) they (observing hard diets, earlie and late houres) make hard shift to subsist from hand to mouth, untill age or sicknesse takes them off from labour and directs them the way to beggerie, and such indeed are to be pittied, relieved and provided for.
>   I have seriously considered when I have (passing the streets) heard the several Cryes, and noting the commodities, and the worth of them they have carried and cryed up and down; how possibly a livelihood could be exacted out of them, as to cry Matches, Smal-coal, Blacking, Pen and Ink, Thred-laces, and a hundred more such kinds of trifling merchandizes; then looking on the nastinesse of their linnen habits and bodies: I conclude if gain sufficient could be raised out of them for subsistence; yet their manner of living was degenerate and base, and their condition to be far below the meanest servant in *Virginia*. (p. 15)

Hammond reveals his literary art when he brings the preceding generalizations to life with a concrete picture of a poor Englishman's misery:

> The other day, I saw a man heavily loaden with a burden of Faggots on his back, crying, Dry Faggots, Dry Faggots; he travailed much ground, bawled frequently, and sweat with his burthen: but I saw none buy any, neer three houres I followed him, in which time he rested, I entered into discourse with him, offered him drink, which

he thankfully accepted of, (as desirous to learn the mistery of his trade) I enquired what he got by each burden when sold? he answered me three pence: I further asked him what he usually got a day? he replyed, some dayes nothing some dayes six pence; some time more, but seldome; me thought it was a pittifull life, and I admired how he could live on it; And yet it were dangerous to advise these wretches to better their conditions by travaile, for fear of the cry of, spirit, a spirit [kidnapper]. (pp. 15–16)

The spirit of self-reliance, the determination to avoid poverty, the dream of a better life, the sympathy for the poor and oppressed, and a concrete realistic picture of poverty—all this creates a passage that will become increasingly typical of American literature.

Hammond describes the farmer's characteristic way of life in the New World and advises the prospective planter how to make a good living there. To conclude this section of the pamphlet, he returns to his favorite theme, the American Dream. In a series of balanced phrases, he insists that there is opportunity for everyone in America: "imployments both for the learned and laborer, recreation for the gentry, traffique for the adventurer, congregations for the ministrie." According to him, some Americans have already risen from poverty and obscurity to wealth and power: "some from being wool-hoppers and of as mean and meaner imployment in England have there grown great merchants, and attained to the most eminent advancements the Country afforded." If men cannot, by diligence and industry, gain estates in America, they will not be able to do so anywhere (p. 19). When he sketches the history of Maryland, he attacks Claiborne and his party, saying that not principles moved them, but greed for "that sweete, that rich, that large Country." In closing, Hammond returns to a statement of his love for the country of America, concluding "in few words, it is that Country in which I desire to spend the remnant of my dayes, in which I covert to make my grave" (p. 28). In a postscript, he pleads with the governor and Council of Virginia to lift their decree against Captain Thomas Thoroughgood, "late Commander of the shipp *Cressent*," who is in danger because he "charitably brought" Hammond to England, "otherwise I had causelesly been put to death" (pp. 29–32).

While Hammond was in England, his wife Ann tried to keep the family's affairs going in Maryland. She must have been a woman of courage and education, for she defended Hammond's interests repeatedly before the Provincial Court of Maryland. Perhaps because the

Puritan party controlled the colony (the governor and Council constituted the Provincial Court), she lost several court decisions. The edict proclaimed by Governor Josias Fendall at the Provincial Court on February 26, 1658/9, that no wives could be admitted as attorneys for their husbands (the women had to select some other attorney) may have been aimed at her. In 1660, after the Restoration, Philip Calvert, the proprietor's half-brother, became governor of Maryland, and Hammond was able to return home in safety.[20]

He was back in St. Mary's County, Maryland, by May 8, 1661, when he served as attorney for John Little.[21] On October 11, he petitioned the Provincial Court that he had "brought a considerable Estate into this Country and had severall Ingagements from many of the Inhabitants due to him, but was by command of the then Governor and power acting for the Lord Proprietary imployed in such services as by the dangerousnes of those tymes caused his flight and removeall leaveing behind him a greate charge and confused his Estate both which suffred irrepairably." Hammond charged that his wife had been oppressed and "imprisoned and other wayes dampnifyed Insomuch that she was not onely brought to extreme want, but your petitioner wrapt up in strange and unjust Engagements." Therefore Hammond pleaded "that he may have Reheareings of what hath passed in the severall Courts of this Province and that Execution may be in those cases suspended." The court ordered that in those "Judgements [that] hath not been already executed against him he shall have a *Scire facias.*"[22]

The litigious Hammond was involved in several minor actions before the court in 1661 and served several times on a jury (usually as foreman). Then, on February 14, 1661/2, he appeared before the Provincial Court, requesting that a note that his wife Ann had given to John Lord in the amount of 6,000 pounds of tobacco be declared null and void. Walter Pake testified that

> after the departure of John Hammond out of this Province he was present at a Court holden at Patuxent (William Fuller then ruleing the Country as Governor) where Mrs. Hammond, one John Lord, Captain [William] Mitchell and Richard Hoskegs were conferring together. There they perswaded the said Mrs. Hammond to Sign a

[20] For Ann Hammond's appearances in the Provincial Court, see *Archives of Maryland*, 10 and 41. Gov. Fendall's proclamation is recorded in ibid., 41:233.
[21] Ibid., 41:581.
[22] Ibid., 483. Here and in the following quotations, I have expanded abbreviations.

bill to the said Lord for six thousand pounds of tobacco, and desired
him this deponent to Wittness itt, which with much perswasions of
the said partyes, he did, but would have had the said Mitchell to have
witnessed itt likewise who refused, replying I cannot wittness such a
date because it is knowne I was not in the Country, the same replyed
the said Hoskins.

Evidently Lord somehow (the court record suggests that the reason
had something to do with the Puritans being in power) forced Ann
Hammond to give him a false bill of debt.[23]

On September 16, 1662, Hammond signed an agreement (which
was confirmed by the governor and secretary) with Richard Willan,
the sheriff of St. Mary's County, whereby he agreed to act as under-
sheriff for one-half of all profits and benefits of the office.[24] Later in
1662, Hammond acted as attorney for Marmaduke Snow and for John
Little.[25]

The most interesting and the last case concerning Hammond to
appear in the records of Maryland concerned an attempt by Jacob
Lumbroso to slander Hammond's wife and to make the redoubtable
writer a laughingstock. Lumbroso, a Portuguese Jew who emigrated
to Maryland about 1655, served as a physician, attorney, innkeeper,
storekeeper, merchant, and planter. Though evidently a man of education and ability, he seems to have been an unsavory character (being charged at various times with abortion, attempted rape, and
receiving stolen goods).[26] He quoted a few lines of verse (on the evil
of slander!) in appearances before the Provincial Court in another
case, and he and Hammond probably shared an interest in literature.
On June 26, 1662, Lumbroso sued Hammond for a debt of 1,000
pounds of tobacco, itemizing his goods at 500 pounds for one "anker
[10 gallons] of Brandy, 400 pounds for one hundred pounds of sugar,
and 100 pounds for two turkeys." Hammond acknowledged receiving
these goods from Lumbroso but claimed that the prices Lumbroso
cited were not those agreed upon. Two weeks later, "Att a Court
held att New Towne for the County of St. Marys the 5th of August,"
Hammond introduced a witness, William Price, who testified that he
and some companions were drinking at Hammond's inn about the end

---

[23] Ibid., 528–29.
[24] Ibid., 49:300–301.
[25] Ibid., 41:572 and 581.
[26] For Lumbroso (sometimes called John Lumbrozo), see the *DAB* account,
and the supplementary information in the *Archives of Maryland*, 53:1–li, and
60:xlii–xliii.

of "January last" when Jacob Lumbroso came in and "called for a bottle of Liquor saying Mr. Hammond I must not pay soe deere as the rest in regard I am to gett nothing by you in the same goods." According to Price, Hammond agreed to this. Further, Price testified that he had gone with one of Hammond's sons when Lumbroso gave them two turkeys for delivery to Hammond. Price had asked Lumbroso "upon what account they were delivered," and he replied, because "Mrs. Hammond made and washt his Linnen."

At this same court session, Hammond petitioned against Lumbroso for slandering his wife. Hammond asserted that he had purchased of Lumbroso "certain Goods for a Sume of tobacco by them agreed on payable att the Crop" and that he had offered Lumbroso a note "which he delayed to take, he professing very much kindnes and severall extraordinary Curtesyes to him your petitioner." Thereafter, Lumbroso visited Hammond's frequently "and by some descourse dropt from his wife and the said Lumbroso, he found cause to forwarne him his howse." After this, Lumbroso demanded a greater sum than Hammond owed. When Hammond refused to pay the extravagant amount, Lumbroso reported that he had trusted Hammond with goods and could not receive payment. According to Hammond, Lumbroso also publicly alleged that Hammond "would have had him layn with his wife for satisfaction." He said that Lumbroso repeated this malicious lie "soe Confidently and frequently that itt became a Generall discourse and hath soe blemisht your petitioner that he is become the by word and Scoff of many." Walter Pake[s] testified that he had heard Lumbroso say that Hammond "had proffered him his wife to lye with her in sattisfaction of some Goods." Pake[s] further testified that after hearing this he recriminated with Hammond, who said that "he asked the said Lumbroso why he gave his wife an Elle of fine Holland and the said Lumbroso answered him, that he gave itt her for the times he had layne with her, And the said Hammond swore many Bloody oathes and called the said Lumbroso Rogue and Villaine and said he had forwarned him his howse." Another witness also testified that he had heard Lumbroso say that Hammond offered him "to lye with his wife" in payment of the debt.

On October 10, 1662, the case was decided. The jury concluded that Hammond did not owe Lumbroso anything, but that Lumbroso, for defaming Hammond and his wife, had to pay Hammond "five thousand pounds of tobacco damages with Costs of suite." As the editor of the *Archives of Maryland* laconically remarked, "Dr. Lumbroso and Mr. Hammond fell out and the evidence in the case was quite discreditable to the physician."[27]

John Hammond evidently died sometime in late February or early March, 1662/3. He witnessed a deed on November 25, 1662, and he was still alive at some time in February, but there is a reference to him as deceased in March, 1662/3.[28] Like Andrew White, Hammond was not a professional writer and probably cared nothing for literary reputation. He wrote his first pamphlet to urge his—and Lord Baltimore's—side of the case; and he evidently wrote the second pamphlet for pay. He published nothing in America, for there were no printing presses south of Boston and the population was too small to furnish a profitable market for books. Besides, he was not a writer, but a planter, innkeeper, and attorney. Nevertheless, his promotion tract was a definite advance in American literature.

Moses Coit Tyler has high praise for *Leah and Rachel*: "This, indeed, is genuine American talk. Here, certainly, in these brusque sentences, do we find a literature smacking of American soil and smelling of American air. Here, thus early in our studies, do we catch in American writings that new note of hope and of help for humanity in distress, and of a rugged personal independence, which, almost from the hour of our first settlements in this land, American began to send back, with unveiled exultation, to Europe."[29] Hammond's attack on tavern-roaring ministers, unrealistic utopian schemes, and negligent and idle housewives probably marks the earliest appearance of these now-familiar humorous subjects of American satire. Even more striking are the emerging American attitudes: the spirit of self-reliance, the determination to avoid poverty, the dream of a better life, the pity for the poor and downtrodden, the disregard for social classes, and a tough-minded attitude toward the economic facts of life. Although Hammond shows that he loves the Chesapeake Bay area and that he believes his future lies in America, he does not think of himself as an American, even though Londoners regarded him as an alien. The term *American* (first used by Cotton Mather about 1698 in

27 *Archives of Maryland*, 41:588–91 and xiv.
28 Ibid., 41:602; 49:202. His widow, Ann, married Pope Alvey some time between Oct. 17, 1663, and Jan., 1663/4. See ibid., 49:156. Pope Alvey, a cruel planter, is known to have beaten one indentured servant to death. See ibid., xix–xx and 453. Of Hammond's children, at least Mordecai and Daniel survived their father. See ibid., 452–53, 455, 496.
29 *History of American Literature*, 56–57.

the *Magnalia*) did not yet exist, but another word for the same idea (*creole*, a person born or living in America of European descent) was current. Hammond thought of himself as an Englishman who lived in America—but he revealed that the English at home were, by their ignorance and intolerance, deliberately separating the English abroad from them and driving the future Americans along the road to their own nationalism. Even while revealing that a national self-consciousness did not yet exist among Americans, Hammond demonstrates both the reasons why such a consciousness would come about and a set of what we now recognize as nascent American characteristics. *Leah and Rachel* makes a major step toward national identity and contains the fullest seventeenth-century statement of the American Dream.

GEORGE ALSOP

ADVERTISER

George Alsop's witty *A Character of the Province of Mary-Land* (London, 1666) uses the current literary fashions to win his audience: the background of the new science; the tradition of learned wit, especially the elaborately rhetorical low style characteristic of Thomas Nashe; the Restoration frankness about sex; comic wordplay, including paradox, pun, incongruous personification, extravagantly extended figures of speech, and word coinages; and finally, an unusual number of folk sayings, maxims, allusions, and colloquialisms. All these make up a racy prose, altogether extraordinary for a promotion tract. Alsop's *Character* is one of the most witty and scurrilous books of colonial America.

George Alsop was the elder of two sons of Peter and Rose Alsop, of London. He was baptized at St. Martin-in-the-Fields on June 19, 1636. The will of Peter Alsop reveals that he was a tailor, who probably was hard-pressed to provide his family with a reasonable standard of living.[1] Although the allusions in the *Character* prove that George Alsop was well-read and knew Latin and French, no information concerning his education has come to light. An outspoken

---

[1] "Georgius Alsopp" was baptized on June 19, 1636, the son of "Petri et Rosae" Alsop. J. V. Kitto, comp., *The Register of St. Martin-in-the-Fields, London, 1619–1636*, Harleian Society Publications, vol. 66 (London, 1936), 127. The will of Peter Alsop, the father of George Alsop, is in PCC Eure, 1672, folio 117. I am indebted to the Principal Probate Registry for furnishing me with a photostat. For an attempt to show that the George Alsop born in Westminster is the same George Alsop who wrote *A Character of the Province of Mary-Land* (London, 1666), see the Appendix, pp. 343–45.

Royalist, George Alsop indentured himself to four years' service as a bondservant in Maryland because of his disgust for the political and religious situation in Cromwellian England.[2] On August 19, 1658, he wrote, "I have lived with sorrow to see the Anointed of the Lord [Charles I] Tore from his throne by the hands of Paricides, and in contempt haled, in view of God, Angels, and Men, upon a public Theatre, and there murthered."[3] Needless to say, England was not then a safe place for a man who dared to write such opinions. A devout Anglican, he was outraged by the triumph of the Puritan forces:

> I have seen the sacred Temple of the Almighty, in scorn by Schismatics made the Receptacle of Theeves and Robbers; and those Religious Prayers, that in devotion Evening and Morning were offered up as a Sacrifice to our God, rent by Sacrilegious hands, and made no other use of, then sold to Brothel-houses to light Tobacco with.
> (p. 74)

Alsop, Anglican and Royalist, emigrated to Maryland to escape the conditions in England. According to the information in *A Character of . . . Mary-Land* he had spent two years as a "Handicraft" apprentice (p. 31) in London before becoming an indentured servant for four years in Maryland; while he was in Maryland, his brother, "P. A." (Peter Alsop), was serving an apprenticeship at Joiners' Hall in London.[4] George Alsop had some reputation as a writer before leaving England. His letter dated "From the Chimney Corner upon a low cricket, where I writ this in the noise of some six Women, Aug. 19 Anno 1658," replied to a request for a poem on the king's murder. In Maryland, too, he became known for his literary ability. In the province, "some Gentlemen" asked him to write a poem about a purple hat he had received from England (p. 107).

Alsop arrived in Maryland in December, 1658, or early January, 1658/9 ("after a five months dangerous passage," p. 91) and before January 17, 1658/9, had become an indentured servant to Thomas

---

[2] Harrison T. Meserole, Walter Sutton, and Brom Weber, eds., *American Literature: Tradition and Innovation* (Lexington, Mass., 1969), 27, speculate that Alsop may have been arrested for slandering Cromwell and the Puritan regime and punished by being transported to the colonies as an indentured servant. But he clearly states in the *Character* that he freely indentured himself.

[3] *A Character of the Province of Mary-Land*, 73–74. Hereafter page references will be given in the text.

[4] A Peter Alsop became a member of the livery of the Joiners' Company in 1689. This is probably George Alsop's brother. Henry Laverock Phillips, *Annals of the worshipful company of Joiners of the City of London* (London, 1915), 105.

Stockett (p. 97) for four years. Like Alsop, Stockett was a Royalist and had only emigrated to Maryland a year before. He had settled near the head of the Chesapeake Bay, south of the Susquehanna River, by the present town of Havre de Grace. In 1658, this was the frontier, and Stockett lived on the edge of the wilderness, with the Susquehanna Indians as his neighbors. Here Alsop spent his four years (1659–62) as an indentured servant, perhaps as Stockett's secretary and accountant. Thomas Stockett purchased Harmer's Town, June 30, 1659, and Bourne, June, 1661. The name of George Alsop, as one of Stockett's servants, is found on the patent recording the latter transaction. By 1661, Stockett was a captain in the militia and a leading citizen of Baltimore County. He was elected to the state legislature in April, 1661, and in May was appointed one of the two agents for the Susquehanna Indians. Any Susquehanna Indian who wanted to travel among the English plantations had to stop at Stockett's house (or at Jacob Clauson's) and secure a pass. Any English runaway servant who joined the Susquehanna Indians was to be returned by them to Stockett's. Obviously Alsop must have seen these Indians frequently and probably traded with them.[5]

By December 11, 1662, Alsop had gained his freedom. What he did during the time of his indentureship and afterwards is unknown. When he wrote his cousin Ellinor Evins on December 9, 1662, he said that he was sending her a present of some furs. This may suggest that he was trading with the Indians, perhaps still working for Stockett. All that is known for certain is that he remained in Maryland until after April 9, 1663, the date of the last letter printed in *A Character*. He returned to England in late 1663 or sometime in 1664, for he evidently wrote the book in London in 1665.[6]

[5] For Stockett, the account in John D. Gilmary Shea's edition of Alsop's *Character* (New York, 1869), 13–15, is valuable. For Stockett's land purchases, see Record of Patents, Liber 6, folio 159, and Liber 2, ff. 442–44, Maryland Hall of Records; Harry H. Kunesch, Jr., ed., George Alsop's *A Character of the Province of Maryland: A Critical Edition* (Ann Arbor, 1970; in *Dissertation Abstracts*, 31 [1971]:4775-A), 1–4, 42. Gust Skordas, comp., *The Early Settlers of Maryland* (Baltimore, 1968), 443, records that Stockett emigrated in 1658. For his political career and dealings with the Indians, see *Archives of Maryland*, 1:396, 426, 460; 3:421, 424, 487. For the present location of Harmer's Town, see Paul Wilstach, *Tidewater Maryland* (Indianapolis, 1931), 184–88.

[6] Alsop, pp. 105–107. Although the letters are dated only by day and month, the year can be ascertained from internal references. Kunesch gives the years in brackets in his edition, but he mis-dates, I believe, the last four letters, making them all a year later than they actually are. In his last letter to his brother, dated at the end "Dec. 11." (p. 112), Alsop says he has "made a shift to unloose

Moses Coit Tyler said of Alsop's *Character* that there was "but one other American book produced in the seventeenth century that for mirthful, grotesque, and slashing energy, can compare with this."[7] But Nathaniel Ward, in writing *The Simple Cobler of Aggawam in America*, had an easier task than Alsop: for Ward wrote a satire; Alsop, a promotion tract. Even the choice of a title shows that Alsop chafed against the restrictive form and content of the typical promotion tract, for his title tells the reader that he is giving a "character-book," a popular seventeenth-century genre, consisting of abstract character-sketches (usually satiric) of representative types, such as a "character of a ranting minister" or a "character of a dunce." Because of the popularity of the character books, numerous imitations appeared. Of Owen Felltham's *Resolves* (a book cited by Alsop), the *Literary History of England* says that it "can be best described as a collection of short essays written in the style of the character books."[8] Writers before Alsop had published characters of various countries (including Owen Felltham, *A Character of the Low Countries*), but Alsop's was the first and only "character" of any American colony. Alsop opens *A Character of the Province of Maryland* with a dedication to Lord Baltimore, saying that what he writes he knows to be true, "It being an infallible Maxim, *That there is no Globe like the occular and experimental view of a Country*" (sig. A3–A3ᵛ). Alsop immediately begins creating the wild and careless *persona* that is among the book's chief delights:

> If I have wrote or composed any thing that's wilde and confused, it is because I am so my self, and the world, as far as I can perceive, is not much out of the same trim; therefore I resolve, if I am brought to

---

my self from my Collar now as well as you" (p. 106). Kunesch, p. 144, dates this letter 1663, which would mean that Alsop spent five years (or at least four years and eleven months) as an indentured servant. But Alsop refers to his "four years" indentureship on numerous occasions in *A Character* (e.g., A3ᵛ, 7, 31, 32–33, 37, etc.). Since we know that Alsop was already indentured to Thomas Stockett and was somewhat familiar with the Maryland scene by Jan. 17, 1658/9 (see pp. 91–95), he would have completed his four-year indentureship in Dec., 1662 (or at latest, early Jan., 1663). Therefore, the letter dated "Dec. 11." referring to the completion of his indentureship should be dated 1662. And the following letter, dated "Decem. 13." (p. 114), which begins "This is the entrance upon my fifth year" in Maryland, also supports a dating of 1662, rather than 1663.

[7] *History of American Literature*, 58.

[8] Albert C. Baugh, ed., *A Literary History of England* (New York, 1948), 604, n. 12.

the Bar of *Common Law* for anything I have done here, to plead *Non compos mentis*, to save my Bacon.

There is an old Saying in English, *He must rise betimes that would please every one.* And I am afraid I have lain so long a bed, that I think I shall please no body; if it must be so, I cannot help it. (sig. A4–A4ᵛ)

In another dedication "To all the Merchant Adventurers for *MARYLAND*, together with those Commanders of Ships that saile into that Province," Alsop tells that he wrote the "major part" of his *Character* during "the intermitting time of my sickness." "H. W." (author of a prefatory poem) adds that a *Character* was "Composed in such a Time, when most men were/Smitten with Sickness, or sur-priz'd with Fear" (sig. B2). Since this evidently refers to the comet and great plague of 1665, Alsop probably wrote the pamphlet while recovering from some sickness in London in that year. His reference to London as "here" (e.g., below, p. 59) tends to confirm this reasoning.

George Alsop's "Preface to the Reader" satirizes with paradox and proverb his own egotism in publishing a book: "I am so self-conceited of my own merits, that I almost think I want none." A prefatory poem, "The Author to his Book," again refers to his illness while writing the tract and compares his book to a child, calling it "The Bastard Off-spring of a New-born wit":

> Farewel, poor Brat, thou in a monstrous World;
> In swadling bands, thus up and down art hurl'd;
> There to receive what Destiny doth contrive,
> Either to perish, or be sav'd alive.
> Good Fate protect thee from a Criticks power,
> For If he comes, thou'rt gone in half an hour,
> Stifl'd and blasted, 'tis their usual way,
> To make that Night, which is as bright as Day.
> (ll. 29–36)

After attacking critics for twenty more lines, Alsop prophesies the ordinary readers' reaction: they will damn the book for fear that other strange creations will come from America. And so he will be hanged —but Alsop concludes with a promise of rebirth for his "Genius."

> Asses and Captious Fools, not six in ten
> Of thy Spectators will be real men,
> To Umpire up the badness of the cause,
> And screen my weakness from the rav'nous Laws,
> Of those that will undoubted sit to see

How they might blast this new-born Infancy:
If they should burn him, they'd conclude hereafter,
'Twere too good death for him to dye a Martyr;
And if they let him live, they think it will
Be but a means for to encourage ill,
And bring in time some strange *Antipod'ans*,
A thousand Leagues beyond *Philippians*,
To storm our Wits; therefore he must not rest,
But shall be hang'd, for all he has been prest:
Thus they conclude.—My Genius comforts give,
In Resurrection he will surely live.

(ll. 55–70)

Three more poems conclude the introduction: one by William Bogherst;[9] one by "H. W., Master of Arts"; and one by "Will. Barber."[10] "H. W." also contributed the lines that accompany Alsop's portrait:

View here the Shadow whose Ingenious Hand
Hath drawne exact the Province Maryland
Display'd her Glory in such Scenes of Witt
That those that read must fall in Love with it
For which his Labour hee deserves the praise
As well as Poets doe the wreath of Bays.

(frontispiece)

The body of the *Character* is organized under six headings. The first part, "The Scituation, and plenty of the Province" follows the usual scholastic pattern of the colonization literature of the day, moving from the general to the specific. Thus the topics are the geography of Maryland, vegetable life, animals (wild and domestic), birds (divided into migratory species and annuals), fish, and, finally, grain.[11] Alsop begins by praising the climate and abundance of Mary-

[9] I believe that this is William Boghurst (1631?–85), a well-known London apothecary. Henry B. Wheatley reprints his advertisement from the *Intelligencer*, no. 59, for July 31, 1655, in *Pepysiana*, vol. 9, pt. 1 of *The Diary of Samuel Pepys* (New York, 1900). E. Ashworth Underwood et al. give some account of Boghurst in *A History of the Worshipful Society of Apothecaries of London, 1617–1815* (London, 1963), 112. There is an altar tomb for his wife, Elizabeth Boghurst, who died on Dec. 31, 1688, at Waterden Church, Brothercress Hundred, Norfolk. Edmund Farrer, *The Church Heraldry of Norfolk* 2 (Norwich, England, 1889):343. Boghurst also wrote *Loimographia: An account of the great Plague of London in the year 1665* (London, 1894) and a long unpublished poem "Londinologia, Sive Londini Encomium, The Antiquities and Excellencies of London," British Museum, Sloane MS 908, folios 72–84.
[10] I have been unable to identify "H. W." and "Will. Barber."
[11] I quote the chapter titles as they are given on the title page. The best discussion of the usual organization of promotion tracts is by Theodore Horn-

land. Mixing sexual metaphors with garden imagery, Alsop, like Hammond, portrays Maryland as a fruitful mother:

> Pleasant, in respect of the multitude of Navigable Rivers and Creeks that conveniently and most profitably lodge within the armes of her green, spreading, and delightful Woods; whose natural womb (by her plenty) maintains and preserves the several diversities of Animals that rangingly inhabit her Woods; as she doth otherwise generously fructifie this piece of Earth with almost all sorts of Vegetables, as well Flowers with their varieties of colours and smells, as Herbes and Roots. (p. 2)

Echoing the biblical imagery of the Garden of Eden, Alsop dwells on the plenitude of the province and almost claims that Maryland is paradise:

> Neither do I think there is any place under the Heavenly altitude, or that has footing or room upon the circular Globe of this world, that can parallel this fertile and pleasant piece of ground in its multiplicity, or rather Natures extravagancy of a superbounding plenty. For so much doth this Country increase in a swelling Springtide of rich variety and diversities of all things, not only common provisions that supply the reaching stomach of man with a satisfactory plenty, but also extends with its liberality and free convenient benefits to each sensitive faculty, according to their several desiring Appetites. So that had Nature made it her business, on purpose to have found out a situation for the Soul of profitable Ingenuity, she could not have fitted herself better in the traverse of the whole Universe, nor in convenienter terms have told man, *Dwell here, live plentifully and be rich.* (pp. 3–4)

He claims that the "Trees, Plants, Fruits, Flowers, and Roots" that grow in the province are "Emblems or Hieroglyphics of our Adamitical or Primitive situations" because of their beauty and lovely odor. Using synesthesia, he asserts that "Their dumb vegetable Oratory" tells the inhabitants that they need look no further "for any other Terrestrial Paradise to suspend or tyre their curiosity upon, while she is extant" (p. 4). Alsop continues to use the ideas associated with the Garden of Eden and a primitive Golden Age by comparing Maryland favorably with "those parts of the Creation that have borne the Bell away (for many ages) for a vegetable plentiousness." Showing that he has read and been bored by promotion tracts which exhaustively

---

berger, "Promotion Tracts," in Walter Blair, Theodore Hornberger, and Randall Stewart, eds., *The Literature of the United States* (Chicago, 1953), 17–18.

catalog plants, he says that he will forbear to enumerate "those several sorts of vegetables that flourishingly grows here" lest his book look more like "an Herbal, than a small Manuscript or History" (p. 6). His flippant attitude toward the usual contents of the promotion tract helps establish the comic (sometimes burlesque) tone.

To the Englishmen of Alsop's day, venison was a delicacy that could be afforded only by the wealthy nobles who owned large private parks where poaching was forbidden. But in Maryland, claims Alsop, the people have as much deer as they can eat (p. 6). Indeed, he adds that "the Gentleman whom I served my conditional and prefixed Time withall, had at one time in his house fourscore venisons, ... so that before this Venison was brought to a period by eating it, it so nauseated our appetites and stomachs, that plain bread was rather courted and desired than it." These are the same deer, he assures his readers, that are such a luxury in England. And he hyperbolically compares America to a nobleman's park, where the deer roam free, "bounded and impanell'd with no other pales than the rough and billowed Ocean." Thoreau, in the second paragraph of the chapter "Higher Laws" in *Walden*, makes the same comparison when he writes that the "hunting and fishing grounds" of New England boys "were not limited like the preserves of an English nobleman, but were more boundless even than those of a savage." Alsop uses a bawdy comparison to London prostitutes to point up the tameness of the deer: "They are also mighty numerous in the Woods, and are little or not at all affrighted at the face of a man, but (like the Does of *Whetsons* Park) though their hydes are not altogether so gaudy to extract an admiration from the beholder, yet they will stand (almost) till they be scratcht" (p. 8). Besides using a familiar London allusion to shock the reader, Alsop implicitly comments on the social order of England and contrasts it with America. England is identified with nobleman's parks, aristocracy, social stratification, and now with the social ills of prostitution and its concomitant connotations of crime, evil, and the breakdown of the social system. Maryland, on the other hand, is like one enormous nobleman's park, where real deer live in a state of fearlessness like that which once existed in Eden and exists now in America, away from the social ills that beset English civilization. As he wrote in a letter to his father on September 7, 1658, when leaving England: "The World's in a heap of troubles and confusion .... I am now bound for Mary-Land, and I am told that's a New World, but if it prove no better then this, I shall not get much by my change; but before Ile revoke my Resolution, I am resolv'd to put it to adventure, for I think it can hardly be worse then this is" (p. 83). Later, Alsop explicitly attacks the evils of contemporary English civilization.

The indentured servant unwittingly supplies ammunition for the French philosophes of the next century (who were to maintain that men and animals degenerated in America) when he attempts to reassure the prospective emigrants that the "Wolves, Bears and Panthers" of America are not really dangerous:

> As for the Wolves, Bears, and Panthers of this Country, they inhabit commonly in great multitudes up in the remotest parts of the Continent; yet at some certain time they come down near the Plantations, but do little hurt or injury worth noting, and that which they do is of so degenerate and low a nature, (as in reference to the fierceness and heroick vigour that dwell in the same kind of Beasts in other Countries) that they are hardly worth mentioning: For the highest of their designs and circumventing reaches is but cowardly and base, only to steal a poor Pigg, or kill a lost and half starved Calf. The Effigies of a man terrifies them dreadfully, for they no sooner espy his but their hearts are at their mouths, and the spurs upon their heels, they (having no more manners then Beasts) gallop away, and never bid them farewell that are behind them. (pp. 8–9)

Attributing human characteristics to animals is in itself humorous, but suggesting a courteous mode of behavior in connection with a surprise meeting between a man and a bear is burlesque situational humor. Alsop's incongruity between diction and subject is a perfect example of the burlesque, as later defined by Richard Lewis (see below, pp. 129–30).

The other wild animals are merely listed, though Alsop points out that the furs of several species are valuable. While describing the waterfowl, he incongruously uses legal jargon (as well as apt assonance and consonance) in an artistic manner:

> The Swans, the Geese and Ducks (with other Water-Fowl) . . . arrive in millionous multitudes in *Mary-Land* about the middle of *September*, and take their winged farewell about the midst of *March*: But while they do remain, and beleagure the borders of the shoar with their winged Dragoons, several of them are summoned by a Writ of *Fieri facias*, to answer their presumptuous contempt upon a Spit. (p. 12)

An eight-line poem concludes the first chapter.

"The Laws, customs, and natural Demeanor of the Inhabitant"

continues the idyllic picture of the province. Catholics and Protestants live happily together. There are no beggars and no left-wing
sects (like England's Fifth-monarchy men and Adamites). Maryland's
winters, Alsop sarcastically says, would abruptly halt the Adamites'
nakedness:

> Nor did I ever see (here in *Mary-Land*) any of those dancing Ad-
> amitical Sisters, that plead a primitive Innocency for their base ob-
> scenity, and naked deportment; but I conceive if some of them were
> there at some time of the year, between the Months of *January* and
> *February*, when the winds blow from the North-West quarter of the
> world, that it would both cool, and (I believe) convert the hottest of
> these Zealots from their burning and fiercest Concupiscence. (pp.
> 17–18)

After discussing the system of government, Alsop takes up the
courts. Since there are few disputes and consequently few lawyers,
the courts have little business. He then mounts an attack on that
standard humorous butt, the lawyer, comparing him unfavorably to
the farmer:

> Here if the Lawyer had nothing else to maintain him but his bawling,
> he might button up his Chops, and burn his Buckrom Bag, or else
> hang it upon a pin untill its Antiquity had eaten it up with durt and
> dust: Then with a Spade, like his Grandsire *Adam*, turn up the face
> of the Creation, purchasing his bread by the sweat of his brows, that
> before was got by the motionated Water-works of his jaws. (pp.
> 20–21)

Once again, England and America, as symbolized, respectively, by
a lawyer and a farmer, have been implicitly contrasted.

There are no crimes, prisons, or "common alehouses" in Maryland
and the children are better brought up (because they are given work,
discipline, and responsibility) than in England. Alsop says that the
parents, "especially those of the Masculine Sex," are "generally conveniently confident, reservedly subtle, quick in apprehending, but
slow in resolving; and where they spy profit sailing towards them
with the wings of a prosperous gale, there they become much familiar" (p. 24). This early characterization of Americans is significant
for its contribution to the idea of the American as a shrewd business-
man—the sharp trader with a genius for profit. It is remarkable that
the English in America were already thought of as a people with
their own characteristics. The indentured servant made the same
point at greater length in a letter of January 17, 1658/9, to "Mr.
M. F.," who had asked Alsop's advice about sending a shipment of

goods to Maryland. Evidently tales of Americans swindling "raw
and unexperienced" English merchants (who of course assumed that
they were superior to the rustic Americans) were rife in Maryland,
for Alsop could not have been in America for more than six weeks
when he wrote:

> *Sir*, If you send any Adventure to this Province, let me beg to give
> you this advice in it; That the Factor whom you imploy be a man of
> Brain, otherwise the Planter will go near to make a Skimming-dish
> of his Skull: I know your Genius can interpret my meaning. The peo-
> ple of this place (whether the saltness of the Ocean gave them any
> alteration when they went over first, or their continual dwelling
> under the remote Clyme where they now inhabit, I know not) are
> a more acute people in general, in matters of Trade and Commerce,
> then in any other place of the World; and by their crafty and sure
> bargaining, do often over-reach the raw and unexperienced Mer-
> chant. To be short, he that undertakes Merchants imployment for
> *Mary-Land*, must have more of Knave in him then Fool. (pp. 96–97)

As we will see, just such an inexperienced factor is the persona of
Ebenezer Cook's *Sot-Weed Factor*. Alsop continues his chapter on the
government and inhabitants of Maryland with an appreciation of
Maryland girls, which may reflect his own failure (and reasons for
the failure) at courtship: "All Complemental Courtships, drest up in
critical Rarities, are meer strangers to them, plain wit comes nearest
their Genius; so that he that intends to Court a *Mary-Land* Girle,
must have something more then the Tautologies of a longwinded
speech to carry on his design, or else he may (for ought I know) fall
under the contempt of her frown, and his own windy Oration" (pp.
24–25). Alsop satirizes the Maryland Quakers, remarking that they
are the only puritans of any number in Maryland, and concludes with
a brief poem which echoes his earlier call to *"Dwell here, live plenti-
fully, and be rich."*

In chapter three, "The worst and best usage of a Maryland Servant,
opened in view," Alsop justifies degrees in social order, citing the
Great Chain of Being in support of his position, and particularly
attacks the doctrines of the Levellers. He decries England's supposed
overpopulation and (with a possible Hamlet reference) claims that
the English poor, "their bodies like a Sentinel must continually wait
to see when their Souls will be frighted away by the pale Ghost of a
starving want" (p. 30). He commends the position of the Maryland
indentured servant: "the four years I served there were not to me so
slavish, as a two years Servitude of a Handicraft Apprenticeship was

here in *London*" (p. 31). Like Captain John Smith, William Bradford and other promoters of America, Alsop says that Americans should be hardy and tells the effeminate rich to remain in England "lest the roughness of the Ocean, together with the staring visages of the wild Animals, which they may see after their arrival into the Country, may alter the natural dispositions of their bodies, that the stay'd and solid part that kept its motion by Doctor *Trigs* purgationary operation, may run beyond the byas of the wheel in a violent and laxative confusion" (pp. 31–32). The virile, however, and especially the poor should emigrate to the new world, where they will find opportunity, respect, and self-respect. Alsop lists the terms of servitude in Maryland and attacks America's slanderers:

Then let those whose chaps are always breathing forth those filthy dregs of abusive exclamations, which are Lymbeckt from their sottish and preposterous brains, against this Country of *Mary-Land*, saying, That those which are transported over thither, are sold in open Market for Slaves, and drawn in Carts like Horses; which is so damnable an untruth, that if they should search to the very Center of Hell, and enquire for a Lye of the most antient and damned stamp, I confidently believe they could not find one to parallel this: For know, That the Servants here in *Mary-Land* of all Colonies, distant or remote Plantations, have the least cause to complain, either for strictness of Servitude, want of Provisions, or need of Apparel. (pp. 34–35)

Burlesquing the concept of America as a land of opportunity, Alsop praises the abundant sexual opportunities of the servants, using bawdy humor to ridicule at least one aspect of the American Dream:

The Women that go over into this Province as Servants, have the best luck here as in any place of the world besides; for they are no sooner on shoar, but they are courted into a Copulative Matrimony, which some of them (for ought I know) had they not come to such a Market with their Virginity, might have kept it by them untill it had been mouldy, unless they had let it out by a yearly rent to some of the Inhabitants of *Lewknors-lane*, or made a Deed of Gift of it to Mother *Coney*, having only a poor stipend out of it, untill the Gallows or Hospital called them away. Men have not altogether so good luck as Women in this kind, or natural preferment, without they be good Rhetoricians, and well vers'd in the Art of perswasion, then (probably) they may ryvet themselves in the time of their Servitude into the private and reserved favour of their Mistress, if Age speak their Master deficient. (pp. 38–39)

Alsop's burlesque of the opportunity theme (like his choice of title and his remark about promotion tracts sounding like herbals) suggests that he is chafing against the form and content of the promotion tract.

Craftsmen, Alsop says, should come to Maryland. Maryland needs them, and in England they "dwell so closely and stifingly together in one and the same place, that like the chafing Gum in Watered-Tabby, they eat into the folds of one anothers Estates" (p. 40). Not only would the craftsmen and merchants have a better standard of living in Maryland than in England, but "their conditions" would be "much better, as well in reference to their Estates, as to the satisfactoriness of their minds; having a continual imployment, and from that imployment a continual benefit, without either begging, seducing, or flattering for it, encroaching that one month from one of the same profession, that they are heaved out themselves the next" (p. 40). Thus Alsop condemns the materialism and competitiveness of English society, which forces the merchants and craftsmen to treat one another like rival animals fighting over the same morsel of food:

> For I have observed on the other side of *Mary-Land*, that the whole course of most Mechanical endeavors, is to catch, snatch, and undervalue one another, to get a little work, or a Customer; which when they have attained by their lowbuilt and sneaking circumventings, it stands upon so flashy, mutable, and transitory a foundation, that the best of his hopes is commonly extinguisht before the poor undervalued Tradesman is warm in the enjoyment of his Customer. (pp. 40–41)

Alsop's damning the commercial basis of society and the hypocrisy of merchants and tradesmen anticipates Thoreau's diatribe, in the fourth paragraph of the first chapter, "Economy," of *Walden*, against the ordinary lives led by his neighbors: "seeking to curry favor, to get custom, by how many modes, not only state-prison offences; lying, flattering, voting, contracting yourselves into a nutshell of civility, or dilating into an atmosphere of thin and vaporous generosity, that you may persuade your neighbor to let you make his shoes, or his hat, or his coat, or his carriage, or import groceries for him." Alsop ridicules the boasting hypocrisy of some craftsmen who would rather "take a Bear by the tooth, as think of leaving their own Country, though they live among their own National people, and are governed by the same Laws they have here, yet all this wont do with them." The reason why these braggarts won't leave England is simply because "there's a great Sea betwixt them and *Mary-Land*, and in that Sea there are Fishes, and not only Fishes but great Fishes, and then should a Ship meet with such an inconsiderable encounter as a Whale, one blow with his tayle, and then *Lord have Mercy upon us*" (pp. 41–42). Yet these same men are great boasters of their exploits: one "was the first that scaled the Walls of *Dundee,* when the Bullets flew about their ears as thick as Hail-stones usually fall from the Sky," and others tell similar tales of bravery. But if some one tells them of the storms of a sea voyage, these heroes turn cowards: "and though the Port-hole of their bodies has been stopt from a convenient Evacuation some several months, they'le need no other Suppository to open the Orifice of their Esculent faculties then this Relation, as their Drawers or Breeches can more at large demonstrate to the inquisitive search of the curious" (p. 43).

As we might expect from a chapter directly appealing to servants, the American Dream is the message—come to America and "live pleantious well." In the concluding brief poem, Alsop admonishes masters to use their servants well. Alsop's amplification or drawing-out of anecdotes (while telling of braggarts' tales and of scurrilous details) and his use of nautical imagery (after talking of a sea voyage) are examples of the tract's literary ability.

The fourth chapter, "The Traffique, and Vendable Commodities of the Countrey," begins with a survey of the advantages of trade and commerce. Alsop cannot resist satirizing the physicians and apothecaries of the day who have raised such a hue and cry against Nicholas Culpeper's *Pharmacopoeia.* Their reason was simply because Culpeper translated their obscure terms and euphemisms into plain English: "All Herbs, Roots, and Medicines would bear their original christening, that the ignorant might understand them: *Album grecum* would not be *Album grecum* then, but a Dogs Turd would be a Dogs Turd in plain terms, in spight of their Teeth" (p. 47). Customs-inspectors were at least as unpopular in the seventeenth century as today, and Alsop (with an allusion to Burton's *Anatomy of Melancholy*) pens a vigorous diatribe against the class:

> The (leering) Waiters for want of imployment, might (like so many *Diogenes*) intomb themselves in their empty Casks, and rouling themselves off the Key into the *Thames,* there wander up and down from tide to tide in contemplation of *Aristotles* unresolved curiosity, until the rottenness of their circular habitation gave them a *Quietus est,* and fairly surrender them up into the custody of those who both for profession, disposition and nature, lay as near claim to them, as if they both tumbled in one belly, and for name they jump alike, being according to the original translation both *Sharkes.* (p. 48)

Alsop then says that Maryland has three main commodities, "Tobacco, Furrs, and Flesh." He describes the cultivation, processing, and shipping of tobacco and comments on the lack of ready cash in Maryland and on the pervasive use of tobacco as currency. Alsop reveals an early Southern prejudice against the New England Yankee when he writes:

> I must confess the *New-England* men that trade into this Province, had rather have fat Port for their Goods, then Tobacco or Furrs; which I conceive is, because their bodies being fast bound up with the cords of restringent Zeal, they are fain to make use of the lineaments of this *Non-Canaanite* creature physically to loosen them; for a bit of a pound upon a two-peny Rye loaf, according to the original Receipt, will bring the costiv'st red-ear'd Zealot in some three hours time to a fine stool, if methodically observed. (p. 53)

Alsop's prejudice, like Andrew White's, against the New Englanders arises primarily because of their Puritanism.

After describing the Maryland trade with England and New England, Alsop satirizes the West Indian traders: "And though these Sun-burnt *Phaetons* think to outvye *Mary-Land* in their Silks and Puffs, daily speaking against her whom their necessities makes them beholden to, and like so many *Don Diegos* that becackt *Pauls*, cock their Felts and look big upon't" (p. 54). These "Sun-burnt *Phaetons*" are half-starved traders who "feed upon the undigested rynes of Potatoes." The chapter ends with a ten-line poem on "Trafique."

The penultimate chapter examines the Indians—a usual feature in colonization literature. As his letters show, Alsop tended to view the Indian as a noble savage. Within two months of his arrival in Maryland, he wrote his friend "Mr. T. B." a brief but interesting description of the Susquehannas, whose "sterne and heroick gate and department" impressed the indentured servant. He said that the women were "very well featured, did not their wilde and ridiculous dresses alter their original excellencies." He praised the men as "great Warriors and Hunters" and the women as "ingenious and laborious Housewives" (p. 89). The chapter on the Indians, "A small Treatise on the Wild and Naked Indians (or Susquehanokes) of Mary-Land, their Customs, Manners, Absurdities, & Religion," repeatedly uses the words *noble* and *heroic*. Alsop begins by pointing out that many Indian nations live in America, and that every tribe has different languages, laws, manners, and customs, and that he has only had an "occular experimental view of . . . [the] Customs, Manners, Religions and Absurdities . . . of *Susquehanocks*" (p. 57). He cannot resist putting on his English audience with an exaggerated account of the size and warlike characteristics of the "most Noble and Heroick Nation of *Indians* that dwell upon the confines of America." Captain John Smith had described the Susquehannas as "great and well proportioned men" who "seemed like Giants" with voices that sounded "from them, as it were a great voice in a vault, or a caue, as an Eccho." Smith included an engraved portrait of the "greatest of the Susquehanocks" in his map, and claimed that "the calfe of whose leg was 3 quarters of a yard about and all the rest of his limbs so answerable to that proportion, that he seemed the goodliest man that euer we heheld."[12] Alsop echoes Smith's description. He claims that the Susquehanna Indians are "a people cast into the mould of a most large and Warlike department, the men being for the most part seven foot high in latitude, and in magnitude and bulk suitable to so high a pitch; their voyce large and hollow, as ascending out of a Cave; their gate and behavior strait, stately and majestick, treading on the Earth with as much pride, contempt, and disdain to so sordid a Center, as can be imagined from a creature derived from the same mould and Earth" (p. 58). Alsop departs from Smith (who described their "attire" as the "skinnes of Bears, and Wooluves") and further puts on his English audience by writing that the Indians, "Men, Women and Children" go "all naked" even in the "nipping frosts of a benumbing winter," except for a small covering over their private parts.

After describing their characteristic body-painting, Alsop says that the Indians pull out all their hair, except that which grows on their head, thus implying that the Indians pull out their pubic hairs as well as their beards. The tattooing "with much difficulty and pain" of "pictures of the Devil, Bears, Tigers and Panthers" on the Indians is counted "a badge of Heroick Valour, and the only Ornament due to their Heroes" (p. 60). The Susquehannas are "great Warriours," keeping their Indian neighbors "in a forceable obedience and subjection." He does not understand their government, which is "wrapt up in so various and intricate a Laborynth, that the speculativ'st Artist in the whole World, with his artificial and natural Opticks,

---

[12] Captain John Smith, *A Map of Virginia* (1612), in Philip L. Barbour, ed., *The Jamestown Voyages Under the First Charter, 1606–1609*, 2 (London, 1969; The Hakluyt Society, ser. 2, vol. 137):342–43. Since Alsop refers to Samuel Purchas (p. 60), he may have been familiar with this description as reprinted in Samuel Purchas, *Hakluytus Posthumus, or Purchas his Pilgrimes*, 18 (Glasgow, 1906; The Hakluyt Society, extra ser., vol. 31): 427–28.

cannot see into" it (p. 60). And he maintains that Samuel Purchas was wrong in calling their government a monarchy. Alsop, in characterizing it, takes the opportunity to satirize England's system of advancement: "he that [is] most cruelly Valorous, is accounted the most Noble: Here is very seldom any creeping from a Country Farm, into a Courtly Gallantry, by a sum of money; nor feeing the Heralds to put Daggers and Pistols into their Armes, to make the ignorant believe that they are lineally descended from the house of the Wars and Conquests; he that fights best carries it here" (p. 61). After slyly attacking English practices, Alsop portrays the war-dress of the Susquehannas and describes with grisly gusto their torturing of prisoners. Alsop may have witnessed Indian barbarities, or he may be presenting an account based upon oral reports:

> The common and usual deaths they put their Prisoners to, is to bind them to stakes, making a fire some distance from them; then one or other of them, whose Genius delights in the art of Paganish dissection, with a sharp knife or flint cuts the Cutis or outermost skin of the brow so deep, untill their nails, or rather Talons, can fasten themselves firm and secure in, then (with a most rigid jerk) disrobeth the head of skin and hair at one pull, leaving the skull almost as bare as those Monumental Skelitons at Chyrurgions-Hall; but for fear they should get cold by leaving so warm and customary a Cap off, they immediately apply to the skull a Cataplasm of hot Embers to keep their Pericranium warm. (pp. 63–64)

This ghoulish humor arises in part because of the incongruity between the horrifying subject matter and the comic tone, and in part because of the joke upon the Indian's concern for the welfare of the suffering captive. It is identical with the cruel humor (perhaps bred by contact with the hardships of the frontier—but probably attributable to the possibilities of facetiously putting on a supposedly superior audience) of the Southwestern frontier. As for its appearance in a promotion tract, one must assume that Cecil, second lord Baltimore, thought that any publicity was good publicity, and that Alsop thought that Indian barbarity was a subject the English wanted to read—and so he surpassed their expectations.

According to Alsop, the captives "sing the summary of their Warlike Atchievements" with "Heroick Courage" while the Indians sear "their bodies with hot irons," cut "their flesh off," and eat it "before their eyes raw while they are alive." And after the death of the captives, "they immediately fall to butchering of them into parts, distributing the several pieces amongst the Sons of War, to intomb the ruines of their deceased Conquest in no other Sepulchre than their unsanctified maws" (p. 65). Alsop perhaps is spoofing the credulity of his reader when he solemnly says that the Indians sacrifice a child to the devil every four years "in acknowledgement of their firm obedience to all his Devillish powers, and Hellish commands." Their priests are like "Those that attended upon the Oracle at *Delphos*" and can command "a pro or con from the Devil" or "raise great Tempests" (p. 67). He also tells of their religion and (perhaps revealing the influence of Sir Thomas Browne's *Hydriotaphia*) portrays in considerable detail their burial customs. The social system also (e. g., marriage, role of women and men) receives discussion. He takes the opportunity to satirize feminine dominance in some English families (and to joke about the Indians' nakedness): "I never observed all the while I was amongst these naked *Indians*, that ever the Women wore the Breeches or dared either in look or action predominate over the Men." He praises the beauty of the Indian women, saying (perhaps alluding to Shakespeare) that there are "as amiable beauties amongst them, as any *Alexandria* could afford, when *Mark Anthony* and *Cleopatra* dwelt there together" (p. 71). Alsop ends the description of the Susquehannas with a bawdy Latin joke and with an unseemly, yet exact, examination of their unusual manner of urinating. Here the humor arises partially by the parody of scientific jargon. Alsop portrays the Indians as noble and heroic because of their hunting ability, courage in warfare, ability to withstand pain, personal beauty, and because of some aspects of their manners. He is no doubt also influenced by the implicit and explicit classical comparisons and, of course, by his satire, direct or implied, of English society.

The last section of *A Character of the Province of Maryland* is "A Collection of Historical Letters," consisting of a selection of Alsop's letters to his family and friends. A not-infrequent device of promotion literature, the letters supposedly guarantee the truthfulness of the statements. Like the third chapter, the letters try to lure servants to Maryland. Although these letters were probably written by Alsop to correspondents, they have undoubtedly been included because of the happy picture they present of the condition of servitude in Maryland. There are twelve in all, several containing poems. Four are addressed to his parents, four to his "much Honored Friend Mr. T. B."; two to his brother; and one each to his "much Honored Friend Mr. M. F." (on sending a shipment of goods to Maryland) and to his cousin Ellinor Evins (thanking her for sending medicine dur-

ing his sickness). The letters range in date from August 19, 1658, just
before he sailed for America, to April 9, 1663, which was probably
shortly before he returned to England.

In his letters, Alsop refers to several other writings, including a
poem "written in haste upon the Kings coming to the enjoyment of
his Throne, with a reflection upon the former sad and bad times." Of
these verses Alsop writes, "I have done them as well as I could, considering all things." The missing poem is probably similar in sentiment and ability to the one written on the occasion of receiving a
purple velvet hat from his brother in England. There he queried
whether the purple hat once graced Cromwell's head:

> Say, didst thou cover *Noll*'s old brazen head,
> Which on the top of *Westminster* high Lead
> Stands on a Pole, erected to the sky,
> As a grand Trophy to his memory.
> From his perfidious skull didst thou fall down,
> In a disdain to honour such a crown
> With three-pile Velvet? tell me, hadst thou thy fall
> From the high top of that Cathedral?
>
> (ll. 13–20, p. 109)

Alsop accuses the hat of being Hebrew, Catholic, and Episcopal, and
ends the poem with sarcastic aspersions on Presbyterians:

> 'Twere best I think I presently should gang
> To *Edenbrughs* strict *Presbyterian*;
> But Caps they've none, their ears being made so large,
> Serves them to turn it like a *Garnesey* Barge;
> Those keep their skulls warm against North-west gusts,
> When they in Pulpit do poor *Calvin* curse.
> Thou art not *Fortunatus*, for I daily see,
> That which I wish is farthest off from me:
> Thy low-built state none ever did advance,
> To christen thee the *Cap of Maintenance*;
> Then till I know from whence thou didst derive
> Thou shalt be call'd, the *Cap of Fugitive*.
>
> (ll. 41–50, pp. 110–11)

In this same letter, Alsop, like a soldier just discharged from the
army, discovers that liberty is not all roses:

> I Have made a shift to unloose my self from my Collar now as
> well as you, but I see at present either small pleasure or profit in it:
> What the futurality of my dayes will bring forth, I know not; For
> while I was linckt with the Chain of a restraining Servitude, I had all
> things cared for, and now I have all things to care for my self, which
> makes me almost to wish my self in for the other four years.

Liberty without money, is like a man opprest with the Gout, every step he puts forward puts him to pain; when on the other side, he that has Coyn with his Liberty, is like the swift Post-Messenger of the Gods, that wears wings at his heels, his motion being swift or slow, as he pleaseth. (pp. 106–107)

In the last two letters in the book, one to his "Honored Friend Mr. T. B.," dated December 13, [1662], and the other to his parents, dated April 9, [1663], Alsop tells of his long and nearly fatal sickness; but he comforts himself in the former by citing John Donne, "sometimes Dean of St. Pauls": "the bodies diseases do but mellow a man for Heaven, and so ferments him in this World, as he shall need no long concoction in the Grave, but hasten to the Resurrection" (p. 111).

Evidently the former indentured servant left Maryland in 1663 or 1664. His basic reason for emigrating to Maryland was his disgust for life in Interregnum London. Thus his reason for going to America was similar to Thoreau's for going to live in the woods. Thoreau stayed two years and two months and two days at Walden, and Alsop stayed at least four years and four months in his wilderness home, Maryland. And like Thoreau, who ultimately brought back *Walden* from his sojourn in the woods, Alsop too brought forth a report on his wilderness sojourn, *A Character of the Province of Mary-Land*. After writing *A Character*, Alsop managed to take orders as an Anglican minister (his devout Anglicanism and his literary ability suggest that the role of minister would have been natural for him) and served as curate to the Reverend William Paris at Tilney, Freebridge Hundred, Norfolk County. On February 19, 1669/70, Paris wrote to Peter Alsop, the father of George Alsop, testifying that "while acting as my curate," George Alsop "has demeaned himself soberly, studiously, virtuously, and painfully; and that his preaching and living have made him to be generally beloved by all the town." Alsop also obtained certificates from John Henson, vicar of Terrington St. Clement and St. John and rector of St. Edmond, North Lynn, and from Thomas Wilde, vicar of Wigenhall St. Mary and of Islington, that "George Alsop, curate of Tilney, is a man of sober life and conversation, a painful preacher, and a true lover of God's Church."[13]

---

[13] Public Record Office, S. P. 29/255, no. 238. There are also testimonials from John Henson (vicar of Terrington St. Clement and St. John, and rector of St. Edmond, North Lynn, etc.), and Thomas Wilde (vicar of Wigenhall St. Mary and of Islington) praising Alsop's "sober life and conversation" and certifying that he is "a painful preacher" and a "true lover of God's church." Public Record Office, S. P. 29/256, no. 56. I am grateful to the Secretary of the

At about this time (c. 1668–70), he petitioned the king—evidently unsuccessfully—for presentation to the vicarage of Walpole in Marshland, Norfolk.[14] After the resignation of the Reverend Jacob Crooke, George Alsop was appointed Rector of Chipping Ongar, Essex, on the recommendation of Elizabeth Goldesburgh, widow of Thomas Goldesburgh.[15] While rector of Chipping Ongar, Alsop had, on orders from Humphrey, bishop of London, attempted to read divine service in the Quakers' meetinghouse in Gracechurch Street, in the early summer of 1670. Despite a "guard of soldiers" to protect him, the Quakers managed to attack Alsop, "pulled him by the neck, and otherwise ill-used him, by bruising his knee and breast, and calling him a Popish priest and Jesuit, and excited the people to pull off his long robe, as it was the garment of the beast; so that, apprehending further mischief, he with great difficulty made his escape."[16] After his resignation from Chipping Ongar, Alsop was succeeded by the Reverend Mesech Smith, on May 7, 1673.[17]

Peter Alsop, his father, made out his will on September 14, 1672, and died shortly thereafter. He left "to my two sons George Alsop and Peter Alsop to each of them one shilling a piece in full of their childs' parts or portions out of my estate and I give and bequeath all the rest of my goods Chattels' money and personal estate whatsoever unto my loving wife Rose Alsop."[18] After these few glimpses of the later life of George Alsop, he drops out of sight. Evidently he never published again. There was a George Alsop who died in Calvert County, Maryland, in 1703, in debt in the amount of £1 1s. 1d.; but his administrator was a Quaker, Richard Johns, and I doubt that this Marylander was our author.[19]

A Character of the Province of Mary-Land uses nearly every gimmick in promotion literature's bag of tricks—and it invents a few. The organization of the tract, the reference to Samuel Purchas, and the collection of letters, all reveal Alsop's thorough acquaintance

---

Public Record Office for furnishing photostats of these documents relating to Alsop.
  [14] Public Record Office, S. P. 29/450, no. 127.
  [15] Richard Newcourt, *Reportorium ecclesiasticum parochiale londenense* (London, 1708–10), 2:451.
  [16] Public Record Office, S. P. 29/277, no. 14.
  [17] Newcourt, 2:451.
  [18] Pcc Eure, 1672, folio 117. See n. 1.
  [19] Inventory and Accounts, 1703, Liber 23, folio 50; and Testamentary Papers, 1703, box 13, folder 75, Maryland Hall of Records.

with the genre. What make this tract superior are the style, the satire, and Alsop's self-characterization. The grand baroque prose of *A Character* is equalled in seventeenth-century America only by Nathaniel Ward, Edward Johnson, Cotton Mather, and John Cotton of Virginia. Alsop's pervasive satire of the ills of English society is not surpassed in American literature until Thoreau condemns his own countrymen for materialism, hypocrisy, and competitiveness—ills that Alsop earlier found in English society. By the end of the pamphlet, Alsop, as madcap, wit, poet, satirist, Anglican, and Royalist, has won the reader's admiration. The creation of this *persona* is an amazing feat: in fiction, it would be a success; in the promotion tract, it is a triumph. Through this narrative mask, Alsop wittily satirizes customs-inspectors, doctors, lawyers, policemen, shopkeepers, braggart tradesmen, timid adventurers, permissive parents, English society, money-hungry Americans, Maryland Quakers, the New England Puritans, and a host of other religious sects. Erudite and slangy, reverent to king and God while scurrilous and scatological to men and manners, poetry mixed with prose, numerous literary allusions (mainly biblical and classical), an extraordinary delight in assonance and consonance, and a plenitude of rhetorical devices—all characterize Alsop's Menippean satire. *A Character of the Province of Mary-Land* is a jewel in the genre of promotion literature. No one can be certain of the literary influence of George Alsop, but this tract is the earliest of a long line of distinguished Southern works in baroque prose.

EARLY EIGHTEENTH-CENTURY LITERATURE

THE PLANTER

2

In 1700, Maryland contained—excluding Indians—an estimated 29,604 people. The capital had just moved from St. Mary's to Annapolis, but it was still only a small village. The wilderness had receded before the land-hungry planters, and the abundant wildlife was continually diminishing as the forests were systematically destroyed to make way for tobacco plantations. By the beginning of the eighteenth century, the tidewater area had been almost denuded of trees. Deer, bear, and turkey were growing ever scarcer, while buffalo, wolves, rattlesnakes, and beaver were already rare. During the early eighteenth century, the first laments for the disappearing wilderness appear in American poetry, as both Richard Lewis and Ebenezer Cook decry the greed of the American farmer and point out the permanent damage done to the environment.

Nearly everyone in the sparsely populated colony was directly or indirectly dependent on King Tobacco. The colony was composed, essentially, of planters. Tobacco was the medium of exchange in the Chesapeake colonies throughout the colonial period, and Maryland's economic fortunes rose and sank with its fluctuating price. Although fur-trading was still carried on, the number of traders was small, and they had moved from the tidewater area to the Piedmont plateau, above the fall line (i. e., above the falls in the rivers). A few industries existed—ship building, lumbering, and iron mining—and some men earned a living by catching fish, oysters, and crabs, but the planters and tobacco merchants dominated.

In 1708, Ebenezer Cook, who, like his father, was a Maryland planter and merchant, published in London a burlesque poem *The Sot-Weed Factor: or, a Voyage to Maryland.* An ambivalent poem, perhaps reflecting that Cook divided his time between England and America and did not know whether he considered himself an American (the word *American* usually meant an Indian and had only in the prior decade been also used to mean a person living in America) or an Englishman, *The Sot-Weed Factor* portrays the initiation of an English merchant into the rough life of the American frontier. In satirizing the American planters, Cook presented such an outlandish and distorted portrayal that any Englishman who believed that the poem represented the truth thereby revealed his own ignorance and credulity. In the latter part of his life, Cook resided continuously in Maryland, where he was known as the mock poet laureate of the colony. He continued writing poetry, especially elegies, but never again achieved the success of his first anti-promotion tract, *The Sot-Weed Factor.*

Thomas Bordley gave up his position as attorney-general of the colony to lead the popular party against the proprietary party (i. e., the followers of Lord Baltimore). To publicize the cause of the popular party, Bordley arranged to have an English printer, William Parks, come over to Maryland. Although the colony had several printers before Parks (William Nuthead, Dinah Nuthead, Thomas Reading, John Peter Zenger, and possibly Michael Piper), only Thomas Reading (fl. 1700–13) left a sizable body of printed material, none of it of literary interest. After William Parks came to Annapolis in 1726, the conditions of printing in Maryland changed. He encouraged local writers, not only by printing their broadsides and pamphlets, but also by publishing a newspaper intermittently from 1727 to 1735, thus stimulating the Maryland authors and providing an outlet for essays and poems. Although Cook's first publication had appeared in London, all his later extant works were printed in Maryland. The population of the colony more than tripled between 1700 and 1730 (from an estimated 29,604 to 91,113), while Annapolis and its immediate vicinity similarly increased (according to the vestry records of St. Anne's, as reported by Walter B. Norris) from 374 in 1696 to 809 in 1729. In addition, Parks established relations with his fellow printers in the major cities of the American colonies (Philadelphia, New York, and Boston), as well as with some London printers. They regularly exchanged newspapers and sold each other's publications. Also, travel between the colonies was growing more common, and by 1729, a stage was operating between Annapolis and Philadelphia. Virginia poets sometimes published in the *Maryland Gazette*, and Marylanders could send their writings to the Philadelphia printers.

When Richard Lewis (1700–34), an Annapolis school teacher and Baltimore planter, appeared on the literary scene in 1728, the colonial press was vigorously active. Through subscriptions, he was able to begin his literary career with a lovely edition of a popular Latin poem, Edward Holdworth's *Muscipula*, accompanied by his poetic English translation, *The Mouse Trap* (Annapolis, 1728). The existence of a population large enough—and with enough interests in literature—to pay for the printing of a 68-page quarto Latin and English poem marks a significant step in the development of Maryland literature. Lewis published other poems in Parks's newspaper and in broadsides and pamphlets; various colonial newspapers reprinted them; and when he sent a copy of his "Journey from Patapsco to Annapolis, April 4, 1730" to an English correspondent, it was printed in the English newspapers and magazines. Lewis applied the pastoral tradition to American scenery and thus became the first American nature poet. Although an English emigrant, he was, in his verse, an American chauvinist, claiming that American nature offered a better subject for poetry than English or European nature and arguing that the English and classic poets would have written greater poetry had they been writing of America. With the advent of Lewis, there was finally competition and challenge between comtemporary Maryland authors. White, Hammond, and Alsop had been, in effect, writing in solitude, for none of them had peers of literary ability. Lewis and Cook, however, knew one another, and, as we shall see, Cook's later poetry reveals the influence of Lewis. Furthermore, evidence exists of a literary feud between them. They also knew the literary men in the neighboring colonies: Cook visited the Virginia literary circles (John Fox and John Mercer both left references to him), and Lewis visited Philadelphia and praised the Philadelphia writers (including Franklin and Joseph Breintnall).

By the early eighteenth century, American writers were already using and reacting against the conventions of American literature. *The Sot-Weed Factor*, which probably reflected a popular anecdote, was clearly an anti-promotion tract. But it carried the spoof a step further, and mocked the satires upon promotion tracts as well as the promotion tracts themselves. Since Americans were increasingly portrayed by the English as barbarians, Cook reduced this image to an absurdity by portraying even the lawyers and justices as titanic, selfish, greedy, illiterate, fighting, drunken wild men. (In the next generation, the Reverend Thomas Cradock in his "Maryland Eclogues in Imitation of Virgil's" attempted the same subjects, but with less complexity, and America had to await the Southwestern school of humorists for a better handling of the subject.) And Lewis, writing in more formal genres, also revolted against the promotion tract myth of an Edenic America. George Alsop had personified America as an innocent deer, contrasted with England, which was identified with prostitution and cuckolded men. But Lewis found that the innocent deer had disappeared from tidewater Maryland and that the former Edenic wilderness (which he identified with the vanishing Indian) had given way to the troubled complexities of modern man. Lewis decried the passing of the American wilderness, lamented the fall of the American from innocence, and portrayed such American social ills as the uprooting and killing of the Indian—thus pointing the way to a much longer and more vital tradition in American literature.

BENEZER COOK

POET LAUREATE

Although Ebenezer Cook[1] (c. 1667–1733?) is known today mainly by his notoriety as the dubious hero of John Barth's *The Sot-Weed Factor* (New York, 1960), he was in his own time infamous as the mock poet laureate of Maryland. Ebenezer Cook composed the original *Sot-Weed Factor* (London, 1708)—a satirical poem supposedly describing the conditions, customs, manners, and people of the colony—in the jingling, humorous rhyme Samuel Butler used in *Hudibras*. *The Sot-Weed Factor* burlesques America's crude frontier life and slyly ridicules English assumptions about America. Today's readers usually think that the satires of primitive frontier conditions are a nineteenth-century product; but the tradition of Southern humor is directly descended from such colonial ancestors as John Hammond, George Alsop, and William Byrd II, and from the satiric poetry of Ebenezer Cook. In addition to *The Sot-Weed Factor*, Cook wrote several elegies, a poem on the economic plight of Maryland, and a long Hudibrastic version of John Cotton's "The History of Colonel Nathaniel Bacon's Rebellion in Virginia."

The date and place of Ebenezer Cook's birth are unknown, but his parents were married in London on August 1, 1665, and he was probably born within a few years thereafter.[2] The earliest extant

[1] The poet himself spelled his surname *Cook* or *Cooke*, but he used the former more frequently.

[2] Lawrence C. Wroth, *The Maryland Muse by Ebenezer Cooke: A Facsimile, with an Introduction* (Worcester, Mass., 1935), 6. Wroth's pamphlet is reprinted from the American Antiquarian Society *Proceedings* 44 (1934):267–335. Edward H. Cohen, "The 'Second Edition' of *The Sot-weed Factor*," *American Literature*

record of his life is his signature on a petition of 1694 against the re-
moval of Maryland's capitol from St. Mary's to Annapolis.[3] He must
have been an adult at this time and was probably assisting his father,
Andrew Cook, a London merchant and "sot-weed factor" who plied
the tidewater tobacco trade and who owned "Cook's Point," at the
mouth of the Choptank River, Dorchester County, Maryland.[4]

The Sot-Weed Factor: Or, a Voyage to Maryland (London, 1708)
was Cook's first and best poem. As the title page declares, *The Sot-
Weed Factor* (sot-weed=the weed that makes one drunk, i. e., tobacco; factor=merchant) satirizes *the laws, government, courts and
constitutions of the country; and also the buildings, feasts, frolicks,
entertainments and drunken humours of the inhabitants of that part
of America.* Although Ebenezer Cook was an old Maryland hand by
1708 (the notes to the poem, Cook's connections with Maryland,
and his presence in Maryland in 1694—all prove this fact), the poem's
speaker is a greenhorn, or, to use George Alsop's words, a "raw and
unexperienced Merchant" (see above, p. 58). As Alsop's description
proves, anecdotes about the rustic Americans swindling the sophisticated English factors were popular in Maryland. What Cook may
have done in *The Sot-Weed Factor* was to versify and embellish a
popular oral tale. During the course of the poem, the speaker is called
a "Merchant Stranger" (l. 451) and simply a "Stranger" (l. 683),
thus emphasizing his inexperience. The ostensible purpose of the narrative, hudibrastic poem is to warn and prepare possible emigrants:
"That Strangers well may be aware on, / What homely Diet they
must fare on" (ll. 52–53). The ludicrous rhymes and breathless,
awkward, iambic tetrameter rhythm complement the satirical, exaggerated, outraged, and burlesque tone. The poem chronicles the adven-
tures of a tobacco merchant, and although seemingly anti-American,
the poem is actually a double-edged satire.

The Sot-Weed Factor opens with the speaker's reasons for the
voyage:

> CONDEMN'D by fate to way-ward Curse,
> Of Friends unkind, and empty Purse;
> Plagues worse than fill'd *Pandora's Box*

---

42 (1970):298 n. 22, has written "according to the unpublished papers of the
Cooke family, Ebenezer Cooke was born in the early months of 1667," but I have
not seen these papers.

3 *Archives of Maryland* 19:75.

4 Wroth, *Maryland Muse by Ebenezer Cooke,* 7. See also Elias Jones, *Revised
History of Dorchester County, Maryland* (Baltimore, 1925), 281–83.

I took my leave of *Albion's* Rocks:
With heavy Heart, concern'd that I
Was forc'd my Native Soil to fly,
And the Old World must bid good-buy.[5]
(ll. 1–7)

The tenderfoot describes the voyage, the landing at Piscataway (a small town at the juncture of Piscataway Creek and the Potomac River, just south of the present city of Washington), and the Maryland planters who gather to gawk at the ship ("a numerous Crew, / In Shirts and Drawyers of Scotch-cloth Blue. / With neither Stockings, Hat, nor Shooe"). The use of *Drawyers*, primarily meaning underpants or hose, ridicules the planters by suggesting that they are so poor and so barbarous that they do not have trousers. Also, calling their clothes "Scotch-cloth Blue" (Cook explains in a note that planters "generally wear Blue Linnen") suggests that the planters are all Scotch Presbyterians, for eighteenth-century readers knew that blue was worn by the Scotch Presbyterians in opposition to the Royalist red. This may also echo Butler's description of Hudibras's religion as "*Presbyterian* true blew" (*Hudibras*, part 1, canto 1, l. 189). To the cultivated, if naive, Londoner, these "Sot-weed Planters" looked:

> ... as tawney as a Moor:
> Figures so strange, no God design'd
> To be a part of Humane Kind:
> But wanton Nature, void of Rest,
> Moulded the brittle Clay in Jest.
> (ll. 28–32)

The stranger, satirizing theories which traced the origin of the American Indians to biblical personages, says that Marylanders are descendants of Cain:

> At last a Fancy very odd
> Took me, this was the Land of *Nod*;
> Planted at first, when Vagrant *Cain*,
> His Brother had unjustly slain;
> Then conscious of the Crime he'd done,
> From Vengeance dire, he hither run;
> And in a Hut supinely dwelt,
> The first in Furs and Sot-weed dealt.
> (ll. 33–40)

[5] *The Sot-Weed Factor* ... (London, 1708), ll. 1–7. Hereafter, line citations will be given in parentheses in the text. A modern reprinting is available in Bernard C. Steiner, ed., *Early Maryland Poetry*, Maryland Historical Society *Fund Publication, No. 36* (Baltimore, 1900), 11–31.

Americans are "a detested Race" who have emigrated to the New
World because "They cou'd not live at Home" (ll. 42–43). The
would-be merchant also characterizes America as a "Shoar, where no
good sense is found, / But conversation's lost, and manners drown'd"
(ll. 54–55).

In the following lines, Cook uses the unfamiliar Indian word *canoe*,
a hudibrastic feminine rhyme, an incongruous periphrasis, and a weird
simile—all to build humorous effect. He writes that he crossed the
Piscataway River

> In such a sining odd invention,
> I scarce can give its due Dimention.
> The *Indians* call this watry Waggon
> *Canoo*, a Vessel none can brag on;
> Cut from a *Popular-Tree*, or *Pine*,
> And fashion'd like a Trough for Swine . . . .
> (ll. 59–64)

When Cook describes the "merchant stranger" as "Standing Erect,
with Legs stretch'd wide" (l. 67) while crossing a river in a canoe,
the poet knows that every American reader will scoff at a tenderfoot
so ignorant that he does not sit down in a canoe. The passage continues:

> We paddled to the other side:
> Where being Landed safe by hap,
> As *Sol* fell into *Thetis* Lap.
> A ravenous Gang bent on the stroul,
> Of Wolves* for Prey, began to howl;
> This put me in a pannick Fright,
> Least I should be devoured quite:
> But as I there a musing stood,
> And quite benighted in a Wood,
> A Female Voice pierc'd thro' my Ears,
> Crying, *You Rogue drive home the Steers.*
> I listen'd to th'attractive sound,
> And straight a Herd of Cattel found
> Drove by a Youth, and homewards bound . . .
> (ll. 68–81)

The American reader realizes that the greenhorn tobacco merchant
has, as night fell and he found himself in what he thought was a wilderness forest, imagined (in his "pannick Fright") that he has heard a
pack of wolves howling. What he has actually heard, although Cook
does not directly tell his audience of Londoners so, is a herd of cattle bawling. The poet emphasizes the greenness of the tobacco mer-

chant by comparing him to the *Babes in the Wood* (one of the most popular ballads and chapbook stories of the seventeenth and eighteenth centuries), when he describes the factor as "musing . . . quite benighted in a Wood." The greenhorn has been too frightened to perceive his error, and he assures his London readers in a note that "*Wolves are very numerous in Mary-Land." The extreme subjectiveness of the *persona* is amusingly stressed when the factor finds the strident "female" imprecation an "attractive sound." Marylanders such as Thomas Bordley who dubbed Cook their mock "Poet Laureate of Maryland" recognized that Cook's real object of satire was the ridiculous notion of Englishmen that America was a complete wilderness.

The stranger asks the youth who is driving cattle where he can get a room for the night, and is suspected of being a runaway servant. He, however, lustily lugs out his sword at the insinuation, thereby demonstrating (says the ironic poet) that he is a man of honor; and so he finds his way to a poor planter's house where he is hospitably invited to share the miserable dinner: he has "syder-pap" (cider and small hominy) as an appetizer, "pon" (bread made of corn), mush (hastypudding), milk, hominy, and more syder-pap. The poem's first smutty allusion occurs in the description of the planter's pipe:

> Then out our Landlord pulls a Pouch,
> As greasy as the Leather Couch
> On which he sat, and straight begun,
> To load with Weed his *Indian* Gun;
> In length, scarce longer than ones Finger,
> Or that for which the Ladies linger.
> (ll. 120–25)

The impecunious planter shares his keg of rum with the stranger. Although the liquor makes him nauseous, the stranger is not too drunk to characterize the indentured female servant, "one who pass'd for Chamber-Maid; / Tho by her loose and sluttish Dress, / She rather seem'd a Bedlam-Bess." He hears the whore's patently false story of fleeing home to avoid a hated marriage, and then gives his own interpretation:

> Whate'er the Wanderer did profess,
> Good-faith I cou'd not choose but guess
> The Cause which brought her to this place
> Was supping e'er the Priest said Grace.
> (ll. 170–73)

81

When the sot-weed factor tries to sleep in the bed in the chimney corner, the animals who share the room with him keep him awake, and he finally wages a mock-heroic battle with them:

> But soon a noise disturb'd my quiet,
> And plagu'd me with nocturnal Riot;
> A Puss which in the ashes lay,
> With grunting Pig began a Fray;
> And prudent Dog, that Feuds might cease,
> Most strongly bark'd to keep the Peace.
> This Quarrel scarcely was decided,
> By stick that ready lay provided;
> But *Reynard* arch and cunning Loon,
> Broke into my Appartment soon;
> In hot pursuit of Ducks and Geese,
> With fell intent the same to seize;
> Their Cackling Plaints with strange surprize,
> Chac'd Sleeps thick Vapours from my Eyes:
> Raging I jump'd upon the Floar,
> And like a Drunken Saylor Swore;
> With Sword I fiercely laid about,
> And soon dispers'd the Feather'd Rout....
>
> (ll. 180–97)

The dogs came running to the "Place of Combat . . . Exactly as the Field was won."

Finding himself "Fretting and hot as roasting Capon, / And greasy as a Flitch of Bacon" (ll. 204–205), the factor goes outside into the cool night air, only to be bothered by the noise of frogs:

> Hoarse croaking Frogs did 'bout me ring,
> Such Peals the Dead to Life wou'd bring,
> A Noise might move Their Wooden King.
> I stuff'd my Ears with Cotten white
> For fear of being deaf out-right,
> And curst the melancholy Night:
> But soon my Vows I did recant,
> And Hearing as a Blessing grant;
> When a confounded Rattle-Snake,
> With hissing made my Heart to ake:
> Not knowing how to fly the Foe,
> Or whether in the Dark to go;
> By strange good Luck, I took a Tree,
> Prepar'd by Fate to set me free;
> Where riding on a Limb a-stride,
> Night and the Branches did me hide,
> And I the Devil and Snake defy'd.
> Not yet from Plagues exempted quite,

The curst Musketoes did me bite;
Till rising Morn' and blushing Day,
Drove both my Fears and Ills away;
And from Night's Errors set me free ...
(ll. 213–34)

In this farce, the tenderfoot is irritated by the call of frogs (a sound that most Americans find pleasing); and blinded by darkness and half-deaf because of the cotton in his ears, he hears a hissing which he imagines to be a rattlesnake, and climbs a tree to escape the reptile, only to find himself bitten by mosquitoes. But he has imagined the rattlesnake—the hissing that the tenderfoot heard was the whine of mosquitoes. The greenhorn never realizes his "Night's Errors," and perhaps the English audience does not (even though, in the numerous popular accounts of American rattlesnakes in the seventeenth and eighteenth centuries, the snakes always rattle, never hiss, before strik-ing), but the American reader should appreciate the absurd portrait of the fearful "superior" Londoner who spends the night perched in a tree.

After a hearty planter's breakfast of "rashier broil'd of infant Bear" (l. 238), the merchant-stranger sets out with a horse (an "aged Rhoan") loaned by the planter, and with the planter's eldest son as a guide:

Steering our Barks in Trot or Pace,
We sail'd directly for a place
In *Mary-Land* of high renown,
Known by the Name of *Battle-Town*.
To view the Crowds did there resort,
Which justice made, and Law their sport,
In that sagacious County Court....
(ll. 252–58)

The packed syntax states that the greenhorn went to Battletown to view the crowds, who, in turn, came to make fun of the justices and lawyers of the county court. On the journey to the Calvert County seat, the factor and his guide encounter some Indians, who are, with some sexual allusion, characterized and compared to England's ancient Picts:[6]

But *Indians* strange did soon appear,
In hot pursuit of wounded Deer;

[6] John White, governor of the ill-fated Roanoke colony, had earlier made this comparison, which is, in fact, an application of the anthropologist's com-parative method. Paul Hulton, *The Watercolor Drawings of John White From the British Museum* (Washington, D. C., 1965), 24–25 and 53 (nos. 95–104).

No mortal Creature can express,
His wild fantastick Air and Dress;
His painted Skin in colours dy'd,
His sable Hair in Satchel ty'd,
Shew'd Savages not free from Pride:
His tawny Thighs, and Bosom bare,
Disdain'd a useless Coat to wear,
Scourn'd Summer's Heat, and Winter's Air;
His manly Shoulders such as please,
Widows and Wives, were bath'd in Grease
Of Cub and Bear, whose supple Oil
Prepar'd his Limbs 'gainst Heat or Toil.
Thus naked Pict in Battel fought,
Or undisguis'd his Mistress sought;
And knowing well his Ware was good,
Refus'd to screen it with a Hood . . . .
(ll. 261–78)

Alarmed by the Indian's appearance, the sot-weed factor tries to gallop away, but can not rouse his plodding roan:

But Rhoan who better knew than I,
The little Cause I had to fly;
Seem'd by his solemn steps and pace,
Resolv'd I shou'd the Specter face,
Nor faster mov'd, tho' spur'd and lick'd,
Than *Balaam's* Ass by Prophet kick'd.
Kekicknitop the Heather cry'd;
How is it Tom. my Friend reply'd,
Judging from thence the Brute was civil,
I boldly fac'd the Courteous Devil . . .
(ll. 284–93)

In this archetypal story of the greenhorn's encounter with the Indian, Cook makes even the tenderfoot tobacco merchant realize that his expectations about Indians (the stranger automatically thinks that the Indian will want to murder and scalp him) are foolish. These three accounts of the greenhorn's expectations of America (a land full of wolves, rattlesnakes, and hostile Indians) are microcosms of the poem: just as the sot-weed factor's absurd expectations of America are burlesqued in these anecdotes (usually without the greenhorn's ever realizing the truth of the situation, though the reader cannot help but smile at the absurd position of the *persona*), so in the macrocosm, the poem as a whole, the English reader's expectations of what life is like in the wild frontier of America are burlesqued. If the reader does not realize it, then it only proves that he is the victim of foolish and unbelievable notions, and thus himself a fool.

After the Indian goes his way, the stranger and the planter's son, in a passage again satirizing the theories concerning the ancestry of the Indian, argue whether the Indians are descended from the Chinese or the Phoenicians. During this exchange the Englishman mocks the American and the English college student:

> I smil'd to hear my young Logician,
> Thus Reason like a Politician;
> Who ne'er by Fathers Pains and Earning
> Had got at Mother *Cambridge* Learning;
> Where Lubber youth just free from birch
> Most stoutly drink to prop the Church . . . .
>
> (ll. 320–25)

After referring to the folk story of a bear living by sucking its paws, and then deliberately echoing *Hudibras* ("He that complies against his will, / Is of his own Opinion still"),[7] the speaker satirizes Catholicism and reflects on the futility of religious arguments:

> And when that both had talk'd their fill,
> We had the self same Notion still.
> Thus Parson grave well read and Sage,
> Does in dispute with Priest engage;
> The one protests they are not Wise,
> Who judge by Sense and trust their Eyes;
> And vows he'd burn for it at Stake,
> That Man may God his Maker make;
> The other smiles at his Religion,
> And vows he's but a learned Widgeon:
> And when they have empty'd all their stoar
> From Books and Fathers are not more
> Convinc'd or wiser than before.
>
> (ll. 362–74)

In Battletown, the greenhorn and the planter's son can't find lodging, and so they join a group of drunken planters sitting in a circle. These friendly drunks are, it turns out, the lawyers and judges of Calvert County, and the open field actually serves as a court:

> We sat like others on the ground
> Carousing Punch in open Air
> Till Cryer did the Court declare;
> The planting Rabble being met,

[7] Samuel Butler, *Hudibras*, ed. John Wilders (Oxford, 1967), 293 (pt. 3, canto 3, ll. 547–48).

Their Drunken Worships likewise set:
Cryer proclaims that Noise shou'd cease,
And streight the Lawyers broke the Peace:
Wrangling for Plaintiff and Defendant,
I thought they ne'er would make an end on't:
With nonsense, stuff and false quotations,
With brazen Lyes and Allegations;
And in the splitting of the Cause,
They us'd such Motions with their Paws,
As shew'd their Zeal was strongly bent,
In Blows to end the Argument.
A reverend Judge, who to the shame
Of all the Bench, cou'd write his Name;
At Petty-fogger took offence,
And wonder'd at his Impudence,
My Neighbour *Dash* with scorn replies,
And in the Face of Justice flies:
The Bench in fury streight divide,
And Scribbles take, or Judges side;
The Jury, Lawyers, and their Clyents,
Contending, fight like earth-born Gyants . . . .

(ll. 384–408)

Satirical gibes at the hard-drinking, irascible, and illiterate American pioneers had already become, by Cook's time, a recognizable feature of American (and anti-American) literature—but no one before Cook had portrayed these standard butts of American humor in so lively a fashion or so well. The poet even adds a note, solemnly assuring the reader that "in the County-Court of Mary-land, very few of the Justices of the Peace can write or read." Of course the note (like the description of the drunken, fighting lawyers and justices, and the supposed lack of a court house, as well as the earlier portrayal of planters without hats, stockings, or shoes) actually burlesques the English reader who thought that Americans were barbarians. Americans of the seventeenth and eighteenth centuries frequently expressed dismay concerning the English ignorance of America and especially the English assumption that all America was a wilderness, completely without civilization. The English were even surprised that English-speaking white men lived in America.[8] Cook's double-edged satire is the earliest full-scale reply to this assumption of superiority, and *The*

[8] One of Colonel Robert Bolling's (1738–75) favorite anecdotes concerned his grandfather John Bolling (1676–1729), who excited the awe of a Yorkshire lady because he spoke English "as well as we do." To which John Bolling ungallantly replied that his English was considerably better than hers. See Robert Bolling, *A Memoir of a Portion of the Bolling Family* (Richmond, 1868), 4.

Sot-Weed Factor thus belongs to a tradition of American folk humor culminating in Mark Twain and William Faulkner. Battletown, the site of this imaginary court scene, had been the seat of Calvert County for nearly half a century. As recently as January 11, 1697/8, the Council of Maryland had met at the court house in the town, and there is a reference from 1703 to the "Court House in Battle Town in Calvert County."[9] So, as one would expect, and contrary to Cook's portrayal, there was a court house in Battletown c. 1707. Moreover, a recent assessment of the procedure of a new frontier court in late seventeenth-century Maryland concludes that "the procedural law displayed . . . would compare favorably with many of the local courts of England."[10] Since so many modern readers have apparently been taken in by Cook's description, it is worth pointing out that the historical evidence bears out the literary evidence (of *persona* and tone) and proves that the portrayal of men and manners in Maryland is at least grossly exaggerated. The purpose of such exaggeration is to expose the ignorance and credulity of the reader. If the English readers did not believe *The Sot-Weed Factor*, they were in effect asserting (what Cook and other Americans knew) that Americans were not barbarians; and if the readers believed the account, they revealed their own ignorance and credulity—not only of America, but of literature as well.

The greenhorn goes next to an inn where he finds a confused medley of "dead drunk" planters, while "others were fighting and contending." Finally, the speaker, "Just then beginning to be drunk," goes upstairs and falls asleep in an old corn-loft. Waking in the morning, he finds "My Shoes were vanish'd quite; / Hat, Wig, and Stocking, all were fled / From this extended *Indian* Bed" (ll. 495–97). Furious, he searches for those articles and finds that they have been burned. Cook solemnly assures his readers in a note that " 'Tis the Custom of the Planters, To throw their own, or any other Person's Hat, Wig, Shooes or Stockings in the Fire." Then he sees his friend, the planter's son, lying naked on a table:

> A Sight so dismal to behold,
> One wou'd have judg'd him dead and cold;
> When wringing of his bloody Nose,
> By fighting got we may suppose;

[9] *Archives of Maryland* 23:367; 25:167.
[10] Joseph H. Smith and Philip A. Crowl, eds., *Court Records of Prince Georges County, Maryland 1696–1699* (Washington, D. C., 1964), cxv.

I found him not so fast asleep,
Might give his Friends a cause to weep:
Rise *Oroonooko*, rise, said I
And from this *Hell* and *Bedlam* fly.
(ll. 463–70)

Several allusions are fused in these lines: there is a mock-religious suggestion in Cook's calling the dead to life; he reminds the readers in a
note that the planters are often called "Oroonoko" from their planting
Oroonoko tobacco; and the appalling sight of the naked, bloody body
would probably remind the early eighteenth-century reader of Aphra
Behn's mutilated hero in her popular prose-fiction work *Oroonoko*
(London, 1688).

The planter's son gets up, finds his horse missing, and sets out in
pursuit of it, not to return again. The stranger is stranded, but a
wealthy planter offers him a horse and takes him to his home, where
he enjoys punch and apple juice, conversation, and a good night's
sleep. The next day there is a sumptuous dinner:

Wild Fowl and Fish delicious Meats,
As good as *Neptune's* Doxy eats;
Began our Hospitable Treat;
Fat Venson follow'd in the Rear,
And Turkies wild Luxurious Chear . . . .
(ll. 519–23)

And they top it off with a prodigious quantity of madeira. After a
catnap, the sot-weed factor joins the women around the fire and
characterizes them as fishwives. The next day he awakens with a
terrific hangover and a quenchless thirst. He goes through the usual
emigrant's seasoning, but in his case, it lasts "from *March* to cold
December" (l. 594). Finally recovered, he goes to Maryland's Eastern Shore to sell his "*British* Ware" for tobacco. Here Cook writes
a satiric sketch (which may allude to John Dryden's character
of *Shimei* in *Absalom and Achitophel*, ll. 585 ff.) of a Quaker
planter and delightfully employs dialect, oxymoronic combinations
and other antitheses, jargon, and special Quaker characteristics (e. g.,
not swearing):

To this intent, with Guide before,
I tript it to the Eastern Shoar;
While riding near a Sandy Bay,
I met a *Quaker*, *Yea* and *Nay*;
A Pious Conscientious Rogue,
As e'er woar Bonnet or a Brogue,
Who neither Swore nor kept his Word,

But cheated in the Fear of God;
And when his Debts he would not pay,
By Light within he ran away.
With this sly Zealot soon I struck
A Bargain for my *English* Truck . . . .
                                        (ll. 611–22)

The Quaker cheats him, and so the sot-weed factor has recourse to a lawyer who is also a doctor, and a quack in both professions:

On due Revenge and Justice Bent,
I instantly to Counsel went,
Unto an ambodexter *Quack*,
Who learnedly had got the knack
Of giving Glisters, making Pills,
Of filling Bonds, and forging Wills;
And with a stock of Impudence,
Supply'd his want of Wit and Sense;
With Looks demure, amazing People,
No wiser than a Daw in Steeple;
My Anger flushing in my Face,
I stated the preceding Case:
And of my Money was so lavish,
That he'd have poyson'd half the Parish,
And hang'd his Father on a Tree,
For such another tempting fee . . . .
                                        (ll. 637–52)

Seeking justice, the greenhorn goes with his lawyer to Annapolis ("A City Scituate on a Plain, / Where scarce a House will keep out Rain," ll. 666–67) to sue the Quaker for payment. But his lawyer has been bribed, and so the stranger is paid unmerchantable ware:

And least I shou'd the better get,
Brib'd *Quack* supprest his Knavish Wit.
So Maid upon the downy Field,
Pretends a Force, and Fights to yield:
The Byast Court without delay,
Adjudg'd my Debt in Country Pay;
In Pipe staves, Corn, or Flesh of Boar,
Rare Cargo for the *English* Shoar:
Raging with Grief, full speed I ran,
To joyn the Fleet at *Kicketan*;
Embarqu'd and waiting for a Wind,
I left this deadful Curse behind.
                                        (ll. 688–98)

The "Merchant Stranger" closes the poem with a curse for the New World: he implores that cannibals be shipped to Maryland to prey upon the inhabitants "as they have done on me"; asks that no merchant may ever again visit this "Inhospitable Shoar"; prays that the inhabitants turn savage and lose their religion; and, finally, exclaims "May Wrath Divine then lay those Regions wast / Where no Man's Faithful, nor a Woman Chast" (ll. 711–12).

This narrative, hudibrastic poem has a clear structure. The introduction (ll. 1–21) gives the sot-weed factor's background and describes the voyage to America. The landing at Piscataway (ll. 22–95) lists his first impressions of America. The way of life of a poor planter is then described (ll. 96–251). The center of the poem tells of the trip to Battletown (ll. 252–374) and the events there (ll. 375–481). Balancing the account of the poor planter's way of life, the hospitality of a "cockerouse" or wealthy planter (ll. 482–606) is described, while the food and accommodations are implicitly contrasted to the earlier account. The penultimate section tells of the merchant's selling his wares (ll. 607–99), and the poem concludes with a curse on the New World (ll. 700–12).

The structure and general contents of *The Sot-Weed Factor* were familiar to English and American readers before the poem appeared in 1708. Not only were anecdotes about Americans cheating "raw and unexperienced merchants" common, but "The New England Ballad," a popular song of the mid-seventeenth and early eighteenth centuries, tells essentially the same story. The first stanza of "The New England Ballad" introduces the subject of false hopes for America; the second tells of the emigrant's expectations of abundance in America:

> Before Ise went Thither, Lord, how Voke did Tell
> How Vishes did grow, and how Birds did dwell,
> All one amongst T'other, in the Wood and the Water,
> Ise thought 'thad been True, but I found no such Matter.

The third and fourth stanzas portray the strange sights that greet the emigrant in the New World—the buildings are makeshift and temporary "like the standings at *Woodbury* Fair," and there is not a bell in any church in town. The fifth through the ninth stanzas satirize the Puritan Sunday service, baptism and wedding ceremonies. The tenth stanza portrays the town (Dorchester, Massachusetts), the penultimate stanza describes the emigrant's homesickness—and his outrage on learning of the high cost of passage back to England. And in the last stanza he departs for England, leaving behind him a curse for the New World.

Although *The Sot-Weed Factor* is much longer than "The New England Ballad," its structure and contents are similar to the popular song. The sot-weed factor's first impressions of America are comparable to the amazement of the emigrant in "The New England Ballad." The exaggerated portrait of the lack of learning of the judges, lawyers, and Americans in general is similar to the effect of illiteracy attained by the use of mock dialect in "The New England Ballad." Cook's description of the crude, new houses of Annapolis (which resemble "*Southwark* Fair" rather than those at "*Woodbury* Fair") does not outdo the description of the temporary houses of New Dorchester. The Maryland poet's satire of the pious, cheating Quaker is more memorable than the description of Puritan ceremonies—but both satirize the "Left Wing" of Protestantism. And in the old ballad, as in the Maryland poem, the American sharpsters "take" the greenhorn—who leaves with a curse for America. Cook may not have known "The New England Ballad"[11] but he probably did. The structure of Cook's poem is modeled upon "The New England Ballad" or upon some similar burlesque of the New World.

A key difference exists between the old ballad and Cook's poem: "The New England Ballad" is anti-American, and *The Sot-Weed Factor* is typically American. The relationship between "The New England Ballad" and *The Sot-Weed Factor* may indicate why American literature has always had a self-condemning, satirical strain as a major ingredient. The inflated rhetoric and exaggerated claims of promotion literature led naturally to statements that contradicted such rosy and false pictures. These replies to the promotion literature satirize not only the American environment (e. g., the claims of abundance) but also the Americans themselves. Such writings must have been as familiar to Americans as the promotion tracts, and these satires were imitated and burlesqued by American writers (e. g., "New England's Annoyances")[12] almost as soon as writing began in America.

[11] "The New England Ballad" appeared in the great early eighteenth-century collection of songs: Thomas D'Urfey, *Wit and Mirth: or Pills to Purge Melancholy*, 4 (London, 1719):52–54. A mid-seventeenth-century version of the same ballad, entitled "A West-Country Man's Voyage to New England," appeared in *Merry Drollery Compleat . . . The Second Part* (London, 1661). Charles H. Firth, in *An American Garland* (Oxford, 1915) reprints the latter version, 32–34, and speculates that it "may have been written twenty years or more before the date [1661] of its publication" (xxvi).

[12] "New England's Annoyances," a popular American song in the seventeenth and eighteenth centuries, is conveniently available in Evert A. Duyckinck and George L. Duyckinck, *Cyclopaedia of American Literature*, ed. M. Laird Simons, 1 (Philadelphia, 1875):73; and in Harrison T. Meserole, *Seventeenth Century American Poetry: An Anthology* (New York, 1968), 423.

Although Cook's poem clearly satirizes the men and manners of the New World, it also mocks the Englishman's attitudes toward America. There is a boundary between (1) an exaggeration of New World manners for the purpose of satirizing them, and (2) an account of New World manners so distorted that it burlesques the ignorance and credulity of anyone believing such nonsense. When Ebenezer Cook writes that "In the County-Court of *Maryland*, very few of the Justices of the *Peace* can write or read," he has crossed the boundary and is burlesquing his English readers' notions of how ignorant and savage Americans are. When he satirizes the poor planter's son for his arguments concerning the origin of the American Indian, he also satirizes the Cambridge student: the implication is that Maryland youths are as advanced—and as ignorant—as Cambridge students. In a close reading of the total poem, several elements stand revealed as part of a burlesque upon the English ideas of what the wild and wooly frontier across the Atlantic must be like. Besides, the Englishman who comes to Maryland as a would-be sot-weed factor and who scoffs at the ignorance and manners and customs of the Marylanders is, in fact, easily bested by these same barbarians. Although many of the motifs of *The Sot-Weed Factor* are to be found in *Hudibras* and especially in Aphra Behn's *The Widow Ranter: or the History of Bacon in Virginia* (London, 1690), Cook's poem is radically different from them and is typically American. It is a put-on. But even on the surface, the supercilious city-slicker who is the representative Englishman is a fool. He does not appreciate the continual hospitality of the Americans; and naturally, when he trusts a complete stranger with his money, he is promptly cheated. The fault, of course, lies in the sot-weed factor, who comes to America, according to his own words, because of "Friends unkind, and empty Purse" (l. 2). Just as this city slicker failed the test of city life, so too, when given a new chance on the American frontier, he proves unworthy of friends or success.

The best hudibrastic poem of colonial America, *The Sot-Weed Factor* satirizes the numerous rough edges of life in the new country. The poem has some obvious faults: we are told at the beginning that the "Merchant Stranger" is going to open a store at Piscataway—but then, inexplicably, he roams around the countryside. The "Indians" whom the poet and the planter's son encounter become one Indian in the next sentence. But these are minor faults. The hard-drinking, illiterate planters, their sloppy and sluttish wives, the hypocritical religious Puritans, quack doctors and lawyers, half-tame Indians, drunken justices—a whole menagerie of American types is ridiculed with entertaining, irreligious, and scurrilous rakishness. A century later, Washington Irving's "The Legend of Sleepy Hollow" displaced Cook's *Sot-Weed Factor* as the best short humorous piece by an American with an anti-hero as subject. Like Irving, Cook was concerned with American identity, and he helped to create that identity by his characterizations.

Ebenezer Cook's father drew up his will on December 31, 1711, leaving two houses in London and "Cook Point" at the mouth of the Choptank River to his son Ebenezer and his daughter Anna. Andrew Cook must have died either later that day or the next day, for the will was probated by Ebenezer and Anna Cook on January 2, 1711/12.[13] The poet had returned to Maryland before 1717, when he sold his share of Cook's Point to Edward Cook, who was probably his cousin.[14] On April 26, 1721, Henry Lowe ("Agent and Receiver Generall for the Right Honourable Charles Lord Baron of Baltimore") appointed Cook his "lawful and sufficient Deputy . . . and in my behalf to occupy and exercise the said office of bailif and collector of his Lordships manner lying upon the head of Gunpowder River in Baltimore County."[15] After the death of Lowe in 1721, Bennett Lowe, Henry's brother, became receiver-general, and Cook also acted as his deputy. In 1721 and 1722, Cook, as Lord Baltimore's agent, rented various properties in Cecil and Baltimore counties.[16] Cook also practiced law during this period. A hitherto unnoticed poem by John Fox of Virginia (a minor poet known for his London periodical of 1717, *The Wanderer*) proves that Cook was practicing law in Maryland before 1722. On January 10, 1722/3, John Fox wrote a letter and long poem to Thomas Bordley, attorney-general of Maryland, requesting Bordley to take him on as a law clerk.[17] To prove that a poet could turn to law, Fox cites the career of Ebenezer Cook: "Yet could I hope from his Example, / To tread the Rode great Lawyers Trample" (ll. 331–32). Fox also throws light on the position of Cook as "Poet-Laureate

---

[13] Wroth, *Maryland Muse by Ebenezer Cooke*, 6–7.

[14] Jones, 281–83.

[15] Deeds, Baltimore County 1717–21, Liber T.R., no. D.S., folio 237, Maryland Hall of Records.

[16] Wroth, *Maryland Muse by Ebenezer Cooke*, 8.

[17] John Fox to Thomas Bordley, Jan. 10, 1722/3, Bordley MSS, Maryland Historical Society.

of Maryland." He writes that if Bordley makes him a clerk, he will "Dab Cook my Poet Laureat too" (l. 343). Fox's verse may suggest that Cook received his title from Bordley; or, since Bordley was attorney-general of Maryland, as well as speaker of the Assembly, Cook may have been the choice of the Assembly, in some unrecorded action, as poet laureate of Maryland. More likely, Cook's title was a joke. The poem also reveals that Fox felt that he was Cook's equal, if not superior, in verse, and indirectly testifies that Cook wrote poetry (which has not survived) during these years.

In the spring of 1726 William Parks set up his press in Maryland. The earliest extant belletristic work printed in the colony was Cook's broadside poem on Thomas Bordley, *An ELOGY On the Death of Thomas Bordley, Esq.*, who died on October 11, 1726, while on a trip to England. In the 49-line poem, Cook tells the Maryland legislators to weep for their dead leader:

> Mourn *Senators*, your heads with Cyprus crown,
> And let the Bar with Sable Weeds hang down;
> The leading Member in your House is Dead
> To *Heaven's* Imperial Court for Justice fled
> There Truth and Equity in Judgment set,
> And the eternal Law, which God thought fit,
> To govern that unruly brittle Span,
> Will final Sentence pass on wretched Man.
>
> (ll. 15–22)

Continuing the law imagery, he complains of death's inexorableness:

> No Quirk in Law the Writ can e'er abate,
> Sign'd by the hand of unrelenting Fate,
> It is a Debt to Nature all must pay,
> Nor can we long put off the evil day ....[18]
>
> (ll. 38–41)

This broadside contains Cook's earliest extant use of the title "Poet-Laureat, of Maryland."

Prince Georges County, Maryland, admitted Cook to the bar during the summer of 1728. On October 28, he witnessed the sale of a prop-

---

[18] Cook's broadside is printed in facsimile in the Parke-Bernet Catalogue No. 1385, *Important Americana...Sale Nov. 25, 1952* (New York, 1952), item 101. A portion of the elegy was quoted by Elizabeth Bordley Gibson, *Biographical Sketches of the Bordley Family of Maryland* (Philadelphia, 1865), 20, who wrote that a number of "Elegies and epitaphs" commemorated Bordley's death. Lawrence C. Wroth briefly discusses Cook and the Bordley elegy in *The John Carter Brown Library Annual Report 1952–1953* (Providence, 1953), 51–54.

erty in Annapolis.[19] Sometime in December, 1728, Cook crossed over the Potomac to Virginia, for the account book of John Mercer, planter, attorney, and poet, shows that Mercer loaned the indigent poet 18s. 8d. "at Colonel Mason's."[20] William Parks had begun printing the *Maryland Gazette* in the fall of 1727, and Cook's next extant poem is found in one of the few remaining issues of Parks's newspaper. "An Elegy on the Death of the Honourable Nicholas Lowe" appeared in the *Maryland Gazette* for December 24, 1728. Cook had been deputy receiver-general under Lowe and had a number of connections with the Lowe family. Lawrence C. Wroth has shown that Lowe was having an affair with a servant, Mary Young, and that Cook evidently felt that Lowe should have married her.[21] The concluding lines of his elegy for Lowe reflect his disapproval:

> [But] tho' none live so just as to be found
> [With] but some Fault that may their Conscience wound,
> [It c]an be said, his Character to blast
> [He liv]'d and dy'd a Batchelor at last.[22]

In the late spring of 1729, Cook testified for Mary Young in her suit against Lowe's estate.[23]

In 1730, the Maryland laureate published *Sotweed Redivivus: Or the Planters Looking-Glass.* The title is perhaps meant to suggest Ed-

---

[19] Wroth (see n. 2 above), 8–9. Annapolis Land Records, 1728, Mayor's Court, Liber B, folio 168, Maryland Hall of Records.

[20] John Mercer's Ledger, 1725–37, p. 91. Bucks County Historical Society, Pa.

[21] Wroth, *Maryland Muse by Ebenezer Cooke*, 9–10. Nicholas Lowe's obituary was reprinted from the *Maryland Gazette* of Dec. 3, 1728, in the *American Weekly Mercury*, Jan. 4, 1728/9: "Annapolis, Dec. 3. Last week, dy'd at his House, in St. Mary's County, Nicholas Lowe, Esq., one of His Lordship's Honourable Council, and Agent, and Receiver-General, of all His Lordship's Revenues, in Maryland." In addition to rehashing the evidence discovered and presented by Wroth, Edward H. Cohen, "The Elegies of Ebenezer Cooke," *Early American Literature*, 4, no. 2 (1969), 49–72, says that several letters by Edward Cooke (an uncle of Ebenezer) "have been discovered in the possession of the last of the descendants of Cooke," and that in one letter Edward Cooke relates that Ebenezer "also took a liking to Mrs. Young and attempted one night to climb into her bedroom window; much to his surprise, he found her already sharing her bed with Nicholas Lowe" (p. 55). Unfortunately, Cohen cites no documentation for this statement: his note says that "further identification and verbatim quotation of this material is here suppressed according to the express desires of the owner" (p. 71 n. 16).

[22] This issue of the *Maryland Gazette* has been trimmed in binding, so that the initial letters of each line are missing. I have used the emendations supplied by Steiner, 54.

[23] Wroth, *Maryland Muse by Ebenezer Cooke*, 9.

ward Ward's *Hudibras Redivivus.* The poem considers the economic plight of Maryland during the depression in the late 1720s and may have been inspired by the poetry of Cook's young rival, Richard Lewis. Like Lewis, Cook recommends that the planters grow less tobacco and instead diversify their crops and increase their trade and crafts. Cook opens the poem with a lively Preface:

> MAY I be canoniz'd for a Saint, if I know what Apology to make for this dull Piece of Household stuff, anymore than he that first invented the *Horn-Book*; all that can be said in its Defence, is, the *Muses* hath taken as much Pains in framing their brittle Ware, as Bruin does in licking her Cub into Shape: And should that carping-Cur, Momus, but breath on it, (vah! *miseris,*) we are quite undone; since one Blast from the Critick's Mouth, wou'd raise more Flaws in this *Looking-Glass,* than there be Circles in the *Sphere*; and when all is said and done, the Reader will judge as he pleases. Well, if it be the Fate of these Sheets, to supply the Use of Waste Paper, the Author has done his Part, and is determined to write on, as often as his Inclination or Interest shall prompt him.[24]

In a prefatory poem addressed "To the Generous Subscribers," the poet states that he is old, sickly, and poor. The "thick Woods" that the poet formerly traveled through (in *The Sot-Weed Factor*) have now been *"Cut down for Fuel by unthinking Swains,"* and he laments that *"mangled Oaks"* lie on the plains (ll. 13–14). The complaint against the destruction of the American forests is notable, coming so early in American history; no one before Cook or Richard Lewis had written against the rape of the virgin American continent. It seems likely that Cook echoes this sentiment from Lewis, who gave it a memorable expression in his "Food for Critics." Cook also writes an early anti-Negro expression in American poetry: the slaves who harvest the tobacco are described as "a Troop of Aetheopian Hands, / *Worse Villains are, than* Forward's Newgate *Bands"* (ll. 18–19). Since the market has more tobacco than it can bear, Cook, paraphrasing similar expressions in Lewis's poetry, writes: *"It's Industry, and not a nauseous Weed, / Must cloath the* Naked, *and the* Hungry feed" (ll. 26–27). Echoing Lewis's poem to Hasting, Cook says that the

---

[24] Wroth, ibid., 22–23, has pointed out that the draft for this preface is preserved in the front fly leaves of a volume by Edward Coke, *Second Part of the Institutes of the Lawes of England* (London, 1642), and that the preface was originally designed for a second edition of *The Sot-Weed Factor.* St. George Leakin Sioussat, *Economics and Politics in Maryland 1720-1750, . . .* (Baltimore, 1903), 37–41, has admirably set the poem in its niche in the economic history of Maryland.

province should ship her products to England in Maryland vessels (ll. 28–35). Cook then apologizes for his poetry, claiming that his subject is innately inferior:

> *THIS thread-bare Theme* the Author's *Muse here sings,*
> *Did never drink of the* Castalian *Springs,*
> *Or bath'd her* Limbs in Heliconian *Streams,*
> *Where fiery Phoebus cools his thirsty Beams ....*
> (ll. 36–39)

(Compare to this, a fairly typical expression of Lewis, "Of ancient Streams presume no more to tell, / The fam'd Castalian or Pierian Well.") Ebenezer Cook claims that he writes a different kind of poetry:

> *SUCH lofty Numbers and heroic Strains*
> *Of sprightly Wit, as* Virgil's *Lays contains,*
> *When elevated with* Phoebian *Fire,*
> *On* Tyber's *Banks, he struck the warbling Lyre,*
> *Are too sublime for her, that ne'er could fly*
> *Above the Pitch of* Grub-street *Elegy,*
> *Or the flat Sound of* Doggerel *Poetry ....*
> (ll. 40–46)

Cook closes the prefatory poem suggesting that, before Marylanders be allowed to marry, the girls should have to make a complete wardrobe for themselves from native homespun, and the men (who now spend their time at cards and horse-racing) should have to grow 3,000 pounds of hemp or flax.

Sotweed Redivivus, like *The Sot-Weed Factor*, is a narrative poem written in jingling, hudibrastic verse. The speaker is supposedly the sot-weed factor who figured in the earlier poem, but he has now grown old and settled in Maryland. He is twice addressed as "old Poet" (I, 84 and III, 126) and is thus a version of Ebenezer Cook. In contrast to the burlesque tone of the former poem, *Sotweed Redivivus* is serious and persuasive, with only occasional satiric flashes. It has less description, characterization, and action than *The Sot-Weed Factor*, but more dialogue. The first of the three cantos of *Sotweed Redivivus* begins with the old poet riding to Annapolis, which is, in 1730, "The famous Beau Metropolis ... grown rich and opulent" since the poet described it in *The Sot-Weed Factor*. The Maryland Assembly is meeting in Annapolis, debating remedies for Maryland's failing single-crop system. Some members are trying to pass a law which would create "a *Current Coin*, / Without Exception, such as may, / Our *Publick Dues* and *Clergy pay*" (I, 27–29). But a number

97

of groups are against the paper money.[25] Cook falls in with a planter, and the two discuss the issue (I, 51–74). In the evening, Cook drinks at a tavern with the legislators. A member of the Assembly with pretensions to learning says that he can't vote for paper currency because

> *Planters,* when in drink
> Wou'd light their Pipes with Paper Chink;
> And knowing not to read, might be
> Impos'd on, by such Currency ....
> (I, 115–18)

When Cook goes to bed, he discovers that his bedmate is the same wealthy planter who had entertained him in *The Sot-Weed Factor*; the planter calls for a bottle of claret, but the mulatto servant at the inn had gone to bed already, and so they begin rehearsing the economic plight of Maryland without liquor's aid.

Canto II begins with the planter's summary of the difficulty. In short, there's too much tobacco for the market. He suggests that the planters should only be allowed to grow a fixed amount per person, that factors should have to pay hard currency for tobacco, and that common warehouses should be erected for storing tobacco. He also thinks that the ministers as well as lawyers should be paid in currency (II, 153–55). During the course of his projecting, the planter proposes cultivating tobacco "without the help of Savage Hands" (II, 84), and also urges the agrarian Marylanders to live in towns and cities (II, 114). Cook and the planter both drift off to sleep before the latter finishes his program of remedies.

Canto III opens with Cook toasting Maryland:

> SCARCE had the *Goddess* of the *Night,*
> Resign'd her Throne to *Phoebus* bright;
> When calling for a Quart Decanter
> Of *Sack,* I thus harangu'd the *Planter*:
> Rise, *Oroonoko,* rise, said I,
> And let us drink Prosperity
> To *Maryland,* before we part;
> Starting, says he, with all my Heart.
> (III, 1–8)

Then the planter (who compares himself to the *Maryland Gazette* essayist, "P. P.") continues with his cures for Maryland's economic

---

[25] Parks reprinted Benjamin Franklin's essay *A Modest Enquiry into the Nature and Necessity of a Paper Currency* (Philadelphia, 1729) in his *Maryland Gazette* for July 22, 1729.

woes. The swamps and marshes should be drained, and hemp, flax, rice, and cotton planted. The herds of sheep and cattle should be increased, and Maryland should build ships for its sea trade. Cook once again reveals the influence of Richard Lewis, echoing his poem to Hastings on the shipwright's art:

> BUT then, perhaps it will be said,
> By those (to venture) are afraid,
> How shall these floating Castles be
> Equipp'd, and fitted for the Sea?
> A Doubt not difficult to solve,
> Wou'd such (in Pence abound) resolve,
> As the *Phoenicians* did of old,
> To plow the Seas in Vessels bold;
> Which *Draft-men* best know how to mould.
>
> (III, 51–59)

When the planter finishes his program for the public good, Cook comments:

> But when all's done, as hath been said,
> It's Industry must force a Trade:
> Upon *Mercator* turn the Tables,
> And cut those Interlopers Cables.
>
> (III, 109–12)

Finally, Cook concludes his poem by urging the Assembly to act and not to deliberate forever:

> Then by the *Poet* be advis'd,
> Said I to him, seem'd much disguis'd;
> His Counsel's not to be despis'd
> Begin, be bold, old *Horace* cries,
> And bravely venture to be wise.
> In vain, he on the Brook Side stands,
> With Shoes and Stockings in his Hands;
> Waiting 'till all the Stream be past and gone,
> That runs, (alas!) and ever will run on.
>
> (III, 126–34)

Partially because of its topicality, the poem is not very interesting today. Cook borrowed the subject and some of the imagery from Lewis's poetry; but unlike the younger poet, he was not able to write interestingly on such innately drab subjects as economics. Cook was a poet in search of a subject, and the topic selected in *Sotweed Redivivus* was unsuited to his satiric talent. Unlike *The Sot-Weed Factor*, this poem was written for a local audience, and the poet did not, unfortunately, distinguish the speaker of the poem from the poet in real life. The poem lacks the amusing story, the sustained humor, the close observations, and the complexity of the earlier work. Although Cook attempts to recapture the spirit of the earlier work and even copied whole lines from it into *Sotweed Redivivus*, this poem is like most imitations—a failure. Moses Coit Tyler contrasted *The Sot-Weed Factor* with *Sotweed Redivivus*: "The first poem has, indeed, an abundance of filth and scurrility, but it has wit besides; the second poem lacks only the wit." [26] Perhaps a little scurrility would have enlivened *Sotweed Redivivus*—but I did not find any.

"The History of Colonel Nathaniel Bacon's Rebellion in Virginia. Done into Hudibrastic Verse, from an old MS" is Cook's longest poem. It appeared in his volume *The Maryland Muse* (with the third edition of *The Sot-Weed Factor*), published in Annapolis in 1731. According to the last note in *The Maryland Muse*, Cook intended to published yearly a miscellany of poetry, but there is no record of any further volume. *The Maryland Muse*, like all Cook's poetry printed in Maryland, survives only in a unique copy. Lawrence C. Wroth has shown that Cook's "old MS" source was John Cotton's history of Bacon's rebellion. Evidently, the Reverend Hugh Jones (the Virginia historian who was at this time a minister in Charles County, Maryland) sent Cook the manuscript history as a suitable subject for the poet's narrative, hudibrastic talent. Although Cook follows Cotton's account fairly faithfully, he also consulted other Virginia historians. He must have had a copy of Hugh Jones's work, and he once cites Robert Beverly's *History of Virginia* (I, 391). Here is "H. J.'s" prefatory punning poem to Cook's "Bacon's Rebellion":

> Old Poet,
>   As *You may remember*,
> *You told me sometime* in September,
> *Your pleasant* Muse *was idly sitting*,
> *Longing for some new Subject fitting*
> *For this Meridian, and her Inditing*,
> *Worth Praise and Pence, for Pains in Writing.*
>   *I therefore (thinking it great Pity*
> *A* Muse *should pine, that is so witty*)
> *Have sent an old, authentick Book*,
> *For Her in Doggrel Verse to Cook*;
> *For since it never was in Print*,
> (*Tho' wondrous Truths are written in't*)
> *It may be worthy* Clio's *Rhimes*,

[26] *History of American Literature*, 488.

> *To hand it down to future Times.*
> *YOU know what never-fading Glory,*
> *Old* Salust *got by* Catlin's *Story;*
> *The Fame* Hyde *gain'd, I need not tell y'on,*
> *By's Hist'ry of the* Grand Rebellion:
> *You know how* Butler's *witty Lays*
> *Procur'd for him immortal Praise:*
> *I'll add no more—But if you please, Sir,*
> *Attempt the same for Ebenezer,*
> *Which you may gain, or I'm mistaken,*
> *If you can nicely* Cook *this* Bacon.

Each of the poem's three cantos is prefixed by a rhymed argument. The first canto narrates Nathaniel Bacon's provocation and the *"rebellious Manner"* in which he displayed *"his Banner."* The satire opens with ludicrously mixed classical and hudibrastic references. Throughout the poem, Nathaniel Bacon is compared to Oliver Cromwell. Cook tells the origin of Bacon's rebellion: Indian tribes attacked Marylanders; the latter asked Virginia for help; and Virginia's Governor William Berkeley sent out an armed party. The Indians ("Who ne'er in vain at Friend or Foe, / a Trigger draw, or bend their Bow, / As able Archers, and as good, / As *Little John* and *Robin Hood"* [I, 49–53]) ambushed a group of the Virginians, but were subsequently defeated. The savages objected to Berkeley's helping the Marylanders, saying that unless given satisfaction, they were determined to wage a full-scale war. This remonstrance was rejected by those Virginians

> Whose Int'rest lean'd the other Way;
> Such as, for Honour or for Pay,
> Made Sword and Pistol their Vocation,
> And held it an Abomination,
> And base Dishonour to their Station,
> On any Terms t'accept a Peace
> From *Infidels*; that, like wild *Geese*,
> Beyond the *Western* Mountain Roam,
> And rarely can be found at Home.
>   (I, 131–39)

Therefore, the Indians assaulted the Virginians, burning and plundering the outlying areas. After Governor William Berkeley proved unable to suppress the savages, Nathaniel Bacon appeared on the scene. Cook thus characterizes him:

> A Man respected by the Mob,
> As a fit Fool to do their Jobb;

Who, Sword in Hand, would rescue Cattle,
And give the *Indians* bloody Battle;
That had from *MAR'LAND* taken Flight,
Dreading with *Bonnett* blew to fight,
Who well they knew (as *Scotch Highlander*)
Was hot, as fiery *Salamander*.

(I, 180–87)

The planters ask that Bacon be appointed a general to carry the war
to the Indians, but Berkeley refuses. While Bacon is at Jamestown
trying to get the commission, he hears that the Indians have attacked
his plantation and killed his overseer. So Bacon charges off, leading
the mob, to attack the Indians:

THUS, great as *Noll*, as *Quixot* stout,
At head of Planters he rid out,
The Woods of Salvages to clear,
Pursu'd by BERKELEY in the Rear,
Who (being obliged by his Station)
Had sally'd forth from *Midd Plantation*,
With Life-Guard, resolutely bent
Impending Mischiefs to prevent;
Make *Lilliputian Cavilero*,
(As Great in Thought as *Spanish Hero*)
On bended Hams *Peccavi* cry;
Or *Bacon* hang on Gibbet high,
For daring contumaciously,
To levy War on Enemy,
Without the general Assent
Of *Governour* and *Parliament*;
Who of the Publick Good to treat,
Were than at *James*-Town call'd to meet.

(I, 218–35)

Berkeley lost Bacon's trail and returned to Jamestown to proclaim
him a traitor. After Bacon put the Indians to flight, he went to his
plantation and was elected burgess. When he reached Jamestown,
Berkeley made him a prisoner of state. Bacon was tried, acquitted,
and subsequently received Berkeley's promise to make him a general.
But the governor later reneged. Bacon then arranged to have a message delivered, saying that his wife was ill. He asked for and received
permission to return home, and here we find the first scatological
allusion in the poem:

NAT having play'd this cunning Trick,
Instead of visiting the Sick,
Before black Messenger rid Post,
(As if the De'el had drove) to th' Host;

To head a factious, stubborn Crew,
(As e're o're Seas for Refuge flew)
Of Servants, Slaves, and Overseers,
At least Five Hundred Mutineers;
That to insult the *Government*,
(By *Bacon's* Preincouragement)
At Nat's Approach began to bluster,
And *Hurley-Burley* soon did muster,
Like Tumble-T———ds got in a cluster.
                              (I, 343–55)

At the head of his forces, Bacon returned to Jamestown and demanded a commission. Berkeley refused to give him one, but the Assembly conferred it. Then Bacon "rid from his Dwelling, / Like *Oliver*, a Colonelling" (I, 372–73). While searching for Indians, Bacon learns of Berkeley's preparations against him and returns to Williamsburg where the rebels "sign the League, which you may see, / Drawn up at large, in *Beverley*" (I, 390–91).

Cook begins Canto II with a description of Bacon's army, a "giddy multitude" composed of "*Bullies, Ruffians, Debauchees, / Cheats, Gamesters, Pimps*, and *Raparees*" (II, 9–10). Bacon digs in for a siege. To protect his men while they are building fortifications, Bacon seizes the wives of the loyal planters, ranging "them on their Works, in View / Of *Citadel* and Cannon too: / So that no Loialist durst fire" (II, 41–43). Behind this living barricade, Bacon prepared for a siege; the poet suggests that the wives of the loyal planters spent their nights in Bacon's bed (II, 70–71).

After completing the fortifications, Bacon released the women, and then Berkeley's "mercenary Troops" attacked. One of the governor's commanders was Hubert Farrell, who was "more us'd t'attack a Cyder Barrel / Than face a Foe upon old Sorrel" (II, 94–95). Farrell tells his men to follow his example, and so Cook pictures the following ludicrous sequence:

> THEN marching on, a Ball from *Nat*
> Laid *Farrell* on his Belly flat;
> Which b'ing observ'd by Farrell's Bands,
> They all fall flat upon the Sands,
> Thinking he did it, as the Token,
> Of what he just before had spoken:
> Whereby a Body of Foot Soldiers,
> Compos'd of Servants and Freeholders,
> That follow'd *Farrell* in the Rear,
> Were forc'd to halt when they drew near;
> Which made a Troop of Horse, behind,

Towards the Marsh about to wind,
To see what should be the Occasion
Of unexpected Retardation;
Who looking over Tow'rds the Main,
Thought all their Forlorn-hope were slain.
So Wheeling suddenly about,
They put their own Reserves to th' Rout;
Which made them all retire for Shelter,
In great Confusion, *Helter-skelter*,
Excepting such as *Bacon's* Shot
Imbargo'd dead upon the Spot,
And One or Two that in Retreat
Were trod i'th' Water under Feet.
(II, 113–36)

None of Bacon's men was hurt, but a number of Berkeley's were killed. The next day, Bacon received reinforcements. On hearing this, Governor Berkeley fled Jamestown to Accomack, on the Eastern Shore, and the rebels burned Jamestown. He then marched to Gloucester where he learned that Colonel Brent was coming with 1,200 men to battle him. Bacon called his men together, told them of the odds against them, and found that they were all resolutely with him. When Brent's men learned that Bacon was preparing for them, they deserted. Bacon next journeyed to the seat of Gloucester County and asked the Gloucester men to join him. They at first refused but later changed their minds and agreed to see him "at a second Meeting, / At *Warner's* house, for farther Treating" (II, 271–72).

A message from the Eastern Shore asked Bacon to cross the bay and take the war to the governor and his party, who were plundering the people. But, in lines that anticipate Edgar Allan Poe's "Raven," Death comes for Nathaniel Bacon:

ON these Designs was *Bacon* harping,
At BERKELEY's Conduct often carping;
When Death at's Chamber door came rapping,
As *Moss* caught Mare, took *Bacon* napping.
(II, 303–306)

The poet compares Bacon's lieutenants to Cromwell's successors and to "*Quixot's Sancho*, Fool and Knave." In a tortured image, Cook claims that maggots bred in Bacon's brains finally felled him, and Cook describes the emerging maggots in gusty and disgusting detail (II, 313–24). To prevent Berkeley's men from exhuming and mutilating the body, Bacon's followers hid his corpse. The second canto concludes:

WHO's born for Hanging (Proverb says)
Ne'er needs fear Drowning in the Seas;
So *vice versa*, 'stead of Tree,
The Fates ordain'd *Nat* to the Sea;
Who justly merited the Halter,
But nought the Fates Decrees will alter;
Tho' t' had been better, had he swung,
Such *Bacon* being best well hung.
    BUT, now beneath the restless Billow,
He rests, who ne'er had Rest on Pillow,
The Year that *Nat* set sail for *Styx*,
Was Sixteen Hundred Sev'enty Six
I'th Month *October*, the 18th day:
So I've no more of him to say.
                                    (II, 354–67)

In the third canto, Governor Berkeley resolves to try to defeat the rebels who are continuing the fight. He strikes "whilst Iron's hot, / And so makes *Traytors* go to pot" (III, 19–20). Cook compares this to Berkeley's quick action in proclaiming Charles II king on learning of Cromwell's death. The first group of Bacon's men whom Berkeley caught was Colonel Hansford and his party, seized at Auborn's house, "By *Auborn's* wanton wife betray'd; / And thence across the *Bay* convey'd, / And hang'd at *Accomack*, 'tis said" (III, 52–54).

Then "*Will* (Who with Friends did live in Clover)" sails over the bay to York River and anchors at Tindall's point. His men go ashore to attack Whaley, another of Bacon's lieutenants. Hubert Farrell ("Who of the Wound, was now quite well, / He got, when he at *James*-Town fell" [III, 80–81]) commanded the attack. Farrell plans to surprise Whaley, but a sentry spots Farrell's men, and the battle commences:

Where long they pelted at each other,
Tho' none was kill'd in all this Pother,
Excepting *Hubert*, who i'th' Chase,
Fell once again upon his Face;
When pop came Ball, from Musquet Barrel
That thro' the Back shot Hubert Farrell.
                                    (III, 111–16)

The men, seeing that Farrell has been slain, break and run for the boats:

Happy the Man, that first can get,
To Shallop, tho' like drown'd Rat wet,
Higgledy Piggledy Malpas shot,
Heels over Heads, away they trot,
'Till safe unto their Boat they got:

105

Ev'n those that others Legs did use,
In getting out (to save their Shoes)
Run on their own Legs now, to choose.
(III, 128–35)

Berkeley raises men from Gloucester and Middlesex counties. When Ingram learns the news, he dispatches Lieutenant Walkett to the fort at Middlesex. Major Smith, Berkeley's commander, tries to take the fort from Walkett, but Walkett's thirty men prove too resolute for Smith's five hundred. Smith retreats to the Reverend Mr. Pate's house. When Smith leaves the house, Ingram takes it, and Cook has a chance to satirize the minister:

> For, *Ingram* having Information,
> That *Smith* had left *Pate's* Habitation,
> Whips in between the House and Major,
> And swore like Tinker in his Rage, Sir:
> "That 'less the Garr'son would surrender
> "On Terms that he should please to tender,
> "He'd Shoot, or Burn, or Hang, or Kill,
> "Each Person that declar'd for *Will*":
> Which naughty Words, or wicked Whoreson,
> Did so affright poor Captain Parson,
> Whom *Smith* had left to guard the House,
> (In Peace a Man, in War a Mouse)
> That, not accustom'd to such Sport,
> He forthwith gives him up the Fort,
> Resolving now to mind his Church,
> And ne'er more leave her in the Lurch;
> But stick to's Text, and mind his Book,
> Since *Mars* had such a dismal Look;
> Ne'er fight the Battle of the Lord;
> And never use a Sword at all,
> Besides the Sword that's spirit'al.
> (III, 159–80)

While Ingram feasts on the provisions at Pate's house, Smith returns. But Smith is leery of attacking Ingram. After some hesitation, the men with Smith decide not to fight, and desert.

Next, Cook satirizes the English merchants trading in the Chesapeake area, revealing that he, like most colonials, thought the ship captains were usuriously profiting from the colonial planters:

> Now comes the trick of Captain *Grantham*,
> Which some think base; but I think handsome:
> He long had traded in the Parts,
> Knew Planters Tempers and their Hearts;
> And had great Infl'ence far and near,

Either for int'rest, Love, or Fear;
As many worthy Traders have,
Who in their Hands still keep the Staff;
By keeping Planters Egg in Nest,
Pray don't be Mad, 'tis but a Jest.
(III, 249–58)

After negotiating a secret pact with Berkeley, Captain Grantham goes to Ingram and says it's a shame that innocent men are dying, claiming that Berkeley is willing to give generous terms if the rebels surrender. Bacon's lieutenants, Ingram and Walkett, arrange terms with Grantham for their capitulation. Then Grantham meets secretly with Ingram's men, who will not capitulate. So Grantham tells them that he sailed over with a fleet of redcoats, who are now moored in the Downs. He proposes that they surrender to Berkeley, who will give:

". . . Indemnity for those
That Freeman are and good Freeholders;
And then for all the listed Soldiers,
Suppose for them I get their Pay,
And get the Servants freed, what say y'?"
(III, 362–66)

And Grantham asks that they keep their terms from Ingram and Walkett. The men agree, and so Grantham brings them the pardon. After the rebels lay down their arms and return to the plantations, the governor and Council take retribution on them:

AND now each Party seem'd at Ease.
Supposing nought could break their Peace,
When Council and Assembly thought,
That some o'th archest *Rebels* ought,
By Death to make some Satisfaction,
For all the Ills of late Distraction,
To frighten Folks from trayt'rous Action.
THEN here and there did Rebel swing,
On Limbs of Trees, like Dogs in String,
To put the Saddle on right Horse,
The vilest hangs in Chains in Course;
So *'Tony Arnold*, who kept *Ferry*,
Was thus preser'd to *Charon's* Wherry.
(III, 411–23)

Cook concludes "Bacon's Rebellion" with a reference to the book's next part, a revised edition of *The Sot-Weed Factor*:[27]

[27] This edition of *The Sot-Weed Factor* (Annapolis, 1731) has frequently been reprinted in the anthologies. But Cook toned down his satire on Quakers for the 1731 edition—and changed the ending. No longer does the poem con-

So much for Hanging and for Killing,
Enough (I hope) for half Five Shillings;
For I've no more of this to tell,
'Ere you read *Sotweed* rest a Spell,
So for the present, Sirs, Farewell.
(III, 438–42)

Cook's poem is competent and occasionally enjoyable—but not as good as *The Sot-Weed Factor*. The speaker in "Bacon's Rebellion" is an uninteresting poet freely working from sources. There is no clear structure, though the events of the war, the death of Bacon, and the reappearance of certain characters (like Governor Berkeley and Hubert Farrell) suggest some pattern. And the multitude of characters and actions make the story difficult to follow. Of course Cook's contemporaries were probably familiar with the chief men and events of the rebellion, so these latter two charges may be unfair. But certainly *The Sot-Weed Factor*, with its central character, complex *persona*, and artistic structure, is a better poem. Although "Bacon's Rebellion" was more suitable for Cook's narrative and hudibrastic talent than *Sotweed Redivivus*, the high seriousness of the actions in "Bacon's Rebellion" works against the form and manner of the poem. Cook effectively combined situational and verbal humor in *The Sot-Weed Factor*, but "Bacon's Rebellion" (with some exceptions) allowed him to play only with verbal humor. The story as found in John Cotton's manuscript (which Cook closely followed) lends itself more to tragedy than farce. Furthermore, Cook never resolved where his sympathies lay and treated both sides with alternating sympathy and condescension.

When Benedict Leonard Calvert died in 1732, at least two elegies were written on his death: one by Richard Lewis and one that has been attributed to Ebenezer Cook. The main reason for attributing "A Poem. In Memory of the Honourable Benedict Leonard Calvert, Esquire" to Cook is the similarity of its opening lines ("What mean these Tears, is Benedictus fled / Gone to the watry Mansions of the Dead") with the opening of Cook's elegy on Nicholas Lowe ("What means this Mourning, Ladies, has Death led / Your Brother Captive to his Earthly Bed?"). Unfortunately, the elegy on Calvert is extant

---

clude with a curse on Maryland; instead Cook gives some watered-down advice to the prospective merchant. In making his poem less offensive, Cook made it a lesser poem.

only in a mutilated copy, for the first letters of every line are missing after the first third of the poem, and the last line is completely missing.[28] Nevertheless, with its reference to Spenser and its echo of James Shirley, it is an interesting addition to Cook's canon. It opens with a horrible picture of Calvert's body on the ocean floor, food for fish, and progresses to the conventional vision of the soul ascending to heaven. The body of the poem praises Calvert's character and his ceaseless efforts for the province's good. The ending alludes to James Shirley's famous lines from his masque *The Contention of Ajax and Ulysses* ("Only the actions of the just / Smell sweet and blossom in their dust"):

> But as the Actions of the Good and Just
> Smell Sweet (when Dead) and blossom in the Dust,
> So his will from the Ocean always Cast
> A Fragrant Scent, and blossom to the last ....
>
> (ll. 49–52)

The last extant poem and last record of Ebenezer Cook is his elegy on the death of William Lock,[29] a justice of Maryland who died in May, 1732. The elegy probably appeared in a now-lost issue of the *Maryland Gazette*, but only a manuscript copy of the poem survives. Cook begins with an elegiac tone of high seriousness, but soon puns on Lock's following the court circuits: "And is that Lamp gone out, extinguished quite, / Which in the Western Circuit shone so bright?" The poet then asks why Richard Lewis, who recently wrote a long elegy on Governor Benedict Leonard Calvert, has not lamented Lock:

> Has Lock refined his Tenement of Clay,
> And to some unknown Somewhere wing'd his way?
> And shall he buried in oblivion lye?
> Is there no Bard to wing his Elegy?
> So are the muses drop't asleep, since they
> To Calvert's Ghost did their devotions pay?
>
> (ll. 3–8)

[28] Together with several poems by Richard Lewis, this elegy is in a manuscript folio notebook at the United States Naval Academy Library, Annapolis. Walter B. Norris, "Some Recently Found Poems on the Calverts," *Maryland Historical Magazine* 32 (1937):116–17, first suggested an attribution to Cook and printed the elegy, 127–28. Cohen (see n. 21 above), 57–60, also argues for the attribution to Cook.

[29] "An Elegy on the death of the Honourable *William Lock*, Esq., one of his Lordship's Provincial Justices, who departed this Life at his Seat in Anne Arundel County, May—,1732. By Ebenezer Cook, Poet Laureate." Printed in the *Maryland Historical Magazine* 14 (1919):172–73; and in Cohen (see n. 21 above), 66–67.

Cook says that if that's the case, then he will write on Lock. He thus arrives at the traditional beginning of the elegy:

Awake, Melpomene! —behold the Dire
Decree of Fate! See on a sable Bier
(O mournful sight) he's quite deprived of Life,
The most impartial Judge of human Strife,
That ever yet, with an unbias'd hand,
The Scales of Justice held in Maryland . . . .
(ll. 13–18)

Cook says that when Lock died "Justice fled to Heaven," and he concludes by asking pardon for his hyperbole (and perhaps should have begged pardon for the pun). The six-line epitaph concludes, "Thou, Reader, as Lock is, prepare to be; / Death's Power is absolute on Land and Sea."

There is no further record of Ebenezer Cook, poet laureate of colonial Maryland. He must have been well over sixty at this time. He may have returned to England, but more probably he died in Maryland soon after this last production. *The Sot-Weed Factor* is Cook's best poem. Lively and humorous throughout its entire length, the poem is excellent satire. *Sotweed Redivivus* attempts to handle the kind of poetry that Richard Lewis wrote. But in Cook's hands, serious poetry is a bore. "Bacon's Rebellion," although occasionally enlivened by humor, is too long, without clear focus, and not unified. The subject is more interesting than the poem. And Cook's occasional poems are all slight. His reputation rests upon *The Sot-Weed Factor*, which satirizes not only America but also the popular English conceptions of America.

$\mathscr{W}$ILLIAM PARKS

PRINTER

$\mathscr{P}$

In 1726, when William Parks started printing in Annapolis, he inaugurated the first flourishing of Maryland literature. A year later he began publishing the *Maryland Gazette*, the first Southern newspaper; and in 1728 he brought out Richard Lewis's *The Mouse Trap*, the first belletristic book published in the South. The appearance of a weekly newspaper which solicited poems and essays stimulated the scattered writers of Maryland. William Parks printed the poetry of Richard Lewis and Ebenezer Cook, and the political polemics and theories of the Reverend Jacob Henderson, Daniel Dulany, and Henry Darnall, as well as the miscellaneous writings of numerous lesser authors.

Parks's antecedents and early life are unknown, but he printed in three English towns before he came to America. His Welsh printing may suggest that he was Welsh. He began printing the *Ludlow Post-Man, or the Weekly Journal* in 1719.[1] He evidently printed in Ludlow only about two years before going to Hereford, where he issued two books (including Benjamin Meredith's Welsh translation of John Bunyan) in 1721.[2] By July, 1723, he had set up business in Reading,

[1] Lawrence C. Wroth, *William Parks, Printer and Journalist* (Richmond, 1926), 36. Another valuable study of Parks is William Henry Castles, Jr., "The *Virginia Gazette*, 1736-1766: Its Editors, Editorial Policies, and Literary Content," *Dissertation Abstracts*, 33:3350-51 (Tennessee). For Parks's English newspapers, see James D. Stewart et al., *British Union Catalogue of Periodicals* (London, 1955-58).

[2] Llewelyn C. Lloyd, "The Book Trade in Shropshire: Some Account of the Stationers, Booksellers and Printers at Work in the County about 1800," *Trans-*

where the first issue of *The Reading Mercury, or Weekly Entertainer*, printed by "W. Parks, and D. Kinnier," appeared on July 8, 1723.

Thomas Bordley, a leader of the Maryland Assembly and a steadfast opponent of the proprietary party, somehow got in touch with Parks early in 1725. Bordley had previously supervised the printing of *The Charter of Maryland, Together with the Debates and Proceedings of the . . . Assembly . . . 1722, 1723, and 1724* (Philadelphia, 1725), engaging Andrew Bradford for the task. In his "An Epistolar PREFACE TO THE *Maryland* READERS," Bordley claimed that the "publick Parliamentary Proceedings of Maryland have commonly been so little known to the Inhabitants of the Province, that they have scarce had any Opportunity of Judging whether they were Served or Prejudiced by their Representatives; whether their Constitution was maintained or prostituted, whether their *English* Liberties were asserted or Neglected by them." Bordley further states that "the want of proper Publication of their Proceedings" has kept the people in ignorance, and that some representatives who have claimed to be friends of the people have actually behaved otherwise. Bordley revealed his own conception of himself and his primary reason for introducing a press in Maryland when he wrote:

> The Character of a great Commoner, so much esteemed in *England*, seems here unknown, or useless, for want of such, as, by a curious Inspection into the Proceedings of former Times, and making themselves well acquainted with all Parliamentary Proceedings and the Rights of their Country, may deserve that Character, which is likewise, in great Measure, owing to the want of Publishing the Votes of our Assemblies: But 'tis hop'd from this beginning and the provision that is made for having a Press amongst us, the Gentlemen of the Country will more readily fall upon this useful kind of Learning, since it will be thereby made so Easy to become proficients in it.

Obviously Bordley engaged Parks primarily for political purposes. At any rate, Bordley, on November 6, 1725, informed the Assembly that he had sent for a printer.[3]

The earliest record of William Parks in Maryland occurs in the Journal of the Upper House of Assembly for March 17, 1725/6, when he presented a petition asking for permission to print the public laws.

---

actions of the Shropshire Archaeological and Natural History Society, 48, pt. 2 (1936), 152–56. William Rowlands, *Cambrian Bibliography*, ed. D. Silvan Evans (Llanidloes, Wales, 1869), 327–28.

[3] *Archives of Maryland*, 35:475–76.

The Upper House referred the request to the Lower House, where Thomas Bordley, Thomas Truman Greenfield, John Rider, Ralph Crabb, and James Hollyday were appointed to meet with a group from the Upper House to arrange terms for Parks's appointment as public printer.[4] On March 21, 1725/6, the Lower House passed a bill to support printing the Journals of the Assembly and "a Compleat Body of the whole Laws" of Maryland.[5] Parks opened his printing office in 1726 and soon became the Annapolis postmaster. Parks's establishment also served as the stage office: an advertisement in the Philadelphia *American Weekly Mercury* for April 4, 1728, mentions that the stage stopped in Annapolis at Parks's post office.

The political climate in nearly every colony was turbulent, with the lower houses of the legislature constantly fighting for privileges against the power of the proprietors or royal governors. When William Parks came to Maryland, the Lower House decided to have its journals printed and published at the public's expense. The Upper House (perhaps wanting the Assembly's quarrels promulgated as little as possible) opposed the proposal. Finally the Lower House prevailed.[6] Parks began printing in Maryland in 1726, issuing three pamphlets as well as Cook's broadside elegy on Bordley.[7] On December 29, 1726, Parks bought a tract of land for £40.[8] And on January 25, 1726/7, he bought Lot T in Annapolis for £180.[9] Evidently, as the printer had told the legislature, he intended to "live and dye" in Maryland.[10] But his stay in Annapolis was comparatively short (only about three and a half years), for he gradually realized that printing in the larger and wealthier colony of Virginia would be more profitable. On December 15, 1726 (probably just less than a year after he came to Maryland), he proposed to the Council of Virginia that he print the laws of that colony.[11] On February 22, 1727/8, the governor

[4] Ibid., 439, 451, 470–71.
[5] Ibid., 475–77.
[6] Ibid., 451, 452, 455, 484, 485.
[7] Lawrence C. Wroth, *A History of Printing in Colonial Maryland, 1686–1776* (Baltimore, 1922), 170–71. The Cook broadside only recently came to light. There is a facsimile in the Parke-Bernet Catalogue No. 1385, *Important Americana*, item 101.
[8] Land Records, Anne Arundel County, Liber *Syl*, folio 255, Maryland Hall of Records.
[9] Ibid., folio 277.
[10] *Archives of Maryland*, 35:451.
[11] Herbert Read McIlwaine, ed., *Executive Journals of the Council of Virginia* (Richmond, 1930), 4:125.

and Council referred to the House of Burgesses his petition and proposals for printing a complete body of the laws of Virginia then in force "and also the Laws to be made hereafter from time to time." The House resolved to print the laws and ordered a committee to meet with Parks regarding the terms. Here, for the time being, the matter rested.[12]

In 1727, Parks brought out *A Compleat Collection of the Laws of Maryland*, a large folio of 312 pages which he sumptuously bound in his own shop in Annapolis. Although the compiler of the *Laws of Maryland* (1727) has previously been unknown, an entry in the account book for 1725–37 of John Mercer (a Virginia poet and lawyer) reveals that he was paid £11 10s. by Parks for "an abridgment of the Laws of Maryland contained in the printed volume," and credited with another £11 10s. for supplying an "Index and etc."[13] On September 12, 1727, Parks printed the first issue of the *Maryland Gazette*.[14] With its publication, belletristic literature began to thrive in Maryland. Parks encouraged native literature by soliciting and printing local writing, including two of the earliest American essay series, Daniel Dulany's political pieces, and many pamphlets and broadsides. Thus the poetry of Ebenezer Cook and Richard Lewis found their way into print and into the literary tradition.

Unfortunately, only a few issues of Parks's newspaper survive. The *Maryland Gazette* for December 10, 1728, number 65, is the earliest extant issue. The last extant issue of this series of the *Maryland Gazette* is for December 22, 1730, number 171; but the newspaper was continued at least until March of the following year, as records of bills and references in other newspapers show.[15] The *Maryland Gazette* was revived late in 1732 by Parks and his Annapolis partner Edmund Hall and was continued at least through number 90, for November 29, 1734.

Parks probably began his newspaper in 1727 with a statement

[12] Herbert Read McIlwaine, ed., *Journals of the House of Burgesses of Virginia 1727–1734, 1736–1740* (Richmond, 1910), 25.

[13] C. Clement Samford and John M. Hemphill, II, *Bookbinding in Colonial Virginia* (Williamsburg, 1966), 150–51. John Mercer's Ledger, 1725–1737, p. 42, Bucks County Historical Society, Pa.

[14] Although no issues of the *Maryland Gazette* for 1727 are extant, Wroth, *William Parks, Printer and Journalist*, 40, item 15, judges that the first issue of the paper is from this date.

[15] Clarence S. Brigham, *History and Bibliography of American Newspapers, 1680–1820* (Worcester, Mass., 1947), 1:218.

similar to the one he used in the first issue of the *Virginia Gazette*. There, he told the readers that "the Design of these Papers, is to inform the Reader, of the most material Occurrences, as well of Europe, and other Foreign Parts of the World, as of these American Plantations;... by which the Readers may be improv'd, amus'd, or diverted: which I shall faithfully collect, as well from the Public Prints, which I have ordered to be transmitted to me, from several Parts of England and the American Plantations, by all Opportunities, as from the private Accounts I may receive from my Correspondents." He also requested literary contributions: "And if any Ingenious Public-spirited Gentlemen, who have Time to spare, will employ their leisure Hours in the Service of the Publick, by Writing any Speculative Letters, Poems, Essays, Translations, &c. which may tend to the Improvement of Mankind in general or the innocent Diversion or Entertainment of either Sex, without Offence to any in particular, they may depend on a Place in this Paper; and their names concealed if desir'd." [16]

Parks began the *Virginia Gazette* with an original essay series entitled "The Monitor" which ran for twenty-two numbers (Parks omitted it whenever important news filled the paper) until February 25, 1736/7. Since the first sixty-four issues of the *Maryland Gazette* are not extant, we cannot now determine what devices Parks used to launch his Maryland newspaper in 1727. But in 1729 he published an essay series in the *Maryland Gazette*. The "Plain-Dealer" essays are the fourth periodical series in American literature. [17] Unfortunately, only the first two essays appear to be original. Parks borrowed the others from various English periodicals, changing them slightly to reflect local conditions. When he repeated this same practice later in the *Virginia Gazette*, he gave the following apology:

> When I first publish'd these Papers, I propos'd to entertain my Customers, now and then occasionally, or when there was a Scarcity of News, with Pieces Instructive or Diverting; in which I flatter'd myself with the Assistance of the Gentlemen of this Country, many of whom want neither Learning, or fine natural Parts, to qualify them for the Task: But I cannot help taking Notice, that either thro' their too great Modesty, or want of Application in the Service of the Pub-

[16] The first issue of the *Virginia Gazette* is no longer extant, but the text of Parks's address was printed in the *Virginia Historical Register* 6 (1853): 20–22.

[17] See the list of periodical essay series in Ernest Claude Coleman, "The Influence of the Addisonian Essay in America before 1810" (Ph.D. diss., University of Illinois, 1936), 402–406.

lic, I find myself greatly disappointed in my Expectations of their
Assistance: And therefore have sometimes been obliged to collect
from Authors, (which perhaps may not be in the Hands of a great
Part of my Readers) such Pieces, as may answer the Ends propos'd.

   The Guardians, Spectators, Tatlers, Magazines, &c. are inexhaustible Treasures, out of which may be extracted everything that is
necessary for the Support of Virtue, the Suppression of Vice, the
Promotion of Learning, Wit, Ingenuity, &c. And when I make Choice
of any of these for my Papers, (which I will adapt, according to the
best of my Judgment, to the several Circumstances of Time, Place,
and Occasion) I may boldly venture them to the Perusal of my most
snarling Critic, upon the Performance; however my Judgment in
The Choice may be approv'd of.[18]

   True to his own advice, Parks borrowed from English authors for
his "Plain-Dealer" essays. He prefaced his first number (written in
the guise of a letter to the editor) with a quotation from Pliny and
said that the editor could not fill the paper with "what is even in the
vulgar Sense called News," but he could "by making Collections from
good Authors" help to "diffuse a Spirit of good Sense, among your
Readers, and inspire them with a Love for sound and close Reasoning,
from such Principles only, as are evidently true; the want of Regard
to which, has been the Foundation of all the errors and Mischiefs
relative to human life." The writer stresses the benefits of reading and
says that the editor has a duty to the readers "to copy from such
Writers as have expressed their Thoughts in the clearest and plainest
Manner, that Persons who have not been trained up to use the barbarous Terms and abstruse Notions of the Schools, may learn to
philosophize with a moderate Application of Mind: And herein he
should act without regarding what is fashionable, or unfashionable;
or what Customs, or Opinions, are generally prevalent in the World,
or espoused by any Party in particular."

   Parks early sounds the rationalistic note that characterizes the
"Plain-Dealer" series, saying that thinking "freely upon all Occasions
. . . ought to be encouraged as the main Support of Virtue, and the
best Security of the Liberty and Property of a People." He hopes
that his readers, after exposure to various viewpoints, will be "dis-
posed to lay aside, one after another, the more gross Prejudices in
Life, whether they be imbibed or constitutional, for the Sake of Virtue and Truth, in which alone the Mind of a rational Creature can
acquiesce." Finally, the "Plain-Dealer" says that he has here practiced

[18] *Virginia Gazette*, Aug. 10, 1739.

"what I advised you to do, and collected a great Part of these Thoughts." If the essays meets with approval, he will supply the paper "with Materials for at least one Month."[19]

In "Plain-Dealer" number two, Parks again says that he is going to borrow writings from various authors. If he doesn't name the authors, the reason is not to rob them of their reputations "but to give my critical Readers an Occasion to exert their Judgment upon Stile." The essay concerns the plight of the author "in a Country where Gentlemen, with little Judgment, are so facetious and satyrical as in this: Such a one raises an Alarm among his Fellow-Subjects, and by pretending to distinguish himself from the Herd, he becomes a Mark of public Censure, and sometimes a standing Object of Raillery and Ridicule." Parks (or the writer he's quoting) defends the role of the author, argues that authors accomplish much good in the world, and points out that writers have more enduring fame than politicians.[20]

One scholar has commented on the essay series: "Perhaps more astonishing than any other echo from England is the deistic tendency of four numbers of 'The Plain Dealer.'"[21] Another thinks that the essays were not deistic.[22] The latter argues that there was no articulate deism in the America of 1728, an argument that rests ultimately upon the absurd notion that there was a "cultural lag" in America—that, somehow, when William Parks came over from England in the winter of 1725/6, he dropped approximately the last fifty years of his intellectual heritage.

Ignoring Franklin's testimony in the *Autobiography* that he was an outspoken deist in Boston before he came to Philadelphia in 1723, one need only examine the productions of the Philadelphia writers in the 1720s to see (as the bishop of London later testified)[23] that there was outspoken deism in America. The most glaring example is proba-

[19] The *Maryland Gazette* for the first several numbers of the "Plain Dealer" series is not extant, but the series was reprinted by Franklin in the *Pennsylvania Gazette*. *Pennsylvania Gazette*, Apr. 19, 1730.

[20] *Pennsylvania Gazette*, Apr. 16, 1730.

[21] Elizabeth Cristine Cook, *Literary Influences in Colonial Newspapers, 1704–1750* (New York, 1912), 159.

[22] Nicholas Joost, "'Plain-Dealer' and *Free-Thinker*: A Revaluation," *American Literature* 23 (1951):37. Joost is quarreling with Alfred Owen Aldridge, author of "Benjamin Franklin and the *Maryland Gazette*," *Maryland Historical Magazine* 44 (1949):177–89.

[23] Thomas Sherlock, *A Letter From the Lord Bishop of London, to the Clergy and People of London and Westminster, On Occasion of the Late Earthquake* (London, 1750), 7–8.

bly the deist pamphlet published in 1728, *A Few Words in Favor of Free Thinking* (Philadelphia, 1728); this author inserted an advertisement in the April 4, 1728, issue of the *American Weekly Mercury*, which satirically assures the public that his opponent, author of *A Looking-Glass, for the Modern Deist* (Philadelphia, 1728), was "an honest religious man." For examples of clearly deistic essays in the colonial newspapers, there is "Philalethes' " letter in the December 9, 1725, *American Weekly Mercury*, and the ghost story in the April 23, 1730, *Pennsylvania Gazette*. Since this latter story follows Franklin's reprinting of Parks's first two "Plain-Dealer" series, it may have been inspired by them. At any rate, the point is that outspoken deism existed in America before Parks printed his "Plain-Dealer" series. The entire series has a rationalistic, and probably a deistic, point of view.

We cannot now positively know whether or not Parks was a deist. The "Plain-Dealer" series and the reprinting of Masonic news (including one of the earliest theatrical notices in an American paper)[24] suggest that he was. But he was nominally an Anglican, and in Williamsburg was elected a vestryman of Bruton Church.[25] In addition to the "Plain-Dealer" series and to the contributions by Cook and Lewis in the *Maryland Gazette*, Parks printed essays and poems from English and American papers and published the minor writers of Maryland. One of his most interesting borrowings, on March 11, 1728/9, was from Thomas Sheridan's and Jonathan Swift's Dublin newspaper *The Intelligencer*. Parks borrowed a story and an accompanying mock-heroic and scatological poem, "The Tale of the T[ur]d." This is the earliest thoroughgoing scatological poem, to my knowledge, in an American newspaper.

A good local poem appeared in the *Maryland Gazette* for March 17, 1729/30. "Verses on St. Patrick's Day: Sacred to Mirth and Good-Nature" is dated "March 16, 1729/30" and signed with the pseudonym "Somerset English."[26] In its concern with economic problems, the poem suggests Lewis's pen, but it lacks the local references and feeling for nature which usually characterize his work. The poem pleads for

---

[24] *Maryland Gazette*, May 26, 1730.
[25] William Arthur Rutherfoord Goodwin, *Historical Sketch of Bruton Church* (Petersburg, Va., 1903), 120.
[26] When Franklin reprinted this in the *Pennsylvania Gazette*, Mar. 25, 1731, he changed the pseudonym to "Philanthropos." Of course, it may be that the author sent it to Franklin a year later with a different signature.

equality among men and nations, and uses the feeling against the enclosure movement to attack patriotism and prejudice:

> Then while we friendly take a cheerful Bowl,
> Let's wish that every Man with honest Soul,
> May gen'rously throw down with noble Scorn,
> Those dire Enclosures shagg'd with prickly Thorn,
> Which some (who ought to meet with much Dispraise)
> Ignobly bent have taken Pains to raise,
> Men born for Social Life to separate,
> And plant twixt Nations everlasting Hate.
> (ll. 83–90)

Literature from other colonies was also published in the *Maryland Gazette*. A poem (probably reprinted from Samuel Keimer's *Barbados Gazette*) appeared in the issue for March 31, 1730, entitled "The Aged Creole; Or, the Way to Long Life in Jamaica." An interesting Virginia poem dealing with early frontier exploration was once featured. When an English versification by the Reverend George Seagood (d. 1724) of the Reverend Arthur Blackamore's Latin poem "Expeditio Ultramontana" appeared in the paper for June 24, 1729, "Ecclesiasticus" explained in a preface that William and Mary College had to pay two original Latin poems every November 5 to the governor of Virginia as quit-rent for its land. "Ecclesiasticus" said that in 1716, "The *November* after Col. *Spotswood*, and his Train, return'd from their Progress amongst the Mountains . . . Mr. *Blackamore*, the Humanity Professor, composed an excellent Poem on this *Mountain Expedition*; which the late Rev. Mr. *George Seagood* turn'd into *English*." "Ecclesiasticus" hoped that the poem would "contribute to the Satisfaction of your Correspondents, that are poetically inclined." In decasyllabic couplets, the poem praises the courage and determination of Spotswood, describes a few scenes from the expedition, and stresses the bounty of the wilderness:

> Yet arn't these Woods without their proper Grace;
> The verdant Earth here shews a cheerful Face.
> This fruitful Soil with richest Grass is crown'd,
> And various Flow'rs adorn the gawdy Ground:
> (Neglecting Order) Nature plants this Land,
> And strews her Riches with a lavish Hand;
> With Fruit her Bounty clothes each well-deck'd Bush,
> The luscious Cherries on the Branches blush.
> Here silken Mulb'ries load the bending Boughs,
> And there the cluster'd Grape luxuriant grows.

119

Here Currants, Peaches, Strawb'ries, Nature tends;
And other Dainties to the Hero lends.

(ll. 120–31) [27]

The chief political writer for Parks's *Maryland Gazette* was "P. P.," whose essays appeared from March 4, 1728/9, until at least May 27, 1729. The essays take a liberal position, "P. P." praising the Maryland planters for their "Sentiments in terms becoming Freemen, wearied with continued Oppression, and groaning under the consequences of repeated Mismanagement (to use no worse a Term)." [28] The "P. P." series (which Ebenezer Cook referred to in *Sotweed Redivivus*) [29] was part of the battle the Maryland planters were waging against the British merchants. The planters were not making money on their tobacco crops and thought that the middlemen, the London merchants, were depriving them of a fair price. [30] Henry Darnall was the major spokesman for the Maryland tobacco planters. He proposed that the Maryland planters send him to London as their representative. There, he would regulate the tobacco trade. Following up his 54-page pamphlet, *A Just and Impartial Account*, which Parks printed in January, 1728/9, Darnall issued "A Letter to the Inhabitants of Maryland" in the February 4 *Maryland Gazette*. Siding with Darnall were "P. P.," Nicholas Ridgely, James Donaldson, and a host of others. [31] Against them were the London merchants, Walter Hoxton (the map-maker), and a few unidentified writers. [32]

Another major political battle which found its way into a num-

[27] Earl G. Swem has edited *Mr. Blackamore's Expeditio Ultramontana* (Richmond, 1960). The payment of the Latin verses evidently continued throughout the colonial period. See *Virginia Gazette*, Nov. 12, 1736. Blackamore's Latin poem is no longer extant, but a few lines of another translation from it by Godfrey Pole were published in the *Southern Literary Messenger* 2 (1836):258. The Reverend Arthur Blackamore was in Virginia from 1707 to 1717, when he was finally discharged for drunkenness. He is better known as the author of two early "novels." See Richard Beale Davis, "Arthur Blackamore. The Virginia Colony and the Early English Novel," *Virginia Magazine of History and Biography* 75 (1967):22–34.

[28] *Maryland Gazette*, May 27, 1729.

[29] Ebenezer Cook, *Sotweed Redivivus: Or the Planters Looking-Glass* . . . (Annapolis, 1730), 20.

[30] Cf. the letter of Benedict Leonard Calvert to the Lord Proprietary, Oct. 26, 1729, *Archives of Maryland* 25:602–603.

[31] Nearly all the extant issues of the *Maryland Gazette* touch on this quarrel, but see especially the numbers for Mar. 18, 25, and Apr. 8, 1729.

[32] Ibid., Apr. 1 and 15, 1729. Walter Hoxton is known for his map, *To the Merchants of London Trading to Virginia and Maryland, this Mapp of the Bay of Chesepeack, with the Rivers Potomack, Potapsco, North East, and Part of Chester* (London, 1735).

ber of pamphlets and into Parks's *Maryland Gazette* and the (Philadelphia) *American Weekly Mercury* was fought by Daniel Dulany and the Reverend Jacob Henderson. Henderson, as commissary of Maryland, represented the Maryland ministers. When the Assembly lowered the ministers' salary, Henderson took the case to England, where he petitioned the king. Unsuccessful at court, Henderson returned to Maryland, where he continued to carry on the ministers' quarrel with the Assembly.[33] "Athanasius Wildfire" (who was probably Daniel Dulany) had an anti-clerical sermon, *The Traditions of the Clergy Destructive of Religion*, printed in Philadelphia in March, 1731/2, with a dedication to Henderson.[34] Henderson replied to this assault with a series of letters in the the *American Weekly Mercury* under the pseudonym "Th' Extinguisher."[35] Parks published Dulany's *A Letter from Daniel Dulany, esq.; to the Reverend Mr. Jacob Henderson*, and Henderson replied with *The Rev. Mr. Jacob Henderson's Fifth Letter to Daniel Dulany, Esq.; in Relation to the Case and Petition of the Clergy of Maryland.*[36]

Parks's most significant political publication was Daniel Dulany's *The Right of the Inhabitants of Maryland, to the Benefit of English Laws* (Annapolis, 1728). In vetoing an act of assembly, Lord Baltimore had directly denied that English statutes were automatically in force in Maryland. The Lower House, in a meeting on October 21, 1723, passed an address to the proprietor, suggesting that he was ill-advised and that English laws applied to Maryland. Daniel Dulany had been one of the three members of the House committee that drafted the address, and he was evidently unsatisfied with Lord Baltimore's final concession, that those "Laws, Rules, Customs and Usages, as are undoubted certain constantly advered to and practiced among

---

[33] *The Case of the Clergy of Maryland* (London, 1729). The date and place of publication are revealed by Daniel Dulany's *A Letter from Daniel Dulany, Esq.; to the Reverend Mr. Jacob Henderson . . . To which is prefix'd: The case and petition of the clergy of Maryland, as published in London by Mr. Henderson, 1729* (Annapolis, 1732). See *John Carter Brown Library Annual Report, 1941–1942* (Providence, 1942), 40–41.

[34] William Bowman's sermon *The Tradition of the Clergy . . .* served as ammunition in several quarrels of the time. For the earlier South Carolina arguments, see Hennig Cohen, *The South Carolina Gazette, 1732–1775* (Columbia, 1953), 161.

[35] *American Weekly Mercury*, Apr. 12 and 20, 1732.

[36] The *Archives of Maryland* 38:453–60, contains more source material for this study. See also Wroth, *History of Printing in Colonial Maryland*, no. 61. Further sources are in William Wilson Manross, ed., *The Fulham Papers in the Lambeth Palace Library* (Oxford, 1965), 41–47 (3:121–32, 143–47, 195, 233–35).

you" were in force. Therefore Dulany prepared his theoretical argument on the English statutes. Prefiguring the claims of the American revolutionists to "natural, inalienable rights" and citing Cato, Sir Edward Coke, John Locke, Samuel Pufendorf, and Hugo Grotius, Dulany argues that because the colonists were English citizens, they were entitled to all the benefits of English laws.[37]

Early in 1728, Parks arranged to print for the colony of Virginia. At first he evidently intended to do the Virginia printing at his Annapolis shop; as late as January 29, 1728/9, when he bought Lot N in Annapolis for £35, Parks probably meant to remain in the Maryland capital. But sometime during 1729, he decided that Virginia offered a better future than Maryland. Edmund Hall, his future partner, must already have been working for him: on October 27, 1729, Parks sold Lot T in Annapolis for £150 sterling,[38] and shortly thereafter left for England to buy a new press for his projected Williamsburg office. When he returned to the province in June, 1730, he thanked the subscribers to the *Maryland Gazette* for contributing to his paper while he had been in England.[39] On July 20, 1730, the Reverend James Blair of Williamsburg wrote the bishop of London, "We have a Printer shortly expected to settle in this towne." Parks moved to Williamsburg and set up his press in late July or early August: for on September 14, Governor William Gooch of Virginia sent the Board of Trade "a printed Copy of the Laws, which will . . . serve as a Specimen of the Product of our Press, where the whole Body of the Laws of the Colony is to be Printed for the Publick Service."[40]

In Virginia as in Maryland, Parks stimulated belletristic productions. Parks's proposal for printing two volumes entitled "The Virginia Miscelleny, Consisting of New Poems, Essays and Transla-

---

[37] See *Archives of Maryland* 34:692–98 and 35:496 and 537. There is a discussion of the background and significance of Dulany's pamphlet in Aubrey C. Land, *The Dulanys of Maryland* (Baltimore, 1955), pp. 76–85; and a fuller account may be found in St. George Leakin Sioussat, *The English Statutes in Maryland* (Baltimore, 1903), where Dulany's pamphlet is reprinted as an appendix.

[38] Land Records, Anne Arundel County, Liber B, folio 172, Maryland Hall of Records, and ibid., Liber T 11, folio 69.

[39] *Maryland Gazette*, June 9, 1730.

[40] Library of Congress, MSS Division, British transcripts, Fulham Palace, Virginia Box I, doc. 131 (Manross, 182 [xii, 152–53]); and Wroth, *William Parks, Printer and Journalist*, 67. Cf. Samford and Hemphill, 38n.

tions ... by several Gentlemen of this Country" appeared in the Philadelphia *American Weekly Mercury*, July 15, 1731, where Parks mentioned that he was living "at his House, near the Capital, in Williamsburg." As there are no other references to the "Virginia Miscelleny," it evidently was never printed. Since Parks published Ebenezer Cook's *Maryland Muse* in 1731, perhaps the projected Virginia venture was meant to be a rival work. The *Maryland Muse* contains a satiric treatment of a Virginia story, *The History of Colonel Nathaniel Bacon's Rebellion in Virginia, Done into Hudibrastic Verse, from an old MS.* As Lawrence C. Wroth has shown, the "old MS" was the Burwell Papers, sent to Ebenezer Cook by the Reverend Hugh Jones. Parks's printing inspired at least two poems: John Markland's *Typographia* (Williamsburg, 1730),[41] and Joseph Dumbleton's "The Paper-Mill, inscribed to Mr. Parks."[42]

Parks's letter, dated from Williamsburg, July 20, 1732, to Dr. Charles Carroll, an influential member of the Maryland legislature, reveals how the printer continued his Maryland operations after moving to Virginia. The printer wrote that the Virginia Assembly had adjourned on July the first, and that he would have come to Annapolis before the opening of the Maryland Assembly: "but that Mr. John Randolph, from whom, as clerk of the Assembly, I have a copy of the new Laws to print, is going to England upon a Great Embassy; and I am oblig'd to finish them before he goes, that he may sign these for the County-Courts." If Parks did not do this, he would "forfeit the Salary of 120 £ per Annum, which the Governor and Assembly have generously been pleas'd to settle on me and as there is seldom an Assembly oftener than once in 3 years, and consequently earn my salary easy, I shou'd have been thought very negligent of my Duty, if I had not Staid to finish these." Parks adds that he is "making all the Haste" he can, and will be through with the Virginia printing "next Week, Time enough to come to Annapolis before the Assembly breaks up." Since Dr. Carroll is "well acquainted with all the Gentlemen of the Assembly," Parks asks Carroll "to excuse me to them;

[41] On Markland, an English poet of some note before he emigrated to Virginia, see J. A. Leo Lemay, *A Poem by John Markland of Virginia* (Williamsburg, 1965).
[42] Printed in the *Virginia Gazette* for July 26, 1744, this poem is extant only because it was reprinted in the *American Magazine* for Aug. 1744, p. 523. For an account of Dumbleton's poetry, see Hennig Cohen, *South Carolina Gazette*, 199 and note, and 203–204, 211–13.

which will I hope be the easier granted, because I have a Partner there who is very capable of performing the Business."[43]

Parks continued to operate this Annapolis shop until sometime in the fall of 1737, but the only extant Maryland publications after 1734 are all of an official nature. He began printing the *Virginia Gazette* in 1736, and by then, obviously, his time and interests were elsewhere than Annapolis. Although Parks's Virginia career lies outside the scope of this work, it is interesting to note that by February 2, 1747/8, Parks's family and establishment in Williamsburg included at least fourteen people. An account of a smallpox epidemic recorded that thirteen of Parks's people had recovered, but that his storekeeper had died. Obviously an esteemed citizen, William Parks was elected an alderman of Williamsburg on February 6, 1738/9, and mayor of the capital of Virginia on November 10, 1739, and again on November 30, 1747.[44]

An incident that illustrates the difficult political position of the colonial printer occurred the year before Parks died. The Virginia House of Burgesses claimed the right to search the Journal of the Council; the Council disagreed, saying that in the past the Council had supplied the House with the records of their Journal when asked to do so—but that it was "a notorious Infringement of their indubitable Rights" to think that the House had a *right* to the examination.[45] On March 27, 1749, the Council sent their argument to Parks to publish in the next issue of the *Virginia Gazette*. When the printer returned from a two-day journey to York, Virginia, on March 30, he found that the Council had delivered the letter to William Hunter, who was setting up the paper in print. Since Parks realized that printing the piece would bring the House down on his neck, he delayed doing so until the Council found fault with him, saying that it was his duty as public printer to print whatever the Council sent him. About May 8, 1749, Parks wrote the Council a letter of apology[46]

---

43 Baltimore Iron Company Records, 1: 25. MSS, Maryland Historical Society.
44 "A True State of the Smallpox in Williamsburg, February 22, 1748," *Virginia Magazine of History and Biography* 63 (1955):269–74, esp. 273; see also Leola O. Walker, "Officials in the City Government of Colonial Williamsburg," ibid., 75 (1967):35–51, esp. 47.
45 Herbert Read McIlwaine, *Journals of the House of Burgesses of Virginia, 1742–1749* (Richmond, 1912), 403.
46 Printed in William P. Palmer, ed., *Calendar of Virginia State Papers and other Manuscripts, 1652–1781* (Richmond, 1875), 248; and in Herbert Read McIlwaine, *Legislative Journals of the Council of Colonial Virginia* 3 (Richmond, 1919): 1569.

and then printed the Council's attack on the House in the *Virginia Gazette* of May 11, 1749.[47] Charles Carter read the issue aloud in the House of Burgesses on that date, and the House resolved that the *Gazette* contained "a malicious and scandalous Libel," and ordered the sergeant of arms to take Parks immediately into custody and to bring him to the "Bar of the House" to be examined. Parks told the House his story, and after the Council confirmed that Parks had published the account only by their direct order, the House released him.[48]

In the winter of 1749–50, Parks put his Virginia affairs in order in preparation for a trip to England. After embarking for England on March 22, 1749/50, he fell ill. On March 30, he made out his will aboard Captain Watson's ship, the *Nelson*; he died two days later, April 1, 1750. The following obituary, evidently reprinted from the *Virginia Gazette* of May 24, appeared in Jonas Green's *Maryland Gazette*, June 13, 1750:

> Williamsburg, May 24
> Since the last *Gazette*, arrived in *York* River, the *Hatley*, Capt Hill, and the *Nelson*, Capt Watson, both from London; by whom we have the Account of the Death of Mr. William Parks, late Printer of this Paper: He took his Passage in Capt *Watson*, and went on board the 22d of *March*; in good Health; but was soon seized with a Pleurisy, of which he died the 1st of April; and was buried at Gosport. His Character was so generally known and esteem'd, by all who had any Acquaintance with him, that it would be vain to aim at it. He was assiduous in his carrying on Public Business, as Printer to this Colony, and gave general Content; so that his Death may be esteem'd a public as well as a private loss.

By encouraging and printing the literature of Maryland and Virginia from 1726 to his death in 1750, William Parks performed an important service for the culture of early America. In view of the high literary quality of the extant newspapers, broadsides, and pamphlets printed by Parks, every student of American literature must regret that so few of his imprints have survived.

[47] No *Virginia Gazette* for 1749 is extant. Parks printed his paper on Thursday. The House had met on Wednesday, May 10. Had the issue of the *Gazzette* containing the "libel" been published the previous Thursday, surely the House would not have waited a week to defend its honor.

[48] McIlwaine, *Journals of the House of Burgesses of Virginia, 1742–1749*, 401–404. Isaiah Thomas, *History of Printing in America* 2 (Worcester, Mass., 1810):143–45, tells the anecdote of Parks's trial for libel for publishing an item revealing that a Virginia burgess had once been convicted of sheep stealing. Thomas took the story "from the newspapers printed more than forty years ago" (p. 143) and noted that it was "republished not many years ago" (p. 145). I have not thus far turned up the source for this amusing anecdote.

RICHARD LEWIS

POET

Although he was a well-known poet in his day, Richard Lewis (1700?–34) has been almost unknown to American literary history. "To Mr. Samuel Hastings" is an early, interesting poem on an American industry. His most famous poem, "A Journey from Patapsco to Annapolis," is good nature poetry, echoed by Alexander Pope in the *Dunciad*. "Food for Criticks," another nature poem probably by Lewis, portrays the Indian as a noble savage. Although Philip Freneau is still generally regarded as the first poet of American nature, Lewis wrote nature poetry over half a century before Freneau. He also wrote a large number of occasional poems, including an exceptionally fine elegy on Governor Charles Calvert (d. 1734). The variety of topics in his poetry, from economic theory and practice to descriptions of American nature, and from philosophical and religious speculations to sentimental portrayals of farmers, Indians, and animals, suggests something of its interest.

Little is known of Lewis's early life. Benedict Leonard Calvert, governor of Maryland and younger brother of the fifth Baron Baltimore, wrote to the antiquarian Thomas Hearne, on March 18, 1728/9, that Lewis was a schoolmaster in Annapolis, "who formerly belonged to Eaton, a man really of Ingenuity, and to my Judgment well versed in poetry." His poem "A Journey from Patapsco to Annapolis" discloses that he was approximately thirty years old on April 4, 1730. In view of his age and the patriotic feeling for Wales displayed by his poetry, it seems likely, as George Sherburn suggested, that the poet was the Richard Lewis who matriculated as a plebeian in Balliol College, Oxford, on April 3, 1718, at the age of nineteen.[1] If so, his father was Richard Lewis of Llanfair, Montgomeryshire, Wales. Lewis stayed a mere thirteen weeks at Balliol, leaving during the week of June 20 to June 26, 1718. Further inquiry at Oxford and in Wales has proven fruitless.

He probably emigrated to Maryland in 1718: a Richard Lewis married Elizabeth Batee in January 1718/9 at All Hallows Parish, Anne Arundel County, Maryland.[2] As I shall show below, the poet's wife was named Elizabeth. The earliest record definitely locating the poet in Maryland was his report to the Royal Society of London that he had heard, on October 22, 1725, an explosion in the air at Patapsco (i. e., by the Patapsco River, probably in or near the present city of Baltimore).

The earliest extant writing by Richard Lewis is his translation of Edward Holdsworth's Latin poem *Muscipula*, which the Marylander entitled *The Mouse Trap, or the Battle of the Cambrians and Mice ... by R. Lewis* (Annapolis, 1728). This handsomely printed volume with a rubricated title page was the first belletristic book published in the South. The elaborately annotated translation is full of antiquarian lore, perhaps reflecting the interests of Governor Benedict

[1] George Sherburn wrote an excellent note on Lewis in Percy H. Boynton, ed., *American Poetry* (New York, 1918), 600–602. Lawrence C. Wroth added some information to this in a *History of Printing in Colonial Maryland*, 65. Walter B. Norris printed several of Lewis's poems from manuscript in "Some Recently Found Poems on the Calverts," 112–35, but the texts are poor. C. Lennart Carlson, "Richard Lewis and the Reception of his Work in England," *American Literature* 9 (1937–38):301–16, follows Sherburn in tracing the printing history of "A Journey from Patapsco to Annapolis"; but Carlson found no American printings of the poem, and he confused the few biographical facts about Lewis that were supplied him by Joseph Towne Wheeler. Calvert's letter is printed in *Remarks and Collections of Thomas Hearne* (Oxford, 1915), 10:109n. Although all previous scholars have interpreted Calvert's letter to mean that Lewis attended Eton school (and the *Eton College Register, 1698–1762*, on the strength of Calvert's reference, includes Lewis among its alumni), it may simply mean that Lewis is from Eaton, near Chester, in Cheshire County, just across the river Dee from Wales; but I have also failed to turn up any references to him in the Chester area. Joseph Foster, *Alumni Oxonienses: The Members of the University of Oxford 1715–1886*, 4 vols. (London, 1889–98), 3:847. Personal letters from R. U. Sayce, editor of the Montgomeryshire Records, dated May 17, 1965, and from D. S. Porter, dated Oct. 20, 1965, of the Department of Western Manuscripts, Bodleian.

[2] The Assistant Librarian of Balliol College kindly checked the Bursary records for me and furnished the date of Lewis's leaving Balliol, in a personal letter dated June 30, 1967. Parish Register, 1700–1724, All Hallows Parish, Anne Arundel County, p. 16, Maryland Hall of Records, Annapolis.

Leonard Calvert, Lewis's patron (who subscribed for ten copies). Lewis injects a patriotic Welsh note when he writes (p. 43) that he has "translated this Account of the *Muscipula*, for the Satisfaction of the *Curious*; and to assure the *Censorious*, on the Word of my Author [Holdsworth], That what they mistake for *Satyr*; was intended for a *Panegyric*, on the Antiquity of the Cambrians, and their Skill in Mechanic Arts."[3]

In a dedicatory poem to Benedict Leonard Calvert, Lewis asks that the governor permit as a visit from the Muse "This FIRST ESSAY of *Latin Poetry*, in *English Dress*, / which *MARYLAND* hath publish'd from the Press." After deprecating his, or any other attempt to translate poetry, he compares the wild Maryland wilderness with Italy's cultivated countryside. He refers to Calvert's conversations on the beauty of Italy and echoes the themes and imagery of Addison's popular poem "A Letter from Italy."

> *There* PAINTURE breathes, *There* STATUARY lives,
> And MUSIC most delightful Rapture gives:
> *There*, pompous Piles of *Building* pierce the Skies,
> And endless Scenes of *Pleasure* court the Eyes.
> While *Here*, rough Woods embrown the Hills and Plains,
> Mean are the *Buildings*, artless are the *Swains*:
> 'To raise the Genius,' WE no Time can spare,
> A *bare Subsistence* claims our utmost Care.
>
> (ll. 31–38)

The allusion to Addison is most obvious in line 33; Addison's line 77 reads, "Here pillars rough with sculpture pierce the skies." The antithesis between Maryland and Italy, the allusion to Addison, and the bitter last couplet (where the word *bare* gains emphasis by its effective internal rhyme) distinguish this poem. Henry James expressed a similar feeling when he wrote, "History, as yet, has left in the United States but so thin and impalpable a deposit that we very soon touch the hard substratum of nature; and nature herself, in the western world, has the peculiarity of seeming rather crude and immature."[4] But, as we shall see, Lewis felt an intense appreciation of American nature, and, indeed, thought its wonders excelled anything offered by Europe. In "A *bare Subsistence* claims our utmost Care,"

---

[3] *Philosophical Transactions of the Royal Society of London* 38 (1733–34): 119–20. Lewis's *Muscipula* was reprinted (although not entirely accurately) in Bernard C. Steiner, ed., *Early Maryland Poetry*. My quotations are from the original.

[4] Henry James, *Hawthorne* (London, 1879), 12.

Lewis anticipates the apology that Americans will make for the next
two centuries for the supposed lack of a vibrant cultural life in
America. According to this often-repeated apology, Americans have
been so busy with the basic necessities of life that they did not have
the time to pursue the arts and sciences.

In the conclusion, Lewis refers to the word "Crime" in his preceding stanza, asks the governor to forgive him the "crime" of these
verses from "an unknown Muse," and (as he later did in his "Verses
... to Benedict Leonard Calvert," *Carmen Seculare*, and "Elegy on
... Charles Calvert") gracefully alludes to Benedict Leonard Calvert's
power to forgive condemned criminals:

> YET—hear me!—While I beg you to excuse,
> This bold Intrusion of an unknown Muse;
> And if her Faults too manifest appear,
> And her rude Numbers should offend your Ear,
> Then, if you please with your forgiving Breath
> Which can reprieve the Wretch condemn'd, from Death,
> To speak a Pardon for her Errors past,
> This First Poetic Crime, shall prove her Last.
>
> (ll. 82–89)

The dedicatory poem demonstrates a competent mastery of the
heroic couplet and is well constructed. It begins and ends with an
apostrophe to Calvert. Within this framework, Lewis considers the
difficulties of his poetic task, assesses the cultural and economic
situation of Maryland, praises the attempts of Governor Calvert to
remedy the situation, and apologizes for his abilities. Even in this
early poem, he demonstrates that he is not afraid to vary his prosody:
there are three triplets (ll. 19–21, 26–28, 79–81) and one off-rhyme
(ll. 57–58); there are numerous metrical variations and one alexandrine
(l. 78). The diction in this dedicatory poem, suitable to its purpose
and genre, is formal.

The "Preface" to the *Muscipula* confesses that Lewis had promised
the book to the subscribers at an earlier date, but he hopes that his
patrons will excuse the delay when they see that he has completely
revised the circulated copy and that the Latin is printed as well as the
translation. He reminds the reader that he "is engaged in teaching
Language," a "very fatiguing Employment." In discussing the genre
of the *Muscipula*, the Maryland schoolmaster shows that he is well-
versed in contemporary literary theory:

> THIS Poem, is of the *Mock Heroic*, or *Burlesque* Kind, of which
> there are *two* Sorts. *One*, describes a *ludicrous Action*, in *Heroic*

Verse; such is The *Rape of the Lock*: The *Other* under *low Characters*, and in *odd*, *uncommon* Numbers, debases some great Event; as *Butler* has done, in his celebrated *Hudibras*; which would have been still more *truly comical* in the opinion of an *excellent Judge*, if it had been written in the *Heroic Measure*.

The "excellent Judge" is Addison, whose definition (*Spectator*, no. 249, December 15, 1711) Lewis adopts, broadens, and brings up-to-date.

After referring to Sir John Denham, and Lord Roscommon on the problems of translation, Lewis echoes Dryden's positions in the "Preface to the Translation of Ovid's Epistles." He writes:

> THAT I might do my Author all the Justice in my Power, I have avoided the *Libertinism* of a *Paraphrast*, on one Hand, and the *Idolatry* of a *mere literal Translator*, on the other. The *Sentiments* of an *Original*, ought to be preserved, with all *possible Exactness*, but they are too frequently disregarded in a Paraphrase Translation. And nothing can be more ridiculous, and unentertaining, than a *too faithful* Attachment to the *Phrase* of a Writer; and a *tyrannic Endeavor*, to confine a *Latin Poet*, to express his Thoughts, in *English*, by the *same* Number of *Lines*, and *Words*, which he thought *sufficient* for *that* Purpose, in the *Roman Language*.

This translation of the *Muscipula* compares well with the other translations of Holdsworth's popular poem.[5] Lewis's appreciation of Holdsworth's intent, as well as the Marylander's knowledge of classical literature, is demonstrated by his note (*i*):

> Pallas, was the Heathen Goddess of Arts and Sciences,—The Original, exactly translated, would be—*At length he builds* a Mouse-Trap, by the Divine Art of *Pallas*: But as the Author has made Use of *Virgil's* Words, wherein he mentions the building of the Horse, which proved so fatal to the *Trojans*; the Translator presumed that it would appear more ludicrous to make the Simile, which is not injurious to the *Author's* Sense, who without doubt, had *that* famous *Machine* in View, when he applied *Virgil's* Expressions on that Subject, to his *Mouse-Trap*.

Thus he justifies his lines "*At length he builds a* Mouse-Trap; *which was made, / Like the fame'd* Trojan horse *by Pallas' Aid*" (ll. 172–73). The annotated translation shows that the Maryland poet had access to a good library of standard reference works on history, antiquity,

---

[5] Richmond Pugh Bond, *English Burlesque Poetry 1700–1750* (Cambridge, Mass., 1932), 219–21, surveys the influence of Holdsworth's poem to the mid-eighteenth century. See also J. H. T. (John Hammond Trumbull) in the *Magazine of American History* 3 (1879):585.

classical poetry, and contemporary belles-lettres, including works by Sir John Denham, Dryden, Addison, James Durham, Thomas Parnell, and Pope.

On July 3, 1729, an anonymous poem appeared in the *American Weekly Mercury*. Since the poem is by someone who lived at a distance from Philadelphia (but close enough to follow the Philadelphia newspapers with interest), since the poem anticipates themes that Lewis used elsewhere in his poetry, and since the poetry is quite good, it seems possible that Richard Lewis was the author. Lewis lived part of the time in the area which is now the city of Baltimore, and he undoubtedly read the Philadelphia papers. The untitled poem is prefaced by the statement, "We have receiv'd the following Lines out of the Country from an unknown Hand, Occasioned by some of our late Publications." The poem opens with a traditional apology: "LET *Philadelphia's* generous Sons excuse, / Th'Officious greeting of a distant Muse." The dominant motif of the poem is the westward migration of the arts—the *translatio studii* idea which perhaps has its best-known expression in Bishop Berkeley's "Verses on the Prospect of Planting Arts and Sciences in America." This was a commonplace in seventeenth- and eighteenth-century thought and has its roots in ancient classical writings. Lewis expresses the motif early in the poem and echoes it again in lines 20–21 and in the ending, "Themis at length she finds, has ventured o'er, / And Arts can flourish on Columbus Shore" (ll. 7–8). The poet claims that Philadelphia is the greatest glory of America:

> But chiefly You the coming Goddess own,
> 'Tis *Philadelphia* most erects her Throne;
> With genuine Wit here every Bosom glows,
> And different thoughts express in polish'd Prose:
> Some pass their Judgment on the Paper Coin,
> And some again in pointed Satyr shine,
> Some *pro* and *Con*, Debate a Party Cause,
> And each has Friends to give the wish'd Applause....
> (ll. 9–16)

These lines allude to Franklin and Breintnall's "Busy-Body" essay series in the *American Weekly Mercury* and especially to Franklin's pamphlet *The Nature and Necessity of a Paper Currency* (Philadelphia, 1729).

Sounding the patriotic note that will recur in Lewis's later poetry, the schoolmaster writes that Pennsylvania (and America) is better off than Europe because the colonies live in peace: "Go on brave Souls, out-rival Ancient Greece / Or Rome, or Britain's Self in Arts of Peace" (ll. 21–22). As in his poem prefatory to *The Mouse Trap*, he alludes to Addison's "Letter from Italy," saying that "The Godess flies th'unhospitable Ground" (l. 31) where war rages. Because of war, Themis has flown to America where she will teach "the sacred Arts to Rural Swains" (l. 33). The poem concludes with a prophecy of America's future greatness:

> Forgive me Sirs, forgive the tedious Strain,
> Still will I sing, nor shall my Song be vain,
> For now methinks I grow indeed possess'd,
> The *Delphick* Godhead Struggles in my Breast,
> And thus by me his Oracle declares;
> E'er Time has Measured out an hundred Years
> Westward from *Britain*, shall an *Athens* rise,
> Which soon shall bear away the learned Prize;
> Hence Europe's Sons assistance shall implore,
> And learn from her, as she from them before.
>
> (ll. 34–43)

It has generally been forgotten that poems on the future glory of America by Nathaniel Evans, Thomas Godfrey, Philip Freneau, and the Connecticut Wits in the 1760s–1780s were manifestations of an ancient theme in Western literature, the westward migration of the arts, and that this theme which had its most famous seventeenth-century expression in George Herbert's couplet "Religion stands on tiptoe in our land / Ready to pass to the American Strand" was known and echoed by seventeenth-century Americans, by Cotton Mather in the opening of the *Magnalia Christi Americana*, and by the poets of America throughout the entire eighteenth century. This occasional poem praising Franklin and Philadelphia is an excellent example of the "future glory of America" genre. The poem was immediately imitated in Philadelphia, for George Webbe's poem in Titan Leeds's almanac for 1730 contains the same theme and echoes phrases from this poem. Jacob Taylor's poem prefaced to Webbe's *Bachelor's Hall* (Philadelphia, 1732) also uses the "future glory of America" theme and echoes the poem.[6]

---

[6] A note in the *American Weekly Mercury* of the previous week says that the poem had arrived too late for inclusion in that issue of the *Mercury* but would be printed the following week. For the vogue of George Herbert's couplet, see Abram E. Cutter, "Poetical Prognostics," *New England Historical and Genealogical Register* 27 (1873):347–51. Scholars have often pointed out that the open-

An occasional poem of 219 lines, "*To Mr.* Samuel Hastings (*Ship-wright* of Philadelphia) *on his launching the* Maryland-Merchant, *a large Ship built by him at* Annapolis," appeared in the *Maryland Gazette*, December 30, 1729, and was immediately reprinted in the *Pennsylvania Gazette*, January 13, and in the Philadelphia *American Weekly Mercury*, January 14, 1729/30.[7] Although the poem is anonymous, the many local references—especially the poet's watching the construction of the ship on the banks of the Severn River (by Annapolis)—testify that the author was a Maryland poet. He was also a nature poet: the first descriptive catalogue of American rivers is found in this poem (ll. 138–96). The author combines classical history and mythology with biblical and Christian history. One might suggest that this comparative technique has only recently received its logical development in the poetry of T. S. Eliot. Previous American writers seem to be thoroughly religious and suggest parallels which are typological and basically Christian. Lewis is comparative and deistic: he interchangeably uses history as mythology, and mythology as history. The discussion of longitude (ll. 175–84) reveals a knowledge of comtemporary science. Finally, the latter part of the poem, (ll. 185–217) is devoted to local economic problems and displays the same attitudes that Lewis expressed in his dedicatory poem (ll. 39–52) to *The Mouse Trap*. As we shall see, all of these topics are characteristic of Lewis's poetry. And probably no other Maryland poet—including the only other one of notable ability, Ebenezer Cook—was capable of the excellent structure and versification of this poem. Richard Lewis wrote it.

---

ing line of the *Magnalia* ("I write the *wonders* of the *Christian religion*, flying from the depravations of *Europe*, the *American Strand*") echoes Virgil (e.g., Peter Gay, *A Loss of Mastery* [Berkeley, 1966], 60); but no one has previously noted the Herbert allusion. Mather uses the *translatio studii* idea elsewhere, notably in his *Theopolis Americana* (Boston, 1710). George Webbe, whom Franklin mentions in the *Autobiography*, wrote the excellent poem in Leeds's almanac for 1730. Webbe's authorship is proven by a reference in the *Gentleman's Magazine* 22 (Aug., 1753):372, and by the attribution in the Du Simitiere Papers, formerly in the Library Company of Philadelphia, now deposited in the Historical Society of Pennsylvania. There is no thorough examination of this important idea as it is found in early American literature, but its vogue in the Federalist period is clearly established by Lewis P. Simpson, "The *Anthology* as a 'Progress Piece,' " *The Federalist Literary Mind* (Baton Rouge, 1962), 31–41.

[7] The *Maryland Gazette* for Dec. 30, 1729, is not extant, but the *Pennsylvania Gazette*, reprinting the poem, notes "From the *Maryland Gazette*, December 30." Alfred Owen Aldridge in "Benjamin Franklin and the *Maryland Gazette*," 177–89, first suggested, 186–89, that Lewis wrote "To Mr. Samuel Hastings."

Lewis opens "To Mr. Samuel Hastings" with a traditional apology (similar to that in the previous poem) for his poetry, and then addresses Hastings:

> Thou wond'rous Architect! whose Palaces
> Bear their Inhabitants o'er deepest Seas,
> Where, while a longsome Voyage they pursue,
> Surprising Scenes of Wonder greet their View:
> Attend! while I the slow Degrees disclose,
> By which the Ship-wright to thy Skill arose.
>
> (ll. 9–14)

The poet begins a chronological progress-piece on the history of shipbuilding with an account of "Adam's Offspring" crossing the Euphrates River on floats. He claims that floats were improved by tying several logs together to make rafts, but that the rafts split up when they struck rocks. Shortly the next step was taken: huge trees were hollowed out to make "canoos" (ll. 15–32). It is noteworthy that Lewis uses the anthropologists' comparative method to sketch the history of ship-development—canoes were unknown by Western men until found in use by American Indians. The art of shipbuilding remained at the canoe stage for "ages," until God, rewarding Noah for his piety, taught him how to build the Ark:

> Within its Womb, the universal Race
> Of Insects, Beasts, Birds, Men obtain a Place,
> Who in due Time should meet a second Birth,
> And with their Offspring fill the future Earth:
> The Rest were by the Deluge swept away.
> While Angels o'er thy Ark their Wings display,
> Their guiding Hands that Ship with Pleasure steer,
> Which safely does its precious Cargo bear
> O'er highest Hills in wild Disorder hurl'd
> On Seas which overwhelm'd the shatter'd World.
>
> (ll. 43–52)

After the Ark lands on Mt. Ararat, Lewis turns from biblical references to classical history and mythology. The Phoenicians modeled their ships on Noah's, and later Daedalus taught mankind the use of sails:

> Their heavy Ships around the neighb'ring Shores,
> Creep slowly by the Help of num'rous Oars;
> 'Till Daedalus, Inventor of the Sails,
> In Canvas Prisons bound the flying Gales:
> And taught his Vessel by their Aid to fly
> Swift as the Birds that range the spacious Sky:

These were the Wings from whence he gain'd his Fame,
These to remotest Climes convey'd his Name.
(ll. 59–66)

When half the world groaned under proud Sesostris' rule, brave
Jason set out in the ship *Argo* and joined with various kings to break
Sesostris' power (ll. 67–75). Lewis concludes the progress-piece with
a summary of the accomplishments of ships and their present importance to America and especially to Maryland. This verse paragraph
wins its effect from the repetition of the key word *ship* and by the
exotic diction and *s*-alliteration of the concluding lines:

Thus did a Ship preserve the Race of Man,
And by a Ship the *Greeks* their Freedom gain:
To Ships, we owe our Knowledge, and our Trade,
By them defend our own, and other Realms invade,
Without their Aid, *America* had been
To all, except its Natives, now unseen:
Her Trees whose stately Tops to Heaven aspire,
Had fall'n a Prey to Worms, or fed the Fire,
Which now with Pleasure shall forsake their Woods,
And fly to distant Lands o'er deepest Floods,
From hence shall bear the Product of these Shores,
And make the Growth of foreign Climates ours:
In Ships of them compos'd, *Barbadoes* yields
To us the Product of her fertile Fields.
Iberias golden Fruit shall zest our Bowls,
And *Florence* send her Wine to chear our Souls.
To form our Cloaths shall *Britain* shear her Sheep,
And *Indian* Curtains screen us when we sleep.
What Nature has to *Maryland* deny'd,
She might by Ships from all the World provide.
(ll. 76–95)

Lewis describes the new ship, the result of two years' work, and
says that wherever it sails, Hastings' fame will go. The poet tells of
a trip he took one night to see the ship: While the poet stood on the
deck, looking at the reflection of the "floating Forest" on the "smiling Surface" of the water, the Muse appeared and revealed a vision:
"A wond'rous Show;—A Triton first appears," sent to "prepare the
Way For Chesapeake, great Ruler of the Bay." In a passage reminiscent of Pope's "Windsor Forest," the major Maryland rivers gather
to hear Chesapeake:

Fair Severn first appear'd to grace his Court,
Patuxent next did to her King resort;
Chester whose Stream o'er ouzy Islands strays;

Patapsco crown'd with Yews his Homage pays;
And *Sassafras*, whose Banks with graceful Pride
Behold their pleasing Prospects in his Tide:
Last *Susquahana*, vext to meet Delay,
O'er rugged Rocks rolls rapid on his Way,
Foaming with hast his Ruler to obey.

(ll. 138–46)

Chesapeake begins his speech with praise for the "graceful form" of the *Maryland Merchant*. Then, revealing that it has been built on the banks of the Severn (the lovely river that flows into the Chesapeake Bay at Annapolis), Chesapeake says that all the Maryland rivers will have to pay, in the form of freight, tribute to the ship. Chesapeake asks Neptune to assuage "Old *Ocean's*" tempests and requests the Moon to grant Hastings, in reward for designing "this stately Ship," the secret of finding longitude. Chesapeake notes that Hastings was born in "that happy Region" that "my fair Streams . . . lave" (l. 183).

Referring to the current troubles between the Maryland tobacco planters and the English merchants, Chesapeake tells the rivers to warn the dwellers along their banks:

> . . . the Factors whom they now employ
> In Britain's Isle their Interest betray . . . .
> To ruin *Maryland* they now unite
> In monstrous Leagues of amicable Spight.

(ll. 189–90, 197–98)

Echoing Henry Darnall's economic plans in the *Maryland Gazette*, Chesapeake advises the citizens to send a Marylander to supervise the selling of tobacco in England, and if they cannot do this, to refrain from shipping any tobacco for a year. His speech ends in the poem's concluding couplet, and the vision vanishes.

The poem's structure consists of an introduction telling the occasion, a chronological progress-piece tracing the history of shipbuilding, a transition section praising Hastings, a vision describing local scenery and economic woes, and an abrupt conclusion. The progress-piece on shipbuilding and the address by the God Chesapeake to the assembled rivers are both excellent vehicles for Lewis's purpose. The abrupt conclusion is, perhaps, a fault. Although another reader might prefer the mythological history of shipbuilding, or the catalogue of the products brought to Maryland (reminiscent in its rich diction of Andrew Marvell's "Bermudas"), or the description of Maryland's economic ills—the high point of the poem for me occurs in the portrayal of the rivers as they rush to answer the Triton's summons; the characters given to the Chester and the Susquehanna rivers still seem apt.[8]

In 1730, Lewis was appointed (perhaps by John Ross, to whom he later dedicated a poem) clerk of an Assembly committee, which was revising the tax laws. He served fifteen days on the committee between May 26 and June 16, 1730, receiving 140 polls of tobacco per day for his services (after one-fourth of this was deducted, he was actually paid £1 16s. 6d.).[9] The next notice of Lewis appears in the *Philosophical Transactions* of the Royal Society of London. Concern with Newtonianism characterized the well-rounded eighteenth-century gentleman. Science was a fashionable interest, indeed nearly essential to the educated, enlightened man. Although Lewis is more in the humanistic tradition of Pope and Addison (cf. the account of his education given in "A Journey from Patapsco to Annapolis," ll. 292–300, below), yet, like Addison, he does not ignore science. Following Isaac Greenwood's "An Account of an Aurora Borealis, seen in New England on the 22d of October, 1732," in the *Philosophical Transactions*, there appears "An Account of the same Aurora Borealis, by Mr. Richard Lewis; communicated in a Letter to Mr. Peter Collinson, F.R.S."[10] The note is dated "Annapolis in Maryland, December 10, 1730." To a brief description of the aurora borealis, he adds, "Dr. Samuel Chew[11] at Maidstone, tells me, that he has for some Days past, at Morning and Evening, observed several Spots in the Sun very plainly with his naked Eye, some of which seemed very large."

Subscriptions for John Pine's engraved edition of Horace were

[8] For an appreciation of the role of the catalogues of rivers in American poetry at a later date, see Eugene L. Huddleston, "Topographical Poetry in the Early National Period," *American Literature* 38 (1966):311. Although Huddleston does not continue his survey of the catalogue to the mid-nineteenth century, it seems probable that the grand catalogues so important in Whitman's poetry stem from this tradition.

[9] *Archives of Maryland* 37:14, 33, 62, 129, 130, and 136.

[10] *Philosophical Transactions* 37 (1731–32):69–70. I do not know when or how Lewis started corresponding with Collinson, nor have I been able to turn up any of the original correspondence. Transcripts of the scientific parts of the letters are recorded in the records of the Royal Society. Collinson, a key figure in the life of Benjamin Franklin, had many business as well as scientific correspondents in the colonies. Collinson corresponded with Marylanders at least as early as Oct. 21, 1721. Collinson to George Robins, Hollyday Papers, Maryland Historical Society.

[11] Dr. Samuel Chew (1693–1743) later became chief justice of the "three lower counties" of Pennsylvania (New Castle, Kent, and Sussex, on Delaware). Maidstone is near West River, Maryland, about twelve miles from Annapolis.

probably collected in America by William Parks about 1730. The subscribers included most of the best-known English and American literary men of the day. Among the American patrons listed in the first volume (London, 1733) were "Mr. R. Lewis of Maryland" (sig. C2^v), "Dr. John Mitchell M. D." (D1), "Mr. William Parks Printer in Virginia" (D1^v), and "Jonathan Belcher Governor of Massachusetts" (Ea^v).

The best neoclassic poem of colonial America was Lewis's "A Journey from *Patapsco* to *Annapolis*, April 4, 1730."[12] The poem appeared in the *Pennsylvania Gazette* for May 21 and was reprinted, abridged, in the *New York Gazette* for June 21, 1731. Although the prefatory comment in the *Pennsylvania Gazette* suggests that this is its first publication, the comment, as well as the poem, may be reprinted from a lost issue of William Parks's *Maryland Gazette*, perhaps from May of the previous year.[13] Lewis sent a revised version to Collinson, who showed it to his literary friends. They promptly published it. When Collinson wrote to Thomas Story on May 27, 1732, he enclosed a copy, saying "A Curious Gentleman From Maryland Sent Mee a Poem of his own Composing w*ch* att the Request of my Intimates was printed Here. I Doubt not but the'l find it very Entertaining, being interwoven with many Diverting Incidents and Fine Reflections."[14] The poem was printed in England at least five times: in the *Weekly Register*, January 1, 1731/2; in the most influential and famous magazine in England, the *Gentleman's Magazine*, March,

---

[12] The poem is briefly discussed by Robert A. Aubin, *Topographical Poetry in XVIII-Century England* (New York, 1936), 245–47, who calls it "the first American journey-poem."

[13] Franklin frequently reprinted from Parks's *Maryland Gazette*. For example, "Verses on St. Patrick's Day: Sacred to Mirth and Good-Nature," was printed in the *Maryland Gazette*, Mar. 17, 1729/30, and reprinted in the *Pennsylvania Gazette*, Mar. 25, 1731. Unfortunately, only a few issues of Parks's *Maryland Gazette* are extant. See Aldridge (n. 7 above) for other Franklin borrowings from Parks.

[14] Quoted from a photocopy of the letter kindly furnished me by the library of the Society of Friends, Friends House, London. Max Hall, *Benjamin Franklin and Polly Baker* (Chapel Hill, 1960), 118, supposes that the poem referred to was Cook's *Sot-Weed Factor*, but this seems improbable. Although Lewis corresponded with Collinson, Cook, so far as we know, did not. Lewis's poem was printed shortly before Collinson wrote to Story; no record of an English *Sot-Weed Factor* of this time has come to light. Finally, it is unlikely that Collinson (a conscientious Quaker) would send Cook's poem to Story—and extremely unlikely that Collinson would think that the scurrilous *Sot-Weed Factor* (with its satire on Quakers) contained "fine reflections."

1732 (II, 669–71); again in the *Weekly Register*, April 7, 1733; in Eustace Budgell's *Bee*, April 14, 1733 (I, 393–404); and in the second most widely read periodical of the day, the *London Magazine*, April, 1733 (II, 204–207). There is no doubt that, as George Sherburn wrote, "The 'Journey from Patapsco to Annapolis' is one of the best poems of its day in America."[15]

It is prefaced in the *Pennsylvania Gazette* by the comment:

We are confident that none who are Lovers of Poetry will be displeas'd to find this Weeks Paper almost wholly taken up with the following beautiful Piece. It is an agreeable Description of the SPRING in these Parts of *America*; the Publication of which the Author modestly declin'd to allow Till another Season; but his Friends were of opinion, that so excellent a Picture would suffer no disadvantage by an immediate comparison with the Original. The religious Turn given the whole, is suitable to the ancient Use and first Design of Verse; the Muse being then only well and rightly employ'd, when she excites to Piety and Virtue.

After quoting seven lines from Virgil's second Georgic, the topographical poem begins with a greeting for the impatiently awaited spring:

AT length the *wintry* Horrors disappear,
And APRIL views with Smiles the infant Year;
The Grateful Earth from frosty Chains unbound,
Pours out its *vernal* Treasures all around,
Her Face bedeckt with Grass with Buds the Trees are crown'd.
In this soft season, 'eer the Dawn of Day,
I mount my Horse, and lonely take my Way,
From woody Hills that shade Patapsko's Head,
(In whose deep Vales he makes his stony Bed,
From whence he rushes with resistless Force,
Tho' huge rough Rocks retard his rapid Course,)
Down to *Annapolis*, on that smooth Stream
Which took from fair *Anne-Arundel* its Name.
(ll. 1–13)

In the change from the sibilant alliteration of line 10 to the cumbrous "Tho' huge rough Rocks," the sound-matching-sense doctrine common to eighteenth-century poetic theory is evident. The metrical variation in "rough Rocks" (a spondee instead of the expected iamb) and "Down to" (a trochee for the expected iamb) helps to make this

[15] In Percy H. Boynton, ed., *American Poetry*, 601. My text is the first revised edition, which appeared in the London *Weekly Register*, Jan. 1, 1731/2, pp. 1 and 2.

effective poetry. Hardly has the poet started for Annapolis before Venus, the morning star, disappears, and the moon grows dim. The first of the many fine descriptive images in the poem portrays the sun as it rises above the pine trees that are gently swaying with the wind:

> O'er yon tall *Pines* the *Sun* shews half his Face,
> And fires their Floating Foliage with his Rays:
> Now sheds aslant on Earth his lightsome Beams,
> That trembling shine in many-colour'd Streams.
>
> (ll. 20–23)

These lines introduce the play of light and color which will be repeated and emphasized in other descriptions in the poem.

Lewis comes to a marsh, wherein, as the mist rises, the trees, emerging into view, seem to rear their "dewy Heads." And the sun, shining on the trees, "brightens into Pearls the pendent Dews" (l. 27). All the animals now joyfully rise "except the filthy *Swine*" (l. 30). He then gives the theme of his poem, a statement of his belief in scientific deism (i. e., that the beauty and order of the universe, which operates according to the laws of Newton and the new science, proclaim the existence of God):

> Thro' sylvan Scenes my Journey I pursue,
> Ten thousand Beauties rising to my View;
> Which kindle in my Breast poetic Flame,
> And bid me my CREATOR's Praise proclaim . . . .
>
> (ll. 36–39)

The first extended description of native flowers and wildlife to appear in American poetry follows:

> First born of *Spring*, here the *Pacone* appears,
> Whose golden Root a silver Blossom rears.
> In spreading Tufts, see there the *Crowfoot* blue,
> On whose green leaves still shines a globous Dew;
> Behold the *Cinque-foil*, with its dazling Dye
> Of flaming Yellow, wounds the tender Eye.
> But there, enclos'd the grassy *Wheat* is seen,
> To heal the aching Sight with cheerful Green.
>
> (ll. 43–50)

The substitution of an initial spondee and a medial trochee (or pyrrhic) for iambs in the opening line of the description testifies to the poet's ability to create emotionally heightened effects through meter. The antithesis of "wounds" (l. 48) and "heal" (l. 50) has interesting implications. Implicitly, nature (the wild "Cinque-foil") is compared to God, for the direct vision of God would blind mortal man. More obviously, the passage says that nature is too crude and violent for man; art (which is, in this context, the cultivation and transformation of the wilderness) is necessary for man to live comfortably.

In a conventional picture of the farmer (ll. 51–60) and of his orchard, the poet sees peach, plum, apple, quince, and cherry trees (ll. 61–68). Lewis describes at length the singing of the "Mimic of the feathery Kind," the mockingbird, who excels the most poetic English bird, the "pleasing Philomel" (ll. 73–90). Then the poet takes up another American bird, one that especially fascinated the early European traveler, the hummingbird:

> Like them [bees] in Size, the *Humming-Bird* I view
> Like them, *He* sucks his Food, the Honey Dew,
> With nimble Tongue, and Beak of jetty Hue.
> He takes with rapid Whirl his noisy Flight,
> His gemmy Plumage strikes the Gazer's Sight;
> And as he moves his ever-flutt'ring Wings,
> Ten thousand Colours he around him flings.
> Now I behold the Em'rald's vivid Green,
> Now scarlet, now a purple Die is seen;
> In brightest Blue, his Breast *He* now arrays,
> Then strait his Plumes emit a golden Blaze.
> Thus whirring round he flies, and varying still
> He mocks the *Poet's* and the *Painter's* Skill;
> Who may forever strive with fruitless Pains,
> To catch and fix those beauteous changeful Stains;
> While Scarlet now, and now the Purple shines;
> And Gold, to Blue its transient Gloss resigns.
> Each quits, and quickly each resumes its Place,
> And ever-varying Dies each other chase.
> Smallest of birds, what Beauties shine in thee!
> A living *Rainbow* on thy Breast I see.
>   Oh had that *Bard, in whose heart-pleasing Lines,
> The *Phoenix* in a Blaze of Glory shines,
> Beheld those wonders which are shewn in Thee
> *That Bird* has lost his Immortality!
> Thou in His Verse hadst stretch'd thy flutt'ring Wing
> Above all other Birds,—their beauteous King.
>
> (ll. 93–119)
>
> * Claudian

As Marjorie Hope Nicholson has shown, *rainbow* was a highly charged word in the eighteenth century, for it, or any catalogue of colors, brought to mind the ideas of the new science, of Newton's

Optics, ideas which suggested a new orientation for man.[16] The New World itself, with its new birds like the mockingbird and the hummingbird, had posed problems for the old scheme of world order. We shall see that the fundamental subject of the poem concerns the order of the universe and man's place in it. Few contemporary readers could help but be pleased by this description of that marvelous American bird that they had heard of, which, like the mockingbird, makes its first important poetic appearance in this poem. The reference to classic poetry (in this case, Claudian's fable of the phoenix's immortality) is a pleasing neoclassic characteristic, and suggests a continuity of culture in a world of new and upsetting discoveries. Notice too, the patriotic note in this passage: American nature is superior to nature in the Old World. Although the description of the hummingbird may echo James Thomson's passage on the hornet in the first edition of *Winter* (1726), it more resembles Robert Beverley's lush description in his *History of Virginia* (London, 1705 and 1722):

> Have you pleasure in a Garden? All things thrive in it, most surpriseingly; you can't walk by a Bed of Flowers, but besides the entertainment of their Beauty, your Eyes will be saluted with the charming colours of the Humming Bird, which revels among the Flowers, and licks off the Dew and Honey from their tender Leaves, on which it only feeds. It's size is not half so large as an *English* Wren, and its colour is a glorious shining mixture of Scarlet, Green, and Gold.[17]

Lewis leaves the "enclos'd Plantation" to go on through the woods where he admires the oak, hickory, and pine trees, and the smooth streams. A storm comes up; a "dreary Darkness overspreads the Skies" (l. 139); "Hush'd is the Musick of the wood-land Choir" (l. 141); "And a dumb Horror, thro' the Forest reigns" (l. 145). Lewis finds refuge from the storm "In that lone House which opens wide its Door" (l. 146). Of course the reader must wonder what significance the "lone House" has—is it religion, nature, friendship? The poet describes a violent April thunderstorm, with rain, hail, and lightning (ll. 149–71). After the brief storm, a rainbow appears:

> Bursts the broad *Sun,* triumphant in a Blaze
> Too keen for Sight—Yon Cloud refracts his Rays,

16 See Marjorie Hope Nicholson's discussion in *Newton Demands the Muse* (Hamden, Conn., 1963), 10, of the significance of the changing colors of the sylphs and syphids in Pope's *Rape of the Lock,* II, 59–68.
17 Robert Beverley, *The History and Present State of Virginia,* ed. Louis B. Wright (Chapel Hill, 1947), 198–99.

> The mingling Beams compose th' *ethereal* Bow,
> How sweet, how soft, its melting Colours glow!
> Gaily they shine, by heav'nly Pencils laid,
> Yet vanish swift,—How soon does *Beauty* fade!
> (ll. 175–80)

The closing *sententia*, a common device in Augustan poetry, is felicitous; and the *tempus fugit* motif will recur.

The storm past, the poet describes the woods after the shower: the pine, dogwood, maple, red-bud (Judas tree), carnation, sassafras, and "vine" are all enumerated. After mentioning the birds' "sweet singing," he writes that "These vernal Joys, all restless Thoughts control, / And gently soothing calm the troubled Soul" (ll. 187–88). The poet climbs from the plain to the top of a hill where he sees a river and tiers of trees below him: "Shade above shade, the Trees in rising Ranks, / Cloath with eternal Green his Steepy Banks" (ll. 204–205). He also sees a hawk which, like the lightning that splits the oak in the thunder storm (ll. 149–52), reveals a jarring discord in the plan of nature:

> But see the *Hawk*, who with acute Survey,
> Tow'ring in Air predestinates his Prey
> Amid the Floods!—Down dropping from on high,
> He strikes the *Fish*, and bears him thro' the Sky.
> The Stream disturb'd no longer shews the Scene
> That lately stain'd its silver Waves with green;
> In spreading Circles roll the troubled Floods,
> And to the Shores bear off the pictur'd Woods.
> (ll. 208–15)

The initial trochee and enjambment of the second line of the description, the caesura in the third line, followed by a medial spondee —all testify to the poet's careful craftsmanship, for he successfully controls the speed of the verse, and the reader's emotions. These lines present the poet's theodicy, for the seeming viciousness of the hawk— and of God—is justified by the hawk's overall view, taken "with acute Survey" (from a position that the fish—and man—is unable to attain). The hawk inflicts pain on the fish and kills it, thus suggesting that pain and death vitiate the wonders of nature and the pleasures of man. Although the hawk takes the fish from his proper, life-giving sphere, "the Floods", yet the fish is raised up into the sky, implying that the fish (an archetypal symbol for Christ) is taken to heaven. That key word "predestinates" implies an ultimate justness of the seeming savagery. A weakness of this theodicy is the implication that the individual is insignificant: the death of one fish (or man) is justified by the overall view. The unimportance of the individual is an uncomfortable thought, and Lewis will treat this modern feeling (the alienation of man in a limitless universe was antithetic to the anthropocentric Christianity of the Middle Ages) later in the poem. The second half of the quoted verse paragraph emphasizes the transience of man's life, which is like the "pictur'd Woods" reflected on the surface of the water. This description implies too that life on earth is not the real life—it is but a reflection of that life, a reflection which is apt to be "stain'd" by troubles.

Still on the "summit," the poet views the varied, cultivated valleys and "mazy thickets," then raises his eyes to the "Far-distant mountains drest in blue" and to the "empty air" (ll. 222–25). In describing the sunset, he again emphasizes changing light and color:

> The rising Clouds usurping on the Day
> A bright Variety of Dies display;
> About the wide Horizon swift they fly,
> And chase a Change of Colours round the Sky:
> And now I view but half the *flaming Sphere*,
> Now one faint Glimmer shoots along the Air,
> And all his golden Glories disappear.
>
> (ll. 288–34)

After the poet describes the advent of night, he views the stars and asks:

> Are these bright Luminaries hung on high
> Only to please with twinkling Rays our Eye?
> Or may we rather count each *Star* a *Sun*,
> Round which *full peopled Worlds* their Courses run?
> Orb above Orb harmoniously they steer
> Their various Voyages thro' Seas of Air....
>
> (ll. 251–56)

Growing out of the new science's speculations (cf. Milton, *Paradise Lost*, VIII, 148–49, "and other Suns, perhaps, / With their attendant Moons thou wilt descry ... "), and reflecting the eighteenth-century doctrine of plenitude, this verse paragraph displays considerable poetic imagination. The passage seems to echo the description of the coming of night in John Gay's *Rural Sports*: "Now night in solemn state begins to rise, / and twinkling orbs bestrow th' uncloudy skies / Millions of worlds hang in the spacious air, / Which round their suns their annual circles steer." The lines diminish the importance of man— an effect pertinent to Lewis's purpose.

The following stanza, with its reference to "vulgar Error," suggests that Lewis has in mind Sir Thomas Browne's *Pseudodoxia Epidemica* (1st ed., 1642), commonly called "Enquiries into Vulgar and Common Errors," especially Book VI, Chapter XIV. The stanza begins with the invocation:

> Snatch me some *Angel* to those high Abodes,
> The Seats perhaps of *Saints and Demi-gods!*
> Where such as bravely scorn'd the galling Yoke
> Of vulgar Error, and her Fetters broke;
> Where *Patriots* who to fix the publick Good,
> In fields of Battle sacrific'd their Blood;
> Where *Pious Priests* who Charity proclaim'd,
> And *Poets* whom a virtuous *Muse* enflam'd;
> *Philosophers* who strove to mend our Hearts,
> And such as polish'd Life with *useful Arts*,
> Obtain a Place; when by the Hand of Death
> Touch'd, they retire from this poor Speck of Earth . . . .
> (ll. 257–68)

This catalogue of Lewis's "*Saints*," though interesting, is deadened by its conventionality. Then the poet again glances at the science of his time:

> While to these Orbs my wand'ring Thoughts aspire,
> A falling *Meteor* shoots his lambent Fire;
> Thrown from the heav'nly Space he seeks the Earth,
> From whence he first deriv'd his humble Birth.
> (ll. 273–76)

Now he turns his "reflective View" inward:

> My working Fancy helps me to survey
> In the just Picture of this *April Day*,
> My Life o'er past,—a Course of thirty Years,
> Blest with few Joys, perplex'd with num'rous Cares.
> (ll. 283–86)

He then traces the ages of man through infancy, childhood, youth (where one finds the trees of science "often bare of *Fruit*, and only fill'd with Leaves" [l. 294], though poetry and history are more rewarding), to the "noontide Beauties" of life, which are frequently deformed by storms. But after a storm, "the *painted Bow* in distant Skies" (l. 307) gives some reason for hope. Lewis compares his life to the journey he has just described: "Thus far *my Life* does with the Day agree, / Oh! may its coming Stage from Storms be free" (ll. 311–12). He asks for the traditional eighteenth-century comforts:

And suffer me my *leisure* Hours to spend,
With chosen *Books*, or a well-natur'd *Friend*,
Thus journeying on, as I advance in Age,
May I look back with Pleasure on my Stage . . . .
(ll. 312–24)

While "thus musing," he finds that he has reached the "River's Margin" and can see Annapolis, "my Journey's End," on the further shore, "To which the Boat attends to bear me o'er" (l. 335). While crossing the river, he raises his eyes to the moon and stars, and "struck with amaze I cry":

ALMIGHTY LORD! whom Heav'n and Earth proclaim,
The Author of their universal Frame?
Wilt you vouchsafe to view the *Son* of *Man*,
Thy *Creature*, who but *Yesterday* began,
Thro' animated Clay to draw his Breath,
To-morrow doom'd a Prey to ruthless Death!
(ll. 344–49)

Thus he intensifies the *tempus fugit* theme of his earlier *sententia*. Lewis now rises to the climax in the poem:

TREMENDOUS GOD! May I not justly fear,
That I, unworthy Object of thy Care,
Into this World from thy bright Presence tost,
Am in th' Immensity of *Nature* lost!
And that my Notions of the *World above*,
Are but Creations of my own *Self-Love*!
To feed my coward Heart, afraid to die,
With *fancied* Feasts of Immortality.
(ll. 350–57)

Here Lewis directly links two ideas—the immensity of nature and the consequent insignificance of man—which were implicit in the earlier descriptions of vast landscapes, empty air, other suns, and "full peopled worlds." The coupling of these ideas marks an important step for poetry written in the English language. The coupling first occurred in Plato, but had been lost to the Christian world (a world in which God was anthropomorphic, and the universe, anthropocentric) until the advances of science proved that the earth was no longer the center of the universe—and not even the center of the solar system. John Donne wrote that the new science calls all into doubt—and Richard Lewis tells us *what* is in doubt. The increase of population, the rise of cities, and the expansion of European peoples into the New World also contributed to the feeling of a single man's insignificance.

An interesting subtlety is found in the application of Lockean psychology to the idea of the immortality of man. The poet asks if the conception of immortality, "of the World above," is not perhaps his own rationalization—because he would like to think that there is an after-life. Thus Lewis attacks the validity of reason itself. Reason, of course, was the most sacred cow of the eighteenth century, and the only other American of the century who reveals a thoroughly complex and sophisticated appreciation of the role of psychology and reason was a person who read the works of Lewis—Benjamin Franklin.[18]

These doubts have been suggested to the poet by "Thy amazing works" (l. 358). But Lewis comforts himself with the thought that, "however mean" he is, he was put "on this Scene" by God's command. Then he asks: "And must I, when I quit this Earthly Scene, / Sink total into *Death*, and never rise again?" (ll. 370–71). And changing Descartes' dictum, he concludes: "No sure,—These Thoughts which in my Bosom roll, / Must issue from a never-dying Soul" (ll. 372–73). Thoughts, he thinks, "could never be bestow'd on *Man* in vain" (l. 377). Lewis ends the poem beseeching God to look with mercy on his infirmity, and attempting to accept stoically the situation of man: "Patient let me sustain thy wise Decree, / And learn to know *myself*, and *honour* Thee" (ll. 389–90).

The poem's major unifying and structural devices are the journey from Patapsco to Annapolis, and the time scheme of one day, from predawn till nightfall. Lewis repeats the key word *journey* (first used in the title) in lines 181 and 337, and uses it metaphorically, *journeying*, in line 323. There are several levels of meaning: the poem describes the poet's journey from Patapsco to Annapolis on April 4, 1730; it allegorizes his journey through life (complete with a catalogue of the ages of man and a boat passage across the river at the end); and, finally, it explores the fundamental questions of an intelligent man's theology in view of the new science and philosophy of the day. Thus the reference to colors, to the rainbow, to "full peopled worlds," and to the meteor, all build a context of contemporary science and specu-

---

[18] Franklin's complex attitude on the limits of reason could easily be the subject of a monograph. See, for example, his parable about the sacredness of life, which ironically concludes, "So convenient a thing it is to be a *reasonable Creature*, since it enables one to find or make a Reason for everything one has a mind to do." Leonard Woods Labaree et al., eds., *The Autobiography of Benjamin Franklin* (New Haven, 1964), 88.

lation in which the poet questions the old anthropocentric religious convictions. His questions and answers are imbued with contemporary philosophy. But he has assimilated the contemporary trends so that his answers, in part, come from Lockean psychology, from Cartesian philosophy, from Newtonian science, and from contemporary literature. The rainbow (l. 307) gives him "some Gleams of Comfort" (l. 308); i. e., the marvels of God's world, their order and regularity (as shown by Newtonian science) testify to God's creating power. The "troubled Soul" is calmed by the description of "vernal Joys" (ll. 187–88), description suggestive of the modern science. Although it is easy to push any one of the symbols too far, there is no doubt that the final religious affirmation is made in the face of, and partly by including and transcending, the major modern currents of thought.

As Sherburn pointed out, the poem is a surprisingly early imitation of Thomson's "Seasons." Lewis echoes Addison's "A Letter from Italy" (cf. Addison's ll. 99–100 to Lewis's ll. 352–53), Gay's "Rural Sports," and doubtless owes something to Pope, Milton, and perhaps even to Chaucer. But his language and subject matter are closest to Thomson. As in Thomson's "Summer" (1727), the progress of the day is even broken by a shower. He borrows Thomson's paraphrasis "plumy people" ("Spring," l. 165) for his line 237. Two Americans probably influenced "A Journey." Lewis evidently knew and echoed Robert Beverley's *History of Virginia*; and an interesting precursor of "A Journey" is James Ralph's *Night* (London, 1728), which contains, in the conclusion of its "First Book" (pp. 15–18), a description of spring in America. (The editors of the *Gentleman's Magazine* added a prefatory title "Description of the SPRING" to "A Journey.") Ralph, who emigrated to London with his friend Benjamin Franklin in late 1724, asked in a preface that his verses be "compar'd with *Nature* (which is its' original) before 'tis declared unworthy of the muse." Although Ralph's lines describing spring in America are brief and generalized, he does include a good description of Niagara Falls and, like Lewis, portrays cattle fleeing before an approaching storm (p. 12). Since Lewis must have known many of the same people with literary interests (including Franklin) whom Ralph had known earlier, the Maryland poet undoubtedly knew of Ralph's poetry and probably read *Night*. "A Journey" is better unified than "Night," its descriptions are more specific and detailed, and its thematic content is more complex. Most important, Lewis is writing good nature poetry. With "A Journey from Patapsco to Annapolis," descriptive nature poetry attained a high point in America, and not until Philip Freneau did America find another notable nature poet.

The popularity and influence of "Journey" also suggest its excellence. It was carried in the pockets of sensitive tourists in Maryland, praised by later writers in the *London* and *Gentleman's* magazines, and imitated by other colonial poets. "A Journey" even had the dubious distinction of being plagiarized, and Henry Baker's poem *Universe* (London, 1734) echoes it in several places.[19] A less enthusiastic reception can be found in Book IV of the *Dunciad*, where Pope alludes to it:

> Yet by some object ev'ry brain is stirr'd;
> The dull may waken to a Humming-bird;
> The most recluse, discreetly open'd, find
> Congenial matter in the Cockle-kind;
> The mind, in Metaphysics at a loss,
> May wander in a wilderness of Moss;
> The head that turns at super-lunar things,
> Poiz'd with a tail, may steer on Wilkins' wings.
> "Oh! would the Sons of Men once think their Eyes
> And reason giv'n them but to study Flies!
>
> (ll. 445–54)

[19] In reprinting an extract from Lewis's *Carmen Seculare* in the *Gentleman's Magazine* 3 (Apr., 1733):209, the editor wrote that it was by "Mr. Lewis, Author of the beautiful Poem inserted in our 4th Number, entitled a Journey from Patapsco to Annapolis." A poet writing under the pseudonym "Sylvius" in the *Gentleman's Magazine* 4 (May, 1734):286, praised Lewis's poetry in the following lines:

> But chief I value the luxurious feasts
> Thy care provides for thy poetic guests,
> Enraptur'd hear thy tuneful muses sing,
> Inspir'd with draughts from the Pierian spring.
> Here Maryland delicious views displays,
> For ever blooming in a poet's lays.

For the best contemporary praise of the poem (which appeared in the *London Magazine*), see the end of the chapter. The Philadelphia *American Weekly Mercury* for Feb. 19, 1739/40, contains a long poem that acknowledged its inspiration from Lewis's "A Journey." Like most plagiarisms, "Description of the Spring, By S.W." in the *New York Weekly Journal*, May 12, 1740, is much worse than the original. Although Baker's *Universe* pervasively alludes to Lewis's "Journey," I will cite only the following three passages: "All these declare from whence their Being came, / Their Maker's goodness and his pow'r proclaim, / And call thee forth, with them, to praise his name . . ." (*Universe*, p. 24). This echoes Lewis's triplet, ll. 38–40. Baker alludes to Lewis's hawk passage (ll. 208–15) in these lines: "Hence, wide around, here piercing eyes survey, / and far beneath mark out the destin'd Prey: / the red-hot Bolt which splits the sturdy Oak, / Flies not more swift, nor give a surer Stroke . . ." (p. 25). And Lewis's ll. 253–59 are paraphrased by Baker, p. 10n.: "that each *fixed star* we see is a *Sun*, round which a set of *Planets* take their regular *Courses*."

The first couplet refers to the description of the hummingbird: Lewis is the first poet—and the only one before Emily Dickinson—to make memorable use of the hummingbird. The second refers to his catalogues of various American plants (and puns on the meaning of *cockle* as a mollusk as well as a weed), and the third to his metaphysical questioning and his journey in the American wilderness. The next-to-last couplet ridicules his interest in science, especially meteors, an interest which Pope identified with John Wilkins, bishop of Chester and a founder of the Royal Society. The last quoted couplet seems to continue the allusion to Lewis, ridiculing his technique of exact description as well as his use of the word *eye* (cf. "Journey" ll. 48, 97, 176, 239–40, 338–39). This passage is part of Pope's attack on scientific deism, and his intention becomes clearer when it is realized that Pope was alluding to Lewis's poem. Furthermore, an awareness of Pope's purpose makes these lines in the *Dunciad* richer, and supplies one more example of Pope's allusive poetic technique.

"Food for Criticks," the best nature poem of colonial America, survives only in two texts that seem to be rewritings of an earlier, better version. I suspect that Richard Lewis wrote the poem and that it first appeared in a now lost issue of the *Maryland Gazette*, sometime before the spring of 1731. The poem survives in the *New England Weekly Journal* for June 28, 1731, and in the *Pennsylvania Gazette* for July 17, 1732. In both extant versions, the poem seems like the product of a local poet. In the *New England Weekly Journal* version, there are references to Fresh Pond, Cambridge, Harvard, and Watertown. In the *Pennsylvania Gazette* printing, there are references to Philadelphia, the Schuylkill River, and Pennsylvania.

Content and style suggest that this poem is by Lewis. There are several fine images of reflections on water, a characteristic of Lewis's verse; and the catalogues of birds, fish, and plants are written with a richness of context and exactness of observation found in no other American poet of the day. As in other poems by Lewis, classical references prove that American nature is fuller and richer than the nature of the ancient world. Moreover, the local references in both extant versions of the poem are clumsy—far below the general quality of the poem. The local references reveal that the poem has been tampered with by lesser poets. For instance, the *New England Weekly Journal* (1731) contains the following lines:

If to the West your ravish'd eyes you turn,
Behold the glitt'ring Spire of *WATERTOWN*,
Thence shaggy Hills prop up the bending Skies,
And Smoaky Spires from lowly cots arise.
(ll. 41–44)

The corresponding lines in the *Pennsylvania Gazette* (1732) version read:

If to the west you turn your ravish'd eyes,
There shaggy hills prop up the bending skies,
And smoaky spires, from lowly cots arise.
(ll. 39–41)

The latter version is superior and probably reprints the original text. The local reference, the "Spire of Watertown," clashes with the general effect of the passage, which is to contrast man's lowliness and insignificance with the marvels of nature. It also seems to me that the various flora and fauna catalogued in the poem are more typical of the Chesapeake Bay area than of the Charles River area. These are the most striking reasons for believing that "Food for Criticks" (untitled in the *Journal* version) is not by a Boston poet.

Why not, then, assume that the *Pennsylvania Gazette* text, though appearing over a year later, represents the original intention of the poet? Although the *Gazette* version is superior to the *Journal*, the *Gazette* text also appears to be a reworking from an earlier poem. The Pennsylvania references are awkward in comparison with the general level of the poem; moreover, the *Gazette* text omits a key couplet found in the *New England Weekly Journal*. A comparison of the two versions strongly suggests that they are adapted from an earlier and better poem.[20]

"Food for Criticks" in the *Pennsylvania Gazette* for July 17, 1732, begins with praise for the Schuylkill River, comparing it favorably to the famous waters of classical antiquity (Ebenezer Cook may have referred to this first couplet in his *Sotweed Redivivus* [1730]):[21]

[20] Evert A. Duyckinck had read and appreciated the excellence of this poem in the *New England Weekly Journal* version, and he printed a large portion of it, attributing it to Francis Knapp, in *Cyclopaedia* 1:77–78. I have shown, however, that Knapp was not an American poet, and that he died in 1716: J. A. Leo Lemay, "Francis Knapp: A Red Herring in Colonial Poetry," *New England Quarterly* 39 (1966):233–37.

[21] Cf. ll. 36–39 of Cook's poem: "This Thread-bare Theme the Author's Muse here sings, / Did never drink of the Castalian Springs, / Or bath'd her Limbs in Heliconian Streams, / Where fiery Phoebus cools his thirsty Beams."

Of ancient streams presume no more to tell,
The fam'd castalian or pierian well;
Skuylkil superior, must those springs confess,
As *Pensilvania* yields to *Rome* or *Greece*.
More limpid water can no fountain show,
A fairer bottom or a smoother brow.
A painted world its peaceful gleam contains
The heav'nly arch, the bord'ring groves and plains . . . .
(ll. 1–8)

(Note the awkwardness of the first local reference in this text: the sense is that the rivers of America are superior to those of antiquity, just as the state of Pennsylvania is inferior to Greece or Rome.) Continuing the water-reflection image, the poet says that "rudest swains" might "commence astrologers" by watching the progress of the stars upon the surface of the water. Lewis then pictures the life along the stream's banks and his description of the pursued hare probably suggested to his reader Sir John Denham's portrayal of the hunted stag in "Cooper's Hill":

Along the brink the lonely plover stalks,
And to his visionary fellow talks:
Amid the wave the vagrant blackbird sees,
And tries to perch upon the imag'd trees:
On flying clouds the simple bullocks gaze,
Or vainly reach to crop the shad'wy graze
From neighb'ring hills the stately horse espies
Himself a feeding, and himself envies.
Hither pursu'd by op'ning hounds, the hare
Blesses himself to see a forest near,
The waving shrubs he takes for real wood,
And boldly plunges in the yielding flood.
(ll. 13–24)

Lewis notes the absence of "noxious snake" and of night birds from this scene of primitive innocence, and then admits that there is one night bird, who "when the groves are still, / Hums am'rous tunes, and whistles whip poor will" (ll. 34–35). (This is the first use of the word *whippoorwill* in poetry and antedates any OED listing.) Lewis writes that "elves in circles Trip" to hear the whippoorwill's carol. Revealing the same tendency to melancholy found in other poems by Lewis, this poet writes that the song of the whippoorwill comforts the "Troubled mind," and that the carol banishes despair. For the first time in American literature, the wilderness has been portrayed as an enchanted, magical land. The presence of elves marks a new departure in the imaginative concept of the American landscape, for this passage anticipates the magical land that Washington Irving later created in "The Legend of Sleepy Hollow" and "Rip Van Winkle."

The next verse paragraph opens with two imitations, first a reference to Addison's *Campaign*, and then an echo of Pope's early pastoral, wherein the hills are whitened by sheep. Lewis pictures how the appearance of the countryside changes with the seasons (ll. 39–62) and closes with a *sententia*:

> How pleas'd, could it be spring throughout the year,
> And in these walks eternity be spent,
> Atheists would then to immortality consent.
>
> (ll. 64–66)

The finest verse paragraph begins with a description of the woods by a river. The scene and the wildlife "Awake the fancy and the poet's fire" (l. 74). In a description that may owe its inspiration to the eighth line of Virgil's tenth Eclogue, the poet argues that models for poetic genres are found in the songs of birds:

> Hither ye bards for inspiration come,
> Let ev'ry other fount but this be dumb.
> Which way soe'er your airy genius leads,
> Receive your model from these vocal shades.
> Wou'd you in homely pastoral excel,
> Take patterns from the merry piping quail,
> Observe the bluebird for a roundelay,
> The chatt'ring pie, or ever babling jay:
> The plantive dove the soft love verse can teach.
> And mimick thrush to imitators preach.
> In Pindar's strain the lark salutes the dawn,
> The lyrick robin chirps the ev'ning on
> For poignant satyr mind the movis well,
> And hear the sparrow for a madrigal;
> For every verse a pattern here you have,
> From strains heroic down to humble stave
> Not Phoebus self, altho the god of verse,
> Could hit more fine, more entertaining airs;
> Nor the fair maids who round the fountain sate,
> Such artless heavenly music modulate.
>
> (ll. 77–96)

Lewis thus poetically asserts the superiority of American nature to the legends of antiquity as models for poetry. As the multifarious impressions of the enchanting wilderness overwhelm and delude the poet, he envisions an Indian who formerly lived here—an Indian summoned back from paradise by the haunting memory of the beauties of American nature:

> Each thicket seems a paradise renew'd,
> The soft vibrations fire the moving blood:
> Each sense its part of sweet delusion shares,
> The scenes bewitch the eye, the song the ears:
> Pregnant with scent, each wind regales the smell,
> Like cooling sheets th'enwrapping breezes feel,
> During the dark, if poets eyes we trust,
> These lawns are hunted by some swarthy ghost,
> Some Indian prince, who fond of former joys,
> With bow and quiver thro' the shadow flies;
> He can't in death his native groves forget,
> But leaves elyzium for his ancient seat.
>
> (ll. 97–108)

This verse paragraph concludes with another view of the river, and a catalogue, echoing Pope's *Windsor Forest*, of the fauna associated with it:

> O happy stream! hadst thou in Grecia flow'd,
> The bounteous blessing of some watry god
> Thou'dst been, or had some Ovid sung thy rise,
> Distill'd perhaps from slighted virgins eyes.
> Well is thy worth in indian story known,
> Thy living lymph and fertile borders shown.
> Thy shining roach and yellow bristly breme,
> The pick'rel rav'nous monarch of the stream;
> The pearch whose back a ring of colours shows;
> The horned pout who courts the slimy ooze;
> The eel serpentine, some of dubious race;
> The tortoise with his golden spotted case;
> Thy hairy musk-rat, whose perfume defies
> The balmy odours of arabian spice;
> Thy various flocks who shores alternate shun,
> Drove by the fowler and the fatal gun.
>
> (ll. 109–24)

The last lines prepare the reader for the poem's conclusion: an early and memorable lament for the passing of the Edenic American wilderness. The slaughter of wildlife and the destruction of the primeval forests are sins that strike against God himself. He created them; man cannot. Here in the primeval wilderness of America exists another Eden—which, like the former, man will destroy:

> Hither oftimes th'ingenious youth repair,
> When Sol returning warms the growing year:
> Some take the fish with a delusive bait,

Or for the fowl beneath the arbors wait;
And arm'd with fire, endanger ev'ry shade,
Teaching ev'n unfledg'd innocence a dread.
To gratify a nice luxurious taste
How many pretty songsters breath their last:
Spite of his voice they fire the linnet down,
And make the widow'd dove renew his moan.
But some more humane seek the shady gloom,
Taste nature's bounty and admire her bloom:
In pensive thought revolve long vanish'd toil,
Or in soft song the pleasing hours beguile;
What Eden was, by every prospect told,
Strive to regain the temper of that age of gold;
No artful harms for simple brutes contrive,
But scorn to take a being they cannot give;
To leafy woods resort for health and ease,
Not to disturb their melody and peace.
                                    (ll. 127–46)

"Food for Criticks" is the earliest nature poem of America. There had been snippets of nature poetry in the colonization tracts, and passages describing American nature in James Ralph's *Night* (1725) and Roger Wolcott's *Poetical Meditations* (1725), but these are not poems primarily about nature. "A Journey from Patapsco to Annapolis," like most of Lewis's poetry, contains some excellent descriptive nature poetry, but it is an allegorical journey-poem. "Food for Criticks," however, is topographical, and the setting is a river in the American wilderness. Lewis combined the "retreat" and topographical genres popular in his day, applied the combination to the American wilderness, and thereby created a new kind of poetry. "Food for Criticks," domiciled American nature for American poets.

Like "A Journey from Patapsco to Annapolis," "Food for Criticks" echoes Robert Beverley's *History of Virginia*. The wilderness-paradise that deludes the senses in lines 97 ff. has a counterpart in the feeling aroused in Beverley by nature:

The clearness and brightness of the Sky, add new vigor to their Spirits, and perfectly remove all Splenetick and sullen thoughts. Here they enjoy all the benefits of a warm Sun, and by their shady Groves, are protected from its Inconvenience. Here all their Senses are entertain'd with an endless Succession of Native Pleasures. Their Eyes are ravished with the Beauties of naked Nature. Their Ears are Serenaded with the perpetual murmur of Brooks, and the thorow-base which the Wind plays, when it wantons through the Trees; the merry Birds too, join their pleasing Notes to this rural Consort, especially the Mock-birds . . . . Their Taste is regaled with the most delicious

Fruits, which without Art, they have in great Variety and Perfection. And then their smell is refreshed with an eternal fragrancy of Flowers and Sweets, with which Nature perfumes and adorns the Woods almost the whole year round.

(Lewis had also echoed this very passage, containing descriptions of the mockingbird and the hummingbird, in "A Journey.") The lament and complaint against destroying the wilderness, as well as the portrait of the Indian as a noble savage, also may echo sentiments in Beverley:

> Thus I have given a succinct account of the *Indians*; happy, I think in their simple State of Nature, and in their enjoyment of Plenty, without the Curse of Labour. They have on several accounts reason to lament the arrival of the *Europeans*, by whose means they seem to have lost their Felicity, as well as their Innocence.[22]

James Ralph's *Night* had also portrayed America as a retreat from the busy world; he had described America in terms of prolific abundance and portrayed the American Indian in the midst of the lush nature:

> —There nature pours with lavish hand her sweets,
> And in profusion ev'ry blessing gives;
> When lively spring returns fresh verdure greens
> The thick'ning forests, and renews the shades;
> Wide o'er the dusky lands they wave aloft,
> And dance, and murmur to the wanton gale,
> Which, fum'd with odours, (from the chearful bloom
> Of teeming trees in purple blossoms gay)
> Wafts up a fragrant vapour to the stars:
> Beneath with scented herbs, and opening flow'rs
> The earth's embalm'd, while down the neighb'ring hills,
> Soft murm'ring roll a thousand gentle streams,
> And lull the thoughtless savage to repose:
> Charm'd with the various joy soft sleep descends,
> And dewy slumbers on his eyelid sheds;
> The silent god sinks easy on his breast,
> And folds his drowzy limbs in midnight down.
> (pp. 16–17)

Although these lines use the usual cornucopia theme, they are notable for their portrayal of the richness of American nature and for their view of the American Indian as the inheritor and enjoyer of nature. "Food for Criticks" goes far beyond these lines both in its celebration

---

[22] Beverley, 298 and 233.

of nature and in its view of the Indian as an integral part of the Edenic wilderness. As in "A Journey from Patapsco to Annapolis," Beverley and Ralph are probably both influences.

Although "Food for Criticks," like William Bradford's great history *Of Plymouth Plantation*, was comparatively unknown by scholars for over two centuries, yet it was famous in its day and passed into the literary traditions of America when it was imitated by writers immediately subsequent to Lewis. Surely Freneau's "The Indian Burying Ground" reveals the influence of "Food for Criticks." Lewis sounds the first of innumerable laments, from Washington Irving to William Faulkner, for the passing of the American wilderness; and, like Irving, Cooper, Hemingway, Faulkner and the conservationists of today, Lewis prescribes a right attitude toward the American wilderness.

A Rhapsody was published in Annapolis on March 1, 1731/2, as a folio sheet, printed in two columns on both sides. It was reprinted in the *Maryland Gazette*, February 9, 1732/3, and in the *Gentleman's Magazine*, IV (July, 1734): 385. Although anonymous, the poem has been attributed to Lewis by all authorities.[23] After prefatory quotations from Tacitus and Quintilian, the setting (ll. 1–33) of the pastoral prayer describes a "Swain . . . musing on the various cares / Of human Life, it's ceaseless Hopes and Fears" (ll. 1–2). The swain takes a "solitary Walk" in a "pleasing rural Scene." When he reaches the "Flood" (i. e., the Chesapeake Bay), he sits on a "couch" made of the roots of a cedar and a pine (reminding the reader of the "mossy couches" in "Food for Criticks"), and looks out on a "Prospect" (ll. 18–33) of woods, cultivated fields, orchards, and grazing sheep. As in "A Journey," the "Landscape sooths the troubled Swain" (l. 34), and so he begins a soliloquy. He proclaims an early version of the topographical fallacy, i. e., the hope for an American literature which will be inspired by and equal to the grandeur of the native scenery:

> Oh lovely Place! What Language can display
> The pleasing Prospects which my Eyes survey!
> Here, might a Philosophic Poet's Mind,
> Fit subjects for her Contemplation find.
> (ll. 37–40)

[23] Wegelin and Wroth both attribute it to Lewis, and Sherburn, who knew only the *Gentleman's Magazine* reprinting of the poem, wrote that "this poem is almost certainly by Lewis" (p 601).

In two extended similes, the speaker compares the sun's daily journey to a man's life and likens the seasonal death of a tree's leaves to the death of successive generations of a family. The first simile is especially interesting:

> THAT rolling *Orb of Light*, the Source of Day,
> From his meridian Station posts away;
> And tho' his Beauties now o'erpower the Sight,
> Soon shall his Brilliant Beams be veil'd in Night.
> Thus, shall the *Soul* which now my Life sustains,
> And sends the Blood swift-circling thro' my Veins;
> The destin'd Time arriv'd, pursue its Way
> To Worlds unknown,—the Body shall decay,
> And be o'erwhelm'd with its parental Clay.
>
> (ll. 45–53)

In these lines, the poet's "Soul" is identified with his heart, which (according to the still recent theory of Harvey) pumps blood throughout the body. After death, the soul will "pursue its Way / To Worlds unknown." Lewis thus uses the scientific imagery that had been effective in "A Journey."

In the high point of the poem, the poet says that man is subject to the ravages of circumstance and the precarious balance of his own mental stability:

> The gentle *Flood* slow-swallowing up the Beach,
> Rejoicing seems its Boundary to reach;
> And as the Waves o'erflow the shelvy Strand,
> Retiring from them flits the unstable Sand.
> Tho' now a Calm forbids the Flood to roar,
> Should Winds arise, subservient to their Pow'r,
> Soon would the Water shift its smiling Face;
> While Sands, and Mud, the Surface would disgrace,
> With foaming Rage its boiling Billows white,
> Would Terror raise, and banish sweet Delight.
>
> (ll. 68–77)

When the mind functions within the limits of custom and reason, the individual can meet the world with assurance and "smiling Face." But just as water is subservient to the power of the winds, so the mind is the pawn of the passions. The passions can obliterate the "smiling Face" and reveal "flaming Rage," "Terror," and "boiling Billows white." Instability and madness lurk beneath the mind's surface. This passage probably alludes to Shakespeare:[24] Lewis may

---

[24] On the role of madness in the eighteenth century, see Northrop Frye, "Toward Defining an Age of Sensibility," in James L. Clifford, ed., *Eighteenth*

have had in mind the passage in *The Tempest* where Prospero speaks
of the return from madness of Gonzalo, Alonzo, and the ship's crew:

> Their understanding
> Begins to swell, and the approaching tide
> Will shortly fill the reasonable shore
> That now lies foul and muddy.
>
> (V. i. 79–82)

But the passage may also echo these lines from Pope's "Essay on
Criticism":

> Nature to all Things fix'd the limits fit,
> And wisely curb'd proud man's pretending wit.
> As on the land while here the ocean gains,
> In other parts it leaves wide sandy plains.
>
> (ll. 52–55)

As Lewis had earlier in "A Journey" found an allegory for his life
in the journey from Patapsco to Annapolis, so in "A Rhapsody" the
swain finds a correspondence between the description of a beach
and the mental condition of an individual:

> When I reflect on this, methinks I find,
> Drawn on these Waves, the Picture of my Mind;
> Tho' now, my Bosom all serene and calm,
> Seems fill'd with soft Content, and pleasing Balm;
> Yet soon, perhaps, with rude resistless Sway,
> Shall rising Passion drive this Calm away:
> The Mind disturb'd, and mad with raging Woe,
> Shall to the Sight a loathsom Bottom show;
> And those Ideas which my Fancy store,
> May be dispers'd like Sands upon the Shore.
>
> (ll. 78–87)

Lines 88–124 are the swain's direct address to God, including a
couplet aptly summarizing the poem's theme: "Whatever Views employ my musing mind, / My weakness, and thy wondrous Pow'r I
find" (ll. 90–91). He prays that God "such Pow'rs my fickle Mind
endue, / That I my future Course may safe pursue" (ll. 100–101).
Locke's characteristics of perception are reflected in the couplet:
"That I may Truth obtain divinely fair, / Let my Perceptions be

---

Century English Literature (New York, 1959), 311–18. Shakespeare was the
most popular playwright of the eighteenth century. Lewis refers to "a wretched
Play, called Locrine; falsely attributed to Shakespeare" in note "u" of his
Muscipula. Steiner, *Early Maryland Poetry*, 98.

distinct and clear" (ll. 111–12). The prayer concludes with a typical expression of the dominant eighteenth-century ideals:

> Be my Life crown'd with Peace, to Thee resign'd,
> Blest with Content, and with a tranquil Mind:
> And when that Duty which on Man is laid,
> To Friends, and to my Family is paid;
> And I with just Endeavours still have strove,
> My Mind with useful Knowledge to improve;
> With virtuous Habits to reform my Heart,
> And act thro' Life a just and honest Part:
> May I, with Decency submit to Fate,
> And find my self in a more happy State.
>
> (ll. 115–24)

The final couplet rounds off the poem with an alexandrine: "Here ceas'd the Swain,—and soon the Ev'ning Hour / Warn'd him to seek the House, and quit his verdant Bow'r" (ll. 125–26).

Lewis's *Rhapsody* is typical eighteenth-century poetry. Many minor eighteenth-century poets would have been proud of it, and no major poet need have been ashamed of its major images. Blemished by the triteness of the ship-of-life image, the poem is in the conventional pastoral meditative genre. Recalling that the pastoral demanded heightened poetic diction, it can hardly be objected that a "swain" musing in a "bower" on "That rolling *Orb of Light*" is theatrical. A pastoral was supposed to be theatrical, to be an imitation of a familiar classical genre. Although the subject and some structural devices are the same as in "A Journey," *A Rhapsody* is not as complex or effective a poem. It lacks the sustaining interest of the physical journey, the clearly reinforced time structure (the reader is not aware of passing time in *A Rhapsody*), the profound questioning of God's existence and goodness, and the brilliant descriptions of American nature of the earlier poem. In *A Rhapsody*, the mutability of life and the frailty of human reason are memorably described.

Lewis's next poem was "verses, to Mr. Ross, on Mr. Calvert's Departure from Maryland, May 10th 1732."[25] Benedict Leonard Calvert,

---

[25] Although this poem was probably printed at the time, it is known only from a manuscript copy in a thin folio notebook in the library of the United States Naval Academy. It was printed by Walter B. Norris, "Some Recently Found Poems on the Calverts," 118–20, with the title "To John Ross Esqr Clerk of the Council." I have used the more definite title cited as a footnote to l. 190 of Lewis's "Verses. To the Memory of his Excelly Benedict Leonard Calvert," Norris, 125. Although Lewis's name is not signed to "Verses, To Mr. Ross," his reference to it in his elegy on Calvert (ll. 189–92) makes it indisputably his.

governor of Maryland, and patron and friend of Lewis, had been ill
in Maryland and was returning to England in hopes of recovering
his health. John Ross (d. 1766), who had subscribed for two copies
of the *Muscipula*, was clerk of the Maryland Council from 1729 to
1764 and register in Chancery from 1729 to 1761. Inscribed to Ross
because of his friendship with the governor, the 67-line poem pays
tribute to Governor Calvert.

Fearful for Calvert's health, Lewis in his imagination follows the
ship bearing Calvert through storm and calm, and the poet projects
his happiness on learning of Calvert's safe arrival in England. Then he
reminisces of Calvert in Maryland:

> Oft shall I recollect each cheerful Night
> By Calvert's converse crown'd, with sweet delight
> When he forgetful of his State would *deign*
> Humane, your Humble Friend to entertain ....
>   (ll. 46–49)

Lewis praises Calvert's skill in government, his eloquence, wisdom,
and humanity. The poet closes with an apology for his verse, a wish
for Calvert's safe voyage, and the exclamation—"Safe may our Patron
Sail!" (l. 67).

But Benedict Leonard Calvert died, June 2, 1732, on the voyage to
England, and Lewis wrote an elegy for him: "Verses, To the Memory
of His Exclly Benedict Leonard Calvert; Late Governour of the
Province of Maryland who died at Sea, June———1732. Humbly
Inscribed to the Honble Edmond Jenings Esq., Secretary of the
Province."[26] After a long quotation from Pliny the Younger's letter to Pompius Saturninus, Lewis begins his 237-line elegy with an address to Jenings: "I did not hope my Numbers could Suspend / The
Tears, that Flow'd for your Departed Friend" (ll. 1–2). Conventionally, he writes that he has waited until Jenings's grief has sub-
sided before giving him "The Lays, Inspir'd by my Lamenting Muse"
(l. 8).[27] Although his verse is insufficient to praise Calvert's virtues,
it is unfit that Calvert (as Achilles says of Patroclus in the *Iliad*)
should "Sleep, unsung, in the Vast Cave of Death" (l. 14). Lewis

[26] Most accounts on Calvert's death give June 1, but the *Gentleman's Magazine* 2 (June, 1732):826, gives June 2. Like the poem to Ross, Lewis's elegy to
B. L. Calvert is known only from the manuscript notebook in the Naval
Academy Library, printed by Norris, 121–27. My quotations are from the manuscript. Edmund Jenings, deputy secretary of Maryland, 1733–54, had subscribed
for two copies of Lewis's *Muscipula*.
[27] Norris, p. 121, prints *Lay*, but the manuscript reads *Lays*.

praises Calvert's learning in the various fields of physics, literature, morality, history, philosophy, and theology. To complete his education, Calvert toured Europe; but unlike other tourists, he learned the customs and histories of the various countries before he set out. Calvert found, as did Addison in his "Letter from Italy," that the most important source of a country's success was its liberty:

> With a Sagacious Prospect, He surveyed,
> Those Cities, that have lost, or gain'd a Trade,
> From Liberty he found their Blessings flow,
> And Slavery occasion'd all their Woe.
> He saw and Shuddr'd at the Mournful View
> How false Religion Triumph'd o'er the True,
> Instruct'd hence, to prize his Native Isle,
> Where Liberty, on all Bestows her smile;
> Where Commerce joyns Mankind in Social Bands
> Where poorest Swains Securely till their Lands
> And none Dare Snatch the Harvest from their Hands.
> Where Conscience Scorns an Inquisition's Chaines,
> And piety o'er Superstitition Reigns.
>
> (ll. 70–82)

After his European tour, Calvert returned to England but was soon sent by his brother, Lord Baltimore, to be governor of Maryland. Lewis eulogizes Calvert's reign as governor and then tells of his "mild Domestic Life":

> Can I forget those Hours, when as a Friend
> To Entertain me He would Condescend?
> Charm'd with the instructive accents of his Tongue,
> On All He said my Thought regardful hung.
>
> (ll. 111–14)

Calvert was, according to Lewis, an amazing source of knowledge on "Social Virtue," well-read "in choicest Works of Antient Wit / And what the best of Modern pens have writ," and, withal, free from "that Scholastic Sickness Pedantry" (ll. 115–24). Calvert was also the best dancer in the province, but what Lewis most appreciated was Calvert's conversation about Italy and about his antiquarian interests:

> But I with Him the Highest Joys have known,
> When I have Seen him in his House alone.
> Then, his Description set before mine Eye
> What e're was Beautiful in ITALY.
> I View'd each fam'd Antiquity in ROME
> I gaz'd with Transport on St. PETER's DOME;
> Next I the places Superb admir'd,

> Whose Paintings' Seem'd with living Warmth inspir'd
> Thro Gardens, Grottos, Labaryinths, I rove,
> And meet Poetick Shades in every Grove . . . .
> (ll. 131–40)

Calvert delighted his friends with his talk and mirth "round the Social Bowl." Thus ends Lewis's character of the former governor. He asks pardon for offering it to Jenings, who knew Calvert much better than he did. And Lewis recalls his last view of his patron:

> Now I behold him in the Sorrowing Throng,
> Thro' which, his Chariot Slowly mov'd along,
> To bear him to the Ship, Whence never more,
> Shall he Descend, alive, to Touch the Shore.
> (ll. 180–83)

Lewis (echoing *Paradise Lost*, I, 84) describes his condition:

> How Chang'd alas? from whom I once had known?
> In him long-lingering Disease has Shown,
> Her Wasteful Rays, and Mark'd him for her own.
> Her Pallid Shrow'd, oerspread his Hollow Cheek;
> And Death had only left him Pow'r to Speak.
> (ll. 184–88)

Referring to the verses he wrote for Calvert's departure, Lewis now admits:

> The Chariot then seem'd Dismal as his Hearse,
> 'Twas then, Despairing, I accus'd* the Verse
> In which, my Hope had Fancy'd He once more
> Should see his Brother, on fair Albion's Shore.
> (ll. 189–92)
> * Verses, To Mr. Ross, on Mr. Calvert's
> Departure from Maryland, May 10, 1732.

Then, developing the trope of the "watchful rays" of disease, Lewis (echoing Milton's *Lycidas*, ll. 168–71) pens the most notable image in the poem:

> No more was He to See his Native Place,
> No more to feel great BALTIMORE's Embrace;
> In one Short Month his Soul Ascends the Skies,
> Deep in the Sea's Vast Vault his Body lies,
>   Thus to the Ocean Wave the Solar Ray,
> Descending bears from us the Cheerful Day,
> Yet then by Power from the ALMIGHTY given
> He Gilds with New born Beams the Eastern Heaven.
>   So BENEDICT, superior now to Pain,
> With Lustre Shines amid th'etherial Plain.
> (ll. 193–202)

Buried at sea, Calvert has no tombstone to preserve his name. But his legacy to the Prince William School will insure that his name will always be remembered by Annapolis scholars:

> His Benefaction on the School bestow'd,
> By which his Love to MARYLAND He show'd,
> Shall Living Monuments for ever raise,
> Who shall in various Tongues Proclaim his Praise.
>
> (ll. 205–208)

Calvert bequeathed the much-needed funds "not to perpetuate his Name" (l. 215) but from a genuine desire to do good; otherwise, "It had on his own Oxford been bestow'd." Lewis hopes, though, that some future product of the Annapolis school will sing his "Benefactor's Praise," because "Thy Funds were Sunk, thy School had soon Decay'd / Unless Supported by his Bounteous Aid" (ll. 220–21).

Referring to the future poet, the product of the Annapolis Prince William School, Lewis writes:

> Let that Blest Bard to Maryland Declare
> That to inform her Sons was CALVERT's Care
> Had Heaven Restor'd him to his Native Land
> If there his wonted Health He had Regain'd
> The Gift He gave was small to what his mind,
> Had to Advance good LIT'RATURE design'd,
> His Pow'rful Entreaties would have mov'd;
> His Noble Friends who useful Learning Lov'd,
> To Build a COLLEGE, where our YOUTH might find,⎫
> Instruction, to Adorn each Studious Mind;   ⎬ T'endow
> And for their Use, his Books were all Design'd. ⎭
>
> (ll. 222–32)

In closing, Lewis asks that Calvert's friends accept his verses—until the future poet appears; and in a final figure of speech, in which "flowers" is a metaphor for his verse, he says:

> Who shows these Flow'rs, Devoted to his Shade,
> Cherished by you, Their Beauties will not Fade;
> Till a more Greatful GARLAND may be made.
>
> (ll. 240–42)

The poem's structure consists of an introduction (ll. 1–14), a sketch of Calvert's life (ll. 15–196), consolation for his death (ll. 197–232), and a concluding apology (ll. 233–42). The sorrowful, informal tone varies slightly throughout the poem, but is everywhere suited to the genre, a lay (here, a short narrative poem) in the form of an elegiac verse epistle.

"Congratulatory Verses, wrote at the Arrival of Our Honourable Proprietary" appeared in the *Pennsylvania Gazette* for August 21, 1732. This anonymous, occasional poem celebrating Thomas Penn's arrival in Pennsylvania may be by Lewis. It contains a catalogue of rivers reminiscent of the same device in Lewis's poem on Samuel Hastings; the author compares Italy and Pennsylvania (as Lewis did in his dedicatory poem to Calvert in the *Muscipula*, and in "Verses to Calvert"); and the poem shows the keen appreciation of nature and use of history typical of Lewis.

Lewis opens the poem by saying that he praises the ardor of those who "run or ride" to meet the proprietor, but that he chooses to sit down in private and write this welcoming poem. The poet sees in his imagination the trees raising up their branches as if to "look out with eager Eyes" (l. 10) for the arrival of Penn. The second stanza portrays the happiness of the rivers because of the proprietor's coming:

> With virtuous Pride, I hear your Rivers boast,
> But *Del'ware* hopes to gain your Favour most,
> For his good Service every Moment shown,
> To wash the Banks of this your rising Town:
> *Schuylkil* some Part would in your Favour claim,
> And in some sort his Service is the same;
> His winding Stream, his Hills, and every Grove,
> Humbly present their Service and their Love.
> And *Susquehanna* large, august and fair,
> Reveres your Name, and longs to see you there.
> *Potomock's* northern Streams, and ev'ry Spring,
> On your Approach with Acclamations sing,
> For Truth and Right they raise their tuneful Song,
> And scorn all Words spoke in their Owner's Wrong:
> They call you Lord, and while the World endures,
> They will belong to none but you and yours.
>
> (ll. 15–30)

Pennsylvania is then favorably compared to England, the American poet pointing out that the province is "vastly larger" than the "native land." Lewis concludes with an appreciation of the accomplishments of William Penn, Thomas's father. Although "Congratulatory Verses" is a slight occasional poem, it prefigures what Lewis later wrote upon the visit of Charles, fifth Baron Baltimore, in *Carmen Seculare*. Perhaps the most significant attitude that Lewis here expresses is the colonists' pride in the size and richness of Pennsylvania —a colony that dwarfs England.

On October 27, 1732, Lewis, at Annapolis, sent another letter to Peter Collinson, who had it read at a meeting of the Royal Society and published in the *Philosophical Transactions*: "A Letter from Mr. Richard Lewis, at Annapolis in Maryland, to Mr. Collinson, F.R.S. containing the Account of a remarkable Generation of Insects; of an Earthquake; and of an explosion in the Air."[28] Lewis minutely describes the metamorphosis of a "Fly, like a Gnat" which he observed with the aid of a magnifying glass. He notes that he has "read Rhedis' curious Treatise of the Generation of Insects,[29] but found no Account therein of any of their Nests like These." Then Lewis tells of an earthquake that "was felt in diverse places in Maryland ... on Tuesday the 5th of September last [1732], about eleven in the Morning." He says that the "most particular Account I have heard of it was from Mr. Chew. It shook his House for some time, and stopp'd the Pendulum of his Clock."

From the third note, concerning an explosion in the air, we learn that Lewis was in Maryland, at Patapsco, on October 22, 1725, for he himself heard the noise of the explosion. He included the account of Captain Richard Smith, who lived about sixty miles from Patapsco and who reported that there was an "appearance of an extraordinary Brightness in the Zenith, resembling Flame, which continued for about 5 minutes." Smith and Lewis both heard noises like "imaginary Guns" which were repeated twenty or thirty times, so disturbing "the Atmosphere, that the Birds lost the Use of their Wings, and fell to the Ground in great Disorder."

Richard Lewis wrote *Carmen Seculare* for the festivities at Lord Baltimore's arrival in 1732, on the occasion of Maryland's first centennial. The poem—signed and dated at the end "Richard Lewis, November 25, 1732"—was printed in Annapolis and reprinted in the *Gentleman's Magazine* 3 (April and May, 1733): 209–10, and 264.[30]

---

[28] *Philosophical Transactions* 38 (1733–34):119-21.

[29] Probably Francesco Redi, *Opusculorum pars prior, sive experimenta circa generationem insectorum...*, 2 vols. (Amstelaedami [Amsterdam], 1686).

[30] Printed just before Lewis's *Carmen Seculare* in the poetry section of the *Gentleman's Magazine* for April is "An Address to James Oglethorpe, Esq.; on his settling the Colony in Georgia." The earliest extant printing of this poem is in the *South Carolina Gazette* for Feb. 10, 1732/3; it was reprinted from there in the *New England Weekly Journal* for July 16, 1733. Because the poem probably could not have been reprinted in the *Gentleman's Magazine* from the *South Carolina Gazette* (too little time had elapsed), because the poem is by a colonial, and because the style and content of the poem are reminiscent of Lewis, it is possible that this poem too is by Richard Lewis.

For this occasional poem, Lewis uses an informal and relaxed diction, justified by a prefatory quotation from Bacon's *Advancement of Learning*:

> Those who write the Rise and first Progress of an Infant State, ought to describe It in Language simple and unadorn'd as are its Manners; while the large Accessions of Art, and Empire, must be painted in all the Elegance and Sublimity that accompany those happy periods.

Opening the poem, Lewis states that Marylanders have followed the news of their proprietor's European travels and now greet him with roaring cannons and bonfires, "Signals of our Joy." He asks Lord Baltimore to accept his address, wishes him well, and tells what the baron will see if he goes on a "Progress" through Maryland:

> If in wish'd Progress, thro' these wide Domains,
> Our Lord shall pass, to cheer his Tenant Swains;
> With Pleasure will be seen th'extensive Land,
> Adorn'd by Nature with a lib'ral hand.
> Of *Chesapeake*, fair Bay! She justly boasts,
> That swells to wash her *East* and *Western* Coasts;
> Whose num'rous, gentle, navigable Streams,
> In Fame would equal *Po*, or nobler *Thames*;
> Smooth-gliding thro' some Poet's deathless Song,
> Had they in Europe roll'd their Waves along.
> (ll. 48–57)

In the next verse paragraph, Lewis describes the abundance of wildlife and fish on the Chesapeake:

> Vast Flocks of Fowl each River's surface hide,
> Amidst them sails the Swan with graceful Pride;
> From these, the Fowler's Gun gains plenteous Prize,
> Those that escape the mimic Thunder rise,
> And clam'rous, in Confusion, soar the Skies.
> Each Flood with watry Wealth Exhaustless stor'd,
> With choicest Cates supplies the Fisher's board.
> (ll. 58–64)

In three short sections, Lewis celebrates the corn, fruit, and flowers of Maryland and then devotes a long verse paragraph to the climate and animals, and to the planters' hospitality. Although Ebenezer Cook in *The Sot-Weed Factor* (which had appeared in Annapolis in a third edition the previous year) had admitted that "Planters Tables . . . are free for all that come and go" (ll. 112–13), Lewis praises the planters' hospitality:

> Here, ev'ry Planter opens wide his Door,
> To entertain the Stranger, and the Poor;
> . . . .
> That good *Old-English* Hospitality
> When ev'ry House to ev'ry Guest was free;
> Whose Flight from Britain's Isle, her Bards bemone,
> Seem here with Pleasure to have fix'd her Throne.
> (ll. 87–98)

It seems possible that Edward Kimber, who quotes from Lewis's "Journey" in his "Itinerant Observations," was echoing these lines when he wrote: "All over the Colony [Maryland], a universal Hospitality reigns; full tables and open Doors, the kind Salute, the generous Detention, speak somewhat like the old roast-Beef Ages of our Fore-fathers, and would almost persuade one to think their Shades were wafted into these Regions, to enjoy with greater Extent, the Reward of their Virtues."[31]

Lewis then begins another variation of the progress theme. He tells the history of the taming of Maryland; and the description of the wild animals and fierce Indians in early Maryland contrasts markedly with the condition of Maryland at its first centennial.

> Such, gracious Sir, your Province now appears,
> How chang'd by Industry, and rolling Years,
> From what it was! ———————
> When, for the Faith your Ancestors had shown
> To serve Two Monarchs on the English Throne,[32]
> Cecilius, from the Royal Martyr's Hand
> Receiv'd the *Charter of this spacious Land.
> Incult and wild its mazy Forests lay,
> Where deadly Serpents rang'd, and Beasts of Prey:
> The **Natives jealous, cruel, crafty, rude,
> In daily Wars declar'd their Thirst for Blood.
> (ll. 99–109)

> * In the Year 1632.
> ** Indians

Conventionally, the poet hopes that the muse will inflame him with spirit equal to his "glorious Theme." Cecil Calvert spent a fortune to cultivate his infant colony. Lewis states in a note: "Ld. Cecilius was at the Charge of sending Ships, with People, and Provisions, to seat and cultivate Maryland; which Charge amounted to Forty Thousand Pounds, the Interest of which Money, He never receiv'd, by any

[31] [Edward Kimber], "Itinerant Observations in America," *London Magazine* 15 (July, 1745):323.
[32] A reference to George Calvert's services to James I and to Charles I.

Profits he had from thence. See Ld. Baltimore's Case, deliver'd to the Parl. of England, in 1715, by Ld. Guildford."

Referring to the Act of Religious Toleration "in 1640, allowing Liberty of Conscience to All, who profess'd their Belief in Jesus Christ" (Lewis's note), and to the wars of the commonwealth period, Lewis wrote:

> Maturest Wisdom did his Act inspire,
> Which Ages must with Gratitude admire;
> By which, the Planters of his Land were freed
> From Feuds, that made their Parent-Country bleed:
> Religious Feuds, which in an evil Hour
> Were sent from Hell, poor Mortals to devour!
>
> (ll. 122–27)

Then, taking his cue from Butler's *Hudibras* (I, 189–202), Lewis continues:

> Oh, be that Rage eternally abhorr'd!
> Which prompts the Worshippers of one mild Lord,
> For whose *Salvation* one Redeemer dy'd,
> By War their *Orthodoxy* to decide:
> Falsely religious, human Blood to spill,
> And for God's† Sake, their Fellow-Creatures kill!
> Horrid Pretence! ———
>
> (ll. 128–34)

† Tillotson.

This is one of two breaks in the heroic couplet in this 300-line poem; both, of course, are used to good effect. Lewis has already devoted two stanzas to praise for Cecilius' religious position, and in the third stanza he chauvinistically says:

> What Praise, oh Patriot, shall be paid to Thee!
> *Within thy Province* Conscience *first was free!*
> *And gain'd in* Maryland *its native Liberty.*
>
> (ll. 140–42)

In the concluding stanza on religious freedom, Lewis reveals that he had checked the facts in the original records:

> That Men of diff'rent *Faiths* in Peace might dwell,
> And All unite t'improve their public Weal;
> * *Opprobrious Names*, by which blind Guides engage
> Their blinded Proselytes, in deadliest Rage;
> Sunk in Oblivion, by the wise Decree
> Of Calvert, left his Land from Faction free.
>
> (ll. 149–54)

* By the said Act, a fine was imposed on such as should *call* Their Fellow-

After one more stanza on Cecil Calvert, Lewis moves on to the time of the third Lord Baltimore, Charles. Lewis describes the Indian attacks associated with Bacon's rebellion:

> To drive away the Planters from their Lands,
> Th'outrageous *Natives* came in hostile Bands:
> Revengeful, cruel, restless, they persu'd
> Their Enemies, and ruthless, shed their Blood:
> Returning from his daily Toil, at Night
> The Husband often saw with wild Affright,
> His darling Wife, and Infants, robb'd of breath,
> Deform'd, and mangled by dishonest Death.
>
> (ll. 166–73)

Finally, Charles manages to bring peace to his war-torn land. But the return for his expenses was, according to Lewis, small. Then Lewis reaches the succession of the current Lord Baltimore, who must, if he is to continue making money from Maryland, aid his colony:

> At length, to You, Great Sir, has Fortune paid
> The Int'rest of the Debt, so long delay'd;
> And ev'ry future Year that runs his Race,
> Shall to your Revenue add large Increase:
> If You, My Lord, afford your gen'rous Aid,
> If You inspirit our decaying Trade.
>
> (ll. 189–94)

The poet concludes his chronological survey of Maryland history, claiming that the present Lord Baltimore has already shown his concern for his people by the lieutenant-governors he has chosen; and so Lewis praises Captain Charles Calvert, Benedict Leonard Calvert, and Samuel Ogle.

Yet the province is beset by economic problems; the Maryland schoolmaster, appealing to Lord Baltimore's interest both in the people of Maryland and in his revenue, makes a number of suggestions. A major problem arises from the single-crop system:

> Too long, alas! *Tobacco* has engross'd
> Our Cares, and now we mourn our Markets lost;
> The plenteous Crops that over-spread our Plains,
> Reward with Poverty the toiling Swains;
> Their sinking *Staple* chills the Planters Hearts,
> Nor dare they venture on unpractis'd Arts;

Planters any of Those Party-Names by which the Factions of Religion Then in England were unhappily distinguish'd. See Old Rec. Book, in Secr. Off. Annap.

> Despondent, they impending Ruin view,
> Yet starving, must their old Employ persue.
> (ll. 232–39)

In their distress the planters turn to Calvert: "Your happy Station in the British Court, / Enables You your Province to support." Suggesting a remedy for the evils that, years later, Goldsmith described in the "Deserted Village," Lewis says:

> By you encourag'd, Artists shall appear,
> And quitting crowded Towns, inhabit here.
> Well pleas'd, would they employ their gainful hands,
> To purchase and improve your vacant Lands.
> (ll. 252–55)

Perhaps with the shipwright Hastings in mind, Lewis continues his proposals for diversifying Maryland's economy:

> While some with sounding Axes thinn'd the Woods,
> And built the Ships to traverse briny floods;
> Others, industrious, would with hasty Care
> The various cargoes studiously prepare.
> (ll. 256–59)

Lewis also suggests fishing, mining, growing flax, cultivating the silkworm, and making wine. He concludes the program of improvements, writing:

> THESE Blessings Nature to This Land imparts;
> She only asks the Aid of useful Arts;
> To make Her with the happiest Regions vye,
> That spread beneath the all-surrounding Sky.
> (ll. 274–77)

In the conclusion, Lewis recurs to the occasion of the poem, Calvert's centennial visit:

> An hundred Suns thro' Summer Signs have roll'd
> An hundred Winters have diffus'd their Cold;
> Since MARYLAND has CALVERT's Race obey'd
> And to its noble LORDS her Homage paid;
> This, for the Year of Sacred JUBILEE:
> This Year, distinguish'd far above the rest,
> That Time hath sent, shall be for ever blest!
> From your kind VISIT, shall the People date
> An happier Æra, mark'd by smiling Fate,
> To raise the Province from its languid State.
> (ll. 278–88)

In the final two stanzas, Lewis says that he would like to be "prophetic of those glorious Times" that "our Children shall behold" but that "A nobler *Bard* must sing those golden Days" (l. 300). The structure consists of an opening telling the occasion; the body in four parts: (1) the imagined progress through the colony, (2) the history of the colony, (3) the current plight of Maryland, and (4) how to remedy it; and a closing which celebrates the occasion of Charles's visit and prophesies future glories for Maryland. Though the poem is uniformly good, the description of the lush Maryland countryside (ll. 58–80) seems reminiscent of Herrick and prophetic of Keats's "To Autumn."

Lewis evidently served the Lower House of the Maryland Assembly in some capacity in the spring of 1733, for the house on April 10, 1733, voted him "Forty Shillings ... for Extraordinary Services done This Assembly." On August 10, 1733, Lewis sent his last letter to Collinson, along with two specimens of insects. Lewis describes the nests of the insects and concludes, "They seem fond of Man, and when taken on the finger will raise their forefeet and gaze earnestly on the person that holds them and use many freakish contorsions with their head, as if they endeavour'd to divert one." And Lewis says that "for this their singular behaviour I have given them the name of Mangazers."[33]

As Bernard Christian Steiner suggested, Richard Lewis may have written the "Proposals ... For founding An Academy at Annapolis for the Education of the Youth of this Province."[34] Certainly Lewis, as teacher of the Prince William School in Annapolis, would be the logical person to write the "Proposals," yet the fact that the two highest teachers in the academy were supposed to be clergymen might well augur a pen other than the poet's. Lewis, however, may have assumed that he could easily take ministerial orders.

The proposed academy was supposed to equal "the best Latin and Greek Schools, (such as Eton and Westminster)," and, additionally,

---

[33] *Archives of Maryland* 39:88. Collinson read the letter at the Royal Society on Mar. 13, 1734, but it was not published. LBC.21.308–309, Library of the Royal Society, London. A microfilm of the letter is available at the American Philosophical Society, exposures 3575–76.

[34] See Bernard C. Steiner, ed., *Archives of Maryland*, 38:456–61; and idem., "Early Classical Scholars of Maryland," *The Classical Weekly*, 14, no. 24 (May 2, 1921), 185–90. The "Proposals" are printed by Steiner in the *Archives*, and my quotations are from this printed edition.

to cover "the principal Branches of the Philosophy which a first Graduate Learns at the Universities." And the author also pragmatically wrote that the students should be taught "some useful and practical Parts of Knowledge" which were not generally taught at the universities. There is a chauvinistic note in the proposal, for the author suggests that Marylanders, educated for the ministry at the academy, should be given first choice of the "Benefices or Livings here." And the proposer hopes that within a few years "Ingenious Men shall be bred up in the Collegiate School, capable of filling the Vacancies without having Recourse to Europe or any extraprovincial Place whatever."

The duties of the five teachers are enumerated, and the proposer reveals that he has been teaching and that he prefers the new "more approvd, expeditious and easy" methods for teaching languages: for the old ways have been "fatally found to be too dry, laborious and discouraging to the tender Capacities of Boys" (p. 459). Concluding, the author says that he has found that the youths' minds are "naturally Very Good, and Capable of great proficiency by a Suitable Cultivation" (p. 461).

In every colonial city, the feast-days of the patron saints of England, Ireland, Scotland, and Wales were celebrated annually. Philadelphia's Welsh society, which met on St. David's Day, arranged an extra-special program for the meeting on March 1, 1733/4, of "The Society of Ancient Britons." The March 6 news notice in the *Pennsylvania Gazette* describes the festivities:

> Friday last being St. David's Day, the Society of *Ancient Britons* had a Sermon in Welch by the Rev. Mr. Hughes, at *Christ-Church*; and an Elegant Feast at Mr. Owen Owen's. Our Hon. Proprietor, Governor, and principal Gentlemen of the City were present, and a greater Number of People than were heretofore on the like Occasion. It being also the Birthday of her most sacred Majesty Qn. Caroline, the Governor entertain'd the Company at his House before Dinner, where all the Loyal Healths were Drank under several Discharges of Cannon on the Hill.

A poem signed "Philo-Cambrensis" appeared in the *American Weekly Mercury* for February 26, 1733/4, "Humbly inscrib'd to the worthy Society of *Ancient Britons*, meeting at *Philadelphia*, March the 1st, 1733-4." The poem is entitled "Upon Prince Madoc's Expedition to the Country now called America, in the 12th Century" and dated "Jun. [Jan.] 29, 1733-4." The anonymous author possessed an antiquarian interest in Welsh history, a thorough classical background, and the ability to write heroic poetry. Style and content argue that Richard Lewis wrote the poem. Moreover, "Upon Prince Madoc" is echoed in an elegy on Lewis; this allusion proves that a knowledgeable contemporary attributed the poem to him.[35]

Lewis opens the poem by saying that he is going "to quit the noted Throng" of "Grecian Heroes," "Roman Arms," and "Saxon worth" which other poets celebrate, "And after Madoc soar in Loftier Song." Greater than Hannibal, Alexander, or Caesar—Madoc "first this Indian World survey'd, Surpass'd, return'd, and conquer'd, undismay'd" (ll. 29–30). Madoc found the New World without a compass to guide him, for he "both thought, and prov'd *The world was round*" (l. 46). The poet writes a series of comparisons for Madoc's ability to rise to the occasion:

> The nimble Stag by Hounds and Horn deter'd,
> And beat from Shelter by the treach'rous Herd,
> Collecting all his Spirits leaps the Pales,
> And reigns in safety in the fenceless Dales.
> From bit'rest Plants the Bee her Honey stills;
> And with rich Stores her new built City fills.
> Deep under-ground rich Mines of Gold are laid,
> From roughest Stones the polish'd Diamond's made.
> The violent Force of harden'd Steel gives vent
> To hidden Fires within the Flint-stone pent.
> Distress and Toil from *Madoc* thus drew forth
> The glorious Treasures of his *innate* Worth.
> (ll. 57–68)

Lewis claims that Madoc's achievements were superior to Alexander's or Caesar's, for the Welshman first discovered the New World. In describing Madoc's feat, Lewis weaves in classical mythology with history:

> No more let *Babylon* of Wonders boast;
> Let *Persian* Feats in this Eclipse be lost;
> Though *Alexander* fills the highest Chair,
> And to the second *Caesar* does repair,
> (*This* by himself, *That* by Historians plac'd)
> When Honor's Table's with their Presence grac'd;
> Where other *Greek* and *Roman* Heroes meet,
> And as they merit, take their proper Seat;
> Yet will The *Welch-man* (to the Worlds surprise)
> In State triumphant far above them rise;
> For *they ALL* ent'ring at the common Gate,

---

[35] See Byfield's elegy at the end of the chapter.

Meet but with Pref'rence of the *second* Rate;
But *HE* th'*Herculian* Pillars *first* remov'd,
Which to the *REST* too hard a Task had prov'd . . . .
(ll. 69–82)

Had the greatest poets known of Madoc's deeds, they would have
sung his praise:

> Were *Homer* now alive to hear of this,
> He'd write his *Madocks*, burn his *Odysses*.
> Could *Virgil* live his *Aeneads* he'd supress,
> And *Madoc's* Prowess in *Heroics* dress.
> Had we a *Miltons* Genius to rehearse
> Great *Madoc's* mighty Deeds in *English* Verse;
> The *new-gain'd World* would be a proper Thing,
> To add to what the *PRINCE OF BARDS* did Sing.
> (ll. 87–94)

Then, in the longest stanza in the poem, Lewis writes that man cannot explain why God has ordained certain things to happen, but that
they are "For some great Ends of *GOD* unknown to us" (l. 108).
Lewis claims his poem is inadequate to Madoc's fame and urges, "Let
Cambria's Sons this Hero's Feats proclaim and to SAINT *DAVIDS*
joyn PRINCE *MADOC'S* Fame" (ll. 124–25).

Like Lewis's *Muscipula*, "Upon Prince Madoc" compliments the
Welsh people and suggests that the poet may have been Welsh. A
source for the poem was the ode sung at the St. David's Day celebrations: "The Cambrian Glory: An Ode: Or, Memoirs of the Lives and
Valiant Actions, of the Ancient Britons; to be Sung every St. David's
Day."[36] Both "Upon Prince Madoc" and "The Cambrian Glory"
celebrate the pantheon of Welsh heroes, but the Maryland poet emphasizes the imaginary exploits of Madoc in the New World. The

---

[36] "The Cambrian Glory" was first printed in the second edition of Thomas
D'Urfey, *Wit and Mirth*, 3:32–36. See Cyrus L. Day and Eleanor B. Murrie,
English Song Books 1651–1702: A Bibliography with a First Line Index (London,
1940), 187, no. 438.
    Lewis's poem evidently revived the myth of Welsh Indians in America. On
St. David's Day, March 1, 1733/4, a group of six Welshmen in Philadelphia
wrote a letter to the "British Society," proposing that they jointly send some
"adventurous" men to search for these Welsh descendants, because "Some
reliques of the Welsh tongue being found in old and deserted settlements about
the Mississippi, make it probable that he [Madoc] sailed up that river." See
Morgan Edwards, *Materials Towards a History of the Baptists in Pennsylvania*
(Philadelphia, 1770), 128–29, "Appendix VIII." For a recent examination—
which does not, however, mention Lewis or his poem—of the Madoc legend,
see Richard Deacon, *Madoc and the Discovery of America* (London, 1967).

comparison of Madoc to Caesar and other heroes of classical history and mythology is extremely interesting. As in several other poems, Lewis argues that exploits performed in conquering the New World are greater than the achievements of the old heroes. Perhaps Lewis's comparisons may be viewed as an aspect of the "ancients versus moderns" controversy, but these comparisons are significant in the development of American culture. They mark an early identification of American explorers and frontiersmen with the mythic heroes of the old world. By the mid-nineteenth century, the identification of such frontiersmen as Davy Crockett with the classical heroes would be accepted and expected in literature. The beginnings of the tendency to identify the frontiersmen with classical heroes are perhaps found in the Puritans' practice of likening themselves to biblical personages (especially the Israelites); but the more probable origin is the comparisons, by Lewis and later writers, of the early American explorers and frontiersmen to the classical gods and heroes.

On Saturday, February 2, 1733/4, Captain Charles Calvert, president of the Council, former lieutenant governor, and a subscriber for four copies of Lewis's *Muscipula*, died.[37] An anonymous elegy on Calvert appeared in the *Maryland Gazette* for March 15, 1733/4: "An ELEGY on the much lamented Death of the Honourable CHARLES CALVERT, Esq.; formerly Governour in Chief of the Province of Maryland; and at the Time of his Decease, Commissary-General, Judge of the Admiralty, Surveyor-General of the *Western* shore, and President of the Council. Who departed this Life, February 2, 1733–4." The author prefaced the poem with:

> Mr. *Parks*,
> HAVING been requested for a larger Number of Copies of the following Elegy that I am able to comply with; in Gratitude to my Good Benefactors, whose Respect to the Worthy CHARLES CALVERT, Esq.; deceased has been expressed by their Generosity to the Author, I intreat the Favour it may be inserted in your News Paper; and at the same Time beg that those Gentlemen who have desired a particular Copy, would be pleased to accept this Publication, in Lieu thereof.

Since the only extant copy of this newspaper (pages 1 and 2 only, which were completely filled by the poem) was found in the same manuscript folio notebook containing several other Lewis poems,

---

[37] His obituary was reprinted in the *New England Weekly Journal* of Mar. 18, 1733/4, from a no-longer-extant issue of the *Maryland Gazette* of Feb. 8.

and since the contents and style suggest that Lewis wrote the poem, I believe that there is little doubt of his authorship.

Lewis's elegy of 221 lines is, befitting its genre, in a heightened and formal diction. It opens with a picture of the "Genius of the Country" in mourning:

> Her Hair untouch'd the Iv'ry Comb forbore,
> And Dress employ'd her busy Thoughts no more;
> The Spear and Shield aside neglected lay,
> And *Cornucopia*'s Harvest droop'd away:
> Pale Grief had chas'd the Beauties from her Face,
> Nipp'd all her Bloom, and rifled every Grace;
> Excess of Sorrow, heighten'd by Despair,
> Rent her said Breast, a dire Intruder there.
>
> (ll. 5–12)

Finally able to speak, the mourning genius laments Calvert's death. After two brief stanzas (ll. 23–28) attacking death, the "Genius of Maryland" laments:

> He's gone too soon to his Eternal Home,
> The bright Example of the Age to come:
> He's gone too soon, and with regret we find
> He scarce had left an Equal here behind.
>
> (ll. 46–49)

Although not the equal of Dryden's memorable "Farewell, too little and too lately known" (the opening of "To the Memory of Mr. Old-ham," which the repeated "too soon" seems to echo), Lewis's lines rank with the best verses of any elegy written in colonial America, including Urian Oakes's elegy to the Reverend Thomas Shepard. The substitution of two spondees (with their slow and weighted effect) for iambs in lines 46 and 48 is an example of good craftsmanship (perhaps learned from Dryden's example).

Next, Lewis celebrates Calvert's achievements. Speaking of his heroism in battle, Lewis reflects the subject matter and sentiments of Addison's "Campaign" and ends with a reference to Marlborough:

> Let *England*'s Sons with loud Applause express,
> And grateful MARLBOROUGH's worthy Shade confess
> If CALVERT had not fought, His triumphs had been less.
>
> (ll. 58–60)

Charles Calvert was "Alike well vers'd in Arts of Peace as War," and came to Maryland "Our sinking Trade and Country to retrieve" (ll.

63 and 69). Using antithesis and zeugma, Lewis praises Calvert's administration:

> He, he alone, the secret Skill could find
> At once to govern and to please Mankind;
> To strike at once a Pleasure with an Awe,
> And give a Satisfaction with a Law,
> While ev'ry Subject yields with grateful Mind
> Obedience, rather courted than enjoin'd.
>   (ll. 71–76)

Lewis then catalogues the ills that did *not* disturb Calvert's reign and tells of Maryland's prosperity and security under Calvert:

> Secure beneath his kind protecting Shade,
> The planter saw his honest Labour paid;
> Secure the Merchant plows the watry Main,
> While wholesome Laws defend his well-got Gain;
> Secure the Artist gives his Rule the Praise,
> And dates his thriving Trade from CALVERT's Days;
> Secure *Minerva's* Infant glimm'ring Light,
> With rising Dawn dispell'd the Clouds of Night,
> Far driving barb'rous Ignorance away;
> And CALVERT's Morning usher'd in the Day . . . .
>   (ll. 87–96)

The repetition of "secure" and the image of "rising Dawn" are both effective.

The Genius of Maryland rises to rapture in describing Calvert's widow: "O mourning Relict of the best-lov'd Lord, / The Only Treasure that his Soul ador'd!" (ll. 119–20). Bewailing "With Parent Throes my best departed Son," the Genius is finally overwhelmed by grief. Then an Angel appears and addresses the mourning spirit:

> GENIUS of *MARYLAND*, immortal Fair,
> Why thus resign'd a Victim to Despair;
> You who contain within your pregnant Womb
> Heroes unborn, and Empires yet to come,
> Arise! thy Province claims thy Guardian Aid,
> Nor longer Heav'ns Divine Decrees upbraid . . . .
>   (ll. 147–52)

The Angel tells the spirit of Maryland that

> Since he who form'd the animated Clay
> Has deem'd it meet to take its Breath away,
> Let unavailing Grief be laid aside,
> And follow Resignation's better Guide,

> Your empty Pray'rs for his Return forsake;
> 'Twere next to Sacrilege to wish him back.
> (ll. 157–62)

After comforting the Genius of Maryland with a description of Calvert's divine bliss and pointing out that Maryland is also happy under Ogle's reign, the angel departs. Lewis ends his last poem with the thought that Charles Calvert will not be forgotten:

> While *Chesapeak's* luxurious Waves repay
> Their tributary Rivers to the Sea;
> While deep *Patowmack's* Spring remains unknown,
> And *Indian* Kings our Lord's Dominion own,
> So long shall CALVERT's Honour, Praise, and Name,
> Shine in the Annals of Immortal Fame:
> So long shall future Times his Actions tell,
> And faintly copy what they never can excell.
> (ll. 214–21)

The traditional two-part structure of the elegy (first the lament for the death of the deceased and then the consolation that he has gone to heaven) is demarcated by the appearance of the angel. The meter has more spondees than is usual in Lewis's poetry, thus helping to create a stately, slow, elegiac feeling. Although none of the lines seem especially memorable or excellent, the poem in its entirety is calm, measured, restful, and beautiful.

Richard Lewis died intestate in late March of 1734. His widow, "Betty" (i. e., Elizabeth) renounced the administration of his estate on April 10, 1734. John and Benjamin Howard posted a bond of £300 (which means that Elizabeth Lewis received from them approximately £150—a fairly large amount in those times) and were appointed executors.[38] On March 27, 1735, Doctor George Walker and John Moales of Baltimore County were appointed "to appraise the Goods and Chattels of Richard Lewis late of Ann Arundel County deceased as were in Baltimore County."[39] However, no inventory or account of Lewis's estate appears in the records. After Benjamin Howard (Lewis's executor) died, Catherine Howard, his widow and

---

[38] Testamentary Papers, 1734, Anne Arundel County, box 39, folder 4, Maryland Hall of Records. I am indebted to Mrs. Lois Green Carr, then at the Maryland Hall of Records, for the estimate of the amount that Betty Lewis received.

[39] Testamentary Proceedings, 1735, Anne Arundel County, Liber 30, folio 23, Maryland Hall of Records.

executrix, issued a citation of August 14, 1740, "to the Sheriff of Baltimore County against Elizabeth Lewis Widow of Richard Lewis late of Ann Arundel County Deceased to show cause why she conceals several of the Goods and Chattels of the said Richard Lewis." On August 10, 1741, Elizabeth Lewis finally replied that she had "delivered to Mrs. Benjamin Howard and to John Howard his Son all the Effects that she . . . had of the said Richard Lewis's (her own wearing apparel excepted)."[40]

Richard Lewis had at least one child, a son of the same name, who was apprenticed in March, 1735, to Richard Tootel, a saddler in Annapolis, by Daniel Dulany for a fee of £20.[41] Richard Lewis's business advertisements later appeared in the *Maryland Gazette*, November 22 and 29, 1745 (the advertisements note that Richard Lewis had served his time with the late Mr. Tootel), March 7, and September 22 and 30, 1747. He is also mentioned in the issue for July 20, 1748. The son of the poet is probably the Richard Lewis who married Virlendah Wheeler in Annapolis on January 9, 1746.[42]

An elegy and epitaph on Lewis, by W. Byfield, "late of New-Castle upon Tine," appeared in the *Pennsylvania Gazette* for December 5, 1732: "An ELEGY on the much to be lamented Death of Mr. RICHARD LEWIS, late Master of the Free-School of the City of ANNAPOLIS." Though inferior verse, it is short and shows the esteem in which Lewis was held by his contemporaries: Byfield (imitating Lewis's poem on Madoc) compares Lewis to Milton, Cicero, and Virgil, writing:

> This City's lost their Pedagogue of Art,
> More exquisite than any in this Part.
> As to his versifying Parts, I may,
> Without Presumption, absolutely say
> He was a Second *Milton* and cou'd chime
> In lofty Strain, when he was pleas'd to Rhime.
> He was more Eloquent, (tho' cropt more Young,)
> Than learned *Cicero*, or a sweeter Tongue.
> And could but *Virgil* see his lofty Strain,
> He wou'd condemn his own to th'Flames again.
>   Peruse his Works, and you will quickly find
> His Breast retain'd an Heav'nly enamell'd Mind.

[40] Ibid., folio 206.
[41] "Richard Lewis Son of Richard Lewis late of Annapolis Schoolmaster." Judgements, Anne Arundel County, I.B. No. 1, 1734 to 1736, folio 417, Maryland Hall of Records.
[42] St. Ann's Parish Records, 1:144, Maryland Hall of Records.

My dearest Friend, Oh! that I could rehearse
Thy living Virtues with a fitting Verse!
But when the best of my Endeavour's done,
I shall but light a Candle to the Sun,
Who am griev'd to th' Heart, thy Glass so soon is run.

An interesting letter accompanies the elegy and epitaph. The anonymous author obviously considers himself a judge of superior taste. He satirizes Byfield's elegy on Lewis and the poetry of Pennsylvania's best-known contemporary poetic hack, John Dommett; and he praises that "fine Poet," Richard Lewis. In an age when every author seemed eager for a literary quarrel, no one contested his opinion. He mentions the "Character which Mr. Lewis has left behind him among People who have a true Taste for Learning" and refers to Franklin's reprinting "several of his beautiful Pieces of Poetry." He also proposes an "Expedient, whereby all mean Writers, who scribble because of their Poverty or their Loving-Kindness," will be rewarded. The "Expedient" may reveal the identity of this author, for it is similar to a proposal made by Joseph Breintnall in the "Busy Body No. 5." It would be especially suitable for Breintnall to write the appreciation of Lewis, because Breintnall was, as Franklin said in the *Autobiography*, "a great Lover of Poetry reading all he could meet with, and writing some that was tolerable."[43]

Proof exists of the continuing reputation of Lewis. Not only did many of his contemporaries flourish into the mid-eighteenth century, but later immigrants with literary interests, such as the Reverend Thomas Cradock (who arrived in Maryland in 1742) knew his poetry. In "The Maryland Divine," an imitation of Virgil's fourth eclogue, Cradock satirized the irreligious ministers and citizens of Maryland. As he concludes the poem, Cradock says that if his abilities were commensurate with his desire, he would write more on this subject and that *not even* Lewis would be read with more admiration and respect:

Oh had I strength but equal to my Will,
These glorious Wights shou'd be my Subject still;
Nor shou'd e'en Lewis, poor, unhappy Bard,[h]

---

[43] "The Busy-Body No. 5" is printed in Leonard Woods Labaree, ed., *The Papers of Benjamin Franklin* 1 (New Haven, 1959):127–33; see 130. For Breintnall, in addition to the note in the Franklin *Papers* (1:114), see F. B. Tolles, "A Note on Joseph Breintnall," *Philological Quarterly* 21 (1942):247–49, and J. Philip Goldberg, "Joseph Breintnall and a Poem in Praise of Jacob Taylor," *Pennsylvania Magazine of History and Biography* 86 (1962):207–209.

Be read with more Delight or more Regard.
Lewis, on whom the Muse her Favours Shed
And yet to want her Favourite betray'd.

Obviously Cradock and the litterateurs of Pre-Revolutionary Maryland held Lewis in high esteem. Cradock's note "h" comments that Lewis was a good poet and also that he, like so many men of the eighteenth century, was irreligious (we have seen that he was a scientific deist—Cradock's note suggests that Lewis, like Franklin, was not a Christian): "A gentleman, who has a pretty Vein in Poetry, & like other sons of Parnassus, was very poor; he was also a fine Gentleman, & laught at Religion with the rest."[44]

A recent survey of American topographical poetry of the late eighteenth century concluded: "The widespread currency of poems that delineated the variety and grandeur of American nature lays open to doubt claims that Philip Freneau was 'The pioneer nature-poet in America' and that he 'heralded our literary independence, so far as themes are concerned, by bringing into poetry for the first time truly American nature.'"[45] Of course these claims are false. Richard Lewis preceded Freneau and the poets of the late eighteenth century by fifty years. Clearly American nature was one of his favorite and best subjects. Although the number of Freneau's poems nearly as good as "The Wild Honeysuckle" suggests that Freneau's achievement is greater than Lewis's, Freneau is not a better nature poet.

The investigation of colonial American poetry has hardly begun. Those few poets generally known to the student of today are the ones included in the first anthologies of American poetry made by the Connecticut Wits and their friends at the end of the eighteenth century—featuring, naturally enough, the Connecticut Wits and their friends. The Connecticut Wits were aware of the seventeenth and early eighteenth century New England writers, but not of those from the Southern, or even the Middle, colonies. Colonial America may, in this respect, be compared to medieval Europe: the literary achievements of one generation in one area were largely unknown to those of a later generation in a different location. The few books of poetry published before the American Revolution were unknown and un-

---

[44] Cradock Papers, MS 196, Maryland Historical Society. The fair copy of the fourth eclogue gives only the first and last initials of Lewis's name, but the name is spelled out in a draft of the poem, also in the Cradock Papers. I am grateful to my friend Professor David Curtis Skaggs for this reference.
[45] Eugene L. Huddleston, "Topographical Poetry," 310.

available to later writers in a different colony. Broadsides and newspapers were ephemeral. Even today, after more than a century of assiduous collecting and despite the bibliographies of early American literature, many poems and poets are irretrievably lost. But what remains has been inadequately assessed. One thing is certain. Lewis is better than the usual handful of colonial neoclassic poets mentioned in the literary histories: William Livingston, Benjamin Colman, Benjamin Church, or (the best of them) Joseph Green and Mather Byles.

No other neoclassic American poet was so widely reprinted; and, indeed, it is practically impossible to imagine a cultivated, well-educated man of the time caring for any other contemporary American poet, in the way that the following quotation shows that Edward Kimber (later editor of the *London Magazine*) cared for Richard Lewis:

> The next Night we got to the Line that divides *Maryland* from *Virginia*, being about 30 miles, thro' a Road whose delightful Scenes constantly refresh'd the Senses with new and beauteous Objects. And here I can't help quoting Mr. Lewis, when speaking of another Road in this Colony, he says,
>
>> But now the enclos'd plantation I forsake,
>> And onwards thro' the woods my journey take;
>> The level road the longsome way beguiles,
>> A blooming wilderness around me smiles;
>> Here hardy *oak*, there fragrant *hick'ry* grows
>> . . . .
>> Here stately *pines* unite their whisp'ring heads,
>> And with a solemn gloom embrown the shades.
>> See there a green savanna opens wide,
>> Thro' which smooth streams in wanton mazes glide;
>> Thick branching shrubs o'erhang the silver streams
>> Which scarcely deign t' admit the solar beams.
>
> And, indeed, I can't help, every now and then, taking him out of my Pocket in this Country; for his descriptive Part is just and fine, and such a Warmth of Sentiment, such a delicate Vein of Poetry, such an unaffected Piety runs thro' the Whole, that I esteem it one of the best Pieces extant.[46]

Richard Lewis's major achievement was to make American nature a suitable subject for poetry. Two-thirds of a century later, William

---

[46] [Edward Kimber], "Itinerant Observations," 327–28. For an account of Kimber, see Sidney A. Kimber, "'Relation of a late expedition to St. Augustine,' with biographical and bibliographical notes on Isaac and Edward Kimber," *Papers of the Bibliographical Society of America* 28 (1934):81–96.

Bartram made American nature a great subject for prose; and at approximately the same time, Philip Freneau took up the very themes that Lewis and the innumerable lesser poets had used in their verse since 1730. Richard Lewis was the first important American nature poet, and the finest Augustan poet of the New World.

MID-EIGHTEENTH-CENTURY LITERATURE

THE CLUB

3

Between 1740 and 1770, the population of Maryland increased from slightly over 100,000 to more than 200,000. By 1750, with an estimated 141,073 people, the colony had numerous small towns and a capital that attracted itinerant lecturers and entertainers and traveling theater companies. From the Chesapeake Bay and the navigable rivers, there stretched, as far as the eye could see, plantations and small villages. The wilderness had vanished from the tidewater area and from much of the Piedmont plateau. The Reverend James Sterling traced the destruction of the wilderness in a poem on the planter's progress. When "a large wild Bear" rampaged across several tidewater plantations killing hogs, the event was uncommon enough to be newsworthy, appearing in the *Maryland Gazette* for August 2, 1753. Buffalo were featured as rarities kept in gardens. Even the rattlesnakes had almost disappeared from the lowlands: when one "of prodigious size" was killed near Cambridge in Dorchester County, it was reported in the paper for August 10, 1748. At the same time that the wilderness was disappearing east of the Appalachian mountains (the second third of the eighteenth century), life on the frontier was crystallizing into a distinctive culture that had borrowed and adapted many aspects of Indian life. The earliest name for the frontiersman, *buckskin*, was recorded in 1743, revealing that the frontiersmen themselves had by then a sense of the distinctiveness of their way of life.

King Tobacco still reigned supreme in Maryland's economy, but with the increasing settlement of the Piedmont plateau and with the rapidly growing German population, corn and wheat were assuming an important place in the colony's agriculture. Samuel Galloway had a shipyard on West River within two miles of his plantation, Tulip Hill, and in 1765, a French traveler recorded that this small shipyard had already built several vessels. By the middle of the eighteenth century, the various ironworks near Baltimore were making fortunes for their owners; and land speculation was an important sector of the economy. Despite the diversification of the Maryland economy, purportedly the richest man in America in 1749 was Richard Bennett, a tobacco planter and merchant whose major plantation was on the Wye River, on the Eastern Shore. Not far from Bennett's, Robert Morris, the father of the financier of the American Revolution, also made his fortune as a planter and merchant. Slightly earlier, Anthony Bacon, who became one of England's wealthiest tycoons, got his start as a factor in the Maryland tobacco trade. The price of tobacco remained the index to Maryland's economy.

The planters were no longer isolated. In the golden age of colonial culture, the club was a dominant social institution. Nearly every colonial tavern was the home of at least one club, whose members meeting daily, weekly, fortnightly, or monthly, gathered together to drink, talk, and play music. The freemasons was the best-known international club of the day; during this period, lodges started at several Maryland towns, including Annapolis, Chester, and Upper Marlborough. When Dr. Alexander Hamilton journeyed through the Middle and New England colonies in the summer of 1744, he visited a variety of clubs, from the drunken club which he found just leaving Tradaway's Tavern, in the country near Joppa, Maryland, to the aristocratic Governor's Club which met every evening at the Old Tun Tavern in Philadelphia. He enjoyed clubs with specialized interests, like the physicians' Physical Club at Boston, which met at the Sun Tavern, where Dr. William Douglass dictated to a group of followers; the Music Club of Philadelphia, where Tench Francis played an excellent violin that had earlier belonged to Governor Charles Calvert of Maryland; and the Philosophical Club of Newport, which met every Monday evening to discuss science. More typical were the daily clubs meeting at Withered's tavern in Boston, where a "pot bellyd doctor" presided and the Hungarian Club, which met at Todd's Tavern in New York and included the New Jersey poet Archibald Home.

The most famous colonial Maryland club (only Franklin's Junto is better known) was Dr. Alexander Hamilton's Tuesday Club. After flourishing for over ten years, it influenced succeeding Maryland clubs: both the Forensic Club (1759–63) and the Homony Club (1770–73) imitated the apparatus which Hamilton created for the Tuesday Club. The Reverend Jonathan Boucher, the leading literary light of the Homony Club, left references to the Tuesday Club mock name for the Reverend Thomas Bacon, thus revealing Boucher's knowledge of, and indebtedness to, the Tuesday Club. The accounts of Baltimore's nineteenth-century Delphian Club suggest that the Tuesday Club traditions were still influential in Maryland a century later. According to Hamilton's rather fanciful chapter on the history of Maryland clubs in his "History of the Tuesday Club," a number of groups, such as the Red House Club and the Ugly Club, preceded the Tuesday Club. Newspaper references exist to the Loyal Club of Upper Marlborough, and various records, including membership lists, testify to the activities of "The Loyal and Ancient South River Club."

Amateur musicians like Henry Callister, the Reverend Thomas Bacon (whose musical compositions were esteemed by contemporaries in Ireland and England, as well as in America), James Hollyday, and Samuel Chamberlaine, banded together and constituted themselves a musical society. When the "famous Signior Palma" (Juan di Palma) visited the Eastern Shore with his harpsichord, there took place, according to Bacon, "the most delightful concert America can afford." A plethora of Annapolis musical talent was drawn upon freely by the Tuesday Club: the Reverend Alexander Malcolm, author of a standard eighteenth-century musical treatise, played second violin; the Reverend Thomas Bacon played first violin; Jonas Green played the French horn; William Lux played the harpsichord; Samuel Hart, the flute; Thomas Richison, the dulcimer; Daniel Dulany, Jun., Robert Morris, and John Woolaston played the violin; and Hamilton and Bacon played a variety of instruments. When the professional musician and actor Charles Love (whom Hamilton judged "expert") visited the Tuesday Club in early July, 1755, he rendered the "Quaker Sermon" on the violin. The club as a dominant social institution implied a convivial group, often with interest in a special subject such as literature, music, politics, or science. By the mid-eighteenth century, Maryland and the other colonies had a sufficient population for the existence of numerous clubs.

After William Parks finally abandoned his Maryland printing operation, the way was clear for another printer. Jonas Green moved to Annapolis and set up shop in 1738, but his finances were evidently too precarious to risk printing belletristic material immediately. When Green started the *Maryland Gazette* in 1745, the last and major flourishing of colonial Maryland literature began. Green personally knew the Philadelphia printers and most of the New England printers. He established exchanges not only with the printers to the north of Annapolis but also with Parks in Williamsburg and with the succession of printers in Charleston. Green offered to print Dr. Alexander Hamilton's writings and undoubtedly asked the Scots doctor to help him secure literary materials for the paper. Hamilton provoked a literary war with two Baltimore poets, the Reverend Thomas Chase and the Reverend Thomas Cradock, and attacked them with burlesque essays in the paper. The "Annapolis Wits" versus the "Baltimore Bards" enlivened the early issues of Green's paper. When the *Maryland Gazette* was just over three years old, Hamilton wrote a literary history of the newspaper, criticizing his contemporaries in a full assessment of the colony's literary scene. Green began printing sermons in 1746 and issued his first almanac in 1750. But he did not publish broadside verse, and his only volume of poetry was Thomas Cradock's *A New Version of the Psalms* (Annapolis, 1756).

During the summer of 1744, Dr. Alexander Hamilton kept a travel diary, the *Itinerarium*, when he journeyed by horse from Annapolis to Maine and back, visiting all the major population centers along the way, and commenting on the art, music, literature, pastimes, personalities, and social conditions. Thus we have a fascinating picture of the colonial American scene. Within a year of his return, Hamilton organized the Tuesday Club, had himself elected secretary, and began the voluminous and painstaking minutes. He revised and re-revised the minutes, recorded the poems that Jonas Green wrote for the special club occasions, and transcribed the music that the Reverend Thomas Bacon composed for Green's odes. The Tuesday Club was a mock imitation of English society and history, burlesquing the forms sacred to English society from a point of view that combined the Scriblerian tradition and the supposedly ignorant American barbarian outlook. In addition to writing essays for the newspaper, Hamilton composed a comic mock history that, while imitating well-known English historians, combined the form of Fielding's *Tom Jones* with the attitudes of *The Memoirs of Martinus Scriblerus*, and thus produced a humorous mock epic, "The History of the Tuesday Club."

Generally recognized by his contemporaries as Maryland's best poet of the mid-eighteenth century was the Reverend James Sterling, who had achieved some renown as a playwright and poet before becoming a clergyman and emigrating to America in 1737. Sterling versified most of the significant public events of the day and specialized in light complimentary poems and *vers de société*. He also composed progress-pieces which used the *translatio* motif and applied the developing sentimental traditions to American subjects. *The Poetical Works of the Rev. James Sterling* was published in Dublin in 1734—but the poetry that he wrote in Maryland between 1737 and 1763 is more interesting and has never before been assessed or even, in great part, identified.

Since Maryland was known as the most lucrative colony for Anglican priests, many prominent ministers settled there. Those with literary reputations included Henry Addison, William Brogden, Thomas Chase, Thomas Cradock, John Gordon, Jacob Henderson, and Hugh Jones—but none outshone the Reverend Thomas Bacon. Although best known as the compiler of the most beautifully printed book of colonial America, *The Laws of Maryland* (1765), Bacon was a preacher of extraordinary ability—and a poet, musician, composer, and political writer. His sermons on the education of slaves and on charity schools were frequently reprinted in England. He published more titles than any other Maryland writer. In an age when clergymen dominated literature and society, Bacon led the Maryland clergy.

Although the earlier major Maryland poets, Cook and Lewis, were not known personally by Green, Hamilton, Sterling, or Bacon, the latter authors heard anecdotes about them and knew their work. Some of the earlier literary men, like Daniel Dulany, the Reverend Jacob Henderson, and the Reverend Hugh Jones, were still active. Four of the seven founding members of the Tuesday Club—William Cumming, Robert Gordon, John Lomas, and Captain William Rogers —had subscribed in 1728 to Richard Lewis's first publication, the *Muscipula*, along with Hamilton's brother, Dr. John Hamilton. Other *Muscipula* subscribers who visited the club include Nathaniel and Samuel Chew, John Galloway, Richard Hill, James Hollyday, Philip Key, Michael Macnemara, John Ross (to whom Lewis dedicated a poem), and Colonel Richard Tilghman. Two Virginia subscribers to the *Muscipula*, the Honorable Philip Lee and Colonel George Mason, were still alive; and the Virginia poet and planter, John Mercer, who loaned Cook money, published poetry in Green's *Maryland Gazette*. William Parks himself lived until 1750, and his file of early publications was consulted by such mid-century figures as Stephen Bordley.

In mid-century Philadelphia, at least Benjamin Franklin and Joseph Breintnall were among the men of letters who had known the works of Cook and Lewis. Although the identities and works of Cook and Lewis were unknown to American scholars in the nineteenth and early twentieth centuries, it would be a mistake to suppose that they were unknown to or had no influence on the writers who immediately followed them; and the same, of course, is true of Green, Hamilton, Sterling, and Bacon, for their immediate successors, the authors of the Revolutionary and Early National periods.

The eighteenth century was an age of litterateurs and intellectuals. Writing was a fashion as well as an avocation. Men of learning prided themselves upon their essays, poems, and letters—which they cultivated as assiduously and with the same general public interest as today's population cultivates sports. Although there were no professional men of letters in colonial America (it would require at least two more generations before American society was sufficiently large to support, however meanly, professional writers), there can be no doubt that such litterateurs as "Loquacious Scribble" (as Dr. Hamilton dubbed himself) and the Reverend James Sterling (none of whose literary manuscripts are extant) were prolific writers—and as such were not atypical of their time.

*J*ONAS GREEN

P. P. P. P. P.

Jonas Green, public printer of Maryland from 1738 until his death in 1767, was a master printer of colonial America. His edition of Thomas Bacon's *Laws of Maryland* "was not exceeded in dignity and beauty by any production of an American colonial press."[1] He was also a poet and, with Dr. Alexander Hamilton, a leading wit of the Tuesday Club. Green carefully kept a file of the *Maryland Gazette* (which he published from 1745 to 1767) which is still extant at the Maryland State Library—a beautiful and complete file of a major colonial newspaper. As the Tuesday Club poet laureate, he was often called upon by the club for a poem—sometimes to the members' consternation and regret. He wrote numerous anonymous pieces for his newspaper and was famous for his punning articles (his delightfully outrageous puns turn up even in such unlikely places as an obituary and the announcement of the Stamp Act's enactment). As the publisher of the Reverend Thomas Bacon's sermons, Henry Callister's natural history essays, the Reverend Thomas Chase's poems and sermons, the Reverend Thomas Cradock's poems and translations, the Reverend John Gordon's sermons, Dr. Alexander Hamilton's satires and acute criticism, the Reverend Hugh Jones's sermons and anti-Catholic propaganda, the Reverend James Sterling's poems and sermons, Dr. Adam Thomson's poetry and medical essays, and of John Webb(e)'s political essays—and as the publisher of a host of anony-

---

[1] Lawrence C. Wroth, a *History of Printing in Colonial Maryland*, 95. Wroth's account of Green, 75–94, and the list of Green's imprints, 185–230, are invaluable.

mous, minor writers in the *Maryland Gazette*—Green made a major contribution to colonial Maryland's literature.

Jonas Green was descended from a family of printers. His grandfather, Samuel Green (who arrived in America on September 4, 1633), had succeeded the Dayes (first printers in America) as the printer in Cambridge, Massachusetts. Timothy, Jonas Green's father, was born in Cambridge in 1679, served his apprenticeship there, and printed in Boston before moving to New London to become Connecticut's public printer in 1713. Timothy Green married Mary Flint in Boston on January 28, 1702, and their son Jonas was born in Boston on December 28, 1712. Jonas Green grew up and learned the printing business in New London.[2]

In 1734 Jonas Green worked for the Boston printing firm of Kneeland and Green, and in 1735 he independently printed in Boston the earliest American imprint in Hebrew, *Dickdook leshon gnebreet, A Grammar of the Hebrew Tongue*, by Judah Monis. In 1736, he evidently moved to Philadelphia and worked as a journeyman printer for Andrew Bradford; he is entered as a Philadelphia resident in the list of subscribers to Thomas Prince, *A Chronological History of New England* (Boston, 1736). On November 24, 1737, Green wrote a letter to Mr. "Nathan Prince, Fellow of Harvard College," which was sent free under Franklin's name. Green reminds Prince that he sent him word by the last post that he had not had time "since my arrival here[3] . . . to get so ample an account of the Aurora which was seen on the 11th of August last 1737, as you desired of me." He had asked Franklin about the display, but Franklin had referred him to Joseph Breintnall, "a gentleman very observant of such things." Green enclosed Breintnall's account and apologized for not making notes on the display: "You may remember that I told you at Boston that I took but very little notice of it." He also told Prince of the most recent notable natural curiosity: "Last Saturday Evening precisely at Five, a Meteor was Seen in the Air, by many in this city."[4]

About the latter part of November, 1737, Jonas Green printed his

[2] Wroth's account of Green's family, 67–76, is supplemented and corrected by William C. Kiessel, "The Green Family, A Dynasty of Printers," *New England and Genealogical Register* 104 (1950):81–93.

[3] The contents make it obvious that Green had returned to Boston for a visit shortly before he wrote the letter.

[4] Jonas Green to Nathan Prince, Nov. 24, 1737. MSS, Historical Society of Pennsylvania.

first work for the Maryland colony. Governor Samuel Ogle wrote, on November 22, 1737, that he was having "a good Number of Proclamations printed" in Philadelphia, "as we have not a Press here at present."[5] When the agent sent these proclamations to Philadelphia for printing, Green saw an opportunity to set up in business for himself. He secured Bradford's permission and printed these documents under his own name as an example of his ability.[6] The scheme worked. On May 9, 1738, a bill was introduced into the Maryland Assembly to make Green the public printer. An advertisement in the *American Weekly Mercury*, April 13, 1738, reveals that he was still working for Bradford. He probably moved to Annapolis shortly after his marriage to Anne Catherine Hoof in Christ Church, Philadelphia, on April 25, 1738. Since he was paid for being public printer to the province for 1738, and since his first child, John, was born on October 18, 1738, in Annapolis,[7] Jonas Green moved to Annapolis and began printing there in this year—but no issue from his press for 1738 is extant.

Unlike William Parks, Jonas Green did not immediately stimulate literary activity. No belletristic writings appeared during his first seven years in Maryland. Although no Maryland poets as good as Richard Lewis were writing at this time, several (notably the Reverend James Sterling and Dr. Adam Thomson) were productive. The reason for Green's lack of literary publications was probably financial. He evidently went into debt to set up his printing shop; Parks had been an established printer, with his own shop, before emigrating to America. We know that on November 5, 1743, Green borrowed £43 15s. current money of Maryland from Daniel Dulany. Furthermore, Green's unpaid debt to Franklin proves that the Marylander remained short of cash.[8] But after he started the *Maryland Gazette* in

---

[5] Quoted in Douglas C. McMurtrie, *A History of Printing in the United States* ... Vol. II, *Middle and South Atlantic States* (New York, 1936), 425 n. 19.

[6] Lawrence C. Wroth, "A Maryland Proclamation of 1737," in "Notes for Bibliophiles," *New York Herald Tribune*, Oct. 31, 1926. See also Wroth's "A Correction," ibid., Nov. 14, 1926. Wroth, however, was mistaken in thinking that Green was working for Franklin in Philadelphia: Green's advertisement in the *American Weekly Mercury* for Apr. 13, 1738, reveals that he was working for Bradford. The note in the *Mercury* for Jan. 24, 1737/8, signed "J. G.," apologizing for a printing error in the preceding week's *Mercury* is probably by Green.

[7] St. Ann's Parish Register, 1:123, Maryland Historical Society.

[8] Leonard Woods Labaree et al., eds., *Papers of Benjamin Franklin* 7:277, and 9:388. Deeds, Anne Arundel County, 1743, Liber RB1, folio 325, Maryland Hall of Records.

1745, he presented poetry, essays, and hoaxes in the paper; after he was well established, he printed a number of major works (e. g., Thomas Cradock's *A New Version of the Psalms* . . . 1765) which probably failed to meet printing costs.

With the appearance of Jonas Green's newspaper, literature began to flourish in colonial Maryland. The first issue of the *Maryland Gazette*, January 17, 1744/5, contained an editorial on "The Advantage of a Newspaper." Jonas Green claimed that a newspaper makes public "whatsoever is useful and entertaining, at home or abroad." He intends to publish "a Weekly Account of the most remarkable Occurrences . . . having always a principal Regard to such Articles as nearest concern the American Plantations in general, and the Province of Maryland in particular." Whenever news is lacking, he will publish "the best Materials we can possibly collect." The editor asks his literary correspondents and "ingenious" friends for their writings:

> We take this opportunity of making Application to our Learned Correspondents, whose ingenious Productions, if with such we shall at any Time be favoured, will ever find a Place in this Paper, and lay the Printer under the greatest Obligations; provided whatsoever is transmitted of this Kind, be consistent with Sobriety and good Manners.

Since the public has long wished for a paper, he hopes that people will subscribe "in a sufficient Number . . . whereby the Printer may be enabled to carry on and continue it's Publication." Concluding, Green announces the price ("Twelve Shillings, Maryland Currency, per annum, unsealed; or Fourteen Shillings if sealed and directed") and reveals a justifiable pride in his new types: it "will be Printed on a good Paper, and a beautiful new Letter, the same with this Specimen."

Green was at first unable to continue the paper, for the next issue (the first was January 17) was not published until April 26 and was again labeled "No. 1." Thereafter, the *Maryland Gazette's* publication was uninterrupted until the Stamp Act crisis in 1765. His correspondents responded wholeheartedly to the suggestion that they submit poems and essays. He printed the following note on April 26:

> We have received several Pieces, both in Prose and Verse, from our ingenious Correspondents, which for Want of Room we are obliged to postpone; assuring the Authors that they will be inserted the first Opportunity; and hoping that this seeming Neglect will not in the least occasion a Discontinuance of the Favours conferred by Communications of this Kind.

The first belletristic work in Green's *Maryland Gazette* was an Addisonian essay by "Phil-Eleutherus" on the usefulness and value of studying history. In this same issue of June 7, 1745, Green told his correspondents that he was not going to publish indiscriminately: "Two Leters signed Publicolo, we have received; but they are too prolix, and the Subject has been too often handled, to find a Place in this Paper." On June 14, Green published the first poetry in his paper, "Juba's" 45-line poem "To the Ladies of Maryland." A story of July 12, 1745, is typical of colonial America's best news reporting. The *Cunliffe*, under Captain John Pritchard, bound to Liverpool from Virginia, was attacked by a French privateer on January 7, 1745. In a fierce battle, Pritchard and the crew valiantly defended the ship, which safely "arrived at Liverpool on the 18th of January, with a valuable cargo." A passenger aboard the *Cunliffe* wrote an account of the action, describing the battle and the heroic death of Captain John Pritchard, an old Maryland hand. Green printed a long extract from this account as well as the formal epitaph on Pritchard.[9]

The major literary men of Maryland soon appeared in the *Maryland Gazette*. Dr. Adam Thomson first contributed on November 8, 1745, under his usual pseudonym, "Philo-Muses." In the *Gazette* for December 17, 1745, the literary war between the "Annapolis Wits" and the "Baltimore Bards" came to print. "An infallible Receipt to cure the afflicting and epidemical Distempers of Love, and Poetical Itch," by an Annapolis wit in Dr. Alexander Hamilton's circle, satirized the Reverend Thomas Cradock's poetry. The next issue, December 24, 1745, contained an undistinguished poem of 134 lines "To the Ladies," by "Emolpus." Hamilton's sprightly satire on the commonplace greeting "What News?" was the first thoroughly enjoyable local essay to appear in the paper—January 7, 1745/6. Hereafter, Hamilton and his friend and former Edinburgh school fellow, Dr. Thomson, are frequent contributors to the paper. Hamilton as "Theophilus Polypharmacus," in the *Gazette* for February 4, 1746, continued the literary battle with the Baltimore Bards; and the concluding blow, Hamilton's attack on the Reverend Thomas Chase, was a mock advertisement in the March 18, 1745/6 issue. (The "Annapolis Wits" versus the "Baltimore Bards" is recounted in the next chapter.)

Green also printed items that reflected his scientific interest, like

[9] Pritchard's epitaph is reprinted in the *William and Mary Quarterly* 11 (1954):559–60. Unfortunately, the Liverpool pamphlet containing the account of the battle is no longer extant.

the notice, March 4, 1745/6, of the aurora borealis which "extended a full Quarter of the Compass" and "reach'd near 50 Degrees towards the Zenith." The first local political essay appeared in Green's *Maryland Gazette*, April 1, 1746, when "A. B." (who may have been Daniel Dulany or Robert Morris) proposed a new tobacco law.[10] "Q. B." answered on April 22, and "A. B." replied on May 13. The quarrel continued in the issues for June 17, August 26, and October 28; political journalism is thereafter common in Green's newspaper.

An intercolonial literary quarrel concerned the number of Catholics in Maryland. A Maryland writer on November 5, 1746, took issue with a *New York Weekly Post Boy* article which had been republished in the *Maryland Gazette* on October 21; and the New Yorker's reply was reprinted in the *Maryland Gazette* for March 24, 1747. A more amusing literary quarrel began on April 14, 1747, when Green reprinted the speech of the "Honourable Sir William Gooch, Baronet, his Majesty's Lieutenant-Governor and Commander in chief of the Colony and Dominion of Virginia" to the General Assembly, with the Assembly's answer. On June 16, 1747, Green reprinted Franklin's free-verse parody of the speech. When Green wrote to Franklin on July 25, telling him that he was busy with the public work and that he wished he could get another workman, he also apologized for not paying Franklin and asked him to send down another supply of paper. The letter reveals that Green printed about 600 copies of his paper, "I have about 450 or 460 good Customers for Seal'd Papers, and about 80 unseal'd." Commenting on Benjamin Franklin's poem, Green wrote, "The Virginian's Speech made a deal of Laughter here; and was well approved of by some in that Colony; how the Baronet himself lik'd it I have not heard"[11]

Perhaps Green's compliment influenced Franklin to send Green one of his most famous works. On August 11, 1747, Green printed Franklin's "The Speech of Miss Polly Baker." Green said that the

[10] St. George Leakin Sioussat, *Economics and Politics*, 70 n. 4, suggested that "A. B." was Daniel Dulany. Dr. Alexander Hamilton's respectful treatment of "A. B." lends credence to the suggestion. J. A. Leo Lemay, "Hamilton's Literary History of the *Maryland Gazette*," William and Mary Quarterly, 3d. ser. 23(1966):277. A contemporary, however, wrote that Robert Morris (d. 1750) "gave birth to the inspection law on tobacco–& carried it–though opposed by a powerful party." Charles Henry Hart, ed., "Robert Morris, of Oxford, Md. Extracts from a Manuscript Narrative of the Principal Incidents in the Life of Jeremiah Banning. Written by Himself in 1793," in William F. Boogher, *Miscellaneous Americana* (Washington, D. C., 1895), 45.
[11] Leonard Woods Labaree et al., eds., *Papers of Benjamin Franklin* 3:154.

"following very famous SPEECH has been published in the *London* and *Gentleman's Magazines* for *April* past, as well as in some of the other *British* Papers; but was there printed incorrectly, which, I suppose was occasioned by the Mutilation it suffer'd, in passing through the Hands of Transcribers before it reach'd the Press in *London*: And happening to have a correct Copy of it by me, I cannot think it amiss to give it my Readers, not doubting it's favorable Reception." Although this printing obviously has a different textual authority (which was, according to Green, better), the London text is nevertheless generally accepted as standard. There are, however, good literary reasons which no one has previously indicated for believing that this text is closer to Franklin's original than the London printings.

The longest essay in the *Maryland Gazette* was submitted by Daniel Dulany, who said that it had been given to him anonymously.[12] Dulany praised the essay, which was published in installments on December 9, 16, 23, and 30, 1747. Dulany noted that "an Essay on the Means of Improving the Trade of Maryland" was written "before the passing of the Inspection Law" for tobacco, but that its suggestions were still pertinent.[13] Not infrequently, the same essay appealed to several newspaper editors: when Green reprinted "The Prevalence of Luxury, with a Burgo-Master's excellent admonition against it" in the *Gazette* for March 9, 1747/8, he may not have known that it had already appeared in every major town in the colonies—in the *South Carolina Gazette*, August 24, 1747; the *New York Gazette*, December 21; the *Pennsylvania Journal*, December 29, 1747; and the *Boston Gazette*, January 19, 1747/8. Among other enjoyable colonial literary pieces that Green borrowed was Joseph Dumbleton's "A Rhapsody on Rum" which appeared in the *Maryland Gazette* for November 1, 1749.[14]

The most interesting and heated pre-Revolutionary political quarrel in Green's newspaper arose over the relatively minor issue of levying a tax in Prince Georges County to pay for rebuilding the county court house. In the first five months of 1748, the various parties to this pygmy crisis debated natural rights, taxation, theories of gov-

[12] See Dulany's note in the *Maryland Gazette* for June 2, 1747.
[13] The essay was reprinted in the *Maryland Gazette* for Mar. 9 and 16, 1758.
[14] This poem was printed in the *South Carolina Gazette* for Mar. 20, and the *Gentleman's Magazine* for Sept., 1749. It was reprinted in the *Maryland Gazette* from the *Virginia Gazette* of an unspecified date. For a brief account of some of Dumbleton's other poetry, see Hennig Cohen, *South Carolina Gazette*, 199, 203–204, and 211–13.

ernment, and the liberties of the individual, almost as though the Prince Georges County partisans foresaw that the American Revolution was only twenty-five years away and chose this unlikely pretext as an excuse to debate those doctrines which were going to assume such paramount importance in the Revolution. Green was happy to have good native materials (essays, stories, and poems) to publish; but, like all newspaper editors of the day, he preferred to publish material which the authors paid for. On March 10, 1746/7, he noted that "The Letter signed Philo-Symposius, in which was contained a Sum of Money, (an Example worthy of Imitation) is come to Hand, and will be inserted next week." When he received an essay on the Prince Georges County court house issue with a covering letter asking that the piece be inserted in the next paper, Green published a notice in the March 23, 1747/8, *Maryland Gazette* saying that it had just arrived and could not possibly be included in this issue, but that he would publish it the next day as a *Supplement* and "distribute it at Marlborough the same Day." He reminded the author that he expected "ample amends for my Trouble and Expence" and added that in party disputes, he was an impartial printer. In the following issue, he thanked the "Loyal Club at Upper Marlborough" for their "handsome Gratuity" which paid for the *Supplement*.

Jonas Green was sued for libel by Thomas Chose (or Chase) for an advertisement which appeared in the *Maryland Gazette* of July 28, 1747, written by James Richard, a Baltimore attorney. The advertisement attacked Richard Chase, Christopher Jukox, and Thomas Chose —all of Baltimore County—for spreading a false report about James Richard. When the case came before the Provincial Court on October 3, 1750, Green won, and subsequently published a notice of his vindication in the paper for October 10:

> Last Wednesday [October 3] came on, before the Honourable the Judges of the Provincial Court, then sitting, a Cause, wherein *Thomas Chose*, of *Baltimore* County, Clerk, was Plaintiff, and *Jonas Green*, of Annapolis, Printer, Defendant: The Action was brought for a (suppos'd) Libel, published in the MARYLAND GAZETTE of *July* 28, 1747, No. 118; and Damages were laid at Five Hundred Pounds. After a full Hearing, the Jury gave in their Verdict FOR THE DEFENDANT.

Green's subsequent suing of Thomas Chose for the cost of the case reveals that his lawyer was Daniel Dulany, Jr.[15]

[15] Provincial Court Judgments, EI no. 13, ff. 760–61, Maryland Hall of Records.

On the ninth anniversary of the *Maryland Gazette*, May 3, 1753, Green wrote an apologia, saying that he had been repeatedly abused because of the newspaper. But he hopes that the paper has been "useful, entertaining, and instructive" to most readers, and he knows that he has done his best to make it a good paper. But it is impossible to please everyone, especially the "byassed and prejudiced." (Of course, he intended the scurrilous pun.) And so he reaches the immediate occasion for his defense:

> All judicious and sensible Men will acknowledge the Advantage arising from a public Paper; and that This has been of some Use in this Province, I think I may be allowed to affirm, consistent with the Rules of Modesty, notwithstanding a severe Reflection lately passed upon it by a certain prolix Orator, in a very public Assembly, That it was the common Conveyancer of Scandal and Nonsense; and many other as good natured Observations, too tedious to repeat: A heavy Charge, if true! a charge of such a Nature, that had I asserted Half as much of that Gentleman in my Way, that is, put it in Print, which in effect could not have rendered it much more public than the Method he took with me, I might possibly have smarted for it; but it happens that in some Cases, a greater Liberty is allowed to the Tongue than the Press. All the Reply I shall make to the Usage of that learned and loquacious Gentleman, is, That in the Opinion of a great many, this bold Assertion of his had as much Truth in it, as it had Relation to the Argument he then had in Hand; and it is thought by some tolerable Judges, that had he, with his usual Assurance, Virbosity, and Vociferation, recited a Part of the old Ballad of Chevy Chace, to add Weight to his Reasoning, it might have served his Purpose as well, and been every whit as pertinent, as this [here] Charitable and Humane Reflection.

Green announced the birth of his children in the columns of his paper. The *Maryland Gazette* for December 23, 1746, reported the birth of his son "who is to have the honour of being named after that great General his Royal Highness Duke William." And another son, Frederick, was born "just as the Guns were Firing on account of the Birth of His Royal Highness the Prince of Wales" on January 20, 1749/50. Dr. Alexander Hamilton acted as surety for Green's son Frederick.[16]

---

[16] Most of Green's many children died in their infancy. John was born on Oct. 18, 1738, and died thirteen months and two days later. Rebecca was born on July 22, 1740, and married John Chapman, who was the poet laureate of Jonathan Boucher's Homony Club (which was modeled on the Tuesday Club). Jonas was born on Feb. 12, 1740/1, and died the following Dec.; Catherine, Nov. 4, 1743, to Oct. 28, 1744; Masia, Jan. 7, 1744/5, to Jan. 11; Mary was born on Jan. 9, 1745/6; William on Dec. 21, 1745; and Ann Catherine was born on Jan. 19,

In the "postscript" to the May 18, 1748, *Maryland Gazette*, Green advertised that he did bookbinding "in the neatest Manner," for he had "lately procur'd a good Workman, of that Business, from London." An earlier issue, March 18, 1745/6, reveals that he had two printers named Smith working for him. A correction note reads: "Our Entries last Week should have been Clearances: which Mistake was occasioned by a Blunder of Mr. (little) Smith's." Green confessed in an announcement that he ran in the summer and fall of 1749 that he was "in great want of Money."[17]

Dr. Alexander Hamilton started the Tuesday Club in 1746. A high point in the history of the club occurred when Jonas Green (after having told several members that he would like to join) was voted a member, on the motion of the Reverend John Gordon, February 2, 1747/8. Thereafter, Green and Hamilton were the life of the club. Green shortly was appointed "purveyor, punster, punchmaker General, printer, and poet" of the club—titles indicated by the abbreviation "P. P. P. P. P." In the "History of the Tuesday Club," Hamilton characterized Green:

> This gentleman is of a middle Stature, Inclinable to fat, round-faced, small lively eyes, from which, as from two oriental portals, incessantly dart the dawning rays of wit and humor, with a considerable mixture of the amorous leer, in his countenance he wears a constant smile, having never been once seen to frown; his body is thick and well-set, and for one of his make and stature he has a good sizeable belly, into which he loves much to convey the best vittles and drink, being a good clean knife and forks man, tho' no Glutton, and his favorite Dish is Roast turkey with oisters, and his darling liquor of late is Grog, he professing himself to be of the modern Sect of Grogorians, and as some think the patron and founder of that sect in Annapolis, which we shall have occasion to describe some where in this history, he is a very great admirer, Improver and encourager of wit, humor and drollery, and is fond of that sort of poetry which is called Doggerell, in which he is himself a very great proficient, and confines his genius chiefly to it, tho sometimes he cannot help emitting some flashes of the true sublime, in his club compositions:

1747/8, and died on Aug. 26, 1753. Frederick was born on Jan. 20, 1749/50. Deborah was born on Jan. 19, 1751/2,, and died on Oct. 17, 1761; Elizabeth, Nov. 10, 1753, to Sept. 30, 1755. A second Jonas was born on Aug. 29, 1755, and died on Dec. 26, 1756. Samuel was born on Apr. 27, 1757, and a second Rebecca was born on Apr. 4, 1760. St. Ann's Parish Register, i, 123, 129, 130, 133, 138, 142, 144, 156, 180, 204, 212, 219, 227, 234.

[17] *Maryland Gazette*, Aug. 2, Oct. 11, and Nov. 22, 1749.

puns, conundrums, merrytales and jests, are the favority subjects, on which he chuses to exercise his wit and talents, and we shall find him affording abundance of mirth to the club, in his compositions of this sort, in fine, to sum up all he is really a good humored, smooth tempered, merry, Jocose, and inoffensive companion, a man of the most happy Clubical Genius that ever was known, and a great promoter improver and encourager of Clublike felicity, for were there 50 clubs in the place, he'd be a member of every one of them; he is a passionate admirer of natural curiosities, and certain little knick knacks, produced by the whimsical Inventions of art, of which he has a valuable collection by him, some of which we may have occasioned to mention in this history.[18]

Green's first poetic effort of any length for the Tuesday Club was his "Anniversary Ode" on May 16, 1749, the club's third anniversary. Dr. Alexander Hamilton carried on a mock dispute with Green over who should have the honor of reading it, and the club ruled in favor of Green. The "Anniversary Ode" begins with a "Recitative":

> The Tuesday Club, let the sweet music sound,
> Whose fame is spread from west to eastern clime
> Honor'd in future annals shall be found,
> And Cole's great name endure to th' end of Time.

(Charles Cole, a wealthy, congenial elderly bachelor and leading Annapolis merchant, was President of the club.) Then comes the "Air":

> Her wholesome laws, contriv'd and penn'd so well
> Shall ages hence, her solid wisdom tell,
> In after clubs, a pattern she shall stand
> With that most beauteous Badge of hand in hand.

Next, the "Chorus" was sung by the club musician, William Thornton, to a tune that Samuel Hart, "an honorary member, a gentleman remarkable for his delicate pipes," improvised for the occasion: "Our President we honor and revere / Who most deserv'dly fills our stately chair." This is followed by three more "airs," two "Recitativos," and a concluding "Chorus."

At the club meeting on November 7, 1749, Green asked that his title be changed from "P. P. P. P. P." to "P. L. M. C.," for "Poetica Laureatus, Magister Ceremoniam." His wish was granted. He wrote a poem of thanks to Charles Cole for his sumptuous entertainment of the club on November 21, 1749, and delivered a poetical speech of

---

[18] Dr. Alexander Hamilton, "The History of the Tuesday Club," I, 345–46. MSS, Evergreen House, Johns Hopkins University Library.

thanks to the club's secretary, Hamilton, on December 5.[19] Green also undoubtedly had a large share in the poems by the "Conjoint Muses of the several members of the Club," such as the ones delivered on January 2, 1749/50 ("The Epeceedion of the ancient Tuesday Club, on the mournful Indisposition of Charles Cole Esqr"); on January 15, 1750/1 ("Lugubris Cantus"); and on February 20, 1752/3 ("Carmen Dolorosum").[20] Green's only acrostic was "To Mr. President Cole," which he read on February 27, 1749/50. His "Anniversary Ode" of May 15, 1750, was set to music by Thomas Bacon "in three parts, and to be sung and played on several Instruments."[21]

The following years were a high point in Green's poetic activity. He wrote an 84-line "Anniversary Ode" for the meeting on May 14, 1751.[22] His longest poem, declaimed on August 20, 1751, described the attempt to rob Charles Cole on the night of July 2. Green had reported the burglary in the *Maryland Gazette* for July 3, and by the middle of August, had prepared a facetious poem on the attempted robbery of the club's president:

> Dictate some gloomy muse, my verse
> While I the Tragic scene reherse,
> The tragic Scene, that had almost,
> Transformed his Lordship to a ghost,
> Till valiant John, from sleep uprising
> With courage bold and enterprizing
> Discharged the tremendous gun,
> That made the villain fire and run—[23]

Then Green sets the scene. It's nearly midnight, and Cole lies sleeping, dreaming of various machinations to employ against the members of the club. He hears a noise and cries for his servant, John. But when the door of his room opens, in comes a bandit brandishing a pistol. He grabs Cole by the throat with one hand:

> And while he struggled, well nigh choak'd
> Clap'd to his breast the pistol cock'd
> With—'Damn your blood, you old curmudgeon,
> 'Tis not for nought, I've scald your Lodging,
> 'Where is your money? Quickly tell,

[19] Dr. Alexander Hamilton, "The Records of the Tuesday Club," 163, 165, 173–74. MSS, Maryland Historical Society.

[20] Ibid., 187–88, 286; and Dulany Papers, 1753, Feb. 20, "Carmen Dolorosum," Maryland Historical Society.

[21] "Records," 204, 225–27.

[22] Ibid., 280.

[23] Ibid., 324.

'Or 'S Blood, I'll blow your Soul to hell,
'Your hoard of cash? declare old chuff
'Or damn you, I shall treat you Ruff.
(p. 326)

Green interrupts the action of his doggerel mock-epic to picture Cole's look:

Ah! have you never seen at all,
A Bass relief upon a wall,
Or antique bust or Statue, which
Sly artist cut on tomb or nitch,
Whose stony eye balls, dead and dark,
For ever fix on the same mark,
Whose marble Phiz, tho' hewn with skill
Is motionless and silent still,
His Lordship lookd, just such a look,
When hardy thief by gorge him took.
(pp. 326–27)

The thief ties Cole up, and Cole pleads for his life, saying that he has no money. After the bandit replies that he doesn't want Cole's life but his money, he tries to choke the information out of Cole. Then John, Charles Cole's servant, wakes up and looks out the window to see the bandit's accomplice, who levels his gun at John, warning him not to make a noise. But John ducks back, grabs a gun:

And quickly to the porthole run,
Where taking neither aim nor mark,
He fir'd her boldly in the dark,
For, as the rusty gun had not
Been loaded with or slug or shot,
He wisely judg'd, 'twas all the same,
To shoot at random, or to aim,
For he proposed no further harm,
Than the good neighbours to allarm,
That they assistance might afford,
In tribulation to my Lord.
(p. 328)

The bandit fires his pistol at John, just missing him, and then runs off. The bandit in Cole's room, hearing the alarm, jumps out the window and also flees. The aroused neighbors come but at first think that the burglary was a hoax, one saying that he would have Cole bound over to keep the peace. Cole shows his bound hands, and he and John tell their stories; the neighbors then begin to sympathize with them. Green opens his last stanza:

205

O valiant John, thy fame and glory
Shall cut a————in future story
Thy doughty deeds with wonder fill us,
Like those of Hector and Achilles,
Bards yet unborn shall sing thy praise,
And with thy name adorn their lays.

(p. 330)

Green continues his praise for John, claiming that without his help, the president of the club would have been murdered—and thereby "all" (i. e., those future lavish dinners) would have been lost. Green's travesty of 245 lines did not gain the approval of the club, and the members voted against including it in the minutes. "However in this second transcript of the Records, the Secretary takes upon him to exhibit a faithful copy of it as follows."[24]

On September 4, 1751, the editor published a mock essay, signed "Philo P. P. P.," which evidently alludes to Green. This *tour de force*, which uses the letter *p* as often as possible, is probably another example of Green's amusing ability. When Dr. Alexander Hamilton was absent, on September 17, 1751, Green wrote the minutes for the meeting in verse.[25] Another humorous Tuesday Club entry concerning Green is a long, mocking letter in the form of a legal remonstrance. On October 22, 1751, Green read "An humble Remonstrance ... by Jonas Green ... against Colly Cibber ... the authors and publishers of the Gentleman's and Universal Magazines, and all their abettors and adherents, whomsoever, and wheresoever." Green had sent some of his Tuesday Club poems to Anthony Bacon, the English delegate-at-large of the club, with the request that he publish them in the *Gentleman's* or *Universal* magazines. Bacon had submitted them, unsuccessfully. The brief is Green's remonstrance against the magazines for not publishing the occasional poems of the club (supposing them less important than the public poems on the king!) and against the execrable Colly Cibber, whom Green has imitated so well.[26]

Green declaimed his poem "A Mournful Episode" in the club on March 24, 1751/2, and read an "Anniversary Ode" on May 26, 1752. The latter was to have been "set to music in three parts, but never done, on account of the indisposition of Thomas Bacon." Green wrote a poetical "Lamentation" for the meeting of September 26,

[24] Ibid.
[25] Ibid., 329.
[26] Ibid., 336–40.

View here the Shadow whose Ingenious Hand
Hath drawne exact the Province Mary Land
Display'd her Glory in such Scænes of Witt
That those that read must fall in Love with it
For which his Labour hee deserves the praise
As well as Poets doe the wreath of Bays .

Anno Do: 1666. Ætatis Suæ 28 .   H.W.

An engraving of George Alsop, from the frontispiece of Alsop's *Character of the Province of Maryland* (London, 1666). Reproduced with the permission of the Huntington Library.

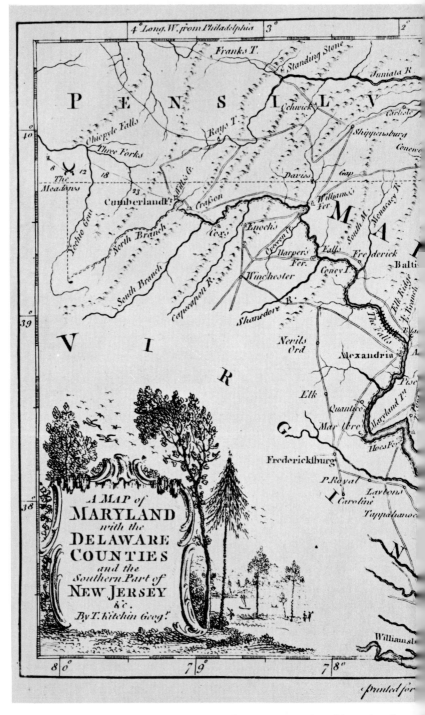

T. Kitchin's Map of Maryland from the *London Magazine* for

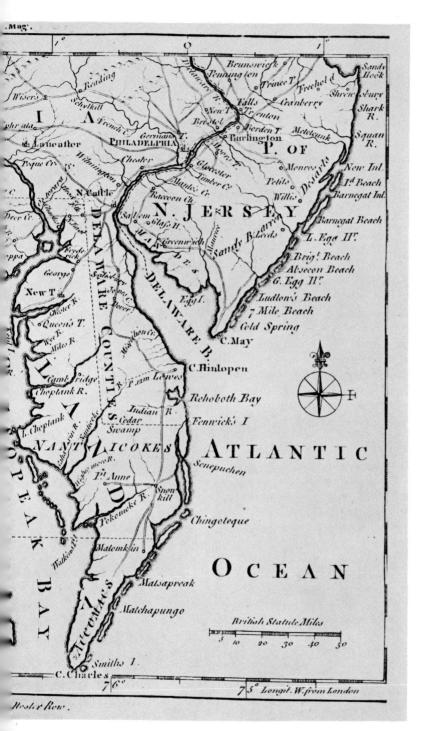

Dr. Alexander Hamilton's facetious caricature of himself as secretary of the Tuesday Club, holding the "RECORD OF THE TUESDAY CLUB." Reproduced from Hamilton's manuscript "The Record of the Tuesday Club" from the collections of the Maryland Historical Society.

1752. His second longest poem was presented at the meeting of October 26, 1752: "A Heroic Poem upon the late grand procession and parade of the Right Honorable Mr. President Cole, and his longstanding members of the ancient and honorable Tuesday Club, in three Cantos."[27] On the same night, Green (according to Hamilton) sang "with great vivacity and humor, the Song of Robin and Jack, and afterwards played it on the French horn."

Green presented his 47-line "Anniversary Ode" to the Tuesday Club on May 15, 1753, and Hamilton recorded his "Eulogium" on Charles Cole's most recent magnificent dinner for the club on November 6, 1753. The printer read "A Lamentable Ode" on Cole's sickness on February 15, 1754, and a "Congratulatory Ode" on Cole's return on March 5, 1754. He declaimed his last recorded "Anniversary Ode" to the club on June 11, 1754.[28] From Hamilton's long, mock-criticism of an anonymous poem that appeared in the *Maryland Gazette* for August 22, 1754, we may reasonably suppose that Green wrote it. Hamilton claimed that the anonymous production appeared to be in the style of their poet laureate. "Memorandum for a Seine-Hauling, in Severn River, near a delightful Spring at the foot of Constitution Hill,"[29] is an enjoyable 22-line poem, in the manner of Matthew Prior:

> Six Bottles of Wine, right old, good and clear;
> A Dozen at least, of *English* Strong Beer:
> Six Quarts of good Rum, to make Punch and Grogg,
> (The latter a Drink that's now much in vogue)
> Some Cyder, if sweet, would not be amiss:
> Of Butter six Pounds, we can't do with less.
> A Tea-Kettle, Tea, and all the Tea-Geer,
> To Treat the Ladies; and also Small Beer.
> Sugar, Lemons, a Strainer, likewise a Spoon;
> Two China Bowls to drink out of at Noon:
> A large piece of Cheese, a Table-Cloth too,
> A Sauce-Pan, two Dishes, and a Cork Screw:
> Some Plates, Knives and Forks, Fish Kettle, or Pot,
> And Pipes and Tobacco must not be forgot:
> A Frying Pan, Bacon or Lard for to Fry;
> A Tumbler and Glass to use when we're dry.
> A Hatchet, some Matches, a Steel and a Flint,
> Some Touch-wood, or Box with good Tinder in't.

[27] Ibid., 354–56, 368–70, 395–96, 400–13.
[28] Ibid., 435–36, 453–54, 463–64, 466–68, and 478–80.
[29] "History," 3:408–13. The poem has been reprinted in the *Maryland Historical Magazine* 52 (1957):251.

Some Vinegar, Salt, some Parsley and Bread,
Or else Loaves of Pone to eat in it's stead:
And for fear of bad Luck at catching of Fish,
Suppose we should carry—A READY DRESS'D DISH.
Annapolis, Aug. 20, 1754.

On September 24, 1754, Green read his 170-line poem "A Tragical and Heroic Episode on the Club Tobacco Box, Pyrated by the Chancellor." His "Extemporary Ode" on Cole's lavish entertainment on November 19, 1754, was made (according to Green) by invoking the Muse, while he was "indeed in the mews, or mew'd up." And on February 25, 1755, he delivered his last two poems to the Tuesday Club: one on the "City of Annapolis" and the other "A Congratulatory Pindaric Ode Addressed to the right Honorable Charles Cole . . . on his having escaped the Cruel Distemper of the Gout." [30]

In 1750 Jonas Green issued the first of his almanacs, which he continued throughout the colonial period. He had published sermons by John Gordon in 1745 and by Thomas Cradock in 1747, and in 1750 he published two sermons preached before the Annapolis Masonic Lodge, one by William Brogden and the other by John Gordon. He also brought out Thomas Bacon's Masonic sermon in 1753. (The three Masonic sermons mention the officers of the Annapolis Lodge; although the wardens are different in each case, Jonas Green always held the office of secretary.) The year 1755 saw the appearance of sermons by William Brogden and James Sterling.[31] Perhaps the influence of the "ancient and honourable" Tuesday Club and the eighteenth-century love for antiquity called forth Green's editorial statement in the March 28, 1750, *Maryland Gazette*, wherein he said that he was going to entertain his readers "with some musty Records from venerable Antiquity, which perhaps may suit their Humor and please them, as People are commonly very attentive to a detail of Occurrences that happened several Thousand Years Ago." He then published "Pulgah to his Daughter Shual, An Antediluvian Epistle," which appeared originally in Henry Baker's *Universal Spectator* and had been reprinted in several other colonial newspapers. Green's editorial statement probably influenced Thomas Bacon's poem, "A Letter, Originally wrote Three Thousand Years ago." [32]

[30] "Records," 500–503, 517–18, 542, 543–45.
[31] See the list of imprints in Wroth, 192–206.
[32] Henry Baker's essay had appeared in the *Universal Spectator*, no. 143, for July 3, 1731, and had been reprinted in the *New York Gazette* for Oct. 11; the

The "Virginia Gazette Day Book, 1750–1752" reveals that Green purchased printing supplies and books from the Williamsburg shop run by the successors of William Parks. Green paid £7 16s. 10½d. for a "Box of Printing Letter" on January 19, 1750/1, and took a shipment of books "with liberty of returning those unsold" on September 3, 1751.[33] He announced in the newspaper for October 5, 1752, that he was lowering the price of the paper from fourteen shillings to twelve shillings sixpence a year.

When Green published a news notice on September 14, 1752, about the time-change to the Gregorian calendar, he commented: "Reader, if the Distance of Time last mentioned (when you and I shall certainly have return'd to our Mother Earth, and be forgotten here, as tho's we had never been) to you seem Long, consider the Contrast, and you will find 'tis far less than a Moment, when compar'd to that Eternity to which we are hastening." Again, the printer couldn't resist moralizing when he printed a news notice, November 23, 1752, about the justices of Anne Arundel County ordering that an offender be whipped for swearing: "If every Magistrate, when out of Court, were to take due Notice of all profane Oaths, and punish the Offenders as the Law directs, without Exception, it would doubtless soon put a stop to that senseless, abominable, and wicked Practice." But Green also printed at least one essay that ridiculed Christianity. The essay signed "Nic Turntype" on the "mysteries" of printing in the *Maryland Gazette* for January 24, 1750, is really a deistic satire on the "mysteries" of religion. The *New York Weekly Journal* reprinted it on March 5, 1750.

Green was elected a "Common-council-man" of Annapolis on October 28, 1755, and he was one of the managers of a lottery for raising £435 to secure the Annapolis dock.[34] During the French and Indian War, he published a number of accounts of the fighting.[35] Like several other newspapers, the *Maryland Gazette* reprinted select numbers of the "Virginia Centinel" essay series.[36] Another product of a

---

Pennsylvania Gazette, Oct. 21; and the *New England Weekly Journal* for Nov. 1, 1731. Thomas Bacon's MS poem is in the Maryland Diocesan Society Library, now housed in the Maryland Historical Society.
[33] Photostats, Research Department, Colonial Williamsburg, Inc., 21 and 64.
[34] *Maryland Gazette*, Oct. 30, 1755, and Mar. 9, 1758.
[35] *Maryland Gazette*, Feb. 26, Mar. 11, 18, and 25, Apr. 1 and 8, July 8, Sept. 2, and Nov. 4, 1756.
[36] The only number of this series extant in the *Virginia Gazette* is the "Virginia Centinel No. X," which appeared Sept. 3, 1756. The *Maryland Gazette* for

Virginia pen, "The Stage Coach from Bourn, imitated, and Addressed to Mr. Hogarth," was published in the *Maryland Gazette* on October 13, 1756.[37] An important Virginia pamphlet that Green printed was John Camm's *A Single and Distinct View of the Act, Vulgarly entitled, The Two-Penny Act* (Annapolis, 1763), which played a part in provoking Patrick Henry's famous speech on the Two-Penny Act.

On June 15, 1758, Green published a humorous, punning article, "Properties of a Gardiner." Since a manuscript addition to the article appears in Green's personal newspaper file, it seems likely that he was the author. Two long articles on insects (the first Maryland essays on entomology), signed "C," are probably by Henry Callister.[38] With the deaths of Hamilton (1756) and Sterling (1763), Green lost his best and most frequent belletristic contributors. On November 26, 1761, he asked for "any divertive, instructive, emolumental Lucubrations" from his readers. The obituary that Green published on January 7, 1762 for "Mr. Henry Crouch, Carver, who was deem'd by good Judges to be as ingenious an Artist at his Business, as any in the King's Dominions," reveals his punning pen. Green concluded that "altho' Mr. Crouch had very little Notice taken of him, and lived somewhat obscurely, yet it must be allowed, that he cut a good Figure in life."

On July 29, 1762, he printed the front page of his newspaper in three different types, "new English, new small pica, and new long pica." The new type had just been imported to print Thomas Bacon's *Laws of Maryland*, a huge folio that occupied the printer for the next several years. When Benjamin Mifflin stopped by Green's on his way through Annapolis on August 2, 1762, he described Green's shop and garden:

Aug. 12, 1756, contains two numbers of the "Virginia Centinel," and the issue for Nov. 25 reprints "Virginia Centinel No. X." As I shall attempt to prove elsewhere, the author was probably the Reverend James Maury (1718–69).

[37] This is "By the Author *The Little Book*," a well-known, poetical miscellany evidently written by John Mercer. The poem is dated "Belmont on Occoquon in Virginia, 31st August 1757." See Richard Beale Davis, *The Colonial Virginia Satirist* (Philadelphia, 1967), and my review in the *Virginia Magazine of History and Biography* 75 (1967):491–93.

[38] *Maryland Gazette*, Dec. 21, 1758, and Apr. 5, 1759. The first article quotes George Adams's *Micrographia Illustrata* (London, 1746). Callister had Thomas Bacon's copy of Adam's *Micrographia Illustrata* in 1746—and had had it in his possession for several years. Calister Papers, 694. MSS, Maryland Diocesan Society Library, housed in the Maryland Historical Society.

Went with Jonas Green to View his printing office which is all below Capacious Airy and convenient—took a walk in his garden where among other things observed a tree which he call the Catolpect Tree planted about 10 years ago and is now about 9 inches thick about 25 feet high. The leaves are large as the Water Beach and grows in regular beautiful order much like the English Elm.[39]

Green vociferously opposed the Stamp Act and generally seems to have sided with the popular party. According to one historian, Green wrote articles signed "Cato" and "Lycurgus" against the Stamp Act—but I see no reason to attribute these to the printer. It was obviously Green's punning pen that informed the Marylanders that the hated Stamp Act had actually been passed: "Friday evening last, between nine and ten o'clock, we had a very smart thunder gust, which struck a house in one part of the town, and a tree in another. But we were more *thunderstruck* last Monday, on the arrival of Capt. Joseph Richardson, in the ship *Pitt*, in six weeks from Downs, with a certain account of the stamp-act being absolutely passed." His highest political office was alderman of Annapolis, to which he was elected on September 29, 1766.[40] When he died on April 11, 1767, he had been an important part of the literary life of colonial Maryland for nearly thirty years. In the *Maryland Gazette* for April 16, this obituary appeared:

> On Saturday Evening last died, at his late Dwelling House, Mr. Jonas Green, for Twenty-eight Years Printer to this Province, and Twenty-one Years Printer and Publisher of the Maryland Gazette: He was one of the Aldermen of this City. It would be the highest Indiscretion in us, to attempt giving the Character he justly deserved, only we have Reason to regret the Loss of him, in the various Stations of Husband, Parent, Master, and Companion.

Much of Green's writing was done for Dr. Alexander Hamilton's Tuesday Club, and under his influence. The printer had literary talent, and his many facetious poems burlesqued serious genres. On occasion he wrote, as his "Memorandum for a Seine-Hauling" reveals, enjoyable poetry in the normal genres. But the majority of Green's poetry, like the proceedings of the Tuesday Club and the writings of Dr. Alexander Hamilton, reveals an ultra-sophistication which is just

---

[39] Victor Hugo Paltsits, ed., "Journal of Benjamin Mifflin on a Tour from Philadelphia to Delaware and Maryland," *Bulletin of the New York Public Library* 39 (1935):432.

[40] Aubrey C. Land, *The Dulanys of Maryland* (Baltimore, 1955), 259. *Maryland Gazette*, Oct. 2, 1766.

the opposite of the stereotype expected in the supposedly culturally deprived, backward provinces. At any rate, the editors of the *Gentleman's* and *Universal* magazines were right in turning down Green's poems for publication—not because they were not good enough (they were as good as the majority of poems published in the magazines)—but because they mocked the forms and ideals of contemporary English society. Like Benjamin Franklin's "Craven Street Gazette," the poems of Green showed that the provincials in America (perhaps because they knew that the English regarded them as provincials) deliberately turned the tables on their English contemporaries, and mocked the cherished forms of English society.

DR. ALEXANDER HAMILTON

WIT

Although Dr. Alexander Hamilton is discussed in every recent survey of colonial American literature because of his travel diary, the *Itinerarium*, he has yet to attain his full reputation. His delightful letters have never been printed; his amusing essays in the *Maryland Gazette* have not previously been identified; and his masterpiece, "The History of the Tuesday Club," remains in manuscript, unknown except to a few scholars. Hamilton was a major writer, and "The History of the Tuesday Club" is the finest humorous work of colonial America. Not until Washington Irving's *History of New York* did America achieve a comparable humorous classic, and although Irving's *History* certainly compares with Hamilton's, it is not greater. In the future, Hamilton will rank as a major American writer of neoclassic prose.

Hamilton was born in Edinburgh on September 26, 1712, the sixth son of the Reverend William Hamilton, principal of the University of Edinburgh, and Mary (Robertson) Hamilton.[1] He grew up there

[1] The best sources for information about the Hamilton family are George Hamilton, *A History of the House of Hamilton* (Edinburgh, 1933); Hew Scott, *Fasti Ecclisiae Scoticanae; the succession of ministers in the Church of Scotland from the Reformation* ... (Edinburgh, 1915-50); Henry Paton, *The Register of Marriages for the Parish of Edinburgh, 1701-1750* (Edinburgh, 1908); and Hamilton's letters in the manuscript collection of the Maryland Historical Society. The children of Principal William Hamilton (1699—m. Feb. 25, 1698—d. Jan. 22, 1732) and Mary (Robertson) Hamilton (c. 1675—Jan. 22, 1760) were: Dr. John Hamilton (c. 1698—Mar. 28, 1768); Jean Hamilton (c. 1700—m. Hugh Cleghorn, July 6, 1718—d. 1743); William Hamilton (c. 1701—*post* 1740); Ann Hamilton (1703—m. the Reverend John Horsley—d. 1735); Gavin Hamilton (1704—m.

and, following in the footsteps of his oldest brother, Dr. John Hamilton, studied medicine at Edinburgh, where he graduated M. D. in 1737.[2] He learned pharmacy in the shop of David Knox, surgeon.[3] His brother Dr. John Hamilton sailed from Greenwich for the New World on February 26, 1720/1, settled in Calvert County, Maryland, and in 1722 married Mary Scott, daughter of Samuel Scott. Probably acting on the recommendation of his eldest brother, Dr. Alexander Hamilton emigrated to Annapolis early in 1739. By April 24, 1739, he had arrived in Maryland and written several letters to his family and friends.[4] He soon became a leading physician in the colony.[5] Writing to his brother Gavin, who became a well-known Edinburgh bookseller, publisher, and bailiff, Hamilton says: "I had rid out 10

Helen Balfour, Mar. 24, 1732—d. 1767); Margaret Hamilton (c. 1706—m. William Tod, May 16, 1731—d. *post* 1740); the Reverend Robert Hamilton (1707—m. Jean Hay, Mar. 31, 1745—d. 1787); Janet Hamilton (c. 1710—m. the Reverend David Smith, Feb. 14, 1731—d. 1773); Dr. Alexander Hamilton (1712-56); and the Reverend Gilbert Hamilton (1715—m. [1] Isabel Smith, Jan. 9, 1742; and m. [2] Margaret Craidie, Mar. 4, 1754—d. 1772). The date of Dr. Alexander Hamilton's birth was kindly supplied me by Mr. A. Anderson, of the Scottish Record Office, in a letter dated June 17, 1964.

[2] *List of the Graduates in Medicine in the University of Edinburgh from 1705 to 1866* (Edinburgh, 1867), 3. His thesis was *Specimen medicum inaugurale, de morbis ossium ipsam substantiam afficientibus, ex causis internis oriundis* (Edinburgh, 1737).

[3] Carl Bridenbaugh, ed., *Gentleman's Progress: The Itinerarium of Dr. Alexander Hamilton 1744* (Chapel Hill, N. C., 1948), 49.

[4] Dr. John Hamilton attended Leyden and received his M. D. from the University of Edinburgh in 1719. R. W. Innes Smith, *English-Speaking Students of Medicine at the University of Leyden* (London, 1932), 107. Dr. John Hamilton's will, 1768, Calvert County, Liber 36, folio 461, Maryland Hall of Records, names six grandsons. Bridenbaugh, p. iii, following Joseph Towne Wheeler, mistakenly identifies Hamilton's brother as the Reverend John Hamilton, but the minister was an Irishman and no relation to Dr. Alexander Hamilton. See Nelson Waite Rightmyer, *Maryland's Established Church* (Baltimore, 1956), 186. Evidently, Dr. Alexander Hamilton did not attend Leyden. His letters to his family of Apr. 24, 1739, are not extant; but his mother, in her letter of July 23, 1739, says that his packet of letters of Apr. 24, arrived on Friday, July 20, and continues, "it was what we was all longing much for, and if it had not been for an account we had from London by a ship that came from Maryland, that your ship was safe at that place and all the passengers well, we had been extremely uneasie." MSS, Maryland Historical Society. I am indebted to Mrs. Edgar Hall of New Orleans for information concerning the emigration and marriage of Dr. John Hamilton.

[5] His mother, July 30, 1739, says that his brother's wife (i.e., Mary [Scott] Hamilton) wrote her of "the good character ye have got already." And on Sept. 12, 1739, Stephen Bordley wrote to Matthias Harris, quoting Hamilton's opinion about a mild epidemic in Maryland. Bordley Letter Book, 1738-40, p. 43, Maryland Historical Society.

or twelve miles that day to see some Patients, and returning in the evening I overtook my Brother going to Annapolis, he delivered me your Letter, together with the poem, which diverted us upon the road for some miles, it is writ with spirit and poignancie, and displays a genius in the author." After two paragraphs describing Maryland's hot summers and cold winters, he concludes with a homesick recollection of his Edinburgh club days, asking to be remembered "to all the members of the Whin-bush club, especially to the Right honourable, the Lord Provost, and other magistrates and officers of that ancient and honourable society." He avows that "every friday, I fancy myself with them, drinking two penny ale, and smoking tobacco." Nostalgically, he declares that he longs "to see those merry days again."[6]

A letter from his brother-in-law, the Reverend David Smith, shows that the droll and witty Hamilton was held in high esteem by his friends and family:

> Yours of the 29th April was very acceptable.... Alas! how much scotch drollery is now transplanted into the American soil: I shall be glad to know by your letters from time to time how it thrives in a warmer climate. I suppose it will refine in proportion to its being cultivated under a more direct ray of Apollo.[7]

But there was, if anything, too much sunshine in the colony, and in the first hot, humid summer he spent in Maryland, Dr. Alexander Hamilton became quite ill.[8] He evidently had consumption, which gradually worsened.

On April 22, 1742, he wrote a letter to "P: J: D——l att Edinburg," acknowledging his letter of April 19, 1741, which gave an account of the Royal Infirmary and asked Hamilton to try to procure subscriptions for it. He implied that he would contribute something himself, but that he could not raise any subscriptions among his fellow Marylanders, though he had "used my utmost Rhetoric." But after all, he wrote, if "our famous Enthusiast and erratic preacher [George] Whitefield, could not work upon them, so as to open their purses," it could hardly be expected that he would be able to.[9]

---

[6] Letter dated Annapolis, June 13, 1739, Dulany Papers, Maryland Historical Society.

[7] Letter dated Innerwick, Oct. 5, 1739, Dulany Papers, Maryland Historical Society.

[8] Mrs. Mary Hamilton to Dr. Alexander Hamilton, dated Edinburgh, Apr. 1, 1740, Maryland Historical Society.

[9] Hamilton arrived in the colonies just in time to witness the Great Awaken-

His poor health in the hot summer of 1743 convinced him that he should leave the New World. A broadside advertisement, dated September 29, 1743, gave notice that he intended to depart soon for Great Britain, but he remained in America. In a long letter to his brother Gavin[10] on October 20, 1743, Dr. Alexander Hamilton tells of his first entry into the rough-and-tumble colonial politics. On election day there was shouting, screaming, cudgeling, and breaking of heads, "so the poles were shut long before they were finished, or determined . . . and they have been afraid ever since to proceed upon the Election, being apprehensive of the same opposition." Hamilton had opposed a "certain creature of the court" for the position of common-councilman of Annapolis. He was elected soon afterward and held the position for the rest of his life.[11]

On November 6, 1743, Hamilton wrote a long letter to an old friend at Edinburgh. He reveals that he has been writing facetious letters, such as "the Epistle writ to Don Grub," which are in a "dignissi, Excellentified stile," worthy to be shown as a curiosity to the president of the Royal Society. He claims that he retains "a little of my native honesty, not having quite lost myself in the American subility and selfishness," and adds:

> I shall only say I am not well in health, and for that reason chiefly continue still a Batchellor. I have more fatigue and trouble than I care for, I find it a very hard matter to live well and grow rich, The longer I live I discover more rogues and fools about me, and see

---

ing. He attacked George Whitefield and the emotionalism of the Great Awakening throughout the *Itinerarium*. Hamilton's father, long a professor of theology at the University of Edinburgh, and his brothers in the clergy were also opponents of excessive emotionalism. The Reverend Gilbert Hamilton debated Whitefield on Tuesday, May 24, 1757, in Edinburgh. George Ridpath, *Diary* (Edinburgh, 1922), 138. Whitefield had been in Maryland where he "preached before the Governor" at Annapolis, between Dec. 7 and 12, 1739. *Pennsylvania Gazette*, Dec. 6, 1739 and Feb. 21, 1739/40.

[10] The letter is actually addressed to "G——H——." Bridenbaugh (xiv) thinks that the letter is to Gilbert Hamilton (who had just married on Jan. 9, 1742). But the reference to the addressee's children proves that the letter must have been sent to Gavin, who had married Helen Balfour on Mar. 24, 1732.

[11] On Feb. 10, 1757, a notice in the *Maryland Gazette* announced that James Johnson, junior, and Mr. Charles Wallace, were chosen Common-councilmen of Annapolis, "in the room of Mr. Simon Duff, removed out of Town, and the much regretted Dr. Alexander Hamilton, deceased." Jonas Green began printing the *Maryland Gazette* in 1745. Since no notice of Hamilton's election appears in the *Maryland Gazette* (and all issues are extant), he must have been elected shortly after the rowdy election of 1743.

more and more into my own folly and Imprudence, I wish well to all men, and mind chiefly my Gallipots and vials, which are my bank stock, and I daily pray God, that I may never be disabled by distemper, or arrive to a helpless old age, and have poverty for a bold companion, for in my way, in this part of the world, there is little grist brought to the mills when the water forsakes the dams....[12]

Sometime in 1744, Hamilton wrote a long letter to his brother-in-law, the Reverend David Smith, "att Innerwich, near Dunbar, Scotland." Smith had recommended a Presbyterian minister, the Reverend James Scougal, who had been "bred up and educated" with Smith. Hamilton wrote that he has received Smith's letter "from Mr. Scougle's own hand" and has seen Scougal twice since then. Scougal indeed seems to be a man "of tollerable parts and good sense"—but he will never do well in Maryland, "where the Established Church is that of England." Hamilton says that if Scougal "could conscientiously take orders from a Bishop," he could get a good living. As a Presbyterian, however, he must expect to eke out an existence. Evidently Dr. Alexander Hamilton thought one religion as good as another. An extremely interesting passage occurs when Hamilton writes of the new vogues in literature:

> You tell me in your first that the place affords as little Entertainment as your Invention. I am positive your Invention is good if you would put it in play, but perhaps The Clog of Studying Sermons, diverts it from more airy Subjects, was I living at Innerwick my Invention would find some exercise upon these same old pendant Stones and ragged rocks that hang over the small rivulet near your house, which you showed me one day, and ever since that time, I cannot help thinking you have a poetical turn, since all people of a lively fancy are much delighted with these ruinous objects, and venerable traces of antiquity whether of art or nature. I shall Imagine myself now near your Ruinous Tower, that stands within view of your house, sitting by the brook side, surrounded with thickets and Romantic objects and thus could I break out, addressing myself to Philosophy, under the notion of a Goddess.

And so Hamilton sends him a 77-line poem, entitled "To Philosophy, a Hymn," cautiously adding: "If these verses are bad, don't tell anybody they are mine."[13]

---

[12] This is Letter III in Hamilton's Letter Book, Dulany Papers, Maryland Historical Society.

[13] Hamilton's letter to Smith is undated, but since he refers to Smith's letter to him of Apr. 27, it could not have been written before the fall of 1743. It was probably written sometime during the winter of 1743-44.

Dr. Alexander Hamilton, a flirtatious, curious, well-educated, experienced, widely traveled, aristocratic Scotch-American physician of thirty-two, wrote a fascinating chronicle of close and accurate description and characterization. The *Itinerarium*[14] surveys manners in mid-eighteenth-century America. Because the hot Maryland summers made Hamilton miserable, he resolved, not to go to Great Britain (as he had planned to do in 1743), but to tour the Northern American colonies. On May 30, 1744, Hamilton set out on a four-month horse-back journey from Annapolis, Maryland, to York, Maine, and back; on the trip he visited and described Philadelphia, New York, Albany, Schenectady, Long Island, New Haven, Newport, Providence, Boston, Ipswich, and numerous other places. He arrived back in Annapolis on September 27. Like his friend Witham Marshe, who traveled to Lancaster, Pennsylvania, during this same summer,[15] Hamilton kept a diary of his trip. In October, he revised the diary and presented a fair copy of it, October 29, 1744, to Onorio Razolini (an Italian who had become a naturalized citizen of Maryland, made an advantageous marriage, and served as armourer and keeper of the stores of Maryland). When Razolini inherited the family estates in Asolo, Italy, he returned to his ancestral home, taking with him, among other treasured mementos of his life in Maryland, the fair copy of Dr. Alexander Hamilton's travel diary, the *Itinerarium*.[16]

On the journey, Hamilton cut an imposing figure. Wearing a brace of pistols, a sword, a green velvet coat, and a laced hat, he set out with

[14] There are two editions of the *Itinerarium*. Albert Bushnell Hart, ed., *Hamilton's Itinerarium* . . . (St. Louis, 1907), and Carl Bridenbaugh, ed., *Gentleman's Progress*. All references are to Bridenbaugh's edition.

[15] Witham Marshe, "Journal of the Treaty Held with the Six Nations by the Commissioners of Maryland and Other Provinces," Massachusetts Historical Society *Collections*, 1st ser. 7 (1800):171–200.

[16] Giovanni E. Schiavo, *Four Centuries of Italian-American History* (New York, 1955), 110, and Donnell MacClure Owings, *His Lordship's Patronage*, 49 n. 50. The best account is Donald Wallace, "Onorio Razolini, Pioneer Italian," *Sons of Italy Magazine*, 15, no. 10 (Nov.–Dec. 1942), 306; 16, no. 2 (Feb. 8, 1943), 2–4. The date of Hamilton's presenting the diary to Razolini is printed in Hart's edition (p. [264]) but omitted by Bridenbaugh. In addition to Hamilton's *Itinerarium*, the Italian took at least eight portraits by Hesselius and Woolaston with him back to Asolo, Italy. See *Maryland Historical Magazine* 22 (1927):307. The physical appearance of the *Itinerarium* (which I have examined in the Huntington Library) suggests that it is a fair copy of Hamilton's diary; internal evidence, like "the landlord's name I cannot remember," confirms the impression that not all of the *Itinerarium* was written on the spot; on the other hand, much of the *Itinerarium* is too specific for the MS to have been written in October without the aid of notes.

his Negro slave Dromo, who had charge of Hamilton's portmanteau and baggage. They were well mounted, and every experienced eye recognized them for an aristocratic gentleman and his servant. But the sensitive Hamilton was amused (and sometimes chagrined) by what people thought of him: he records being mistaken once for a trooper because of his pistols, twice for a peddler because of his portmanteau, and once for an Indian king "upon account of my laced hat and sun burnt vissage" (p. 140). A Boston belle made the most amusing observations concerning his appearance:

> This day I was taken notice of in passing the street by a lady who enquired of Mr. Hughes concerning me. "Lord!" said she, "what strange mortall is that?" " 'Tis the flower of the Maryland beaux," said Hughes. "Good God!" said the belle, "does that figure come from Maryland?" "Madam," said Hughes, "he is a Maryland Physitian." "O Jesus! A physitian! Deuce take such odd looking physitians." I desired Hughes, when he told me of this conference, to give my humble service to the lady and tell her that it gave me vast pleasure to think that any thing particular about my person could so attract her resplendent eyes as to make her take notice of me in such a singular manner, and that I intended to wait upon her that she might entertain her opticks with my oddity, and I mine with her unparallelled charms. (p. 139)

Hamilton's language was a tool of multifarious resources. Colloquial, vivid, blunt, fanciful—it rises to every occasion. The prose of the *Itinerarium* is usually quietly descriptive. But Hamilton had an eye and an ear, a mind and a pen, for romantic scenery, for a graceful expression or woman, for Negro, Scotch, or Dutch dialect, for characteristic dialogue, for proverbs, folk sayings, colloquial expressions, and, most of all, for wit and humor. A good example of Hamilton's facetious humor, his colloquial, picturesque, and allusive diction, and his ability to capture a scene is the description of a drunken group leaving Treadway's Inn, Cecil County, Maryland:

> Just as I dismounted att Tradaway's, I found a drunken club dismissing. Most of them had got upon their horses and were seated in an oblique situation, deviating much from a perpendicular to the horizontal plan[e], a posture quite necessary for keeping the center of gravity within its proper base for the support of the superstructure; hence we deduce the true physicall reason why our heads overloaded with liquor become too ponderous for our heels. Their discourse was as oblique as their position; the only thing intelligible in it was oaths and God Damnes; the rest was an inarticulate sound like Rabelais' frozen words a thawing, interlaced with hickupings

and belchings. I was uneasy till they were gone, and my landlord, seeing me stare, made a trite apology—that indeed he did not care to
have such disorderly fellows come about his house; he was always
noted far and near for keeping a quiet house and entertaining only
gentlemen or such like, but these were country people, his neighbours,
and it was not prudent to dissoblige them upon slight occasions. "Alas,
sir!" added he, "we that entertain travellers must strive to oblige every
body, for it is our dayly bread." While he spoke thus, our Bacchana-
lians, finding no more rum in play, rid off helter skelter as if the devil
had possessed them, every man sitting his horse in a see-saw manner
like a bunch of rags tyed upon the saddle. (pp. 6–7)

Hamilton described every town he visited, commenting on its size,
architecture, setting, and, often, military possibilities, but his best
writing is reserved for characterizations of colonial Americans. Hamilton described nearly every person he encountered. He was interested in people as individuals and as types, and his remarks are
fascinating because of his close observation and witty reporting. His
book is a mine of characters; thumbnail sketches of odd persons
appear on every page. The characters are brought to life with dialogue, wit, and exact descriptions. He even records being struck by
the way some people live up to the idea of their types:

> We were entertained with an elegant dispute between a young
> Quaker and the boatswain of a privateer concerning the lawfullness
> of using arms against an enimy. The Quaker thee'd and thou'd it thro'
> the nose to perfection, and the privateer's boatswain swore just like
> the boatswain of a privateer, but they were so far from settling the
> point that the Quaker had almost acted contrary to his principles,
> clenching his fist att his antagonist to strike him for bidding God
> damn him. (p. 17)

Among the various characters that Hamilton sketches are the would-
be gentleman (pp. 13–14), the tavern keeper (p. 42), the bully (p.
51), the Moravian (p. 58), the ignorant justice of the peace (p. 58),
the soldier (pp. 68–69), the impudent Irishman (pp. 70–71), the
Dutchman (p. 73), the court-spy (pp. 79–80), the old parson (pp.
80 and 82), the learned bully (p. 86), the old sailor (p. 92), the
coward (p. 123), the patriot (pp. 173–74), and the quack (p. 196).
The list could be prolonged. But the most interesting character of
all was Boston's famous physician and historian, Dr. William Douglass. Hamilton devotes several pages to this "man of good learning,
but mischievously given to criticism and the most compleat snarler
ever I knew" (p. 116).

One typically American type especially irritated Hamilton—the inquisitive rustic. In America, unlike Scotland and England, men often greeted perfect strangers, asked them for news, inquired their names and destinations, and pestered the travelers with personal questions. Although this characteristic marks the increasing democratization of manners in America, it was an affront to an aristocratic gentleman—and Dr. Alexander Hamilton, like James Fenimore Cooper a century later, was duly affronted. When an old sailor asked Hamilton "where I cam and whither I went," he replied "I came from Calliphurnia and was going to Lanthern Land" (p. 92). Humor constantly came to his aid. He thus describes a meeting with an "inquisitive rustick" in New Hampshire:

> Having proceeded some miles farther I was overtaken by a man who bore me company all the way to Portsmouth. He was very inquisitive about where I was going, whence I came, and who I was. His questions were all stated in the rustick civil stile. "Pray sir, if I may be so bold, where are you going?" "Prithee, friend," says I, "where are you going?" "Why, I go along the road here a little way." "So do I, friend," replied I. "But may I presume, sir, whence do you come?" "And from whence do you come, friend?" says I. "Pardon me, from John Singleton's farm," replied he, "with a bag of oats." "And I come from Maryland," said I, "with a portmanteau and baggage." "Maryland!" said my companion, "where the devil is that there place? I have never heard of it. But pray, sir, may I be so free as to ask your name?" "And may I be so bold as to ask yours, friend?" said I. "Mine is Jerry Jacobs, att your service," replied he. I told him that mine was Bombast Huynhym van Helmont, att his service. "A strange name indeed; belike your a Dutchman, sir,—a captain of a ship, belike." "No, friend," says I, "I am a High German alchymist." "Bless us! You don't say so; that's a trade I never heard of; what may you deal in sir?" "I sell air," said I. "Air," said he, "damn it, a strange commodity. I'd thank you for some wholesom air to cure my fevers which have held me these two months." (p. 124)

North of Ipswich, Massachusetts, he encountered a young man who boasted of his fine horse and confessed "he had a curiosity to ride to Maryland but was afraid of the terrible woods in the way and asked me if there were not a great many dangerous wild beasts in these woods." Hamilton's reply, which contains the second earliest extant recorded use of the work *buckskin* (i. e., a Southern frontiersman), "put on" the timorous adventurer: "I told him that the most dangerous wild beasts in these woods were shaped exactly like men, and they went by the name of buckskins, or bucks, tho they were not bucks neither but something, as it were, betwixt a man and a beast."

The would-be traveler replied " 'Bless us! You don't say so,' says he; 'then surely you had needs ride with guns' (meaning my pistols)" (p. 123). The existence of the word *buckskin* indicates that the Southern frontiersman had become a distinct type, with his own identity. Although there had been frontiersmen since the very founding of Maryland and although all the earliest settlers were, willy-nilly, frontiersmen, prior to the second third of the eighteenth century no group of Americans born and raised on the frontier considered themselves a separate class from the inhabitants of the towns and the older, settled tidewater area. Hamilton's use of the word shows that it was a local, colloquial expression, which he did not expect the Massachusetts man to know.[17]

Literature was Hamilton's avocation, and his knowledge was extensive. Incidents and scenery call to his mind Rabelais, Cervantes, and Spenser; and, on the trip, he read Montaigne, Francisco de Quevedo Villegas, Fielding, Homer (several times), and two plays by Shakespeare. Of Montaigne's *Essays* he commented that they were "a strange medley of subjects and particularly entertaining" (p. 20). Only two years after the publication (1742) of Fielding's *Joseph Andrews*, Hamilton judged it "a masterly performance of its kind and entertaining; the characters of low life here are naturally delineated, and the whole performance is so good that I have not seen any thing of that kind equal or excell it" (p. 23). The following day he read the second volume "and thought my time well spent" (p. 24). Conversation in colonial clubs often turned on literature: in the Governor's Club in Philadelphia the group discussed "the English poets and some of the foreign writers, particularly Cervantes, author of *Don Quixot*, whom we loaded with eloqiums due to his character" (p. 21). At the Hungarian Club in New York, "Our conversation ended this night with a piece of criticism upon a poem in the news-

[17] Thomas Perkins Abernathy, "The Southern Frontier, an Interpretation," in Walker D. Wyman and Clifton B. Kroeber, eds., *The Frontier in Perspective* (Madison, 1957), 129–42, argues that the first Southern frontier existed in the first third of the eighteenth century between the fall line and the Blue Ridge Mountains. The question of whether frontiersmen existed in seventeenth-century America is simply a matter of definition. To me, the key distinction is that the frontiersmen did not have an identity as a separate class until nearly the middle of the eighteenth century.

In addition to the entries in the *DAE* for the word *buckskin*, it should be noted that Landon Carter used the pseudonym "Buckskin" and "An Honest Buckskin" in the *Virginia Gazette* in the 1750s and 1760s. One of Hamilton's colloquialisms is discusssed by Albert Matthews, "Rattlesnake Colonel," *New England Quarterly* 10 (1937):341–45.

paper" (p. 45). In Boston, Hamilton went to three book auctions. Those volumes that sold best the first time were "Pamela, Anti-Pamela, The Fortunate Maid, Ovid's Art of Love, and The Marrow of Modern Divinity" (p. 112). The second time, disappointed, he records "The books sold so dear that I could not procure such as I wanted" (p. 116); and on the third occasion he "bought a copy of Clerk's Homer very cheap" (p. 116). On Sunday, September 9, Hamilton heard "the first news of the death of our great poet Pope, full of glory tho not of days" (pp. 180–81). And when Hamilton read (reread?) Shakespeare's *Timon of Athens*, he noted that it was "a play which, tho not written according to Aristotle's rules, yet abounding with inimitable beauties peculiar to this excellent author" (p. 191).

Art and music were of course among Hamilton's interests. In Newport he visited Robert Feke, "a painter, the most extraordinary genius ever I knew, for he does pictures tollerably well by the force of genius, having never had any teaching. I saw a large table of the Judgement of Hercules copied by him from a frontispiece of the Earl of Shaftesbury's which I thought very well done." And with his eye for types, Hamilton remarked of Feke, "This man had exactly the phizz of a painter, having a long pale face, sharp nose, large eyes with which he looked upon you stedfastly, long curled black hair, delicate white hand, and long fingers" (p. 102). In Philadelphia, Hamilton observed "severall comicall, grotesque phizzes in the inn wher I put up which would have afforded variety of hints for a painter of Hogarth's turn" (p. 18). (Later, in his Tuesday Club caricatures, Hamilton tried his hand at such sketches.) In Boston he described John Smibert's studio:

> I went this night to visit Mr. Smibert, the limner, where I saw a collection of fine pictures, among the rest that part of Scipio's history in Spain where he delivers the lady to the prince to whom she had been bethrothed. The passions are all well touched in the severall faces. Scipio's face expresses a majestic generosity, that of the young prince gratitude, the young lady's gratitude and modest love, and some Roman soldiers standing under a row of pillars apart in seeming discourse, have admiration delineated in their faces. But what I admired most of the painter's fancy in this piece is an image or phantome of chastity behind the solium upon which Scipio sits, standing on tiptoe to crown him and yet appears as if she could not reach his head, which expresses a good emblem of the virtue of this action. I saw here likewise a collection of good busts and statues, most of them antiques, done in clay and paste, among the rest Homer's head and a modell of the Venus of Medicis. (p. 114)

"Browne Hall," in Denver, Massachusetts, impressed Hamilton with its architecture and setting. He commented that the tapestry by John Vanderbanc "was the best of the kind ever I saw" (p. 121).

Music was a favorite colonial entertainment. Hamilton happily noted in Boston that "Assemblys of the gayer sort are frequent . . . the gentlemen and ladys meeting almost every week att concerts of musick and balls" (p. 146). The organ at Trinity Church, New York, consisted "of a great number of pipes handsomly gilt and adorned." Although Hamilton was disappointed that he couldn't hear it because Trinity Church had as yet no organist, he found that the "vocall musick of the Congregation was very good" (p. 45). Still in New York, he went to a concert at a tavern "fronting the Albany coffee house . . . where I heard a tollerable concerto of musick performed by one violin and two German flutes. The violin was by far the best I had heard played since I came to America" (p. 48). When he visited the Musick Club in Philadelphia, he wrote:

> I heard a tollerable concerto performed by a harpsicord and three violins. One Levy there played a very good violine, one Quin bore another pritty good part; Tench Francis played a very indifferent finger upon an excellent violin that once belonged to the late Ch: Calvert, Govr. of Maryland. We dismissed att eleven o'clock after having regaled ourselves with musick and good viands and liquor. (p. 191)

Perhaps the first American to use the word *romantic* to describe natural scenery was William Byrd.[18] But no writer in America before Dr. Alexander Hamilton was so interested in the wilderness as wilderness, so fascinated by scenery for its picturesqueness, or so absorbed by the variegated face of the American landscape. Hamilton's interest in romantic, melancholic scenery has already been suggested by his letter to the Reverend David Smith, where Hamilton recalls the appearance of various "romantic objects" around Smith's home: "old pendant Stones . . . ragged rocks . . . small rivulet . . . ruinous objects . . . [and] venerable traces of antiquity." Hamilton was sensitive to scenery during his American tour, and several of his descriptions anticipate the "set pieces" popular in the early nineteenth century. His descriptions of the Hudson River anticipate the writings of James Fenimore Cooper and the paintings of the Hudson River School.

---

[18] *The Prose Works of William Byrd of Westover: Narratives of a Colonial Virginian*, ed. Louis B. Wright (Cambridge, Mass., 1966), 254 and 267.

Hamilton wrote that the highlands along the Hudson River "presented a wild, romantick scene of rocks and mountains covered with small scraggy wood, mostly oak" (p. 55). He associated melancholy with the romantic in a way that was to be increasingly popular as the Romantic period grew closer: "This wild and solitary place, where nothing presents but huge precipices and inaccessible steeps where foot of man never was, infused in my mind a kind of melancholly and filled my imagination with odd thoughts, which, att the same time, had something pleasant in them" (pp. 55–56). On the return trip down the Hudson from Albany, Buttermilk Island impressed him: "This appeared a very wild, romantick place surrounded with huge rocks, dreadful precipices and scraggy broken trees" (p. 77). Like the Romantics, Hamilton associated Spenser's *Faerie Queene* with mysterious and melancholic scenes: "travelling thro 12 miles more of stonny, rough road, we passed by an old fashioned wooden house att the end of a lane, darkened and shaded over with a thick grove of tall trees. This appeared to me very romantick and brought into my mind some romantick descriptions of rural scenes in Spencer's Fairy Queen" (p. 98).

Despite his appreciation of nature, Hamilton, like William Byrd,[19] did not believe in primitivism. When an old couple invited him to share their dinner ("a homely dish of fish without any kind of sauce"), he made the following ironic comment on primitivism:

> They desired me to eat, but I told them I had no stomach. They had no cloth upon the table, and their mess was in a dirty, deep, wooden dish which they evacuated with their hands, cramming down skins, scales, and all. They used neither knife, fork, spoon, plate, or napkin because, I suppose, they had none to use. I looked upon this as a picture of that primitive simplicity practiced by our forefathers long before the mechanic arts had supplyed them with instruments for the luxury and elegance of life. (p. 8)

As this passage and the many later ironic tirades against luxury in "The History of the Tuesday Club" demonstrate, Hamilton believed in the benefits of civilization. Incidentally, the use of the words *mess, evacuated* (with its scatological suggestion), and *cramming*, together with the exactness of observation, shows that Hamilton deliberately tried to evoke the reader's revulsion.

---

[19] Byrd, 180 and 248. For a brief characterization of Byrd's purpose in his literary writings, see my review of Wright's edition, *Mississippi Quarterly* 20 (1967):240–42.

A pleasing aspect of nature was its variety. Hamilton commented that the country just north of Trenton, New Jersey, "displays variety of agreeable prospects and rurall scenes" (p. 33). Nature's diversity was especially noticeable by the Hudson; the river "about two miles broad," the Catskill Mountains "caped with clouds," and "large open fields and thickets of woods, alternately mixed," entertained "the eye with variety of landskips" (p. 59). But he also delighted in the idea of landscape as a cultivated garden. He found Newport, Rhode Island, especially lovely: "The island is the most delightfull spot of ground I have seen in America. I can compare it to nothing but one intire garden. For rural scenes and pritty, frank girls, I found it the most agreeable place I had been in thro' all my peregrinations" (p. 157).

Of course Dr. Alexander Hamilton surveyed the doctors and the medical facilities of the various colonies. He carried letters of introduction to most of the best-known physicians of the Middle and New England colonies, and, as we have seen, Dr. William Douglass was his favorite "character," though hardly a favorite person. With Drs. Thomas Cadwalader and William Farquhar of New Jersey, Dr. James McGraw of New York, Drs. John Brett and Thomas Moffatt of Rhode Island, Drs. Phineas and Thomas Bond of Philadelphia, and Dr. John Mitchell of Virginia (who was, like Hamilton, traveling for his health), Hamilton exchanged views. Their conversations afford glimpses into eighteenth-century intellectual ideas. In New York, he found himself talking with two strangers about the influence of climate on people: "the differences of climates in the American provinces with relation to the influence they had upon human bodies" (p. 47). Hamilton's idea of evolution (before the term existed) applies the concept of the Great Chain of Being to creation: "The progress of nature is surprising. . . . She seems by one connected gradation to pass from one species of creatures to another without any visible gap, intervall, or *discontinuum* in her works; but an infinity of her operations are yet unknown to us" (p. 140).

Although the peak (1739–42) of the great religious revival known as the Great Awakening had passed by 1744, such topics as the necessity of rebirth (i. e., the personal, emotional experience of religious conversion), the nature of religious experience, and the profaneness, nay irreligiousness, of all pleasurable activity were still common subjects of conversation among the New Lights or Whitefieldians. Hamilton, a fallen-away Presbyterian and practicing Anglican, detested such New Light doctrines. He repeatedly attacks the doctrines and behavior of the Whitfieldians; not only do they offend his deistic theology, but also his Addisonian aristocracy. Hamilton, who attended Anglican, Baptist, Congregational, Presbyterian, Jewish, and Catholic services on his trip, was a scientific deist. The beauty, regularity, and artistry of nature proved the existence of God, and these teleological evidences were all the reassurance that an intelligent man needed concerning eschatology. But the "mob," the great mass of mankind, needed the threatenings, the ceremonies, rewards, and punishments of orthodox religion. Hamilton, like other typical eighteenth-century gentlemen, believed that the institution of religion had a social utility for the "mob," though not for the intellectual. Hamilton's most thorough religious discussion occurred during a conversation with Dr. Thomas Cadwalader of Trenton, New Jersey:

> To this I replied that priests of all sorts and sects whatsoever made a kind of trade of religion, contriving how to make it turn out to their own gain and profit; yet notwithstanding, many were of opinion that to inculcate religion into vulgar minds we must use other methods than only preaching up fine sense and morality to them. Their understanding and comprehension are too gross and thick to receive it in that shape. Men of sense of every perswasion whatsoever are sensible of the emptiness and nonsense of the mere ceremonial part of religion but, att the same time, allow it to be in some degree necessary and usefull, because the ignorant vulgar are to be dealt with in this point as we manage children by showing them toys in order to perswade them to do that which all the good reasoning of the world never would. The mobile, that many headed beast, cannot be reasoned into religious and pious duties. Men are not all philosophers. The tools by which we must work upon the gross senses and rough cast minds of the vulgar are such as form and lay before their eyes, rewards and punishments whereby the passions of hope and fear are excited; and withall our doctrines must be interlaced with something amazing and misterious in order to command their attention, strengthen their belief, and raise their admiration, for was one to make religion appear to them in her genuine, simple, and plain dress, she would gain no credit and would never be so regarded. (pp. 32–33)

But of course Hamilton went to church on Sunday (when it was convenient)—if only because the sermon still occupied a position of importance in American culture. He regarded the Reverend William Hooper as "one of the best preachers I have heard in America, his discourse being sollid sense, strong connected reasoning, and good language" (p. 130). To Hamilton, a cardinal sin of the minister was to preach above the capacities of the audience: "the language and phraseology of which sacred *rostrum* ought to be as plain to the ploughman as the schollar" (p. 110).

In New London, Connecticut, Hamilton met a brother of Jonas Green, and the brother entertained him with the story of the Reverend James Davenport (a fanatical New Light minister) who nearly offered up his "old, wore out, plush breaches" as a sacrifice. Hamilton commented that it was lucky that his breeches were saved, otherwise Davenport "would have been obliged to strutt about bare-arsed, for the devil another pair of breeches had he" (p. 161). The next morning, August 27, Hamilton visited "Deacon" Green and his wife (Jonas Green's parents) and recorded: "The old man was very inquisitive about the state of religion with us, what kind of ministers we had, and if the people were much addicted to godliness." Hamilton could not pass up the opportunity to satirize religion and Maryland's ministers: he replied that "the ministers minded hogsheads of tobacco more than points of doctrine, either orthodox or hetrodox, and that the people were very prone to a certain religion called *self interest*" (p. 161).

Finally, Hamilton relates several bagatelles. Among the best are the archetypal anecdote of who's the greater quack, the doctor or the peddler (p. 91); the incident illustrating the enmity between General Wade and Lord Loveat (pp. 151–52); the threats of the Mohawk Indian chief, Henrique, to the Eastern Indians (pp. 112–14); and a colonial version of the snipe-hunt:

> I had occasion to see a particular diversion this day which they call *hawling the fox*. It is practised upon simple clowns. Near the town there is a pond of about a quarter of a mile broad. Across this they lay a rope, and two or three strong fellows, concealed in the bushes, hold one end of it. To a stump in view, there is tied a large fox. When they can lay hold of an ignorant clown on the opposite side of the pond, they inviegle him by degrees into the scrape—two people pretending to wager, one upon the fox's head and the other upon the clown's, twenty shillings or some such matter that the fox shall not or shall pull him thro' the water in spight of his teeth. The clown easily imagines himself stronger then the fox and, for a small reward, allows the rope to be put around his waste. Which done, the sturdy fellows on the other side behind the bush pull lustily for their friend the fox who sits tied to his stump all the time of the operation, being only a mere spectator, and haul poor pill-garlick with great rapidity thro' the pond, while the water hisses and foams on each side of him as he ploughs the surface, and his coat is well wet. I saw a poor country fellow treated in this manner. He run thro the water upon his back like a log of wood, making a frothy line across the pond, and when

he came out he shook himself and swore he could not have believed the fox had so much strength. They gave him 20 shillings to help to dry his coat. He was pleased with the reward and said that for so much a time he would allow the fox to drag him thro' the pond as he pleased. (p. 135)

Although Hamilton's journey failed to cure the doctor's ailments, his record of that journey, the *Itinerarium*, is the best single portrait of men and manners, of rural and urban life, of the wide range of society and scenery in colonial America. The *Itinerarium* is generally regarded as one of colonial America's most delightful books, but it was not Hamilton's major effort, nor his best work.

During Dr. Alexander Hamilton's first six years in Maryland, no major medium of publication was available. But when Jonas Green started the *Maryland Gazette* in 1745, Hamilton immediately seized the opportunity to precipitate a literary war between the "Annapolis Wits" and the "Baltimore Bards." The immediate cause of the dispute was trivial: while George Whitefield was preaching in Baltimore County, the Reverend Thomas Cradock wrote an eight-line poem on an attractive girl sitting in the church pew in front of him. Hamilton and his Annapolis circle ridiculed Cradock's effusion, and Hamilton and Edward Dorsey wrote several satirical rejoinders. Cradock's friend and fellow minister in Baltimore County, the Reverend Thomas Chase, also a poet, came to his defense. Chase and Cradock attempted to overcome the Annapolis Wits with a full-scale poetic production on the girls of Baltimore County. Their poem, "The Baltimore Belles," was left lying "on the table in a Tavern," circulated in manuscript, and soon reached the Annapolis group. Someone in Hamilton's circle attacked the poem with "An Infallible Receipt to cure the Epidemical and Afflecting distempers of Love and the Poetical Itch," published in the *Maryland Gazette* for December 17, 1745. Since Cradock and Chase were not daunted by the "Infallible Receipt," Hamilton himself took a hand in the battle. Under the pseudonym "Theophilus Polypharmacus," he published a scurrilous satire on "The Baltimore Belles" in the paper for February 4, 1745/6.

Angered by Hamilton's satire, the Reverend Thomas Chase composed a "dirty Epistle to the City of A[nnapolis]" (Hamilton's title for the poem) in which he lampooned the various Annapolis Wits, characterizing them as dunces and comparing their works to various specimens of excrement.[20] This "prophylactic dissertation" was an-

[20] Unfortunately, neither "The Baltimore Belles" nor the "Epistle to the City

swered by several long mock-criticisms, including one in a grave style by "Martinus Scriblerus" and one in a burlesque style by "Hurlo Thrumbo." Finally, Hamilton silenced Chase with a mock advertisement, supposedly for a runaway servant. The runaway servant (Chase) is described as "a dapper-witted, *finical Fopling*, known by the Name of *Bard*, alias *Bavius*," of dubious mental stability, a person easily identified because he carries around materials stolen from Pope and Prior and because his conversation "turns chiefly on excrementilious subjects." Hamilton slyly suggested that Chase was the anonymous bard when he punned: "any Person who goes upon the *chace* [italics in original] after him" will be suitably rewarded with "the profit of his poems for one hundred years to come." Thus Hamilton, in a mock advertisement signed "Jehoiakim Jerkum," March 18, 1745/6, concluded the Annapolis Wits versus the Baltimore Bards. But he doubly had the last word: he recounted the entire story in his "History of the Tuesday Club." [21]

On January 7, 1746, a satirical essay probably by Hamilton [22] appeared in the *Maryland Gazette*. It satirizes the rustic manners, inquisitiveness, and democratic tendency of Americans, and contains incidental criticism of the *Maryland Gazette* writings. The essay opens, after a quotation from Terence, with aspersions on Green's selections for the paper:

> Mr. Green
>   As you publish a News-paper weekly, for our Entertainment, without which, perhaps, this dull Place would be still duller; and as at some times you seem to be at a Loss for better and more pertinent

---

of Annapolis" is extant, though several lines from the former survive in Hamilton's satire in the *Maryland Gazette* for Feb. 4, 1745/6, and in "The History of the Tuesday Club," 1:181–82, MSS, Evergreen House, Johns Hopkins University Library. Hamilton copied out these poems in his "History," but the relevant pages have been cut out of the MS. Rosamond Randall Beirne, "The Reverend Thomas Chase: Pugnacious Parson," *Maryland Historical Magazine* 59 (1964): 1–14, is a good brief sketch. For Cradock, see Ethan Allen, "Rev. Thomas Cradock, Rector of St. Thomas' Parish, Baltimore County, Maryland, 1745," *Church History* 3 (1854–55):302–12.

[21] Dr. Alexander Hamilton, "History of the Tuesday Club," 1:175–84.

[22] There are several reasons for this opinion, but the best of them is the subject of the essay. Hamilton had written several diatribes against being addressed by rustics with this question ("What News?") in his *Itinerarium*, e.g., 16 and 124. The mixture of aristocracy, wit, morality, and literary criticism seems especially Hamiltonian. Further, the character sketches and ability of the writer suggest Hamilton. Robert R. Hare, "Electro Vitrifrico in Annapolis: Mr. Franklin Visits the Tuesday Club," *Maryland Historical Magazine* 58 (1963):64, n.7, has previously suggested that this essay is in Hamilton's manner.

Subjects, than *Letters from the King to the Queen, From the Dauphin to his dear Mamma, Congratulatory Addresses from a* Dutch *Ambassador to the* French Court, and tiresome Scrolls of *Blank Verses*, to fill up *Blanks* in your *Gazette*; I for this reason, and out of Pity to your *Alphabetic Engine*, which some time ago groaned in dire Labor, and brought forth *monstrous Births* of *Poetry*, have shuffled together a few crude Thoughts in *Prose*, which, if you please, you may dignify with a Place in Paper, when you can find nothing better to insert.

Hamilton asserts that the uncivil question "What News?" is common, "which as it is often impertinently asked, so on many Occasion it meets with a trifling or insignificant Reply: And this, in my Opinion, is just what it deserves." The question arises only because the proposer can think of nothing better to say. And the reply, "when proposed to a silly, weak, or ignorant Man, addicted to talking, must often carry more Harm than Good in it." This is especially true in America:

A Place so barren of News . . . where neither Wit nor Invention abound, to afford innocent Amusements of this Kind, as we have seen by some late *Essays* inserted in your Paper, both in *Prose* and *Verse*, which, instead of being genuine *Streams from Helicon*, are really nothing but *Low Wines*, drawn as one may say, by a single Distillation, from the *Dregs* of *Grub-street*.

Hamilton next sketches several "characters," illustrating what happens when the question "What News?" is proposed to "a silly Fellow, gifted with the Talent of Loquacity"; to "an affected Person, who exposes himself to Ridicule"; to "a professed Tatler"; to a member of the fair sex with a well-stocked fertile fancy; to a half-educated pedant; and to a professional purveyor of scandal. Here is Hamilton's characterization of the "silly Fellow, gifted with the Talent of Loquacity, which most conceited Fops are bless'd with":

The Hearers are presently surfeited with an idle Discourse, which consists of nothing but Fiddle-faddle, or a tedious Story, without Connection or Symmetry of Parts, which answers no Purpose, either to instruct or entertain; and while the Fool is laughed at for his Simplicity, his Vanity suggests to him, that the Company are pleased with his fine Humour, and his own stunning *Horse-Laugh* drowns all the rest. I have often been uneasy at seeing human Weakness so needlessly and wantonly exposed; and tho' some well-bred Persons may make Pastime in thus bandying a Fool, yet the frequent Practice of this Sort of Buffoonry, I think, is inconsistent with that Humanity and good Manners, which ought to adorn the *Gentleman's* Character, and constitute the *Man of Sense* and true *Politeness*.

After Hamilton has presented several "characters with their typical answers, he asks "how shall a prudent Man behave, when this Question is often stated to him?" He replies that "his own Sense and Discretion will direct him," but he also gives three sample replies to the inquiring "Fool." He concludes with a suitable sermon trope (in which the vehicle of the metaphor lightly satirizes boring sermons):

> Sir, if this Sermon to some of your Readers should seem too long, for so short and trifling a Text as What News: let it be remembered, that the Church Doors stand wide open, and if they like it or not, they may without Ceremony walk out, and leave both the Preacher and his Discourse, at whatever Period they please.
> Dated at vwxyz, the
> 30th of the 10th
> Month, the 2d Day of   I am Sir, Yours &c.
> the Week   KLMN PQRST

This slight essay has a graceful yet colloquial style, an aristocratic *persona*, light satire, and a simple structure (with a clearly defined introduction, a body consisting of the several characters, and a conclusion).

On Friday, May 28, 1747, Hamilton married Margaret Dulany, daughter of Daniel Dulany the Elder, and thus became a member of one of the richest and most powerful Maryland families.[23] Stephen Bordley, still a bachelor and a member of Hamilton's Tuesday Club, wrote to Witham Marshe about Hamilton's marriage:

> Yet vain was that hope, since I am now obliged to hold out alone against that numerous and powerful host [of women] we know and formerly provoked by our united hostilities,—for poor Hamilton is gone!—not dead, but married, he was the day before yesterday obliged to surrender discretion to throw himself up to the money of Peggy Dulany, and is already become what you would from your knowledge of the lady now suppose him to be, a very grave sober fellow.[24]

Hamilton enjoyed his marriage; his mother's letters of July 15, 1748, and February 15, 1748/9, both comment on how pleased she is to hear that he is "so happie in your Marriage."[25] On October 18, 1747, Hamilton made out his will, leaving "all my Estate, both Real and personal to my Dear Wife Margaret Hamilton." His friends the Reverend

---

[23] The wedding was announced in the *Maryland Gazette*, June 2, 1747.
[24] Dated May 30, 1747, Bordley Letter Book, 1740–47, p. 179, Maryland Historical Society.
[25] MSS, Maryland Historical Society.

John Gordon, Edward Dorsey, and Henry Cummings witnessed the document.[26]

Dr. Alexander Hamilton wrote the colony's best belletristic essay for the *Maryland Gazette* of June 29, 1748.[27] Signed with the well-known pseudonym of the seventeenth-century author of *Los Suenos*, Don Francisco de Quevedo Villegas, the essay is actually a literary history of the first three years of the newspaper. Hamilton criticizes nearly all the local writings, literary and political, that had appeared in the *Maryland Gazette* since Jonas Green began it early in 1745. Although many earlier examples of American literary criticism are known, Hamilton's "Quevedo" essay is the first criticism of a number of American authors. He briefly characterizes and evaluates every local author who has contributed to the paper. He had read every issue of the *Gazette* thoroughly and critically and kept a file of the paper. Coupled with the evidence given in the *Itinerarium*,[28] this essay reveals that the colonial newspapers were thoroughly read, digested, criticized, and sometimes applauded.

Hamilton skillfully fuses several literary genres in the "Quevedo" essay. The pseudonym tells the reader that the author is deliberately imitating the Lucianic satire, a genre familiar to English readers of the seventeenth and eighteenth centuries primarily through Sir Roger L'Estrange's paraphrase of Quevedo's *Visions*.[29] The tour through hell also recalls Dante's *Inferno*. Thus Hamilton mocks himself and reveals the dilemma of the colonial American author in the very selection of his literary form: for here in the rude New World (or, as he calls it, "This our Woodland Country"), Hamilton satirically compares himself to Dante—and his guide through hell, his Virgil of Maryland, is Jonas Green. Hamilton adroitly uses the popular dialogue genre. The question-and-answer technique provides suspense and allows Hamilton to explore dramatically the characters of the narrator and of Jonas Green. Hamilton portrays Green as a delightful

[26] Hamilton had been security for the Reverend John Gordon for a £100 loan, and William Cumming (possibly a relation of Henry Cummings) had stood security for Hamilton. *Archives of Maryland* 52:24–25.

[27] Reasons for attributing this pseudonymous essay to Hamilton are set forth at length in J. A. Leo Lemay, "Hamilton's Literary History," 274–76.

[28] Bridenbaugh, 45–125.

[29] For an examination of Lucianic satire in the seventeenth and eighteenth centuries, and especially for the popularity and influence of Quevedo's *Los Suenos*, see Benjamin Boyce, "News from Hell," *PMLA* 53 (1943):402–37. See also "Lucianic Sketches" in Henry Knight Miller, *Essays on Fielding's Miscellanies* (Princeton, 1961), 365–419.

boon companion, famous for his "nipperkin of punch" and his constant joking (he cannot forbear punning—even in hell). But he also satirizes Green's foibles, saying that the latter's only test of literary merit is the amount of money an author will pay to have his productions immortalized in the *Maryland Gazette*.

Finally, the essay effectively employs the vision-framework technique. It opens with "Quevedo" reading over his file of the *Maryland Gazette*, which is so dull that it puts him to sleep; and ends when the author is rudely aroused from his dream by a mosquito. That a mosquito bite should end the piece is fitting, for the mosquito was and still is identified with the New World. (From the time of the Pilgrim Fathers to a recent London *Times Literary Supplement*, the English have been saying that the trouble with America is—mosquitoes.)[30] The dialogue, Lucianic satire, and vision-framework genres are skillfully handled. Perhaps only Franklin in colonial America had thus far written a more artful essay.

After quoting the opening of Swift's poem "On Poetry: A Rapsody," Hamilton begins:

Mr. Green,
   The other Night, looking over a Bundle of your News-*Papers*, to which I often have recourse when satiated with more serious and solid Compositions, after I had perused several *Poems* and *Essays* with which you have obliged the Public, I came at last to a *long-winded Paper*, wrote by a *Native of Maryland*; the tedious Prolixity of which lulled me asleep in my elbow Chair, before I had half run over that important and *ponderous Performance*. So soon as the *drowsy god* had clapt his *leaden Cap* over my Temples, I was carried into the *Region of Visions*, and dreamed such a comical *Dream*, that I cannot help relating it to you; and if you think it worth While, you may communicate it to the Public.

Then Hamilton sets the scene for his tour through hell:

   I found myself in a spacious Hall, where were assembled several strange Persons, who, by their Gesture and Discourse, appeared to be *Poets*, *Politicians*, and *Philosophers*: Some wrote, some disputed, others repeated Verses upon various Subjects, and many dispatched certain Pacquets, which all seemed directed to you.

---

[30] William Bradford, *Of Plymouth Plantation, 1620–1647*, ed. Samuel Eliot Morison (New York, 1963), 144. The London *Times Literary Supplement* complained in a review of several books on New Jersey, Nov. 25, 1965, p. 1067: "one thing has not changed: the aggressiveness and deadly power of the Jersey 'skeeter.'"

Jonas Green enters the hall, and Quevedo asks him "who these odd Fellows were, and what they were about?" Green explains that they are his authors, "who oblige me with their *Compositions* in *Prose* and *Verse*, to fill up a Gap in my *Gazette*, in a Scarcity of News." Quevedo requests Green to point out and characterize "the most remarkable of them." Green agrees; and "having prepared a small *Nipperkin of Punch*," they sat at one end of the hall, and "as we handed the Bowl to and again, I made my Questions, which you civilly answered."

After discussing the political essayists who wrote about the proposed Tobacco Inspection Law, Hamilton praises the Reverend James Sterling, who is described as "a tall raw-boned Person" with a "furious Manner." Quevedo questions whether the raving man is "a *Pindaric Poet*, or a *religious Zealot?*" Green replies that Sterling is "the *first Rate Poet* in our *Province*; a most thundering and verbose *Son of the Nine Muses*; he has a Fancy like Lightning; and not only in his *Compositions*, but in his common *Discourse*, he darts out Notions and Conceptions which no Mortal but himself ever thought of." Green adds that Sterling "deals much in *ideal Beings, figurative Personages*, and antient *Pagan Mythology*; and is desirous to be understood by none but People of Taste." (Hamilton here echoes the preface to Sterling's "Epithalamium," *Maryland Gazette*, May 18, 1748.) Sterling's attitude is implicitly censored, because it differs from the neo-classic ideals, which typically held that good literature should be understood by everyone. His attitude was to become common in the Romantic period, and the Maryland poet, according to Hamilton, seems to possess an expressive theory of literature—a theory which was not to have a full statement until the Romantic period, some fifty years later. Hamilton even calls Sterling a "romantic." Quevedo comments that "his must be a strange *Taste* . . . which makes the relishing of what is romantic and obscure to almost all your *Readers*, an essential *Criterion of Taste*." Green replies that "the Gentleman himself is romantic in most Things he does or says; tho' it must be owned, abstracting from this strange volatile Humour, he has a good Measure of Sense and Learning." Quevedo's last statement on the former playwright asks that he "be crowned *Poet Laureat of Maryland*," and Green concludes by wishing that Sterling would "write oftner" for the *Maryland Gazette*.[31]

[31] For identifications of authors and for the dates of the various pieces referred to by Hamilton, see the edition cited in n. 28 above. The discussion above corrects that edition.

Hamilton next writes a satiricial paragraph on Governor William Gooch's speech to the General Assembly of Virginia on the "dreadful Fire that consumed the *Capitol*"; and Hamilton compliments the free verse parody of the speech by a "Northern bard," Benjamin Franklin.[32] Then he pens an appreciation of his "old school fellow," Dr. Adam Thomson, who was Green's most frequent poetic contributor. Hamilton asks, "Pray who is that young dapper Gentleman, so particularly precise and affected in his Carriage, so seemingly pointed, exact and prolix in his Discourse; who seems to dictate to all round him, talks much of Mr. *Pope*, and often quotes *Horace*?" Green replies that he "has a large Share in my Paper, and sets up for a delicate Taste in *Poetry*: As to his Abilities that Way, I am not learned enough to judge; yet those who set up for *Men of Taste and Literature*, in this our *Wood-land Country*, affirm that he is no great Proficient in it." Green punningly adds "However, about this, Doctors differ." Evidently Green is suggesting that Dr. Adam Thomson had a high opinion of his own poetry, while some other "doctors" (e. g., the Reverend Theophilus Swift) thought it inferior. The printer continues:

> His name is *Philo-Musaeus*, sometimes *Philo-musus*: he is Author of several Pieces, some in the *Ode Way*, or as others chuse to call it, in the *Odd Way*,——You'll never forbear punning, Friend *Jonas* ——which relish a little of *Sternhold* and *Hopkins*; tho' some Judges say, that there is a little Fire mixt with his Phlegm. As to his *poetical Pieces*, among others, is *An Ode Upon the taking of Cape Breton*, wrote in *English Saphics*; *Verses occasioned by Colley* Cibber's *Epitaph on* Mr. Pope where is contained a just Panegyric upon Colley, that illustrious *Laureat*; and a *Satyrical Epistle to his Friend*; these two last in *Heroics*; And one Piece in *Doggrel*, upon poor *Teague*, the Author of the Advertisement; where he quits the romantic Name of *Philo-Musaeus*, and becomes Mr. *Town Side*.

Hamilton's last remark is especially interesting: it reveals that Dr. Adam Thomson wrote the satirical verses signed "Town Side" in the *Maryland Gazette* for July 28, 1747; that John Webb(e) was the author of an article signed "A Planter" in the paper for June 23 and 30, 1747; that John Webb, the editor of America's first magazine, was living in Maryland in 1747; and that both Dr. Adam Thomson and

---

[32] Leonard W. Labaree et al., ed., *Papers of Benjamin Franklin* 3:135–40. Hamilton also refers to Franklin's poem in "The History of the Tuesday Club," 2:413 (at "Sederent" 160). Gooch's speech appeared in the *Maryland Gazette* for Apr. 14, 1747, and Franklin's poetic parody in a *Postscript* to the *Gazette* for June 16, 1747.

Hamilton were familiar with and remembered Franklin's brilliant satire of Webb in the *Pennsylvania Gazette* of February 26, 1740/1. Teague (John Webb) "with his *round unthinking Face*" (Hamilton here echoes Pope's description of "Sir Plume" in *Rape of the Lock*, IV, 125) is ridiculed, and so too is Thomson's other foe, "Philo-Kalus" (the Reverend Theophilus Swift).

After discussing Dr. Adam Thomson's "Satyrical Epistle to a Friend" Hamilton characterizes the other Maryland poets:

> Methinks you have got a devilish Clan of *Poets* here.—O yes, Numbers of the *Rhiming Species*. There's *Juba*, the *Monitor of the Ladies*, Here's *Ignotus*, very properly so called, a puny Translator. There's that wonderful imitator of Horace, in his Ode, beginning *Otium divos*, &c. And here is *Eumolpus*, that solemn Dealer in *blank Verse*, The Body of whose *Muse*, too large for her small Wings, like a *squab Gosling*, comes souse down as often as she attempts to soar. ——This Sort of Poetry by some is thought the easiest, but is surely the most difficult; because where the Jingle of Rhime is wanting, there must be a strong Fancy, just Sentiment, and lively Colouring, to make it even tolerable. ——This Gentleman then, said I, has mistaken himself much, if I judge right; for there is little else in that Poem of his, but a Tolerable Cadence and Measure in the Lines. ——He is surely a *dead Poet*: and therefore, here is Peace to his *Manes*.

At this point Jonas Green pulls an emblem out of his pocket and pins it to Quevedo's coat. On the badge is painted "the Device of a *Monkey riding a winged Ass*, and in the *Offskip*, *Mount Parnassus reversed, with its double Top wrapt in a thick black Cloud*." Green tells the surprised Quevedo that this is the badge of distinction for his authors, among whom Quevedo must now be classed.

A paragraph on the "moral or ethical Writers" (containing a reference to Hamilton himself as "the *splenetic Writer* of What News?") is followed by the longest paragraph in the satire, a discussion of the political writers who pretend that their concern is, on one side, "*The Liberty of the Subject*, and the *Security of every Man's Purse and Property*"; and on the other side "The Cause of *injur'd Magistracy*, and . . . the daring and *insolent contempt of Authority*." What these writers on the Prince Georges County Court issue really had at issue, said Hamilton, giving a Marxist interpretation of motives, was simply "whether a *Court-House* shall be built in *this Place* or in *that Place*, agreeable to the Interest, not of the Public, but of either contending Party." Hamilton's own views agreed with the position of "A Freeholder," whose essays appeared in the *Gazette* on January 20, February 10, March 16, and April 20, 1748. He especially ridiculed the logic of "Philanthropos" (whose arguments appeared on April 27 and in the *Postscript* to the issue of May 18, 1748), and implied that "Philanthropos" was in fact the Reverend Jacob Henderson. Hamilton and Green concluded their discussion of the political writers by drinking "a Health to the *Freeholder*, and all true *Whigs*." After this, a personification of Public Opinion appears, "a Person of nice Taste, and hard to please; I never could reconcile him to any of my Authors." To Public Opinion's recriminations, Jonas Green replies that he'll print anything for pay.

Concluding the essay, Hamilton gives a glimpse of the next room in hell, which is, appropriately enough, filled with writers for the Pennsylvania papers, and he abruptly ends the vision: "bit in the Leg by a curs'd *Musketo*, so the whole Vision vanishing, I left off dreaming and fell to scratching."

Hamilton's Lucianic satire is one of the few colonial American critical essays that does not praise or damn a particular work. Instead he assesses the local writings of the *Maryland Gazette* for its first three years. His tone, although occasionally aristocratic and dogmatic, is mainly genial and appreciative—a welcome relief from the acerbic attitude common to eighteenth-century criticism. The cyclic structure of the essay, the contents of the framework (falling to sleep while reading the dull performances and awakening to a mosquito bite), the occupation of the next room in hell by writers for the Philadelphia newspapers, Public Opinion's disapproval of all Green's authors, the satirical badge of distinction of the authors, Hamilton's nonrecognition of these "Minions of Fame," the genre of the essay—all indicate that Hamilton is mocking the authors' delusion of fame. Since Hamilton himself was a major writer for the paper, the essay is partially self-mocking, ridiculing his own vanity and foolishness in hoping for literary fame.

On March 27, 1749, Hamilton was elected a vestryman of St. Anne's Parish Church, Annapolis. He was present at eight meetings and absent from four between 1749 and March 30, 1752, when he was discharged from the office.[33] On April 12, 1749, an essay by "Philotypographus," satirizing the advertisements of the itinerant entertainers of colonial America, appeared in the *Maryland Gazette*. "Philotypographus" may have been Dr. Alexander Hamilton. The

[33] *Maryland Historical Magazine* 9 (1914):166–69.

satire on the colonial medical profession is similar to the attitude that Hamilton expresses more fully in his *Defense* of Dr. Adam Thomson (discussed below), and the attitude toward Jonas Green is similar to Hamilton's in the "Quevedo" essay. "Philotypographus" prints "a genuine Specimen of that odd Sort of Grammar and Orthography, in Use among our Underlings of the Theatre, such as *Rope-Dancers*, *Jack Puddings*, and *Tumblers*." The essay lampoons the ignorance and stupidity of these performers. Hamilton gratuitously adds that the quackery of the itinerant performers is not as bad as the lies of the medical quacks:

> Tho' these itinerant Virtuosi, may be a Degree or two below the Learning and Erudition of our Professors of *Physic* in that Way, or our *Stage-Doctors*; yet it must be observed, that tho' the latter may sometimes write more correctly, yet the Performances of the former come nigher to what they promise then those of the latter; at least if there be any Deceit, they suppose less upon our Senses, then the other Gentlemen do upon our Understanding and Judgment.

Hamilton then sympathizes with the roles of Jonas Green as editor, who must, for the honor of his press, make "Sense out of Nonsense." After this satirical introduction, he quotes "*verbatim* and *literatim*, a true copy" of John William's advertisement of his acrobatic performance.

In 1749, Hamilton and several friends started a Freemasons' society in Annapolis, and Hamilton was elected grand master. The first of the three mid-eighteenth-century sermons which the Annapolis Masons published was the Reverend William Brogden's *Freedom and Love*, which was preached at St. Anne's on Wednesday, December 27, 1749. The sermon was dedicated "To the Right Worshipful Alexander Hamilton, M. D. Master; Mr. Samuel Middleton, and Mr. John Lomas, Wardens." Six months later, the Reverend John Gordon's masonic sermon *Brotherly Love Explained and Enforc'd*, preached at St. Anne's, June 25, 1750, was dedicated to the "Right Worshipful Alexander Hamilton M. D., Master; the Rev. Alexander Malcolm and Edward Dorsey, Esq., Wardens." Accompanying Gordon's sermon is Hamilton's "A Discourse Delivered from the Chair in the Lodge-Room at Annapolis, by the Right Worshipful the Master, to the Brethren of the Ancient and Honorable Society of Free and Accepted Masons." The "Discourse" defines liberty (under three divisions: civic, religious, and moral) and shows how it affects morals, religion, "Polite Literature and Arts," and ethics. Hamilton warns that "true Liberty does not consist in an unlimited *Freedom of the Will*" and concludes by recommending to the Masons "*Charity, Benevolence,* and *Brotherly Love,*" which he calls "the brightest *Jewels of Masonry.*" Like a true citizen of the Enlightenment, Hamilton reveals his belief in cosmopolitanism when he writes, "Confine not your Benevolence to narrow Limits; let not *national, religious,* or *political* Differences break the *Great Cement.*"

The "Discourse" is noteworthy both because it refers several times to the writings of the Third Earl of Shaftesbury and especially because Hamilton averred that the support and encouragement of "*Polite* Literature and Arts" is "one great Part of the Work of a true Mason." He supported this singular opinion and applied it to the subject, "Liberty," with the following argument:

> Men are naturally inquisitive, curious, and fond of new Discoveries; and therefore in a free State, where Wit and Invention are left at large, and there is full *Liberty* of speaking and writing, they will vigorously set about the Discovery of what may be curious, instructive, and profitable; and here a Fountain will be opened of useful Learning and Knowledge, the true *Pierian Spring*, figured out by the Ancient Poets.

On August 12, 1750, the petition of the Annapolis Lodge for a charter was granted by Grand Master Oxnard. The Reverend Thomas Bacon's Masonic sermon, delivered June 25, 1753, was dedicated to Hamilton as master, and to Mr. William Stewart and Dr. Richard Tootell as wardens.[34] In addition to Hamilton as master, the only other constant masonic officer was Jonas Green, secretary.

On November 21, 1750, Dr. Adam Thomson,[35] a playwright, poet, and old schoolmate of Hamilton, delivered a lecture on preparing the

---

[34] John Gordon, *Brotherly Love Explained and Enforc'd* (Annapolis, 1750), 25–26. Hamilton's "Discourse" occupies pp. 23–27 in Gordon's work. Hamilton refers to three works by Lord Shaftesbury (Anthony Ashley Cooper) in his "Discourse": The *Essay on Wit and Humor, Advice to an Author,* and *Letter Concerning Enthusiasm.* The date of the charter of the Annapolis Lodge is given by Edward T. Schultz, *History of Freemasonry in Maryland* 3 (Baltimore, 1884–88):259.

[35] Adam Thomson, *A Discourse on the Preparation of the body for the small-pox: and the manner of receiving the infection* . . . (Philadelphia, 1750). See H. Lee Smith, "Dr. Adam Thomson, the originator of the American method of inoculation for Smallpox," *Johns Hopkins Hospital Bulletin* 20 (1909):49–52. A redaction of Smith's article is in Howard A. Kelly, *Dictionary of American Medical Biography* (New York, 1928), 1206–1207.

body for smallpox in the Philadelphia Academy's Public Hall. In the talk, Thomson proposed the "American method" of inoculation, and he attacked sheer empiricism in medicine, saying that theory and principles were absolutely necessary for the practice of medicine (p. 23). When Thomson's discourse was published, several Philadelphia doctors objected to it. Some thought that the method of inoculation he proposed was wrong, and some evidently felt that Thomson had them in mind in his attack on the empirical school. Several attacks on Thomson appeared in newspapers,[36] and Dr. John Kearsley published *A Letter to a Friend*, wherein he quoted extracts from Thomson's pamphlet and attacked him for his style, lack of learning, technique of inoculation, and lack of originality.[37]

Dr. Alexander Hamilton followed the dispute. After Kearsley's pamphlet appeared, Hamilton wrote *A Defence of Dr. Thomson's Discourse on the preparation of the Body for the small pox and the manner of receiving the infection . . .* (Philadelphia, 1751). The pamphlet, dated Annapolis, April 27, 1751, takes the form of a letter to a Philadelphia physician. Hamilton has read in the newspapers "many ill natured Sneers and rude Reflections thrown upon the Author, without any Cause or Provocation given in the Discourse," and "therefore, tho' the Doctor were an utter Stranger to me, Common Justice and Humanity would incline me to undertake his Vindication; but much more so, as he was my Fellow-Student in Physic, and intimate acquaintance; since it appears to me, that he has been ungenerously used" (p. 3). Hamilton probably addressed the letter to Dr. Phineas Bond, who had studied under Kearsley, and then gone on to school at Paris, London, and Leyden. Bond seems to have been Hamilton's favorite among the Philadelphia doctors during the latter's visits there in 1744.[38] Hamilton asked him to "pardon the Liberty I take, in addressing myself to you, on the strength of the short acquaintance I had with you, while in your City" (p. 3).

The Marylander claimed that most of the newspaper articles were

---

[36] See Carl and Jessica Bridenbaugh, *Rebels and Gentlemen* (New York, 1942), 265–70. The quarrel was carried on in the *Pennsylvania Journal* for Dec. 13, 20, and 25, 1750; Jan. 1 and 8, and the *Supplement* to Apr. 18, 1751.

[37] John Kearsley, *A Letter to a Friend: containing remarks on a discourse proposing a preparation of the body for the small-pox . . .* (Philadelphia, 1751). For an account of Kearsley (1684–1772), see A. C. Jacobson, "John Kearsley, early American physician and architect," *Medical Times* 5 (1923):29–31. One of Kearsley's "medical" sources was Daniel Defoe's *Journal of the Plague Year*.

[38] *Itinerarium*, 29, 189, 213.

"not at all to the Purpose" and that he would therefore ignore them. He challenges Kearsley's objections. Thomson has declared "that he has used a certain antimonial and mercurial Medicine safely, and even, as he thinks, with some Success." His opposers deny this and resort to calling him names for refutation. But "Things of this Nature ought to be proved, or disproved by Experience." If Thomson is wrong, the cases that prove he is in error should be cited. "But not a Tittle of this can I find in what I have seen of the News-Paper Scribble; not any Thing but positive Assertions, without any instances from Experience to Back them" (p. 9).

In answering the attack upon Thomson's lack of originality, Hamilton maintains the typical neoclassic position. Like Pope, Hamilton believed that literature said "What oft was thought, but ne'er so well expressed":

> That our Author *has propos'd nothing* new *upon* the Subject is a very merry Objection: For, granting it to be true, may not an Author write well, and yet say nothing new? Must a Performance, tho' executed with Accuracy and Elegance, be rejected and condemned, because *really* there is *nothing* new propos'd?——If this Rule was to hold, I doubt we should lose many good and valuable Pieces, and retain many trifling Performances, which are altogether Novel, on Account of the strange unprecedented Nonsense they are stuffed with. (p. 9)

Answering the charge that Thomson has offended some doctors by throwing "aspersions" on them, Hamilton wrote a vicious attack on unqualified colonial doctors. He said that the only aspersions in Thomson's paper were contained in what Thomson said "concerning Abuses in the Practice of Physic." Thomson had pointed out that of all the professions in America, "the true Qualifications of a Physician are the least examined into." The reason arises from the "silly Notion" that medical knowledge is acquired only "by bare experience and repeated Practice." It is also necessary, argued Hamilton, to know medical theory and history. The quacks who set up as doctors without such knowledge are only "Guess-Doctor[s]." There are "too many such Practitioners, who impudently impose upon Mankind." Of course, not all doctors without formal medical training are quacks; many are "good Physicians" and "worthy Men," though they have not been "dubb'd a Doctor by the Ceremony of the Imposition of a Square Cap." Study at a university cannot "inculcate Learning and Knowledge, without a good Genius and Proper Application in the

Student." But there are those who "*set up for* Physicians, and trifle with Men's Constitutions, without the least Grain of those necessary Qualifications of Learning and Common Sense." Then, in a passage reminiscent of the satire on the illiterate advertisements of the "itinerant Virtuosi," Hamilton writes:

Have we not heard of, and seen, Fools of forty Years old, who have become *Physicians*, and never studied *Physic* or been capable to study that or any other Science? Have we not many *Stage-Doctors*, who travel about to cure (as they impudently assert) *incurable* Distempers? Are there not *Seventh Sons* who have an inherent Virtue of Curing, and are *born* Doctors? Are there not many piddling Fellows, who pretend to tell all Distempers by Urine? Have there not been Porters, Cobblers, and such like *Gentry* of compleat Education, who have made Estates by their Elixirs, Balsams of Life, Grand specific Tinctures, Pills and Electuaries, and such like Impositions and Fooleries?—In fine, Are there not many that class themselves among the regular Practitioners of the healing Art, whose whole Education has been in the Shop of some half-learned Apothecary; where their chief Study had been to *con over* the Labels of the Drawers, Vials and Gally Pots, and to compound a Recipe secundum Artem? To me it appears as ridiculous to trust such Cattle with Men's Constitutions, as to Thieves and Robbers with their Cash and Treasure. (p. 10)

The people whom Thomson has vilified are only "Quacks, Imposters, and Empirics,"—useful for multiplying the "Fees of Grave-Diggers, Sextons, Undertakers, and such like solemn Gentry."

In ridiculing Kearsley and the anonymous attackers of Thomson, Hamilton tells Swift's fable of "some Apples and a Horse Turd" (p. 13). He makes a typical eighteenth-century scurrilous attack on the author of the article in the *Pennsylvania Journal* for December 20, 1750. According to Hamilton, the author has a

newly discovered Method of curing dangerous Dysenteries, by Means of a certain pneumatic Operation. He informed me of a Patient, dangerously ill with a *Bloody Flux*, at the Point of Death, who, finding some Difficulty in Respiration, desired his Servant, who tended him, to apply his Mouth to his, and blow with all his Force into his Lungs, which the good natured Fellow did several Times; and, to the great Surprize of every Body, the seemingly forlorn Patient recovered. Whether such a Whimsical Cure as this be natural, I leave it to you to judge: For I shall make no Remark upon it; only, I think, the Gentleman might easily make an Improvement on this Discovery by applying his Mouth to a certain Part, through which he might convey his *Air* or *Flatus* more immediately into the Place, where that Distemper has it's Seat.

243

Dr. Hamilton criticizes Dr. Kearsley's logic and style, and satirizes his authorities (especially Dr. Arbuthnot). Although the modern reader is likely to grant Kearsley and his supporters some validity, Thomson and Hamilton evidently had the better medical argument. Hamilton's pamphlet is certainly the most enjoyable and, beyond comparison, the best-written essay in the dispute. The techniques of meiosis, including suggestive diction (e. g., "piddling") and direct tapinosis, demonstrate that he was a formidable writer of invective. The *Pennsylvania Journal* of July 18, 1751, replied with three epigrams on Hamilton, which are notable only for their scurrility and lack of ability.

When Dr. Upton Scott came to America in 1753 from Glasgow, he brought a letter of introduction from his teacher, Dr. Robert Hamilton, professor of anatomy and botany in the University of Glasgow, and Dr. Alexander Hamilton's cousin. Hamilton gave him "a very kindly friendly reception" and their "intimacy gradually increased without the least interruption" while Hamilton lived.[39] In March, 1753, Dr. Hamilton, with Jonas Green and others, was a manager of a lottery "for raising the Sum of Three hundred Pistores, for purchasing a Town clock, and cleaning and securing the Dock, in Annapolis."[40] Hamilton's friend the Reverend Thomas Bacon advertised in the *Gazette* for April 12, 1753, that plans of the buildings for the Talbot County Charity School could be consulted in Annapolis at Dr. Hamilton's.

In 1753 Hamilton played an active part in politics. Once again, Maryland politics was not without excitement. Dr. Alexander Hamilton and Dr. George Steuart, two stubborn Scots physicians, vied for the vacant Assembly seat for Annapolis. The election was close, and the aldermen of Annapolis signed an indenture saying that Steuart had been elected, while the mayor signed one testifying to Hamilton's election. On Tuesday afternoon, October 9, 1753, a week after the General Assembly met for a session, Dr. Alexander Hamilton presented a petition to the Lower House "complaining of an undue Return, made by the Aldermen of the City of Annapolis." The House resolved to look into the matter on the following day and ordered Dr. George Steuart and Dr. Alexander Hamilton to bring in their

[39] Dr. Upton Scott's letter on Hamilton and the Tuesday Club, dated Aug. 28, 1809, is printed on pp. xxv–xxvi in Hart's edition of Hamilton's *Itinerarium*.
[40] *Maryland Gazette*, Mar. 1, 1752/3. News of this lottery is also to be found in the *Gazette* for May 24 and July 5, 1753.

"Lists of the controverted Votes ... with the particular Objection which they intend to insist upon." On the following day Dr. Steuart asked for more time, and the hearing was put off until the 17th. The House heard testimony of witnesses on Wednesday and Thursday, October 17 and 18, and on Friday, "after the most mature Deliberation" decided that Dr. Alexander Hamilton was "duly elected a Deligate for the City of Annapolis." That afternoon Hamilton went with Dr. Charles Carroll and Captain John Gassaway to the Upper House where he took "the several Oaths to the Government required by Law, subscribed the Oath of Abjuration, repeated and signed the Test." He was then seated in the House. Hamilton had summoned seventeen witnesses and Steuart thirteen. The two Scots physicians were ordered to share the hearing cost of £7 10s. 9d.[41]

His literary ability was soon recognized, for the House asked him, with Mathew Tilghman, Dr. Charles Carroll, and Major Henry Fall, to prepare an address informing the governor that the Assembly was not going to raise money and men "at this present Juncture" to help defend the frontier against the French and Indians. On the following day, March 8, 1753/4, Hamilton brought in the committee's address, which was accepted and sent to the governor.[42] Hamilton's last recorded appearance in the House was on Saturday, July 20, 1754, although he probably continued in attendance until July 25, when the Assembly adjourned. The ailing physician probably did not run again. At the next session of the Assembly, begun on December 12, 1754, his friend Stephen Bordley was returned a member from Annapolis in the room of Dr. Hamilton.[43]

On May 14, 1745, Dr. Alexander Hamilton organized the Tuesday Club. The founding members who met at Hamilton's home were John Bullen (d. 1764), commissioner of the Paper Currency Office, alderman, and captain of the Annapolis Independent Company; William Cumming (d. 1752), lawyer, a Scotsman who had been sent to Maryland in 1716 for participating in the Jacobite Rebellion of 1715; the Reverend John Gordon (d. 1790), pastor of St. Anne's, Annapolis, and later of St. Michael's, Talbot County; Robert Gordon

---

[41] *Archives of Maryland* 50:168, 179, 180, 217. Steuart later was elected an Annapolis delegate and has been called "the wheelhorse of the Proprietary party in the house." Ibid., 59:lxiii.

[42] Ibid., 427–28.

[43] Ibid., 587.

(d. 1753), judge of Provincial Court, alderman, and representative; Witham Marshe (d. 1765), secretary to the Maryland Commissioners at the treaty of Lancaster in 1744 with the Six Nations, and later Sir William Johnson's secretary for Indian affairs; and Captain William Rogers (d. 1749), clerk of the Prerogative Office. This group immediately began to frame rules for the society and gradually developed a formal organization. Members were limited to fifteen and had to take turns entertaining the club, which met every other Tuesday. The number of honorary members (persons who were free to visit the club whenever they were in Annapolis but were exempt from the duty of entertaining) was unlimited; "strangers," or invited guests, were also unlimited.

The Tuesday Club gradually changed membership as others were added, while some former members, like the Reverend John Gordon and Witham Marshe, moved out of town; others, like William Cumming and Robert Gordon, grew too old and feeble to attend meetings regularly. Bullen, Hamilton, and, slightly later, Jonas Green and William Thornton (sheriff of Anne Arundel County, church warden for St. Anne's, d. 1769) were the mainstays. The club combined the intellectual and social resources of Hamilton; Green; the Reverend Thomas Bacon; Daniel Dulany and his sons Daniel, Dennis, and Walter Dulany; John Beale Bordley; and Stephen Bordley—and other leading figures of the golden period of colonial culture. The club acted out a mock-heroic commentary on government, history, society, and manners. The club's "gelastic law," a rule ordering everyone to break out in laughter at any mention of Maryland politics, was an attempt to protect the members from the province's bitter party disputes. Following Hamilton's lead, the club gradually took on a distinct character: the meetings satirically recapitulated in miniature the course of English history, and certain members adopted well-known roles. Charles Cole, a wealthy Annapolis merchant (d. 1757), who became president of the club, was arbitrary monarch. Hamilton repeatedly protested the growth of luxury and despotic power in the club, claiming that wealth and greed had undermined the club's native simplicity, democracy, and good fellowship. Meanwhile Hamilton himself deviously organized the extravagant processions through the streets of Annapolis, designed and distributed the silver club medals, created the formal structure of the club (complete with president, chancellor, attorney-general, knight, orator, poet laureate, secretary, council, etc.), and devised a throne and canopy for the president.

Hamilton's pose satirized the prevailing belief in the "noble savage" and in primitivism; the pose also (like nearly everything done in the club) enabled Hamilton to reproduce in miniature the prevailing ideas of the mid-eighteenth century.

Conversation, music, dinner, and drinking were the usual activities of the club, and special delight was taken in the creation of conundrums and riddles. On December 31, 1745, the Tuesday Club held a ball at the State House. The reasons for postponing meetings are interesting: Tuesday, September 29, 1747, was the birthday of Charles, Lord Baron of Baltimore, and since "horse races and other diversions" were to be held in Annapolis, the meeting was put off until October 6. Meeting no. 106, May 31, 1749, was held on Wednesday because a ball was scheduled for the previous night. The club did not meet on Tuesday, September 19, 1749, because of a general muster of the county militia. No meeting was held on Tuesday, October 1, because the members rehearsed for a concert performed on Wednesday, October 2, 1751 "in the Council Chamber, for the Benefit of the Talbot County Charity School."

The meeting on January 7, 1752 was notable because three members entertained the club with music (unfortunately the Reverend Thomas Bacon could not be there): the Reverend Alexander Malcolm played first violin, Daniel Dulany the younger played second violin, and Dr. Alexander Hamilton played violoncello basso. Sometimes the members would meet at one person's house and march in procession with banners and music to another member's (or to a tavern); on October 26, 1752, they met at Richard Dorsey's and marched to Middleton's tavern. Usually five to eight members attended, and one to three guests. The most elaborate meetings were the annual anniversary celebrations in the middle of May. Before the meeting, Jonas Green wrote an ode for the occasion and Thomas Bacon composed music for the ode; the anniversary committee made arrangements for the procession and the feast; and the musicians and singers rehearsed the ode. Present at the anniversary meeting for May 15, 1750, were Captain John Addison, honorary member; the Reverend Thomas Bacon, honorary member; Abraham Barnes, honorary member; John Beale Bordley, member; Stephen Bordley, member; John Bullen, member; Charles Cole, member; Captain Alexander Cumming, guest; William Cumming, member; William Cumming, Jr., member; Richard Dorsey, member; Dennis Dulany, honorary member; Walter Dulany, member; the Reverend John Gordon, honorary member; Jonas Green, member; Dr. Alexander Hamilton, member; Dr. John Hamilton (Alexander's brother), honorary member; the Reverend Alexander Malcolm, member; Robert Morris (father of the financier of the American Revolution), honorary member; and William Thornton, member. These twenty men were all financial, political, and intellectual leaders of Maryland.

The Tuesday Club is a celebrated colonial American club because Dr. Alexander Hamilton left voluminous records of the meetings. Although Witham Marshe began as the secretary, Dr. Alexander Hamilton took over the job when Marshe left for a trip to England at the end of July, 1745. Hamilton kept thorough minutes, and in addition he prepared a "Record of the Tuesday Club, containing the first decade of the Transactions of that Society ... with the heads [drawings] of the honorable the President and the Principal officers and members, and also figures [drawings] of the most material transactions of the club ... with an appendix of Club music composed by Signior Lardini [the Reverend Thomas Bacon], the most favorite Songs us'd in the club ...."[44] This manuscript provides a fascinating portrait of eighteenth-century American club life. For the "Record," Hamilton revised and expanded the minutes taken during the meetings, added poems that were declaimed in the club (including those that the club forbade to be included in the minutes, as unworthy of its genius), and drew a number of enjoyable, if crude, wash caricatures. The "Record of the Tuesday Club" is an elaborate and unified production, complete with preface, appendix, and index (the last, regrettably, missing). References within the minutes to past and future meetings reveal that Hamilton deliberately designed the book as a whole. It is, in many ways, more fascinating than the *Itinerarium*—yet it has never been published. But the "Record of the Tuesday Club" is not Hamilton's major Tuesday Club manuscript.

In September, 1749, the Eastern Shore Triumvirate (a group affiliated with the Tuesday Club and composed of, at that time, the Reverend Thomas Bacon, the Reverend John Gordon, and Robert Morris), proposed that a history of the Tuesday Club should be written. Hamilton, who may well have instigated the idea, greeted the project enthusiastically. He recorded that on October 10, 1749:

[44] Dr. Alexander Hamilton, "A Record of the Tuesday Club," is at the Maryland Historical Society, Baltimore. The original minutes are at Evergreen House, Johns Hopkins University Library.

The Secretary produced an answer to the triumvirates Letter, drawn up by him, according to the order of the Last Sederunt [meeting], but before he read it to the Club, he made the following motion, at the Instance (as he said), of the Worshipful Triumvirate.

That an exact and accurate History of the ancient and honorable Tuesday Club, should be undertaken and penned, from its first foundation, to this present time, and, that an able Historiographer, should be appointed to compose and collect the Same.

To which motion the Honorable the President and the Club gave a Categorical answer in the negative and would by no means consent, that any such History should be compiled, this repulse very much chagrined the Secretary, as he expected to be employed in this great work, being the only proper person for it as keeper, of the Records, for he promised himself not only great Profits, as the Club's Historiographer, but also flattered his vanity, that he should make a very great figure in the Republic of Letters, in quality of an Historian.

Of course Hamilton's reply was facetious, but from this suggestion came the "History of the Ancient and Honourable Tuesday Club." The "History of the Tuesday Club" was carefully planned, painstakingly written, and much revised. Hamilton probably began writing a draft of the "History" before he started the "Record." An early version of the "History" is extant: it is much less elaborate than the revised "History," lacking the overall structure and the facetious names. Hamilton began working on the revised version of the "History of the Tuesday Club" in the early fall of 1754, for the "Dedication to the most Learned, the Attorney General of the Ancient and honorable Tuesday Club and his successors" is dated at the end (p. vii) "From my Study Septr the 9th 1754."[45]

Hamilton uses a highly allusive mock-heroic style in the "History." When he writes a "learned dissertation" in the first chapter of Book II of the "History," he does it in the manner of "the ingenious Mr. Robert Burton"; when he describes the club's civil war, he adopts the style of Clarendon; and when he narrates the literary battles of colonial Maryland, he imitates Pope's *Dunciad*. Although Hamilton

---

[45] Both the draft of the "History" and the three volumes of "The History of the Ancient and Honourable Tuesday Club" are at Evergreen House, Johns Hopkins University Library. Additional Tuesday Club manuscripts are: a continuation of "The History of the Tuesday Club," pages numbering 503 to 564 (of vol. 3), covering the minutes from Dec. 16, 1754, to Apr. 22, 1755, located in the Dulany Papers, Maryland Historical Society; and the minutes of the meetings from May 27, 1755, to Feb. 11, 1756, deposited in the Manuscript Division, Library of Congress.

writes in the Scriblerian tradition, his main literary guide is neither
Arbuthnot nor Gay, neither Pope nor Swift: *The History of Tom
Jones, Foundling* by Henry Fielding contributes more to the structure and style of Hamilton's "History" than any other single work.
In imitation of Fielding, Hamilton writes a rambling seemingly ex-
traneous, but invariably fascinating first chapter for each of the twelve
books. These first chapters are delightful. Each is an essay, complete
in itself—but each also forwards the unified design—an attempt to record a complete philosophy of life. These were Hamilton's closing
years. The physician knew he had not long to live; and at the age of
forty-two, slowly dying, he began to work on his final and most
ambitious manuscript.

In composing the "History of the Tuesday Club" Hamilton made
several major changes from the earlier manuscripts. The "Record"
only gives a straightforward account of the minutes of the meetings.
In the first two books of the "History," Hamilton provides a background and pedigree for the Tuesday Club. Although a satire on
genealogy, these two books contain much information about the
clubs of Scotland and America, describing the ceremonies of Edinburgh's Whin-bush Club (which Hamilton, as we have seen, had belonged to) and the beginning of the South River Club. Chapter I of
Book I is, fittingly, an essay "Of History and Historians." Hamilton
created facetious names for all the club members and visitors. With
his own love of writing in mind, Hamilton dubbed himself "Loquacious Scribble, M. D."; Anthony Bacon, the overseas delegate of the
club (M. P., brother of Thomas Bacon, and one of England's richest
men), is described as "Comely Coppernose"; Thomas Bacon, in view
of his musical achievements, becomes "Signior Lardini"; the witty
John Beale Bordley is characterized as "Quirpum Comic"; Thomas
Cumming, the American delegate-at-large of the club, is labeled
"Coney Pimp Frontinbrass"; Edward Dorsey is "Drawhim Quaint";
Richard Dorsey's appearance (and habits?) elicits "Tunebelly Bow-
zer"; Hamilton's brother-in-law Walter Dulany becomes "Slyboots
Pleasant"; the humorous Virginian who became a Maryland patriot
leader, Colonel William Fitzhugh, becomes "Col. Comico Butman";
Hamilton's friend the learned and suave Reverend John Gordon is
characterized as "Rev. Smoothum Sly"; Jonas Green, in view of his
favorite punch, becomes "Jonathan Grog"; James Hollyday, a musician, is "Joshua Fluter"; Thomas Jennings is characterized as "Prim
Timerous"; the Reverend Andrew Lendrum is unflatteringly de-

scribed as "Rev. Roundhead Muddy"; the smooth-talking Colonel Edward Lloyd becomes "Col. Courtly Phraze"; casual John Lomas becomes "Laconic Comus"; irascible William Lux is "Crinkum Crankum"; the learned author of textbooks on mathematics and music, Reverend Alexander Malcolm, is described as "Philo-Dogmaticus"; his friend Witham Marshe, the Indian expert, is "Prattle Motely, Esq."; Robert Morris, father of the financier of the American Revolution, is "Merry Makefun"; the dashing Captain William Rogers is described as "Capt. Seemly Spruce"; the well-traveled, young Dr. Upton Scott becomes "Dr. Jeronimo Jaunter"; and William Thornton, a musician second only to Bacon, is "Protomusicus Neverout." And the names go on. Hamilton obviously enjoyed creating these humorous appellations, which are an important part of the machinery that make the completed "History of the Tuesday Club" a work of art.

The "History of the Tuesday Club" is more concerned with literature than are the minutes. Not only are there more poems in the "History" (and these additions, written "by a Clubical Bard," I believe to be mainly by Hamilton), but he also writes at length about the literature of Maryland, and gives a number of facetious criticisms. Concerning Green's poem of March 24, 1752, "A Mournful Episode," he writes:

> This poem, the Club seemed to be particularly fond of, esteeming it one of the best performances of their Laureat, Tho others judged, that the first Anniversary ode, the acrostic on the President, and the poetical Entry of Sederant 164, were by much the Compleatest pieces of any that ever that Bard had done, but we need not be much surprized that the Club judged differently from the world in this affair. They looking upon the performances of their poet with milder eyes than the public looked upon them, when they made their Onaccuracies and oversights, which that Ingenious Gentleman from a too great rapidity of Imagination was apt to fall into which could not well escape the nice Eyes of the Critics, and therefore, these Gentlemen were never disposed to spare but would call out with great vehemence, when reading any of his compositions, O horrid!—abominable! shoking stuff!—poor!—mean!—Low!—pish! 'tis intollerable. And other such exclamatory phrazes, commonly used by Critics, but our Laureat Chose to proceed in his own way, not regarding their annotations and Emendations, & indeed, had he suffered his pieces to undergo any alterations, according to the delicate sentiments of these refined gentlemen, it was the opinion of the Club, and of many other Judicious persons, that they would thereby have suffered, as much in their Clubical turn, and humor, as the works of the

Celebrated Shakespeare, suffered in their natural sublime elegance, and beautiful simplicity, by being too much thumbed and beslubbered by the critics in the age next to him.[46]

Another way in which the "History" differs from the minutes is that in the former Hamilton characterizes and individualizes the club members. Thus, instead of the extremely brief records of the first club meeting found in the minutes, Hamilton writes:

> Such of my readers, as have perused the last chapter of the preceeding book, if their memory be not very short will remember, that messieurs Prattle Motely [Witham Marshe] and Loquacious Scribble M. D. [Hamilton himself] the residue of the Ugly Club called to their assistance Jealous Spyplot Esqr [William Cumming], Sergeant at Law, and the Reverend Mr. Smoothum Sly [John Gordon], parson of the parish, in order to form a new Club, and fix it upon a better and more lasting foundation, than any of the Clubs hitherto erected, They presently got four more to join them, vist. Capt. Seemly Spruce [William Rogers], a Jolly boon companion, and no early Starter, being one who usually wore his sitting breeches at a nights compotation. Captn Serious Social [Robert Gordon] of the same kidney, and noted for singing old cock, of surly aspect and few words, but gifted with an excellent musical voice, and a sincere lover of the Bowl and tobacco pipe, these had formerly been members of the Red House Club; and Captn Bully Blunt [John Bullen], a person of a very happy turn to the Burlesque, which made him an exceeding good Club man.
>
> These gentlemen then, meeting upon Tuesday the 14th day of May, in the year 1745, the same month and day on which the Red House Club met, under Mr. George Neilson Sixteen years before, formed and erected themselves into a Club, which they called by the name of the Tuesday Club; they met first at the Lodging of Doctor Loquacious Scribble, who first exercised the office of Steward, and Chairman to the Club; and the Candles being lit, the punch made, and the pipes fairly set a going, after two or three rounds of the punch bowl, they applied themselves to make and pass some wholesome Laws, for the good government and regulation of the Society, In which, they did not trust so much to their own Judgment, and Invention, as some vain people are apt to do, but took for a pattern, the regulations and laws of other Clubs, particularly those of the ancient and venerable Tuesday, (or whin bush) Club of Lunnerie, of which they reckoned themselves a direct continuation, on the same line, and, upon this position, they assumed the name of the ancient and honorable Tuesday Club, of Annapolis in Maryland. . . .[47]

Although more than thirty original poems are recorded in the club's minutes, only one was published. This was "Lugubris Cantus," which

---

[46] "History" 2:533–34.
[47] "History" 1:141.

appeared in the *Maryland Gazette*, January 16, 1750/1. It is no better (and perhaps a little worse) than the majority of the Tuesday Club poems. Perhaps Green published it because it was short and by the "conjoint" muses of the club; or, more likely, Green had a blank space in the paper. Whenever the president, Charles Cole, missed a meeting, the club composed a poem lamenting his absence, which was delivered to him by a delegation on a following day. When Cole was indisposed on Tuesday night, January 15, the club composed "Lugubris Cantus, In Imitation of *Spencer*, Author of the *Fairy Queen*." The first two stanzas depict the melancholy mood of the members. In the third stanza the Genius of the club appears and asks what troubles them. Alarmed at the news of Cole's illness, he cries: "If Cole should Die, your Glory's at an End: / But Courage, I'll back to Olympus fly, / And urge almighty Jove the Fatal Stroke to 'fend." The Genius resolves to "taste your Punch before I go" and afterward proclaims:

> Long then may mighty Cole his Visage show
> In that exalted noble Chair of State,
> And may he Rule a Thousand Years and mo'e,
> This ancient Tuesday Club, e'er he submits to fate.

And the poem ends with a convivial last stanza:

> She spoke, and fled; the Members all uprous'd
>   With new'born Joy each Countenance was crown'd:
> Her kindly Words new Courage soon infus'd,
>   And with a smile the sparkling Bowl went round.
>   The Hall re-echo'd with a joyful Sound,
>   And every Lip dipt deep into the Bowl;
> That soon all Grief in Jovial Mirth was drown'd,
> And all the jolly Song was, Long Live Noble COLE.

As a pleasant, extemporaneous, joint effusion, this poem speaks well of both the ability and reading of its authors.

One of Hamilton's "Asides," Chapter I of Book VIII, "A modest proposal for the new modelling and Improvement of our modern Theatre," contains a short mock play—one more testimonial to Hamilton's interest in every aspect of literature and the fine arts. Hamilton's drawings for his various Tuesday club manuscripts are valuable for visually recording (in caricature) the leading Tuesday Club personalities and some typical club scenes. Hamilton also designed a Tuesday Club medal and a club seal. A wax impression of the seal and four of the medals are extant.[48] When one of the members lost his silver

[48] See Anna Wells Rutledge, "A Humorous Artist in Colonial Maryland,"

medal, he advertised in the *Maryland Gazette* for January 9, 1752, offering two guineas reward for it. The "hieroglyphic" or monogram of the Tuesday Club was 〔 perhaps representing an abbreviation for the society's motto, "Concordia Res Parvae Crescunt." Since the monogram turns up as a signature in John Mercer's "Dinwiddianae," since Jonas Green is known to have been one of Mercer's correspondents, and since William Fitzhugh claimed that he had started a Virginia affiliate of the Tuesday Club (the Hickory Hill Club)—John Mercer of Virginia (who had earlier made Ebenezer Cook a loan) probably communicated with Hamilton's Tuesday Club wits.[49] The symbolic design of friendship on the club medal was two clasped hands within a heart. The earliest college fraternity may have been influenced by the Tuesday Club: William and Mary's "F. H. C." Society incorporated in their medal the design of two hands clasped below (above in one medal) a chevron with a heart at its apex.[50]

The Tuesday Club was well-known in contemporary American society. Nearly all distinguished visitors to Annapolis between 1745 and 1756 were guests at its meetings. Franklin (whom Hamilton dubs "Electro Vitrifrico" in the "History") made a typical clubical pun when he visited the club on January 22, 1753/4.[51] At least one notice appeared in the New York papers about the Tuesday Club. Thomas Cumming (d. 1774) wrote a mock "libel" on the Tuesday Club and its president, Charles Cole, which was published in a New York paper in the spring of 1752.[52] The traditions of the Tuesday Club were continued by later Maryland clubs: the Forensic Club (which flourished from 1759 to 1763), and the Hominy Club (whose president and lead-

American Collector, 16 (Feb., 1947), 8–9, 14–15; Sarah Elizabeth Freeman, "The Tuesday Club Medal," *The Numismatist* 58 (1945):1313–22.

[49] Richard Beale Davis, *The Colonial Virginia Satirist, Transactions* of the American Philosophical Society, vol. 57, pt. 1 (Philadelphia, 1967), p. 6 and n. 8, p. 13, and p. 34, n. 10. "Mr. Mitchelson" and "Mr. Stewart" who were guests at the club on June 23, 1752, requested permission to set up an affiliated society in Virginia. The motto is from Sallust, *Jurgurtha*, X, 6: "harmony makes small states great" (Loeb).

[50] Jane Carson, *James Innes and his Brothers of the F. H. C.* (Williamsburg, 1965). The frontispiece contains pictures of the F. H. C. medals, which are discussed on 3–4.

[51] Robert R. Hare, "Electro Vitrifrico in Annapolis," 62–66.

[52] The "History," 3:37 states that a slander on the Tuesday Club appeared in one of the "New York Weekly Gazettes" about May 12, 1752, but I have not been able to find it in any of the extant New York papers. The Reverend Alexander Malcolm wrote a reply to it which was read in the club on May 26, 1752, but evidently not published.

ing light was the literary man and clergyman Jonathan Boucher) both attempted to emulate the ideas and activities of Hamilton's society.[53] And Hamilton's facetious club name for Thomas Bacon found its way into one of the standard county histories of England.[54]

The artist Charles Willson Peale recalled in his autobiography that he once, when a boy, stopped Dr. Hamilton on an Annapolis street and asked him "What is the best drink for health?" Perhaps Dr. Hamilton had spent the previous night at the Tuesday Club, drinking and singing with his friends; but more likely his immediate and amused reply (which Peale remembered all his life—although Peale may have exaggerated the Scotsman's brogue) is but one more example of Hamilton's quick wit: "Toddy mun. The spirit must hae something to act on, and therefore acts on the sugar and does nae injury to the stomach."[55]

In his closing months Hamilton restrained his slave's economic efforts. He advertised in the *Maryland Gazette* for January 1, 1756, that his Negro "*Dromo*, whom some call *Ben*, a Cooper by Trade" has for the past several years been allowed to increase his trade for his own benefit. Hamilton will no longer allow him to do so, will prosecute anyone who deals with him, and will pay a 10s. reward to persons who inform against anyone doing business with him.

Hamilton died on Tuesday morning, May 11, 1756. A draft for an obituary, probably in the hand of Walter Dulany, says that "he had exquisite parts and was very assiduous in his studies, by which means he became accomplished in all the Refinement of polite literature."[56] And Jonas Green published the following notice in the *Maryland Gazette* for May 13, 1756:

[53] Minutes of the Forensic Club are in Maryland MSS (Misc.), Box 1, Manuscripts Department, New York Public Library. The only published account of the Forensic Club appeared in the Baltimore *Sun*, Aug. 25, 1907. The Minutes of the Hominy Club, 1770–73, are in the Dreer Collection, Historical Society of Pennsylvania. A contemporary account is Jonathan Boucher's *Reminiscences of an American Loyalist, 1738–1789* (Boston, 1925), 66–67. See also Theodore L. Chase, "Records of the Hominy Club of Annapolis," *American Historical Record* 1 (July and Aug., 1872), 295–303, 348–55.

[54] Jonathan Boucher wrote the sketch of Bacon in William Hutchinson, *History of the County of Cumberland* 2 (Carlisle, England, 1794):41.

[55] Quoted in Charles Coleman Sellers, *Charles Willson Peale* 1 (Philadelphia, 1947):37.

[56] Dulany Papers, Maryland Historical Society. Hamilton's death was also announced in the obituary column of the *Gentleman's Magazine* 26 (Aug., 1756): 412.

On Tuesday last in the Morning, Died, at his House in this City, Alexander Hamilton, M. D. aged 44 Years. The Death of this valuable and worthy Gentleman is universally and justly lamented: His medical Abilities, various Knowledge, strictness of Integrity, simplicity of Manners, and extensive Benevolence, having deservedly gained him the Respect and Esteem of all Ranks of Men. —No man, in his Sphere, has left fewer Enemies, or more Friends.

No one before Hamilton responded so well in prose to the influence of American scenery. Arriving in Maryland less than five years after the death of Richard Lewis, Hamilton must have learned of that poet's treatment of American nature, but his letter to the Reverend David Smith demonstrates his appreciation for nature and romantic scenery before his emigration. Even more interesting than Hamilton's attitude toward nature is the response to American society expressed in his various writings. These reveal the reactions of a cultivated and educated man to his American acculturation. Americans, as Hamilton well knew before he emigrated, were regarded as sharp, money-hungry, uncivilized barbarians. Yet Hamilton found (what he must have anticipated from the letters of his brother John) that a large element of the population was as urbane as any group he had ever known. About the time that Hamilton decided to remain permanently in America (the winter of 1743/4), he evidently resolved the problem of his own American identity. His solution was to satirize the forms and prevailing ideas of English society. Later writers would learn to pose as the illiterate sharpsters they were supposed to be—while satirizing the false ideals of English or civilized (Eastern) society. Although Hamilton did not adopt an illiterate dialect (unlike John Mercer, a contemporary Virginia poet), his satire on prevailing standards of English life was more thorough than any contemporary's. Hamilton's major works were not published in his own time, but he was a well-known literary and social figure in the small, colonial society. He dominated literature in mid-eighteenth-century Maryland and helped create a pose increasingly used by American writers. With the publication of Dr. Alexander Hamilton's *Itinerarium* in 1907, students of American literature and culture began to value his genius—but only with the publication of the "Record of the Tuesday Club" and "The History of the Tuesday Club" will the extent of his talent and achievement be fully realized and appreciated.

JAMES STERLING

POET

Maryland's "First Rate Poet," the Reverend James Sterling (1701–63), immigrated to the colonies in 1737 with an established literary reputation. His plays had been performed and published in Dublin and London, his poems had appeared in English and Irish newspapers and magazines (and been reprinted in American newspapers), his poetic translations of the classics were popular, and he had published a volume of his *Poetical Works*. In America, he continued to write poetry; and although his American poetry is better than his earlier work, much of it has not previously been identified. Not so good a poet as Richard Lewis, Sterling was nevertheless a reputable and productive neoclassic poet. He described American nature, used the *translatio studii* theme, and made sustained use of sentimentality.

The grandson of the Reverend James and Helen (Maxwell) Sterling, the son of Captain James and Patience (Hansard) Sterling,[1] James Sterling was born in 1701 at Downrass, King's County, Ireland. After his education at "Mr. Lloyd's" in Dublin, he matriculated at Trinity College on April 17, 1716, and graduated in 1720.[2] With his friend and companion Matthew Concannen, Sterling was one of Dublin's young literary lights.[3] His earliest known published work was

---

[1] For a genealogy of the Sterling family, see Lorton Wilson, "The Rev. James Sterling," *Notes and Queries*, 13th ser. 1 (1923): 13–14.

[2] George Dames Burtchaell and Thomas Ulick Sadleir, *Alumni Dublinenses* ... (Dublin, 1935), 780.

[3] Lawrence C. Wroth, "James Sterling: Poet, Priest, and Prophet of Empire" (Worcester, Mass., 1931), 11; this is an offprint from the American Antiquarian Society *Proceedings*, n.s. 41 (1931):25–76.

a tragedy, *The Rival Generals*, written between his eighteenth and twenty-first years.[4] Published in Dublin in two editions in 1722, the play was reprinted in London in the same year.[5] Despite Concannen's fulsome prefatory poem, *The Rival Generals* is more important for its historical position in the Irish theater than for any intrinsic merit: it was the first tragedy written by a native.[6] Nancy Lyddel, Sterling's future wife, acted in the production, which was performed at the Theatre-Royal in Dublin, perhaps before 1721.[7] He must have married late in 1722 or early in 1723, for "Miss Lyddel" of *The Rival Generals* (1722) had become Mrs. Sterling by October 2, 1723.[8] No doubt he journeyed with his wife to London in 1723—rather than, as legend has it,[9] with his friend Matthew Concanen. At any rate, Sterling's wife, "lately arrived from the theatre in Dublin,"[10] played the part of Desdemona in *Othello* on October 2, and of Marcella in *Don Quixote* (singing "I burn, I burn") on October 4, 1723, at Lincoln's Inn Fields. In 1724, Concanen's collection *Miscellaneous Poems* (London, 1724) appeared, containing three poems by Sterling. The most interesting is "To Robert Lovett, Esq.; Author of a

[4] James Sterling, *The Poetical Works of the Rev. James Sterling* (Dublin, 1734), sig. A2ᵛ.

[5] Daniel Hipwell, "The Rev. James Sterling," *Notes and Queries*, 8th ser. 9 (1896):195–96. La Tourette Stockwell, *Dublin Theatres and Theatre Customs 1637–1820* (Kingsport, Tenn., 1938), 322 n. 58, locates a copy of one Dublin edition in the Trinity College Library. The British Museum *Catalogue*, vol. 229, col. 727, distinguishes between two Dublin editions of 1722: one octavo, and one twelvemo. See especially Carl J. Stratman, *Bibliography of English Printed Tragedy, 1565–1900* (Carbondale, Ill., 1966), nos. 6009, 6010, and 6011.

[6] John Genest, *Some Account of the English Stage from 1660–1830* (Bath, 1832), 10:283, pointed out that *The Rival Generals* would have had to have been acted before Charles Shadwell's *Rotherick O'Connor* in 1720 to be the first Irish tragedy. It seems unlikely that Sterling would have proclaimed that he was the first who "awak'd the Irish Muse to Tragedy" (*Rival Generals*, sig. A3) unless it were so, and more unlikely that Concannen would claim priority for Sterling (*Rival Generals*, sig. A4) unless he thought it true. See also Sterling's verses to Robert Lovett, quoted in the text.

[7] *Rival Generals* (London, 1722), and Sterling's *Poetical Works*, sig. A2ᵛ.

[8] William Smith Clark, *The Early Irish Stage: The Beginnings to 1720* (Oxford, 1955), 162 and 167, mentions Nancy Lyddel. Sterling evidently uses poetic license when he speaks of her as *Emilia* in "Verses on the death of a Beloved Wife," *Poetical Works*, 143–46. Although "Miss Lyddel" of the *Rival Generals* (London, 1722), sig. B2ᵛ, was probably Sterling's future wife, she may have been Mary Lyddel,, who later married Henry Giffard. Nancy and Mary Lyddel were sisters.

[9] Hipwell, 196.

[10] Emmett L. Avery, *The London Stage, 1660–1800: A Calendar . . . Part 2: 1700–1729* (Carbondale, Ill., 1960), 738.

Tragedy, call'd the Bastard." Using travel literature imagery, Sterling likens himself to Columbus, and Lovett to Amerigo Vespucci:

> The Muse, by me, *Columbus*-like, shall boast
> New Worlds discover'd, and an unknown Coast;
> Buskin'd by me, she first essay'd to rage,
> And feebly learn'd to tread an *Irish* Stage:
> But now, Americus divides the Fame;
> The Land I first explor'd, shall bear your Name!
>
> (p. 276)

Although Sterling's next tragedy, *The Parricide*, was not published until 1736, it was probably written and performed as early as 1726.[11] In 1728 he brought out his translation of Musaeus, *The Loves of Hero and Leander*, which was reprinted at least three times.[12] During the late 1720s, his wife became a famous and accomplished actress. She played Lady Ann in *Richard The Third* on March 22, 1731, acted the lead in *The Tragedy of Lady Jane Grey*, and was celebrated for her portrayal of Polly Peachum:

> Mrs. Sterling, who acted Polly Peachum's part in the Beggar's Opera played it with so much applause, that the House called out that she might have a Benefit Night, and obliged the Players to give it her, which she had on Thursday [April 11, 1728] and received one hundred and five Pounds fourteen Shillings, and besides thirty odd Pounds thrown to her on the Stage, it is acted this day again, which is the eleventh time in this Kingdom.[13]

In 1731, she also played Leiza, Reseck's daughter, in James Darcy's tragedy *Love and Revenge*. Darcy wrote that "Mrs. Sterling, in every one's Opinion, as well as in mine, deserves all the Encomiums we can bestow on her."[14] A singular performance was her delivery of Sterling's "A Prologue Spoken on the King's Birth-day, 1731 . . . when a Bill was brought into the House of Commons, by Marcus Anthony Morgan, Esq.; for prohibiting the wearing of Gold and Silver Lace,

[11] Cf. Allardyce Nicoll, *A History of English Drama, 1660–1900* (Cambridge, 1952) 2:357. *The Parricide* was published in Feb., 1736: see "The Register of Books" in the *Gentleman's Magazine* 6 (Feb., 1736): 99. A copy of *The Prologue to the Parricide spoke by Mrs. Sterling the Author's Wife* survives in the Gilbert Collection, Charleville Mall Library, Dublin (see Stockwell, 322 n. 63). Since Nancy (Lyddel) Sterling retired from the stage early in 1732 and died shortly after that, *The Parricide* must have been written at least as early as 1731.
[12] Dublin, 1728; London, 1728; London, c. 1735; and in his *Poetical Works*, in 1736.
[13] *Dublin Gazette*, Apr. 13, 1728; quoted from Stockwell, 61.
[14] James Darcy, *Love and Revenge* (London, 1732), x.

Embroidery, &c."[15] She was a principal actress at Dublin's Smock Alley Theatre, especially noted for her "rendering of medley epilogues of a topical nature, half in song, half in recitation," epilogues probably composed by her husband. Because of failing health, she was forced to quit the stage; her farewell appearance was a performance of the *Beggar's Opera*, at the Smock Alley Theatre, on May 22, 1732, when she recited her husband's poignant epilogue on the occasion. Sterling mourned for her in his "Verses on the death of a Beloved Wife."[16]

After her death, Sterling took a Master of Arts degree and became a minister. Appointed chaplain to His Majesty's "own Royal Regiment of Foot," under the command of Colonel Charles Lanoe, Sterling dedicated *The Poetical Works of the Rev. James Sterling* (Dublin, 1734) to Lanoe. In the Preface, Sterling writes that he has been credited with the authorship of "several anonymous scurrilities, call'd Satires." He denies writing them, saying that he detests slander. But he approves of "general" satire, which "has been not only always thought useful, but necessary to the state." He claims that "even particular satire may be often allowable to chastise flagrant crimes, and vices of which the laws cannot take proper cognizance, or assign a due punishment to; but this must always be done with a view to the good of the community, and never to gratify a private resentment, or the wantonness of a mischievous imagination" (sig. A2). After revealing that he wrote *The Rival Generals* "and many of the following poems" between his eighteenth and twenty-first years (sig. A2ᵛ), he added that he intended to publish a subsequent volume containing the rest of his poetical works, but the sequel was never published. Although none of the poems in his *Poetical Works* proclaims him a major poet, Sterling wrote in a variety of forms, demonstrating constant experimentation. Already his dominant themes had appeared in his verse: trade, empire, and scholarship. Some of the early poems were later expanded, polished, and republished in America.

His wife's brother-in-law Henry Giffard (who had married Mary Lyddel) produced Sterling's *Parricide* at Goodman's Fields Theater in London on January 29 and 31, February 2 and 3, and March 3, 1736. For the January 29 performance, *The Parricide* was advertised as "never acted before," but the *dramatis personae* in the published

---

[15] *Poetical Works*, 28–30.
[16] W. J. Lawrence, "The Rev. James Sterling," *Notes and Queries*, 10th ser. 3 (1905):385–86. Her farewell epilogue is in Sterling's *Poetical Works*, 168–70.

play (brought out on February 2, 1736) differed from the cast for this performance.[17] Sterling's prologue for a performance of *The Conscious Lovers* at Goodman's Fields "in Honour of the Royal Wedding" was published in the *London Magazine* for May, 1736, p. 269. A poem on the Irish Whale Fishery which may be his appeared in Dublin in 1737.[18] Like his later *Epistle to . . . Dobbs*, the poem is dedicated to Arthur Dobbs and is similar to the *Epistle* in subject and technique.

By 1736 the Reverend James Sterling had decided to emigrate to America. He informed the bishop of London early in that year of his "Design of going to Boston in America to supply the new Church there; being invited over by the principal Inhabitants and in particular by Mr. Auchmuty, Judge of the Admiralty, my near Relation."[19] When he learned, on June 15, 1736, "by a ship, just arriv'd from New England," that the Reverend Thomas Harward, lecturer at King's Chapel, Boston, had died, Sterling immediately offered himself "as a candidate to fill" the vacancy. He said that his "sole Motive" for wishing to go to "that remote part of the world is the prospect of contributing more there to the Cause of Religion in my sacred function, than the corruption of the times will allow in my own country."[20] The Bostonians, however, wanted no part of a minister who was a playwright and had been married to an actress. The Reverend Roger Price, rector of King's Chapel, Boston, wrote the bishop of London on November 20, 1736, that some of his parishioners were trying to have a "certain parson" named Sterling appointed as his

[17] Arthur H. Scouten, *The London Stage, 1660–1800; A Calendar . . . Part 3: 1729–1747* (Carbondale, Ill., 1961), 545, 547, and 548. W. A. Henderson, "The Rev. James Sterling," *Notes and Queries*, 8th ser. 9 (1896):196, gives the date of publication. Henderson's source was probably the *Gentleman's Magazine* 6 (Feb., 1736):99.

[18] [James Sterling?] *A Friend in Need is a Friend in Deed, or, A Project, at this Critical Junction, to gain the Nation a hundred thousand Pounds per Annum from the Dutch: by an Irish Whale Fishery, Inscrib'd to Arthur Dobbs, Esq . . .* (Dublin, 1737).

[19] Robert Auchmuty, Judge of Admiralty in Boston, was author of *The Importance of Cape Breton to the British Nation* (London, 1745). See Wroth, 17. Robert Auchmuty's mother, Isabella (Sterling) Auchmuty, was James Sterling's aunt; therefore, Robert Auchmuty was his first cousin. Wilson, 14, and Annette Townsend, *The Auchmuty Family of Scotland and America* (New York, 1932), 1.

[20] Sterling's letter to the bishop of London, dated June 15, [1736], is printed in full by Wroth, "James Sterling," 15–16.

assistant. Sterling, said Price, had been considered by a proposed new church in Boston but did not suit the promoters, for he is rumored to have written a play called *The Rival Generals*—and actually to have *married* an actress! [21]

Sterling received the royal bounty as a missionary on September 16, 1737. Two months later the former playwright had arrived in Maryland. On November 16, 1737, he received an induction to All Hallows Parish, Anne Arundel County, Maryland, where he remained until his resignation on July 18, 1739, the same day he was appointed rector of St. Anne's, Annapolis, by Governor Samuel Ogle. On August 5, he presented his letter of induction to the vestry of St. Anne's.[22] Four months later, while Sterling was still at St. Anne's, the great revivalist minister George Whitefield visited Annapolis on his first colonial tour. Whitefield went "to pay my respects" to Sterling on Thursday, December 6, 1739. Sterling offered the itinerant minister "his pulpit, his house, or anything he could supply me with." About four that afternoon, Sterling took Whitefield and several of the revivalist's friends to a "gentleman's house," where Whitefield recriminated with the company for their strenuous defense of "what they called *innocent* diversions." According to Whitefield "cards, dancing, and such like, draw the soul from God, and lull it asleep as much as drunkenness and debauchery." The Great Awakener pointed out that ministers should be on their guard to protect their parishioners from the "falsely called *innocent* entertainments of the polite part of the world; for women are as much enslaved to their fashionable diversions, as men are to their bottle and their hounds."[23] Sterling thought that Whitefield was an excessively emotional bigot, but, temporarily, the former playwright controlled himself. He later, as

---

[21] William Wilson Manross, ed., *The Fulham Papers in the Lambeth Palace Library* (Oxford, 1965), 71 (V. 205-206). A nineteenth-century authority on the history of the early American theater thought that the Reverend Myles Cooper's 1773 prologue for the benefit of the New York Hospital marked that minister as the only American clergyman who "in any way contributed to the literature of the theater" before the Revolution. See George O. Seilhamer, *History of the American Theatre Before the Revolution*, 1 (Philadelphia, 1888): 323-24.

[22] Gerald Fothergill, *A List of Emigrant Ministers to America, 1690–1811* (London, 1904), 57. For a brief sketch of Sterling as a clergyman, see Nelson Waite Rightmyer, *Maryland's Established Church* (Baltimore, 1956), 213. See also *Archives of Maryland*, 19:521, and 20:94; *Maryland Historical Magazine* 26 (1931):150 and 154; 8 (1913):353; and 26 (1931):157.

[23] *George Whitefield's Journals* (London, 1960), 366-67.

we shall see, viciously replied. On Friday, December 7, Governor Ogle "put aside his court to come to" Whitefield's morning service and invited Whitefield to dine with him at noon. Evidently Whitefield sensed Sterling's coolness: Whitefield recorded that "the minister seemed somewhat affected, and under convictions; but I fear a false politeness, and the pomps and vanities of the world, eat out the vitals of religion in this place."[24]

In the spring of 1740, Sterling served as chaplain to Maryland's General Assembly. On August 26, 1740, he resigned from St. Anne's to accept induction to the more lucrative parish of St. Paul's, Kent County.[25] Sterling lived at Chestertown, on the Eastern Shore of Maryland, until his death over twenty years later. He began accumulating an estate on the Eastern Shore on June 8, 1743, when he rented a parcel of land from the visitors of Kent County's Free School.[26] On September 19, 1743, about ten years after the death of his first wife, Sterling married again. Rebecca Holt, widow of the Reverend Arthur Holt, became the mother of Sterling's only child, Rebecca Sterling, on November 22, 1744.[27] Sterling's wife Rebecca died between 1744 and 1749, for on September 7, 1749, he married his third wife, Mary Smith, granddaughter of Kent County's James Smith.[28]

One of Sterling's friends was Charles Peale, father of the artist Charles Willson Peale. While Sterling was rector of St. Anne's, Charles Peale was master of Annapolis' King William School. Soon after Sterling moved to St. Paul's, Kent County, Peale moved to Queen Anne's County (which is adjacent to Kent County) to be master of the free school there. When Charles Willson Peale was born in Queen Anne's on April 15, 1741, the father proudly took the child to Chestertown where Sterling baptized him. When the Kent County schoolmaster's position became vacant, the minister evidently

---

[24] Ibid., 368.

[25] *Archives of Maryland*, 19:521, and 20:94.

[26] Deeds, Kent County, Liber J. S. No. 24, folio 398, Maryland Hall of Records.

[27] Wroth, "James Sterling," 19. Rightmyer, 190 and 213. Register, 1722–1850, St. Luke's Parish, Queen Anne's County, 51. Vestry Minutes, St. Paul's Parish, Kent County, 88. Maryland Hall of Records. In Nov., 1763, Sterling's daughter married William Carmichael (she is referred to only as "my daughter Rebecca" in his will, dated Oct. 31, 1763, but mentioned as Rebecca Carmichael in the inventory, dated Dec. 1, 1763). See Wills, 1763, Kent County, No. 1166; and Inventories, 1763, Kent County, box 23, folder 39, Maryland Hall of Records. For William Carmichael, see the brief account in the *DAB*.

[28] Register, 1722–1850, St. Luke's Parish, Queen Anne's County, 60. *Maryland Historical Magazine* 18 (1923):192.

recommended his friend; and Charles Peale left Queen Anne's for the Kent County School on December 27, 1742. In 1745, another son, St. George, was born to the Peales. The father later wrote to his sister, "On St. George's Day the 23ᵈ of April last I had a most charming Boy born to me, whom my Friends here particularly Mr. Sterling wou'd for the honr of our English Patron oblidge me to call St. George."[29] (St. George Peale later married the daughter of Henry Callister, who will figure largely in the discussion of the Reverend Thomas Bacon.)

In the latter part of June, 1746, the Reverend George Whitefield came to Chestertown and preached on "St. Paul's Words, I am not mad O noble Festus but speak the Words of Truth and Soberness" (Acts 26:25). His message was that "fine Gentlemen of the World" all regarded truly religious people as Festus regarded St. Paul—quite mad. The following day he preached to the people that "Faith in Jesus" was the "only way to Heaven" and said that good works and good deeds were "not very essential" to salvation. He also, according to Charles Peale, "turn'd Reason quite out of doors"—evidently protesting that reason was useless in religion. After a brief visit in Queen Anne's County, Whitefield returned to Chester "to have the Pleasure of hearing Mr. Sterling." But Sterling was angry with Whitefield's message and perhaps with his manner of preaching. Charles Peale confided what happened to a friend: "Lo the Poor man [Whitefield] I doubt had more Pain, than Pleasure unless his Patience was greater than Jobs, for Sterling under Calvin and his Schism, treated the poor Creature in the most violent, sarcastical, nay I must say Billingsgate terms, making Use of the Terms Montebank, Vagrant, Renegade, guilded Pill, Imposter, Wolf in Sheep's Cloathing, [hideously?] Painted Harlot—in short such terms as I cannot recollect." Peale wrote that Sterling castigated Whitefield (who was in the audience) for an hour, and Peale "felt much pain on both their accounts."[30] Charles Peale evidently knew of Sterling's plans to become collector of the Northern part of the Chesapeake Bay, for the schoolmaster wrote in 1749 that he hoped to obtain a post in the Customs service; but he died in late November, 1750.

---

[29] Charles Peale Letterbook, 1745–1747, p. [6]. American Philosophical Society Library, Philadelphia.
[30] Ibid., pp. [25–26]. This letter is addressed only to "Dear Sir," and it is undated—but it is found in Peale's letterbook between letters dated June 22 and Aug. 1, 1746.

Following the lead of previous scholars, Lawrence C. Wroth identified as Sterling's several poems in Provost William Smith's *American
Magazine*, 1757–58.[31] These, however, represent only a portion of
Sterling's American poetry. An examination of the other sources of
publication available to Sterling has turned up a number of poems that
can be attributed to him. While Sterling was visiting Annapolis in the
spring of 1747 (he was a guest at Hamilton's Tuesday Club on March
27), his first published American poem, "The Sixteenth Ode of
HORACE's *Second Book*, Imitated, AND INSCRIBED to His Excellency
SAMUEL OGLE, Esq.," appeared in the *Maryland Gazette*, March 31,
1747, and was reprinted in the *Pennsylvania Gazette*, April 23, 1747.
Although anonymous, it is extremely similar to Sterling's "The 22d
Ode of the first Book of Horace imitated; and inscribed to the Lady
of his Late Excellency, SAMUEL OGLE, Esquire";[32] therefore I attribute
it to him. Sterling's "Sixteenth Ode" opens with a description of the
motives for war:

> THE pow'rful Prince, by Lust of Empire driv'n
> To tempt, by War unjust, avenging Heav'n,
> While yet his murd'ring Sword lays waste Mankind,
> Prays for a Peace with glorious Ease of Mind,
>   Vain Hope! for mad Ambition knows no Bounds,
>   Swifter than Winds it presses on before;
>   With all the vanquish'd World's collected Crowns,
>   The Macedonian Youth still wept for more.
>
> (ll. 1–8)

In the second stanza, Sterling points out that "contending passions"
are not peculiar to princes, but "Thro' the whole Race extends the
fell Disease" (l. 11). And in the third stanza, Sterling portrays human
restlessness:

> THE bold advent'rous Trader on the Main,
> Whose Chief Delight is Wealth and sordid Gain,
> In Storms forgets his avaritious Care,
> And for an easy Life lifts up his Pray'r:
>   When black'ning Clouds oppress the troubled Sky,

---

[31] Wroth (see n. 3 above), 36–38. Albert H. Smyth, *The Philadelphia Maga-
zines and their Contributors, 1741–1850* (Philadelphia, 1892), 35–41; and Lyon
Norman Richardson, *A History of Early American Magazines, 1741–1789* (New
York, 1931), 119–21.

[32] This poem, which was published in the *American Magazine* for Oct., 1758,
642–43, and reprinted in the *American Museum* for Oct., 1788, 385, is actually a
revision of a poem that Sterling wrote in Ireland: see the *Poetical Works*, 17–21.

And hide these faithful Pilots of the Night
  The Moon and Stars; and whistling Winds reply
To roaring Seas, that gleam a dreadful White;
  His Views of *Cent per Cent* delight no more,
He longs to quit his Trade, and live at Ease on Shore.
  Yet shou'd kind Heav'n vouchsafe the fond Request,
And guide him safely to the wish'd for Port;
  Some further Aim wou'd soon invade the Breast,
Where sateless Passions anxiously resort.

              (ll. 19–32)

After Sterling asks "What can free th'uneasy Mind from Care?" he shows that neither riches nor honors can; echoing the neoclassic retirement poems, he says that one needs a "contented and resign'd" mind (l. 44).

In the sixth stanza, Sterling laments the human predicament and asks why men come to America:

Wʜᴀᴛ endless Schemes perplex the human Race;
And yet, how few their Wants, how short their Space?
Why do we chuse to quit our native Shore,
And other Climes in new-found Worlds explore?
Th'ambitious Man shall there no Succour find;
He cannot leave his restless Soul behind.
Where e'er he goes, still wretched Cares attend,
And urge him headlong, like a treach'rous Friend,
To Fields of Battle, or to cross the Seas,
(The Foe declar'd of comfortable Ease;)
Or, still to render more accurs'd his Case,
Prompt him to fawn and flatter for a Place.

              (ll. 49–60)

To the obsequious climber, Sterling contrasts the man whose passions are gentle, whose reason dictates his desires, and whose "Wish is social Ease and Rest" (l. 64). But the gods permit no perfect bliss here on earth.

Behold the Hero, crown'd with early Bays
  For noble Acts, cut off in youthful Prime.
While some are curs'd with painful Length of Days,
  Strangers to Peace and Honour in their Time.
What one requests, another mourns his Fate,
By turns invidious of each other's State.

              (ll. 69–74)

Sterling concludes the poem with a comparison of the positions of Governor Samuel Ogle and himself. The 88-line complimentary poem to Ogle is competent verse. Dr. Alexander Hamilton, in his "Quevedo" criticism, enthusiastically referred to it as a "wonderful" imitation.

On May 18, 1748, Jonas Green published "an Epithalamium *on the late Marriage of the Honourable* BENEDICT CALVERT, *Esq.*; *with the agreeable young Lady, of your City, his Kinswoman*" on the front page of the *Maryland Gazette*. Although the poem is anonymous, the dateline "Kent *County*, April 29, 1748," indicates Sterling's authorship. (There was, so far as I know, no other Kent County poet of the day.) On April 21, Benedict Calvert, collector of customs for Patuxent District, married Elizabeth Calvert, a distant cousin who was the daughter of former Governor Charles Calvert (d. 1734), whose death Richard Lewis had commemorated. Jonas Green's prefatory note explains that he had heard of the epithalamium and requested the author for a copy. Sterling admonished the printer to be careful in setting the type, for "the least Error, in Performances of this Kind, may not only mar the Harmony of the Numbers, but perplex and obscure the Sense." The poet justifies the introduction of "figurative Personages" and "ideal Beings" as an established way for a bold "Fancy" to operate under the restraint of "cool judgment" (this argument anticipates the explanations of Henry James and others of a *persona*'s function in creating aesthetic distance). He asserted that neither time "nor Inclination will permit me to add any tedious Annotations, explanative of the ancient *Mythology*; since such would be impertinent to People of Taste, and of little Use to *those* who have none." (Since the printed poem has annotations, one wonders if they were added by Jonas Green.)

The opening portrays Maryland's spring:

> Now while the Sun revolving feasts each sense
> With all the Pride, that vernal Blooms dispense:
> While Joys luxuriant the blest Season yields;
> Imbalming the rich Sky from wanton Fields:
> While genial Warmth conspires, with fresh'ning Show'rs,
> To paint th'enamel'd Mead with breathing Flow'rs:
> While *feather'd Warblers* charm th'inchanted Grove;
> And the reviv'd *Creation* wakes to Love.
>
> (ll. 1–8)

The youth Cleon (Benedict Calvert) "Near Severn's streams" (l. 14) addresses Juno, goddess of the "nuptial Bed," asking for the hand of Eliza (Elizabeth Calvert). Juno hears the prayer and promises to grant the marriage (ll. 47–52), assuring Cleon that never was there a more auspicious wedding:

'Not my young Peleus' Marriage-Feast, of Yore,
'Tho' grac'd by Heav'n's bright *Court* was honor'd more,
'Than your's shall be. When *Thetis*, the Divine,
'Match'd with th'*heroic Boy* of mortal Line:
'When all the *Gods*, descending from on High,
'Left vacant for a Day th'ethereal Sky.
(ll. 53–58)

After telling of the roles that Cupid and Cestos will perform at the wedding (ll. 59–64), Juno prophesies that Annapolis will be "As *Pthia* was . . . / The Scene of Wit Divine, and heavn'ly Glee" (ll. 65–66). Momus, Discord, Bacchus, Saturn, and Satyrs shall be excluded. Juno then catalogues the gods that will attend:

'But, in their stead, shall come, in glowing Pride,
'*Flora*; and *Hebe*,[6] with her zone fast-ty'd:
'Kind *Comus*, God of hospitable Cheer:
'And *Ceres*, promising the golden[7] Ear:
'The *Huntress Queen*,[8] with Quiver, shoulder-hung,
'Buskin'd; with Stole succinct; but Bow unstrung:
'*Jove*, now relax'd, and in his pleasing Hour:
'And *Vesta*,[9] bidding Welcome at the Door:
'Aurora, blithsome as her own May-Morn:
'And *Copia*,[10] laughing o'er the Flow'r-crown'd Horn:
'Young *Naids*, sportive *Dryads*, dancing *Fawns*;
'Boasting their native Floods, and Groves, and Lawns!
'But, chief, the *Deities* of Wit, and Sense,
'Manners, and Joy, shall not be absent hence:
'Th'*inspiring King*[11]: The *Muses*, by his Side:
'The Rosy *Loves*, adorn'd with honest Pride:
'The *blue-ey'd Maid*[12] and sprightly *Son* of *May*;
'Shall sit presiding here, and dignify the Day!
(ll. 73–90)

[6] *The Goddess of Youth, who once making an unlucky Slip, dropping her Garments, expos'd some Charms she wish'd to conceal.*
[7] *Corn being now in the Blade.*   [8] *Diana.*
[9] *Whose Statue was plac'd at the Porches of Houses and Temples.*
[10] *The Goddess of Plenty, with the emblamatical Horn.*
[11] Apollo.   [12] Minerva *and* Mercury.

Juno next envisions the singing and the firing of the cannons at the wedding festivities:

'Haste; let the *Pow'rs* of Melody take Wing;
'And all the *Syrens*, in full Chorus, sing:
'Let brazen Tubes, from *Chesapeak's* glad Shore
'To Heav'n's high Vault, in loud Explosion, roar.
'Aloft *Love's waving* Banners be display'd;

268

'While by each *Grace* the *bridal Nymph's* array'd:
'From yon fair Summit[13] let the Trump of *Fame*
'The festal Morn, inflated, strait proclaim:
'The floating Clangor Woods and Hills send round;
'And *Echo* lengthen out the propagated Sound!
                                                    (ll. 91–100)

[13] *The Stadt-House Hill.*

Another indication of Sterling's authorship of "An Epithalamium,"
as well as a minor comment on his poetic practice, is that he used a
variant of this last line in *An Epistle to the Hon. Arthur Dobbs* (Dublin, 1752): "Proud Echo lengthens out the propagated sound" (I, 58).
The poem closes with Juno's description of the "gay Procession" of
bride's-maids, the dancing (with women wearing peacock feathers),
feasting, and each maiden wishing that "Day and Night her own!"

Although numerous poems celebrating marriages were written in
colonial America, Sterling's is one of the few in a heightened, formal
manner. The poem in heroic couplets consists of an introduction of
the setting and characters (ll. 1–16), Cleon's address to Juno, praising
Elizabeth Calvert and asking for her hand (ll. 17–46), and Juno's reply and prediction (ll. 47–100). When Hamilton discussed the "Epithalamium" in his "Quevedo" essay on Maryland writers, he said that
Sterling "deals much in *ideal Beings, figurative Personages*, and antient
Pagan Mythology, and is desirous to be understood by none but
People of Taste." The physician and wit added that though Sterling
was "romantic in most things he does or says," he nevertheless had
"a good Measure of Sense and Learning," was the "first Rate Poet
in our Province," and deserved to "be crowned *Poet Laureat* of
Maryland."[33]

After Hamilton's "Quevedo" essay, no original belletristic material
appeared in the *Maryland Gazette* for six months, and Sterling did not

[33] The entire essay is printed, with an introduction and annotation, in J. A.
Leo Lemay, "Hamilton's Literary History," 273–85. Hamilton's sentence "He
deals much in *ideal Beings, figurative Personages*, and antient *Pagan Mythology*;
and is desirous to be understood by none but *People of Taste*" partially quotes
Sterling's prefatory letter to the "Epithalamium." In my edition of Hamilton's
essay, I confessed that I did not know who the "*first Rate Poet*" was, and I
thought that James Sterling was "Philo-Musaeus" (another productive Maryland poet); however, since I wrote that essay, I have completed compiling a
bibliography of the American poetry in the colonial newspapers and magazines,
in the course of which I turned up a literary quarrel in the *Pennsylvania Gazette*
which proves that "Philo-Musaeus" was Dr. Adam Thomson (d. 1768), a friend
and former school-fellow of Dr. Alexander Hamilton.

submit another poem for six years. By the middle of 1748 he had begun to write *An Epistle to the Hon. Arthur Dobbs, Esq.* (Dublin, 1752; reprinted London, 1752).[34] After the return of two ships, the *Dobbs* and *California*, from an unsuccessful attempt to find a Northwest Passage, Arthur Dobbs resolved to go himself to explore America's northern coast. Sterling's "heroic . . . philosophical . . . descriptive . . . and ethic"[35] poem eulogized Dobbs, and Sterling may have written it as the opening gambit in his play to gain a monopoly on northern trade.

Sterling obviously knew Theodorus Swaine Drage (formerly the "clerk" of the *California* and author of *An Account of a Voyage for the Discovery of a North-west Passage*) when the latter lived in Chestertown, Sterling's home.[36] When Drage wanted to try again to find the Northwest Passage, he persuaded a number of Marylanders to back the scheme. Among Drage's patrons was Sterling's friend, Governor Samuel Ogle, who "was convinced by his arguments, and in November, 1750, gave Drage a document or passport permitting him to make the search."[37] In Philadelphia, Benjamin Franklin, Judge William Allen, and a number of other wealthy citizens organized a Northwest Company. Sterling was among the subscribers. The Philadelphia group raised £1,500 to buy a vessel, the *Argo*, which Drage sailed to Hudson's Bay.

Meanwhile, Sterling left for England about November, 1751. Although he had several surreptitious financial reasons for the trip, he wrote the bishop of London:

> The Desire of availing my Country in its civil, as well religious, Interests, by my Travels, Discoveries, and Observations; (in which I have not been disappointed; as the Lords Commissioners of Trade and Plantations will amply testify) and the Hopes of recovering my Health, much impair'd by the Inclemency of various Climates, and

[34] A copy of the Dublin edition is at the Library of Congress, and a copy of the London edition is at the John Carter Brown Library. See Sabin 91330.

[35] [William Rose,] a review of Sterling's *Epistle* in the *Monthly Review* 6 (1752):237. The reviewer is identified by Benjamin Christie Nagle, *The Monthly Review, First Series, 1749–1789* (London, 1934), 227.

[36] Leonard Woods Labaree, et al., eds., *Papers of Benjamin Franklin*, 4:381. Theodorus Swaine Drage sometimes used the name Charles Swaine. See Percy G. Adams, "The Case of Swaine Versus Drage: An Eighteenth Century Publishing Mystery Solved," *Essays in History and Literature Presented by Fellows of the Newberry Library to Stanley Pargellis* (Chicago, 1965), 157–68.

[37] Bertha Solis-Cohen, "Philadelphia's Expedition to Labrador," *Pennsylvania History* 19 (1952):149.

some disastrous Accidents among Savage Nations, were the true
Motives of my late Return to Europe, as indeed Those of my Going
at First to America were solely consciencious; of which, Sir George
Lyttleton and many other worthy Personages will assure You, I gave
an incontestible and unprecedented Proof by resigning a Presentation
to a Rectory of considerable Income, and the Chaplainship of a Regiment, in Order to pass into a Part of his Majesty's Dominions, where
my Zeal induc'd me to believe I could be more usefull than at Home,
and where the Effects of my Ministry might be extensive.[38]

Since Sterling first visited Dublin (where he evidently did fall ill), he
probably returned partially to see his family and friends. Two years
earlier, he had sent over the manuscript of his *Epistle to Dobbs* with an
"ingenious gentleman"—who died in passage.[39] A minor reason for
his trip was to see this book through the press; a more important
reason, and perhaps the motive for writing the long poem, was to gain
a lucrative civil post, collector of customs for the head of Chesapeake
Bay. Still another motive was his desire to organize a company of
merchants to explore the Northwest Passage. He hoped to win an
exclusive monopoly of Labrador trade.

In London, Sterling and a group of merchants applied for a 99-year
trading monopoly along the Labrador coast as a partial incentive and
reward for their proposed explorations of the Northwest Passage. On
April 16, 1752, Sterling, John Hanbury, Samuel Touchitt, John
Thomlinson, and Mr. Thrale appeared before the Lords Commissioners of Trade seeking "a grant for an exclusive trade upon that coast,
which Mr. Sterling had represented to them as indisputable of belonging to the Crown of Great Britain and that he informed them that
a very valuable trade for furs, whale fins, fish and masts might be
opened there."[40] The Lords of Trade replied to the petitioners that
granting exclusive rights was very difficult and that a limited grant
"would be less liable to . . . objections." Consequently, Sterling, Hanbury, and their associates withdrew proposing to consider proper
limitations. They next presented a petition for exclusive trading rights
on the Labrador coast for sixty-three years. But in view of the Hud-

---

[38] Sir George Lyttleton and Robert, Earl Nugent, were among Sterling's
friends and patrons who were now in power. Sterling's letter to the bishop of
London, April 20, [1752], is printed in full by Wroth in "James Sterling," 20–21.
I have been unable to learn anything of his "disastrous accidents among Savage
Nations."

[39] Sterling's *Epistle* (all references are to the Dublin edition), ii.

[40] Great Britain, Board of Trade, *Journal of the Commissioners for Trade
and Plantations from January 1749–50 to December 1753* (London, 1932), 299.

son Bay Company's prior claims to this coast, Sterling et al. were finally refused.[41]

Back in Philadelphia, Franklin and his associates were furious when they learned of Sterling's attempt to gain a monopoly. In a letter dated November 17, 1752, William Allen, chief justice of Pennsylvania, complained to Thomas Penn that the Philadelphia merchants had been encouraged in the search for a Northwest Passage by the thought that if the main effort were fruitless, they might nevertheless find "a lucrative trade" on the Labrador coast. But, complained Allen, they have just been informed "to our surprise" that "a scoundrell of a parson one James Sterling" has attempted to deprive them of this consolation by applying "to the crown for an exclusive patent." Chief Justice Allen chronicled Sterling's supposed knavery:

> This same Sterling who is a Church of England minister at Newton [present-day Chestertown] in Maryland was concerned with us originally in the undertaking and subscribed to bear a part of the expense but after he had by frequent conversations extracted from the person [Drage] we chiefly depend upon for executing the design all or chief part of the intelligence that he could give he has been base enough to endeavor to circumvent us. As a proof of what I assert I here inclose his original letter wrote with his own hand to Mr. Benjamin Franklin.[42] We have also here our paper of subscription for the carrying on the undertaking signed by the said Sterling. Notwithstanding which as I said before he made a Voyage to London and for his discovery and the proposals he laid before the above gentlemen he has though a parson been rewarded with a collectorship of the Customs at the head of the bay. We conceive ourselves very ill used by this false Brother have therefore transmitted a petition to his Majesty (which comes herewith) praying that no Patent for an exclusive trade may be granted which is humbly submitted to your consideration and I am desired to request that you would be pleased to get it presented if you judge it will answer any good end.[43]

After Thomas Penn received Allen's letter and supporting documents on December 15, 1752, he immediately took steps to block Sterling's petition. On December 17, Penn petitioned the Council of the Board of Trade, which was in session considering Sterling's application. Penn secured a lawyer to present the Philadelphia merchants' side of the affair. At last, after the attorney-general and the solicitor-general

[41] Ibid., 300.
[42] Not extant.
[43] MS, Historical Society of Pennsylvania. See also Edwin Swift Balch, "Arctic Expeditions Sent from the American Colonies," *Pennsylvania Magazine of History and Biography* 31 (1907):421.

of England delivered the opinion that the Hudson's Bay Company's charter precluded an exclusive grant of the Labrador trade, the application of Sterling, Hanbury, et al. was denied.[44]

Showing his characteristic good sense, Peter Collinson (the Quaker merchant and naturalist who formerly corresponded with Richard Lewis) wrote to Franklin on January 27, 1753:

> There is a Sett of Opulent Merchants have been projecting a Scheme for Carrying on a Trade to the Labrador Coast and have laid It before the Board of Trade who approve their Scheme and as it will be attended with a great Expence they Desire a Charter for 20 or 30 years. The Maryland Parson has Sett all this project on foot. He is a Volatile Blade and Great Poet. But this Affair for the present is at a Stand. Your Petition no doubt, but will have its Effect—for all Trade ought to be open and Free to all Our Kings Subjects.[45]

While in London, Sterling drew up a memorial creating a new customs district (which ran from the Chester River on the Eastern Shore around the head of the Chesapeake Bay to Baltimore) as a separate collectorship, and presented the memorial to the Lords of Treasury, where he had powerful friends, including Sir George Lyttleton. The Lords of the Treasury sent the memorial to the Commissioners of the Customs on April 30, 1752, who replied, May 2, with a sarcastic note about the necessity for such an office—but recommended granting it, "at the Salary of 80 £ per Ann." Consequently, on May 12, 1752, the Treasury Board granted Sterling the post.[46]

Nearly everyone objected to the Reverend James Sterling's collectorship: Maryland's popular party resented supporting the Established Church, and especially resented a minister's holding a civil position; the proprietary party resented Sterling's method of obtaining the post—for the governor and the proprietor felt that official Maryland sinecures should be within their patronage; and Franklin and his associates in the Northwest Company resented Sterling's collectorship because they believed that he had betrayed them. But Sterling, richer by 80 pounds a year, was willing to fight; although, at first, the various parties felt they could take the post away from him, they learned different. On January 11, 1753, Penn wrote Chief Justice Allen of the steps he had taken and informed him that John

---

[44] Labaree et al., eds., *Papers of Benjamin Franklin* 4:382.
[45] Ibid., 413–14.
[46] These documents are quoted in full by Wroth, who recounts at length the politics of Sterling's commission. "James Sterling," 22–25.

Hanbury, one of the chief London merchants, felt that Sterling had also deceived the London merchants. Penn reported with satisfaction that Sterling was in trouble. Lord Baltimore too was working to have Sterling's collectorship of customs taken from him. On February 27, 1754, the merchants in the Maryland trade presented a petition to the hands of Trade asking that Sterling's office be discontinued. Despite the petition and the continued urging of Maryland's Governor Horatio Sharpe that his own favorite be given the collectorship, no action was taken. Sir George Lyttleton was still a member of the Board of Treasury, and Sterling's other friend and patron, Robert Nugent, was appointed to the board on April 6, 1754. Sterling's opponents were powerless.[47]

Sterling's *Epistle to Dobbs* was a major eighteenth-century American poem. In the address "To the Public," Sterling says that, reviewing the work, he sees that some lines are "defective in Diction, and some Sentiments too warmly express'd." He apologizes for the faults, saying that ill health brought on by a change of climate made him overlook them. They will be amended if he publishes a second edition, for "but a very few Copies are now printed, by Way of Trial, at his own Expence." The subsequent London edition, however, made no substantive changes.[48]

In the "Advertisement," Sterling says that he wrote the poem in Maryland, over two years ago, "*after the Return of the* Dobbs *and* California *from their Expedition to explore the North-West Passage.*" He sent a copy at that time to England for publication, but the "*ingenious Gentleman*" to whom he consigned the manuscript died on the trip. In the preface, Sterling apologized that the nature of his subject

> led him to mention his own Travels, and to glance at some Incidents, chiefly relative to himself, but connected with those main Designs, where he shows, how by cultivating and improving, in its various Climates, our large and fertile Empire on the Continent, and by introducing new and invaluable Staples of Trade, the maternal Kingdom would be greatly strengthened and inriched, the Dependency of our Colonies better secured, and the ambitious Schemes of France to rival us in Trade, and maritime Power, rendered abortive.

Sterling opens Part I of his *Epistle* with a compliment to Dobbs. He praises Dobbs's attempt to discover a Northwest Passage and asks

[47] Wroth, "James Sterling," 27–33; and Solis-Cohen, 158.
[48] See the bibliographical note on Sterling under American Publications, no. 4.

Dobbs to listen to the tune of a "wand'ring Muse." By referring to himself as a "tuneful Savage" living in the "uncultured Paradise" of America, the Irishman reveals that he has adopted an American identity:

> Hark! in wild Notes the tuneful Savage sings;
> And for no vulgar Height prepares her Wings!
> Lo, thro' th'uncultured Paradise she roves,
> And first inchants *America's* charm'd Groves
> She dares, (while Desarts hear th'heroic Lyre;
> While in full Pomp thine Images inspire)
> Like Nature's greater Works to raise her Song,
> Irregularly bold, beneficently strong.
>
> (I, 17–24)

"Inchants" (l. 20) suggests that his poetry will "enchant" the American wilderness (i. e., that it will mythologize the landscape), and it also says that the poet will sing (chant) the American wilderness. (The former suggestion may echo Lewis's "Food for Criticks.") Sterling, like Lewis, writes an early version of the topographical fallacy: i. e., his poetry, "Irregularly bold" (l. 24), is to be an imitation of "Nature's greater Works" (l. 23), the landscape of America.

He briefly describes Maryland and his plantation on the Chester River:

> Where *Sesquahanah* foams with rock-rais'd Sprey,
> And swells loved *Chesapeak's* capacious Bay.
> Or where *Potowmac* with its placid Waves
> *Maria's* Shores and verdant Meadows laves;
> Where *Europe's* Monarchs scarce transfer their Name;
> Thy Merits are convey'd by loudest Fame;
> Amazed, All heard; All bless'd the great Design;
> And Gratulations hail'd the Scheme Divine.
> The gen'ral Voice pierced thro' my shady Seats,
> Where Speculation to her Grot retreats;
> Where in my green Arcades o'er *Cestria's* Stream,
> Of distant Friends in vacant Hours I dream.
>
> (I, 25–36)

For the English reader, Sterling identifies the Susquehanna and the Potomac rivers, explaining that "Maria's Shores" is Maryland and that "Cestria's Stream" is "the fine River Chester, dividing the Counties of Kent and Queen Anne, where the Author's Plantations are situated." He describes the tulip tree, Niagara Falls, and the Appalachian Mountains, before warning of the French schemes for empire in America: "A Fate, like Louisburgh's, Quebeck foredates, / And hears brave Pepp'rel thund'ring on her Gates" (I, 75–76). The poet commends Dobbs's plans for discovering a Northwest Passage, which will bring civilization to the Far East, and, like Richard Lewis, Sterling praises Enlightenment cosmopolitanism (I, 121–26).

In an imaginary speech, Dobbs, the future Georgia governor, extols the Indians. The speech reveals that the poet believed in the comparative method and the stage theory (i. e., that Indians were in the same "stage" of civilization that Europeans had gone through some time ago):

'O *Britons*, what disgrace
'To injure these?—These, a fraternal Race!
'What Jewels here inestimable shine;
'Rude from rough Nature's adamantine Mine!
'Such were our Ancestors; e'er *Caesar's* Sword
'Imposed the Yoke of a tyrannick Lord!
(I, 141–46)

He damns the Spanish Catholics who enslaved the Indians:

'Christians; who like *Pizzaro*, or the Pest,
'Massacre Millions, and inslave the Rest;
'By Extirpation prove their Right supreme,
'And swim to Empire thro' a purple Stream!
(I, 157–60)

Like Robert Beverley and Richard Lewis, Sterling claims that the Indians were happy before the white man arrived in America. So Dobbs, cast in the role of a chronological primitivist, opens a long speech: "Happy *Peru*! ere *Spaniards* saw your Coast!" (l. 171). After praying for the powers of Shakespeare (I, 269–72), the poet urges Dobbs to explore a Northwest Passage:

Thy Course thro' frozen Continents explore,
And hear the Tempest impotently roar;
Nerved with celestial Fortitude sustain
The drifted Dust of Sleet and solid Rain:
Where Pyramids congeal'd in verdant Spires
Menace the Clouds, and scorn the solar Fires.
(I, 285–90)

The terrors of the arctic voyage and the grandeur of Dobbs's final triumph are pictured before the Marylander praises commerce (I, 411–16) and eulogizes Dobbs's merits (I, 437–50). He calls on the greatest contemporary English poets for help:

Thou pure of Spirit, *Addison*, attend;
Music and Fire, Master of Numbers, lend;
Or both in One, *Pope*, without rival born,

My various Theme in vary'd Stile adorn.
Bid Art and Nature breathe thro' ev'ry Line;
Thou, delicate of Phrase, with Sentiment Divine!
(I, 451–56)

The crafty minister lauds a number of contemporary English politicians: Chesterfield (ll. 501–508); Granville (ll. 518–30); Halifax
(ll. 531–48), who is "The Friend of *West*; and ev'n a Friend to Me!"
(l. 558); "*Pollio*" (ll. 568–80); and Sir Robert Walpole. The first
part ends with a description of the ideal gentleman (ll. 623–56).

Part II opens with an address to Dobbs. Sterling traces Dobbs's
route by poetic salutations to the personages whose feats are associated
with particular places along the route to Hudson's Bay. The poet
predicts that the aurora borealis will cause Dobbs to see visionary
scenes (and Sterling's diction may allude to the return of the deceased
Indian in Lewis's "Food for Criticks"):

Boreal Aurora on the Welkin play,
And wild Refractions toss the sportive Rays.
Aerial Gambols charm the Sailor's Eyes:
Tremulous Landscapes of Inchantment rise;
Around the visionary Figures dance;
Woods, marshal'd Armies, and group'd Towns advance!
Now pleas'd he views the Meteor's bursting Streams,
And wide Effusion of successive Gleams:
Toils are forgot 'midst the fantastic Glow;
While traverst Corruscations quiv'ring flow.
The vary'd Scenes delude the tedious Night,
Supply the Sun, and shed an aw'd Delight;
And, while the sheen Phaenomenons amuse,
Cheering and cheer'd, the Voyage he pursues.
(II, 135–48)

Like the earlier poetry of Richard Lewis, Sterling's verse reveals the
influence of James Thomson and also applies the new vogue of sensibility to an American subject.

Next, in an early imaginative portrait of the whale in American
literature,[49] Sterling describes a whale's splashing waves over the "tall
Quarter" (l. 153) of Dobbs's ship. Dobbs addresses the great mammal,
deducing, in the scientific deistic manner, proof of God's existence
from the wonders of the earth. Sterling also describes the whalers

[49] At approximately this same time, Dr. James Kirkpatrick of South Carolina
in *The Sea Piece* (London, 1750) and Charles Hansford of Virginia in "Bar-
zilla" (see James A. Servies and Carl R. Dolmetsch, eds., *The Poems of Charles
Hansford* [Chapel Hill, 1961]) both wrote short poetic descriptions of whales
and whaling.

slaughtering their prey. After Dobbs reaches Labrador (l. 268), the poet again asks for artistic help—this time of Milton and Raphael: Nature's "full Glories in high Pride demand / Milton's rais'd Spirit, or strong Raphael's Hand: / To paint what free Magnificence has made" (ll. 280–83). He imaginatively describes the mighty mountains of the north, the Bosphore, and then Thule:

> Join'd by its Isthmus to the Mountain's Sides,
> See prominent etherial *Thule* rides!
> In Act to fall, and fill the threaten'd Strait:
> With Pow'r to crush proud Cities by its Weight;
> Or dash to other Planets *Ocean's* Floods,
> And load new Atmospheres with foreign Clouds!
> Sure its huge Basis, by some Earthquake rent,
> Or not augments yon rocky Continent;
> Deserting its broad Top: or in vast Piles
> Its rolling Fragments form yon *Savage* Iles!
> (II, 319–28)

The existence of cold and ice is justified by the concept of the Great Chain of Being (ll. 377–96). After Sterling portrays the collapse into the sea of a great glacier wall (ll. 457–70), he compares Dobbs to previous Arctic explorers:

> Think on the Worthies of *Eliza*'s Days;
> And let dead Merit Emulation raise:
> By vet'ran Chiefs with high Ideas fir'd!
> Such *Davis* once! Such *Frobisher* inspir'd!
> Such *Anson* too! the living *Drake*! whose Sales
> Triumphant swell'd with either *India*'s Gales!
> (II, 471–76)

Sterling hopes that, when Dobbs reaches Hudson's Bay, he will address that "nautic Martyr's honour'd Shade!" (l. 492). The poet closes the second part of his *Epistle* as Dobbs finds the passage to India that will henceforth carry his name, insuring for Dobbs fame equal to Magellan's or Le Maire's.

In the beginning of Part III, Sterling breaks off his description of Dobbs's future journey and presents a vision. The poet is wafted to the deck of Dobbs's ship where (citing the examples of St. Paul's conversion and Constantine the Great's vision) he sees heaven's portent:

> From op'ning Heav'n now tiding Glory flow'd;
> And in the midst the North's Arch-Angel show'd.
> Intolerable Lustre circumvolved;

And Hills of Snow in spreading Lakes dissolved!
His stellate Wings, th'extended Bay o'erspread:
More than a Rain-bow waved around his Head!
Southward of West, two Suns, his Eyes, he cast;
While his strong Tube utter'd its mighty Blast!
The rock'd Globe's Atmosphere confess'd the Sound:
East heard, and sent the Undulation round:
Eccho'd the Poles': shook to its Center Earth;
And Triumph'd Wonder in its second Birth!

(III, 43–54)

Thus Sterling presents his idea of creation. Then the poet envisions the twelve apostles repeating the story of the son of God (ll. 76–82). Four great rulers of England are present: Alfred, Elizabeth, William III, and George I. "The gen'rous *Prince*, who late espoused thy Schemes" (l. 127) is not present only because the sight of him would completely unman Dobbs. Next, the great naval heroes of Britain appear, and Sterling sees "great Parker's Shade" (Elizabeth's archbishop of Canterbury) bestow on Dobbs the "sacred Code" (l. 172). Sterling characterizes Walsingham "The great Patron of the first Adventurers for the Discovery of a North-West Passage" (note to l. 193); Drake (the modern Alexander), "He, who in Glory's Search disdain'd a Bound, / And sigh'd to find that Earth so soon was round" (ll. 221–22); Raleigh (ll. 225–60); and Earl Stanhope (ll. 261–80).

Stanhope summons "*Aetherial Excellence*," a divinity who closes Sterling's *Epistle* with a speech addressed to "Briton." "*Aetherial Excellence*" begins by eulogizing trade. The spirit says that the search for the Northwest Passage should only be undertaken with a cosmopolitan attitude (ll. 317–22). She tells the future monarch of England the truths that have rewarded "his Sire." In the conclusion of the poem, the Spirit asks the king to diffuse religion to "realms unseen" (l. 371), in order to be the most famous of kings:

'His Glory, Theme of ev'ry Age and Clime,
'Blazing, o'erpass the Bounds of Space and Time;
'Nations Antipodal his Worth proclaim;
'Both Hemispheres his Pow'r; Futurity his Name!"

ll. 379–82)

To today's reader, Sterling's poem has little merit. Its interest is the kind that the casual viewer gives to the fossil bones of a dinosaur. But in Sterling's day, the *Epistle* caused Peter Collinson to think him a "great poet." The review in the best contemporary critical magazine said that the poem did not fit any known genre, but consisted "of a mixture of the heroic, the philosophical, the descriptive, and the ethic." According to the reviewer, Sterling's purpose was "to shew, how, by cultivating and improving, in its various climates, our large and fertile empire on the continent, and by introducing new and valuable staples of trade, the maternal kingdom would be greatly strengthened and enriched, the dependency of our colonies better secured, and the ambitious schemes of *France* to rival us in trade, and maritime power, rendered abortive." The critic judged the poetry "manly, spirited, warm, and ornamented with a variety of invention; but withal his fire, in general is irregular, his diction often incorrect, and his numbers are sometimes inharmoniously turned."[50]

The Dublin edition of Sterling's *Epistle* was published by John Smith, probably in January, 1752; the London edition, by Dodsley, in March.[51] Sterling's description of Maryland and his portrayal of the aurora borealis, of whaling, and of Thule are among the better passages in the poem. In heroic couplets, the *Epistle* is in a formal, heightened diction. The tone increases in ardor throughout the three parts, which, respectively, describe the author and Dobbs, and present a chronological progress-piece of past attempts to discover the Northwest Passage; part two describes the projected voyage; and part three chronicles other great achievements in English history, concluding with "Aetherial Excellence's" speech on the benefits that Dobbs's voyage will bring. Unlike Richard Lewis, Sterling does not herald a new sensitivity toward America or nature, but he continues the trends that Lewis had inaugurated; and his lines on the Susquehanna and Chester rivers, like his passage on the aurora borealis, suggest that he read Lewis's poems.

On April 20, 1752, Sterling wrote the bishop of London, requesting financial help to return to Maryland. He claimed that he had traveled extensively for his health and that his funds were exhausted. For the second time he received the Royal Bounty for going abroad as a missionary,[52] and he left London for Maryland early in June, aboard the *Nancy*, Captain Henry M'Lachlan, accompanied by the Baltimore lawyer Richard Chase. They arrived in Annapolis on

[50] *Monthly Review* 6 (1752):237.
[51] It was reviewed in the *Monthly Review* for March and noted in "The Monthly Catalogue for March and April, 1752," of the *London Magazine* 21 (1752):195.
[52] Manross, ed., 47 (3:247-48), and Wroth, "James Sterling," 20-21.

Friday, August 7, after a nine weeks' voyage.[53] On August 27 and September 21, 1752, Sterling ran an advertisement in the *Maryland Gazette* notifying all traders and captains of vessels that he was now "Collector of his Majesty's Duties . . . from the River of Chester on the Eastern Shore, and round the Head of the said Bay, to the River of Patapsco, inclusive on the Western Shore." All traders and ship commanders were required to visit him "at his office in New Town on Chester River; or with his Deputy, Mr. William Lux, at Patapsco."

When Sterling returned to Annapolis for a meeting of Maryland's Anglican clergy in the summer of 1753, he also visited Hamilton's Tuesday Club, August 21, 1753, for the second and last time. He brought to the ministers' meeting proxies for the votes of the Reverends George W. Forester, Richard Harrison, and Hugh Jones. Sterling and the Reverend Thomas Bacon prepared the ministers' address to the governor, which was delivered on August 22.[54]

An anonymous and undated poem *"Occasioned by his Majesty's most gracious Benevolence to his* British *Colonies in* America, *lately invaded by the* French" appeared in the *Maryland Gazette* for December 12, 1754, and was reprinted in the *Pennsylvania Gazette*, January 14, 1755. War and empire, the subjects of the poem, suggest an attribution to Sterling; the hope for a union of the American colonies was, within the month, repeated by Sterling; and the references in lines 84–85 to conversation and friendship with Governor Horatio Sharpe make the attribution to Sterling extremely probable. The prefatory letter concludes with a wish that the poem will *"contribute to a Coalition of the* British *Colonies, and to that Union, which is, at this time, so desirable."* In the opening lines, Sterling claims that he has not been writing recently:

> The Muse that us'd in Silvan Strains to sing,
> To sport in Fields, and chaunt the blooming Spring,
> Or erst (a more ungrateful Task) to storm,
> At Party Wiles, and Factions hideous Form;
> In lofty Trees, in verdant Fields, in Streams,
> That gently mur'ring creep along her Themes,
> No more delights, no more a wicked Age,
> Provokes her Anger, and exalts her Rage.
>
> (ll. 1–8)

---

[53] *Maryland Gazette*, Aug. 13, 1752.

[54] Dr. Alexander Hamilton, "Record of the Tuesday Club," Maryland Historical Society. [Thomas Bacon,] "Proceedings of the Parochial Clergy," *Maryland Historical Magazine* 3 (1908):265. A full discussion of this meeting is given in the Bacon chapter.

But King George has inspired him to write. King George will defeat the French and Indians ("Savage Men, impatient of the Light, / That stroling howl, and prowl like Wolves in Night," ll. 13–14). And *"Ohio's* Banks, shall ring his glorious Name, / His care paternal, to no Bounds confin'd" (ll. 18–19).

Virginians have fought but suffered "the Carnage of unequal Fight." When the monarch heard of their plight, "his Noble Breast" desired "Revenge and Slaughter." Sterling urges the ships to hasten that are bringing relief to America:

> Breathe, breathe, ye Winds, rise, rise, ye gentle Gales,
> Swell the Ship's Canvass, and expand her Sails;
> Ye Sea green Nymphs, the Royal Vessel deign,
> To guide propitious, o'er the liquid Main;
> Freighted with Wealth, for noble Ends design'd,
> (So will'd great George, and so the Fates inclin'd).
> The Pond'rous Cannon o'er the Surges sleep,
> The murd'rous Muskets, swim the raging Deep,
> The flaming Swords, conceal'd in Scabbards sail,
> And pointed Bayonets, partake the Gale.
> Ah! quickly waft her, to the longing Shore,
> In Safety land her, and we ask no more.
>
> (ll. 51–62)

The poet describes the rejoicing at the ships' landing, praises the choice of Governor Sharpe as commander-in-chief, and eulogizes the Maryland governor:

> The active SHARPE with noble Ardour burns,
> Impervious Ways, and cragged Mountains, spurns,
> Nor Hills, nor Woods, his rapid Conquests stay,
> Freedom and Victory direct his Way . . . .
>
> (ll. 78–81)

Then Sterling predicts victory and a reign of peace and plenty. An early use of the word *Ohio* in American poetry is found in this poem, and Sterling's plea for unification of the American colonies has not hitherto been noted. The passage urging the ships to hurry to America perhaps echoes Francis Quarles.[55]

When Governor Horatio Sharpe called a special meeting of the legislature to raise revenue for the defense of Maryland in the French and Indian War, he asked Sterling to deliver the Assembly's opening sermon. Consequently, Sterling preached at St. Anne's, Annapolis,

[55] Francis Quarles, *Argalus and Parthenia* (London, 1632).

December 13, 1754, on empire, virtue, learning, the villainy of the French, and the rights of Englishmen. Sterling had a particularly suitable subject, a timely occasion, and a receptive audience. He opened with a prayer (which was omitted from the London edition) [56] asking that "honesty and industry, Loyalty and Public Spirit, with a Charity extensive to our Species, flourish through all Ranks of our Fellow-Subjects." He pleaded for the "glorious Gospel" to "speedily illuminate this great Continent," thus asking that the French Catholics and the pagan Indians be converted to Protestantism. Sterling's text was taken from chapter 4, verse 18 of the Epistle of Paul to the Galatians, "It is good to be zealously affected always in a good Thing." He opened with a short statement stressing the doctrine's importance and said that he would take up the theme under three headings: (1) the true meaning of the words; (2) their historical proof; and (3) "a particular Application to my respectable Auditors." Sterling recapitulates the history of St. Paul's struggle, and the sermon reveals that he has read the Bible with an eye for effective images: "As the Practice of his Master's Dispensation was very properly stil'd a Warfare; what forceful Images, what bold Figures, does he borrow from the military Art and Roman Discipline, to train up his Pupils by the holy Exercise for glorious Exploits in the Combats they were destin'd to; for the various Lists they were to wrestle in" (p. 12). Shortly after, Sterling again comments on St. Paul's literary art: "Again in being obliged to propose himself, as a Pattern to them of Patience and Fortitude, while he industriously guards against Imputations of Vanity, with what persuasive, what resistless Eloquence, does this consummate Orator (scarce less humanly learned, than divinely inspir'd) insinuate himself into the Hearts of his Readers, and captivate their Passions, while he convinces their Understandings" (pp. 12–13).

Sterling quotes and changes St. Paul's "Are you [they] Hebrews? So am I!" (2 Cor. 11:22) to foreshadow the conclusion of his sermon (thereby emphasizing its cyclic structure): he demands of his audience "Are you Englishmen? Are you, my Hearers, Britons? —You are: All are: So am I" (p. 13). The minister tells the Maryland legislators

---

[56] James Sterling, *A Sermon, preached before his Excellency the Governor of Maryland, and both Houses of Assembly at Annapolis* ... (Annapolis, 1755). The sermon was immediately reprinted in London as *Zeal against the Enemies of our Country Pathetically Recommended* ... (London, 1752). My quotations are from the Annapolis edition.

283

that they should be zealous "for the Honour of God, for the Interest and Propagation of our holy Religion; for the Benefit of our Species, for the Prosperity of our Country," but he also warns them against being overzealous. Just before the close of his first section, Sterling brings up a favorite theme—liberty and the rights of Englishmen. He praises the "disciplin'd Ardour of a Hamden" who equally employs

> His Tongue in the Senate, and his Sword in the Field, in Defence of his Country's unalienable Rights: Of Liberty invaded: —Social Liberty! Mankind's original and universal Charter from Heaven! —Hamden, —I say; almost singly at first steming the Torrent of Royal Incroachments and Ministerial Oppression; who, living, stood the Bulwark of the State; and dying, fell the Emulation of Heroes. An Example, alone sufficient to rouse undegenerated Britons in any Time of public Distress (whether foreign or civil) into somewhat *more* than ancient Romans; as much *more*, as our Constitution in State is preferable in all Respects, to their boasted Republic; and our Protestant Christianity to the (almost-similar) Idolatry of old, or modern Rome!

Under the heading of historical proof, Sterling attempts to prove his advice is true and chauvinistically claims that present-day Maryland is superior in climate, situation, and fertility to the Jewish promised land. In resounding eloquence, the minister praises the choice of Horatio Sharpe, governor of Maryland, as commander of British forces in America. Sterling briefly summarizes Jewish history, claiming that the reverses suffered by the Jewish people were occasioned by a lack of zeal, and their successes, by zeal. He asks how "that minute Spot of the Globe, not half so large as Maryland, nor attended, as I hinted, with so many natural Advantages" achieved such wealth and population. He claims that Judea accomplished these prodigies by "selfish Attachments to public Interests; (for *self* and *social*, if justly stated, will be found to be but the same thing in the End, or concentering in one Point)." In telling how Judea gained such wealth, he proposes, in effect, a plan for the economic development of Maryland and examples Holland as a nation that has flourished by zealously pursuing its interests.

After examining the histories of Greece and Rome—which flourished and foundered through zeal and lack of zeal—Sterling applies the moral to the present situation of his auditors. He defines the meaning of zeal, recapitulates the events that led to the special emergency session of the legislature, refers to England's 80-million-pound debt

(p. 34), and urges Marylanders to take part in the war. He excoriates the French and warns of France's imperialistic plans for America:

> You shou'd consider, How well acquainted they [the French] are with the defenceless Condition of our various Colonies, and that they are hence embolden'd to undertake these destructive Projects; that, while they are carrying on a Chain of Forts of incredible Length behind us, almost from the *Tropic* to the Polar Circle, from new *Orleans* and the Bay of *Mexico* to beyond that of *St. Lawrence* Northward, and within a trifling Distance of our Chief Places for the Fur-Trade at the Bottom of James's Bay; that while they are ever and anon edging on us from the West, and striving to confine us to a comparatively narrow Slip of Land by hemming us in between the Appalachian Hills and the Ocean; that while they are laying the Foundations of a Monarchy, greater than the four ancient Ones together, and extend their enormous *Louisiana* in their impudent Maps and hot Imaginations to the very South-Seas, and perhaps to *Japan*; that while they are doing, or contriving, to do all this, we lie expos'd to their Insults and Depredations, without Fortifications, Magazines, and warlike Stores, or even a disciplin'd *Militia* to defend us against any sudden Hostility; so that if they were to take it into their Heads (which they are very capable of doing, even without waiting for a Proclamation of War) to make a quick March upon this, or either of the two bordering Colonies, with but Two Thousand Men of the regular Troops of *France*, attended with as many of their Wood-rangers and *Indian* Allies, they wou'd find nothing to obstruct their Course till the Atlantic Ocean stopp'd them; but wou'd over run us at once, and with the same Rapidity and Violence that the back Forests sometimes suffer, when at a general Hunting the Woods are set on Fire by the Natives. (pp. 36–37)

Sterling warns the legislators that the French are shrewd enemies; that their design is to unite "Canada with ... Mississippi; that they plan to establish Garrisons on all the navigable Straits of the mighty Expanse of Mediterranean fresh-water Seas, *Ontario, Erie, Huron, Illinois,* and the *Superieur Lake*" (and he suggests that other, unknown channels connect with these to form a Northwest Passage from Hudson's Bay to the Pacific Ocean); and that the French will need a "commodious Port on the Atlantic Main"— either the Hudson River or the Chesapeake Bay.

Since the French are united under the governor-general in Canada, they have an advantage. An association of the English colonies is necessary, says Sterling (p. 40). But when "a manifest Tendency to Anarchy and Confusion" exists within the legislative bodies of only *one* province—how can the colonies themselves be expected to join together? But the colonies must unite, proclaims the poet, or they will be overwhelmed by the French:

> The Enemy are at our Doors: They are entrenching, and fortressing our Borders: They have slaughter'd our *Virginian* forces, and driven from their Habitations great Numbers of Distrest, out-lying Families, and industrious Adventurers, who might otherwise, by rapid progress, advance the British Frontiers and the Christian Religion. They have intercepted our beneficial Southern Fur Trade, and by the vilest Artifices render'd us cheap and suspectable in Eyes of our ally'd Indians; particularly the Five Nations, some Tribes of Whom have seceded from their League and migrated to themselves; as, if not more powerful Protectors; yet to be rely'd on, as more stedfast Friends.
>
> (p. 41)

Sterling predicts a glorious future for America's Middle West, comparing it to Europe's most famous garden-spots. His sermon contains an early, effective portrait of the Middle West as the Garden of the World: [57]

> They wou'd now by Preoccupation, in order to ground a Right to future, and still-growing Claims, engross that charming Country, from the Sources of the Ohio to its Conflux with the Ouahbach, which is truly worth fighting for in a righteous Cause, and is compar'd for delicious Prospect and Fertility, to the Plains of *Milan*, the Garden of *Italy*, surrounded, and interspers'd with celebrated Lakes and Rivers; if indeed great Things, without being too much degraded, may admit a Comparison with small; a widely-expanded landscape with a Pocket-Picture in Miniature; such a Brook as the *Po* with the Mississippi; or such little Fishponds as *Garda*, and *Maggiore* with such *Euxines* and *Caspians*, as the waters of the *Erie* and the *Hudson*.

Although Richard Lewis had previously compared America with Italy and compared American rivers to the most famous rivers of the Old World, Sterling need not be echoing Lewis, for the promotion literature of the seventeenth and eighteenth centuries frequently makes the comparison. Nevertheless, Sterling probably knew Lewis's poetry, and no one before Lewis had used the comparison so memorably. In addition, Sterling may echo the diction in Lewis's poetry (cf. "if great things with mean we may compare," l. 234 of *The Mouse Trap*).

The minister then directly addresses the "Gentlemen of both Houses," asking them to "secure those blissful Regions, as a Jewel of

---

[57] Cf. Book Three, "The Garden of the World," in Henry Nash Smith, *Virgin Land, the American West as Symbol and Myth* (New York, n.d.), and especially ch. 20, "The Garden as Safety Valve."

the greatest Magnitude and Splendor in the British Crown." He says that the West will be "exhaustless Reservations for your own Children, when these multiplying Provinces are overstock'd with People, as they will soon be from the natural Increase only" (p. 42). In a series of eloquent parallel sentences, Sterling urges the Assembly to think of the New Englanders' example at Cape-Breton, of the Marylanders at Carthagena, of the excellence of General Sharpe—and also to consider what failure will mean for the future. He recalls the time not long ago when the citizens of Annapolis ridiculed the possibility that the French might become formidable in America's interior. He reminds the legislators of France's imperialistic history and warns that they must guard their religion as well as their frontiers. Sterling reminds his audience too that there is also an enemy within—Maryland's Roman Catholics: "Then without Cruelty to their Persons, or overstraining the Laws, let us muzzle the *Bear*, or cut off Tyger's Fangs, and take all speedy, Parliamentary, and Christian Methods for Self-Security" (p. 46).

In conclusion, he calls his audience Britons, defines that word in the patriotic terms of the Glorious Revolution, and maintains that only those men deserve the name who are ready to fight and die for their rights. Sterling's last sentence, using anaphora, apostrophe, and hyperbole, fittingly concludes his sermon:

> O then, as you wou'd deserve that glorious appellation; as you are intimately concerned in the consequences of the momentous event, that has summoned you now extraordinarily; as you are under the more peculiar obligations of honour, trust, and conscience, to promote the happiness of the community; of which you are not bare members, but rulers and patrons: as you will answer it to your God; your king; your young and noble proprietary; and your own constituents: O permit not the zeal of a true public spirit to cool in your breasts; but on this, and all other worthy occasions, improve it in yourselves; kindle, increase it in others; and transmit the hallowed principle to your Children's children, to latest posterity; till only the day of Judgment and the Kingdom of Christ put a period to the British dominion in our *new world*; or till time shall be lost in eternity! And for this you will be attended with public prayers and blessings upon earth, as universal benefactors; and shine in distinguishable glory hereafter, even as the *stars of light in firmament of heaven, for ever and ever!—Amen!—*

Sterling's advocacy of colonial union and his appreciation of the future role and future myth of America's interior are early and previously unremarked instances of these important ideas. Delivered by that "noble, elegant and pathetic Preacher," the Reverend James Sterling, the effect of the sermon was instantaneous. That afternoon the members of the Lower House of Assembly resolved that Sterling be thanked and ordered that William Fitzhugh, Lloyd Buchanan, John Henry, William Hicks, Henry Casson, and Alexander Williamson "acquaint him, that he is requested, by this House, to allow the same to be printed."[58] Jonas Green probably printed about 350 copies of the sermon; the House paid for 300 copies, and he advertised the sermon for sale on July 3, 1755, in the *Maryland Gazette*.

On August 12, 1756, an essay urging Marylanders to fit out privateers appeared in the *Maryland Gazette*. This essay, signed "Philopatris," the pseudonym of a Kent County writer when it recurs in the *Maryland Gazette*, is evidently by a minister, for it accompanies an extract from a sermon of Sunday, August 1, praising the war efforts of England and the king, and inculcating "a ready and sincere and active obedience to our first and wise Government." The minister urges his auditors to fit up a privateer, as one profitable way to fight. Further, the *Maryland Gazette* for September 2, 1756, reveals that the men of Chestertown, Kent County (where Sterling lived), have sent out a privateer, the *Sharpe*, under the command of Captain Edward Scott. This data, in conjunction with the style and subject of the essay, strongly suggest that Sterling was "Philopatris."

When Arthur Dobbs, now governor of North Carolina, journeyed to Philadelphia in 1757, he stayed at "Mr. Hutchings's on Kent-Island" on Friday, February 18, setting out for the Quaker city the next morning.[59] One wonders if Sterling troubled to go and see the hero of *An Epistle to . . . Dobbs*. James Sterling encouraged Provost William Smith's *American Magazine* (which has been called "the most vital and original literary magazine published in America before the War of the Revolution"),[60] and submitted to Smith several of his most ambitious poems. "The most remarkable poem in the magazine"[61] was

[58] *Archives of Maryland* 50:598, and 602–603.
[59] *Maryland Gazette*, Feb. 24, 1757. Speeches by Dobbs were reprinted in the *Maryland Gazette* on Jan. 30 and May 15, 1755.
[60] Richardson (see n. 31 above), 99.
[61] Smyth (see n. 31 above), 35. The broadside is reproduced in E. R. McClintock Dix, "An Early Eighteenth-Century Broadside on Printing," *Royal Irish Academy Proceedings* 27 (1908–1909):401–403. The broadside contains two poems: Sterling's 54-line piece begins "Say, Cadmus, by what Ray Divine inspir'd"; the other poem, by Constantia Grierson, begins "Hail Sacred Art! . . ." David F. Foxon, in a letter dated Mar. 14, 1967, kindly informed me that

a carefully rewritten and much expanded version of Sterling's "The Art of Printing," which had been originally written in 1728 for the Stationers' Company in Dublin, and reprinted in the (Boston) *New England Weekly Journal*, November 25, 1728, and in the Philadelphia *American Weekly Mercury*, December 24, 1728. Sterling's revised and enlarged work, dated *"Kent County in Maryland, December 15th, 1757,"* was "A Poem. On the Invention of Letters and the Art of Printing, Addrest to Mr. Richardson, the Author and Printer of Sir Charles Grandison, and other works, for the Promotion of Religion, Virtue and polite Manners, in a corrupted age." Sterling probably submitted it sometime during the early winter of 1757–58; for the Reverend William Smith, in his introduction to the "Poetical Essays for February, 1758," apologized for not publishing the poem then: "The ingenious author of the *Poem on the Invention of letters*, will excuse us for this month, when he sees a collection of inferior productions inserted in the room of his performance, which, we think, will do honour to our undertaking, when we can give it entire, together with the learned notes belonging to it. . . . After that the Pastorals [probably Sterling's "A Pastoral," discussed below] that have been so long on hand will be inserted, with this advantage, that they will then be thrown into the Spring months, or pastoral Season."

When Smith published "On The Invention of Letters" in the March, 1758, *American Magazine or Monthly Chronicle*, he revealed that the anonymous author was *"a gentleman of acknowledged* taste *and* learning, *in a neighbouring government."* According to Smith, Sterling had apologized for writing a poem *"on a subject of so great dignity"* and would not have done it *"if he could have seen any other person likely to undertake it."* He claimed that during the time of his *"intimacy"* with Alexander Pope, he told *"that great* Poet, *above twenty years ago, that it was peculiarly ungrateful in him, not to celebrate such a subject as the* INVENTION OF LETTERS, *or to suffer it*

---

there are two other editions of this broadside at the British Museum (cf. British Museum *Catalogue*, vol. 92, cols. 321-22). Sterling's poem (slightly revised) was included in his *Poetical Works*, 118-21.

Sterling's and Grierson's poems appear to be the first ones on printing which were published in America. The first written and printed in America seems to be John Markland's *Typographia* (Williamsburg, 1730). Perhaps the second one was "Verses on the Art of Printing" in the *Pennsylvania Gazette*, Sept. 2, 1731.

Smyth, *Philadelphia Magazines*, 37; Lyon Norman Richardson, 119–20; and Wroth, "James Sterling," 36, have all previously attributed the poem to Sterling.

to be disgraced by a meaner hand." Smith added his own opinion of the subject and of Sterling's achievement:

> Mr. Pope, *no doubt, saw that it was a very unpromising theme; and our ingenious Author himself seems conscious of this when he complains of the* "difficulty of keeping clear of vulgar thoughts, on such an occasion, and of expressing in verse those that are abstruse, with perspecuity and precision." *We think, however, he has happily affected both, and has likewise given as much harmony to his periods, and spirit to this expression, as the nature of the piece would well admit. There are, indeed, many beautiful passages in it, equally worthy of the* Poet *and of the* Philosopher.

Sterling opens the poem with an address to his readers, describing himself as "industriously obscure":

> THESE lays, ye *Great!* to RICHARDSON belong;
> His *Art* and *Virtues* have inspir'd the song.
> Forgive the bard, who dares transfer, from you,
> A tribute to superior merit due;
> Who, midst war's tumults, in flagitious times;
> And regions distant from maternal climes
> Industriously obscure, to heav'n resign'd,
> Salutes the friend and patron of mankind.
>
> (ll. 1–8)

Sterling addresses Cadmus and, using materials from his earlier poem, asks him:

> Say, by what principle divine inspir'd,
> Thou for a world's instruction greatly fir'd;
> Rapt in what vision, say, thou God-possest,
> Dawn'd the vast image in thy lab'ring breast?
> The figure of ideas to display,
> And colour forth the intellectual ray;
> In speaking silence the dumb voice impart,
> And sounds embody by creative art;
> By sight alone to edify the ear,
> To picture thought, and bid the eyes to hear!
>
> (ll. 19–28)

> *Phaenices primi, famae si credimus, ausi*
> *Mansuram rudibus vocem signare siguris.*
>
> (Lucan)

Sterling says that Cadmus should be praised by all "who gratitude can pay" for first making connections " 'Twixt arbitrary signs and alien things" (l. 34). Sterling thus pictures the state of learning before the invention of letters:

Before thy art, tradition vainly told
Legends confus'd, and oral tales of old;
Or painted symbols, tree, plant, bird and beast,
Laws, Rites and memorable facts express'd.
Thus *Mexico*'s plum'd envoys sent to court
Of strange invaders a *portray'd* report.
(ll. 49–54)

* See the history of the expedition of *Cortez* by *An. de Solis.*

Using a chronological progress theme, Sterling traces the rise of the art of letters from Mexico to China to Egypt to Greece. As one might expect, Sterling gives the highest praise to Greece (ll. 83–94).

The process of transcribing by hand was costly and inaccurate, so that books "In dark alcoves and stinted numbers lay, / Shut up, like eastern kings, from public day" (ll. 115–16). Then, the first printer (who, according to Sterling, was "Laurence John Koster" of Haerlem) arose: "Ah! let not *Faustus* rob great Koster's name; / Like *Him*, [Americus] who since usurp'd Columbus' fame" (ll. 121–22). (The thought and diction in this couplet is similar to Sterling's earlier "To Robert Lovett," cited above.) Sterling then traced the evolution of printing and celebrates its effects:

Now floods of day *Cimmerian* gloom succeed:
The clergy think; and laymen dare to read.
Fair tomes enrich the cultur'd student's room,
And the trim'd lamps their midnight oil consume.
Now, to invent new arts, or old to find,
Becomes the glory of th'ingenuous mind.
To polish manners, and embellish life,
Nation with Nation view in gen'rous strife;
Now, from the exhaustless fund of classic writ,
True taste emerges and *Augustan* wit.
Learn'd critics rise, explore the sense perplext,
And re-establish the collated text.
Prescribing rules to judge the old, the new
The just, the false, the spurious, and the true.
(ll. 133–46)

After chronicling the advances in biblical scholarship, in recapturing the "*Grœcien style*" in architecture, and in the displacing of the ancients by the moderns in philosophy, Sterling lists the achievements of the new science:

Astronomy now wings a bolder flight,
And darts her ken beyond our solar light;
Thro' systems, worthy of a God, she runs,

Bids earths to roll, and fixes central suns.
Now num'rous moons th'*Italic* tube* descries,
Peoples the planets, and reveals the skies.
Elliptic comets, hurl'd by laws divine,
Their orbits know, nor with rash terrors shine.
Commerce from pole to pole its course explores,
Lights up new stars, and glads antarctic shores.
The stormy cape of *Hope* and *Horne* o'ercome,
From East and West, we bear their treasures home;
And, where the late-found magnet points our way,
Around the measur'd globe, we chace the day.
(ll. 169–78)

* Galilaeo's Telescope

The poet praises reason, which is "religion, truly understood" (l. 196). Printing will make it possible for real merit to be rewarded, and no longer will great minds ever be wholly lost: "While latest times *Newton* entire shall boast, / Nor mourn a Bacon, Locke, or Milton lost" (ll. 213–14). But "new dangers" are in the world—France and Rome, who hate "each learn'd, and free mercantile state" (l. 227). Sterling calls on the "Genius of Albion" to protect the rights of Englishmen. He points out how the spirit is operating in Samuel Richardson:

Mark, how thy dictates *Richardson* obeys;
Assertor of thy rights in impious days.
His *Virgin-sheets* no prostitution stains,
His moral ink no venom'd gall profanes.
O'er *Elizivir* or *Bleau** his worth to raise
Gives but mechanic fame and vulgar praise.
To shine first printer is his lowest sphere;
While the good man and author all revere.
(ll. 255–62)

* Celebrated printers.

Sterling concludes the poem with a compliment for Richardson:

See him, like *censer'd* Aaron, dauntless stand,
'Twixt wrath divine and a devoted land!
From his pure Press, see, hallow'd increase rise,
As from an altar, grateful to the skies!
See, for his country obstinately brave,
He still persists, nor yet despairs to save.
Men, whom as man he loves, he wishes saints;
And lives himself the *Grandison* he paints.
(ll. 263–70)

Sterling's poem is built around two chronological progress themes: the first and longest on the invention of letters, and the other on the rise of printing. Throughout the poem runs the motif that man faces never-easing dangers. The greatest former enemy, ignorance, has been defeated by printing and by the Enlightenment. The great modern dangers are political (which the Hanover family settles) and moral (which Richardson overcomes). In a series of long learned notes, Sterling discusses, among other things, the claims of Laurens Janszoon Coster, Johann Fust, Johann Gutenberg, and Johann Mentelin as the first printer. Following the opinions advanced by George Sandys in a translation of Coster's epitaph, and by Ellis in an article in the *Philosophical Transactions*, Sterling honors Coster as the first printer. Sterling's earlier poem "The Art of Printing" has been expanded and revised, and the finished product is among the better Augustan American poems. That Sterling celebrates Richardson is indicative: Richardson is inextricably linked with the vogue of sentimentality that became dominant in England in the last half of the century, and we shall find Sterling writing sentimental poetry.

Sterling's anonymous, undated poem "The Patriot" appeared in the *American Magazine* for April, 1758.[62] It evidently complimented an American, who is compared to a number of contemporary English politicians, but his name (which no doubt originally was the first word of l. 22) is not given. The poem opens with a general indictment of political corruption (ll. 1–14) and makes special reference to the situation in the colonies:

> In humble miniature, when this, we fear,
> Like each *European* vice, is mimick'd here;
> Tho' stationed guilt should persecute my rhymes;
> Since praise to worth is censure on the times;
> Fain would th'advent'rous muse, to merit just,
> Redeem the patriot's honour'd name from dust;
> And proud a theme so glorious to display
> ———to thee she consecrates the lay;
> And in the celebrated list of fame,
> Charm'd with thy conduct, would enrol thy name.
> (ll. 15–24)

Sterling asks the Patriot not to disdain "the author of these lines" and describes himself as "A friend to generous worth where'er it shines" (l. 26). He portrays the ideal character of the patriot (ll. 31–60), contrasting him with "slaves to power, or prostitutes to gain" (l. 63).

After discussing corruption and the patriot in England (ll. 77–84),

[62] Pp. 332–35. This poem is attributed to Sterling by Lyon Norman Richardson, 121, and Wroth, "James Sterling," 36.

Sterling describes the man who is truly great (ll. 85–98), attacks corruption (ll. 99–106), and then applies his principles to the English political scene. He concludes with a generalized portrayal of true patriots. Sterling notes the allusions to Thomson, Pope, and to Bolingbroke's *Dissertation upon Parties*. The student of American literature might be surprised that all specific political references in the poem are to English, rather than American, politicians; but English politicians, like English fashions and literature, were well known in the colonies.

"The Dame of Cyprus" appeared in the *American Magazine* between "The Patriot" and another poem by Sterling, and is also, I believe, by him. The poet tells of Peter, the cruel tyrant of Cyprus, who forced both men and women to work for him. One day, when Peter was near, a woman appeared for work—in the nude. When her fellow workers expressed surprise and shock at her action, she replied that since there were no men present (for surely *men* would not stand for the oppressive rule of Peter), there was no reason not to appear in the nude. The shamed men then rose up against the tyrant and killed him. Sterling applied the story to the present French and Indian War:

> O would some fair-one of distinguish'd merit,
> Equal this *Cypriot* in her public spirit,
> A while forget her sex and native fear,
> And in the lovely *Deshabille* appear,
> Grasping the deadly sword or glittering spear.
> Soon would our drowsy *Statesmen*, stung with shame,
> Be taught to emulate their fathers' fame;
> At length would hear their bleeding country's cries
> And fir'd with rage and gen'rous pity rise,
> To drive the savage murd'rer from the plain,
> And give their harrass'd brethren peace again.
> (ll. 19–29)

This poem (like *Zeal against the Enemies of our Country*) testifies that Sterling sided with the proprietary party in the struggle between the proprietary and popular parties over the financing of the French and Indian War.

Sterling's third poem in the *American Magazine*'s "Poetical Essays" section for April (pp. 332–36) is a good example of his classical training as well as a charming bit of *vers de société*. Accompanying the poem was an explanatory letter, dated "Kent in Maryland":

A Thunder-gust, happening to cease immediately after the arrival of a young lady at my house, where she took refuge from the rain, gave an occasion of complementing her with the following epigram; which with its *Latin* translation, waits on you in order to find a place among the lighter performances in your magazine.

The complete English epigram follows:

> LEDA's twin-sons,* when they together shin'd,
> Smooth'd the rough sea, and calm'd the raging wind.
> But Lo! your single presence quells our storms;
> And one bright maid more, than two gods, performs.

Castor and *Pollux*.

The entire poetry section of the *American Magazine* for May, 1758, was taken up with Sterling's "A PASTORAL. *To his Excellency* GEORGE THOMAS, *Esq.; formerly Governor of* Pennsylvania, *and now General of the* Leeward *Islands.*"[63] The poem had been written in 1744, upon the death of Alexander Pope. Evidently Sterling sent the poem to the Reverend William Smith soon after the latter announced his plan to start a magazine. After several months passed and Smith had still not published Sterling's "Pastoral," he complained that Smith gave "unjust preference" to lesser pieces of poetry. Smith replied that the "Pastoral" was the longest poem he had on hand, that some of those printed before it "were *occasional* and required immediate notice, while others were of prior date and had been promised to the public on our cover." But Smith nevertheless apologized to Sterling: "As the author of the *Pastoral* was one of the first encouragers of our *Magazine*, and a gentleman of education and genius, he could not imagine that it was our interest or intention to disregard any performance of his."[64] Smith published portions of Sterling's letter accompanying the poem:

> As this *poetical Brat* was conceived in *North-America*, you may, if you please suffer it to give its first squeak in the world, thro' the channel of the American Magazine. But if it should appear of a *monstrous* nature, stifle the wretch by all means in the birth, and throw it in the river *Delaware*, from whence, you will observe, it originally sprung. The parent, I can assure you, will shed no tears at the funeral. If *Saturn* presided at its formation, instead of *Apollo*, it will want no *Lead* to make it sink, but fall quickly to the bottom,

[63] Contemporary MS annotations in the British Museum and Library of Congress copies of the *American Magazine* attribute this poem to Sterling: Smyth, *Philadelphia Magazines*, 37; Lyon Norman Richardson, 120; and Wroth, "James Sterling," 36. The poem has been incorrectly attributed to Francis Knapp by Agnes Marie Sibley, *Alexander Pope's Prestige in America, 1725–1835* (New York, 1949), 85. But see J. A. Leo Lemay, "Francis Knapp," 233–37.
[64] *American Magazine*, May, 1758, p. 390.

by its own natural *Heaviness,* as I doubt not many other modern productions, both in prose and verse, (*Sinking from thought to thought—a vast profound!*) would have done, had they been put to the trial.

After this allusion to Pope's *Peri Bathous,* Sterling says that George Thomas "was Governor of *Pennsylvania* at the time it was written, saw the manuscript, and gave his consent to its publication almost exactly in the present form." The "Pastoral" is in two parts. The first is a statement of American literary nationalism and the second a lament for the death of Alexander Pope. In the opening, Sterling combines the *translatio studii* motif (the ancient idea of the westward movement of arts and empire) with a description of the New World:

> Pierian nymphs that haunt *Sicilian* plains,
> And first inspir'd to sing in rural strains;
> Vouchsafe to teach my trembling reed to play,
> And woods to join in concert with my lay.
> Our *Indian* woods, as yet unus'd to sing,
> When taught by you, with harmony shall ring.
> O waft your way from fam'd Parnassus' height
> (The muses love a bold adventurous flight)
> And westward steer—*Phoebus* will lead the way,
> You'll reach our mountains e'er the close of day;
> And there behold, what sure must highly please,
> *Apollo's* steeds plunge in the western seas.
> Soon as the ocean hides his sacred head,
> You'll see the golden curtains of his bed . . . .
>
> (ll. 1–14)

The American beach as the "golden curtains" of the ocean's bed is a striking image. Then Sterling writes a direct statement of the *translatio studii* idea:

> A western course had pleas'd you all along;
> *Greece, Rome,* and *Briton,* flourish all in song.
> Keep on your way, and spread a glorious fame,
> Around the earth let all admire your name.
> Chuse in our plains or forests soft retreats;
> For here the muses boast no antient seats.
> Here fertile fields, and fishy streams abound:
> Nothing is wanting but *Poetic* ground.
> Bring me that pipe with which *Alexis* charm'd
> The *Eastern* world, and every bosom warm'd.
> Our *Western* climes shall henceforth own your power;
> *Thetis* shall hear it from her watry bower;
> Even *Phoebus* listen as his chariot flies,
> And smile propitious from his flaming skies.
>
> (ll. 17–30)

JAMES STERLING

These lines and the following perhaps echo the occasional poem that
Lewis wrote welcoming Thomas Penn to Pennsylvania in 1732:

> Haste lovely nymphs, and quickly come away,
> Our sylvan gods lament your long delay;
> The stately oaks that dwell on *Delaware*
> Rear their tall heads to view you from afar.
> The Naids summon all their scaly crew
> And at *Henlopen* anxious wait for you.
>
> (ll. 31–36)

Sterling repeats his incantatory urging of the muses to come to
America:

> Haste lovely nymphs and quickly reach our shore;
> Th'impatient river heeds his tides no more,
> Forsakes his banks, and where he joins the main,
> Heaps waves on waves to usher in your train.
> A numerous fleet rich with what *Ceres* yields
> (*Ceres* the goddess of our fertile fields)
> With ensigns waving in the prosp'rous gale
> For want of water scarce can bend a sail;
> The goddess vows to stop her liberal hand—
> Haste lovely nymphs, and save a sinking land.
>
> (ll. 37–46)

Here Sterling, referring to his introductory letter and to the idea
of poor poetry as "sinking," ironically undercuts his own verse.
Of course, like Lewis in *Carmen Seculare*, he is obviously referring
to Maryland's economic plight. He next wishes for an end to the
bitter struggles between the political parties: "Harmonious Nine,
bring harmony and peace, / Unite our hearts, and bid all discord
cease" (ll. 47–48).

Finally, the muses arrive in America: "But hark they come!—the
Dryads crowd the shore, / The waters rise, I hear the billows roar!"
(ll. 49–50). The Indians prepare wampum belts "and loud YOHAWS
shout thro' the trembling air" (l. 64). When a blaze appears in the
skies, the Indians are "hush'd in deep amaze" (l. 66) and then ask
what "these wonders" mean. The muses exclaim that "the rude are
polished, soon as we appear" (l. 76) and remind the Americans that
the muses' first appearance in England brought forth a Chaucer
(l. 84). After the muses vanish, Sterling addresses Governor Thomas:

> O thou distinguished by a far-spread fame,
> Obtain'd by merit, not thy honour'd name;
> Whether you strive, by strong persuasive sense,
> To urge a naked province to defence,

297

Or wisely dreading savage *Indian* foes,
By friendship's chain avert tremendous woes;
Hear and accept harmless rural lay . . . .

(ll. 95–101)

Sterling's praise of Thomas concludes the first part of the poem.

The second part (ll. 105–218) of "A Pastoral" is a pastoral elegy: in the spring season, Moeris comes upon Palaemon, who is lamenting and neglecting his flock. When Moeris asks the trouble, Palaemon answers that Pope (called "Alexis"—from his name in his second pastoral) is dead:

'Tis not a private loss afflicts my soul,
A Part we both may bear, but not the whole.
For nations weep, and with one voice deplore
The musical *Alexis* now no more!
From *England's* coast, see yonder distant sail;
But now it pass'd, swift as the flying gale;
They call'd aloud, and stun'd the list'ning shore,
Weep shepherds weep, *Alexis* is no more.

(ll. 129–36)

Moeris replies to the news with a long and effective lament, containing several allusions to Pope's "Windsor Forest":

Then art thou gone! and with thee every art
To please, to check, to sooth, to rouse, the heart?
Who now shall charm the nymphs with heav'nly strains?
Or spread the flowers on *Windsor's* verdant plains?
Who sing thee *Loddon*, and thy weeping streams,
Thy shaded waters, cool as *Cynthia's* beams?
Go tell thy sorrows in thy parent's ears
And grateful *Thames* shall drown his banks with tears.
Sweet as their dying songs, his swans shall mourn;
And murmur grief each tributary *urn*.
    Hang all your leaves, with brilliant drops, ye trees,
And shed them gently on the trav'ling breeze;
Ye moisten'd dales, fly swift to *Cooper's* hill,
That rocks may weep, and swell each purling rill.
Not *Colin's* self, in *Rosalinda's* praise
E'er sung so sweet, so moving notes as these . . . .

(ll. 137–52)

Besides alluding to Denham and Spenser, Sterling quotes from Pope's second pastoral. In concluding the poem, the Marylander follows in his imagination the great English poet to heaven and portrays his reception there. Although this is one of Sterling's better poems, its structure is poor. The pastoral elegy is supposed to fulfill the prediction of the *translatio* motif: with the death of Pope, the muses have left England for America. Nevertheless, the two parts of the poem are joined, rather than unified.

Sterling appended to the poem a number of notes, identifying his poetic sources, defining obscure words, and listing his "imitations" of Virgil. His major critical ideas could be gathered from a study of the introductions and notes to the poems. For example, he wrote the following note to line 146: "In Mr. Pope's elegant poetical language, every smaller stream that empties itself into the *Thames* is a *Tributary Urn*. It is reckon'd one of the greatest beauties in pastoral poetry to give life, action, feeling and intelligence to inanimate things, as *Virgil* finely expresses it, Non canimus surdis, respondent omnia sylvae."

Sterling's next poem in the *American Magazine* was, according to him, "hastily composed . . . for the entertainment of a select group of publick-spirited friends, who gave me a short notice of their intention to dine with me, and drink the protestant champion's health, as they termed the king of Prussia." At his friends' insistence, Sterling sent off the poem written for the occasion to Smith who published it in the August issue, pp. 550–52. "The Royal Comet" is written in rhyming couplets of anapestic tetrameter. Sterling apologized for the unusual meter by saying that it was written for a convivial drinking party and he added: "I hope no reader will think the dignity of the subject, lessened merely by the familiar strain, in which it is written; when they consider that such seemed most suitable to the occasion, the verses, consisting of eleven feet, are to be read, like the *Greek Jambics* (which were anciently much used in convivial festivities) with less solemnity and more rapidly, than the common heroic measure of ten feet in our language will admit." Dated "*Kent in Maryland, July 14th*, 1758," the anonymous poem,[65] which celebrates the achievements of Frederick, king of Prussia, compares Austria's past glories with her present ones under Frederick. In the only reference to America, the poet says that Frederick shall animate, "O *George*, thy new world" (l. 24). In a vicious denunciation of Indians, he claims that they are less than human:

> Our laws, our religion, our rights he befriends,
> And conquest o'er savage invaders portends;

[65] This has been attributed to Sterling by Lyon Norman Richardson, 121, on the basis of an annotation in the Library of Congress copy of the *American Magazine*, and by Wroth, "James Sterling," 37, because of the dateline.

O'er christians miscall'd, who their nature disgrace,
Bely human form, and god's image deface.
(ll. 25–28)

The poem was written during the French and Indian War, and Sterling undoubtedly knew Thomas Bacon's son John, who had recently been killed and scalped by the Indians, as well as others who lost their lives in the battles.

"An Epitaph on the late Lord Howe" appeared in the *American Magazine* for September, 1757, pp. 604–605.[66] This anonymous poem, dated *"Kent in Maryland, August 14th,* 1758," was written

as a tribute of not only *Public* but *Personal,* gratitude, which ought not to be confined to a benefactor, but extended to his posterity; for, please to know, that the grandfather of the late Lord Howe, when in a high employment in the reign of Queen Anne, was a generous patron to the father of the author of these lines, by presenting to her majesty a memorial of his long services in the wars of *Ireland, Spain,* and *Flanders*; and by further promoting his pretentions to an honourable post in the army, of which he shou'd have been otherwise deprived by a court-interest in favour of a younger and unexperienc'd officer.

Sterling's biography, as well as the dateline, evidences his authorship. In heroic couplets, the "Epitaph" opens with an address to *"Britannia*'s mighty *Dead,"* asking them to receive Howe's "heroic ghost," who is compared to the ideal man of the Renaissance, Sir Philip Sidney: "In foreign fields, like *Sidney* young and brave, / Doom'd to an early not untimely grave." Lord Howe saw the advancement of *"Luxury* and *France,"* Britain's "worst foes," and he fought against them "as soldiers fought, in *Marlbro's* days." As he died, Howe predicted that Britons would revenge his death.

Two Latin poems by Sterling are in the *American Magazine.* A 34-line "Elogium" dated *"E Comitatu Cantii in Mariae Provincia,"* which appeared in the September issue, acclaims the soldiers fighting in the Canadian campaign. The other poem, *"Apollinis* Querela, Sive Epigramma," commends the Latin poetry of John Beveridge, who was teaching at the Philadelphia Academy and contributing Latin poetry to Smith's *American Magazine.* When Beveridge reprinted Sterling's

---

[66] Smyth, *Philadelphia Magazines,* 39; Lyon Norman Richardson, 119; and Wroth, "James Sterling," 37, have attributed the epitaph to Sterling. Green reprinted the poem in the *Maryland Gazette,* Nov. 16, 1758, and it was also reprinted in the *New Hampshire Gazette,* Mar. 2, 1759, and in the *New York Gazette,* Mar. 19, 1759.

Latin compliment years later, he wrote that Sterling was among the "best of my Latin correspondents." [67]

The last issue of the *American Magazine* contained Sterling's "*The 22d Ode of the first Book of* Horace *imitated; and inscribed to the Lady of his late Excellency* SAMUEL OGLE, *Esquire.*" This anonymous[68] imitation, dated "*Kent in Maryland, October 25th, 1758,*" was occasioned by Sterling's visit to Governor Ogle's country seat. While walking in the governor's garden, Sterling jumped in alarm when he suddenly encountered a buffalo kept by Ogle. The governor later wrote the minister and "humorously rallied me on my supposed fright, and made a comparison between his *American* wild beast and *Horace's* wolf in the *Sabine* wood." Sterling recalled the Twenty-second Ode and "struck out" the stanzas. He hoped that the lines might "prove some entertainment to those readers of your Magazine, who can taste the original, and who wou'd not be displeased to see an imitation of it with reference to our own times and circumstances."

Sterling opens the poem with a definition of the "christian hero" (who is, of course, like Ogle):

I.

The christian hero, pure from sin,
Serene, and fortify'd within,
Defies the rage of civil jars,
Assembly-feuds, and foreign wars;
    Nor wants the troops, brave *Amherst* led.
He, safe in sanctity of life,
From the *French* sword and *Indian* knife,
Nor dreads a circumcision of the head . . . .

Having established "the Christian hero's" (by implication, Ogle) fearlessness in the face of scalping, the second stanza takes him through the wilds of America:

[67] Wroth, "James Sterling," 37, correctly attributes "Elogium" to Sterling; but Lyon Norman Richardson mistakenly attributes it to John Beveridge, 118 n. 83. For the authorship of "Apollinis," see John Beveridge, *Epistolae Familiares* (Philadelphia, 1765), 46–47. The most recent account of Beveridge is Leo M. Kaiser, "John Beveridge: Latin Poet of Two Worlds," *Classical Journal* 58 (1963):215–23.

[68] On the basis of a contemporary manuscript notation in the Library of Congress copy of the *American Magazine*, Lyon Norman Richardson, 121, attributed it to Sterling; Wroth, "James Sterling," 37, ascribed it to him because of the dateline. It is actually a revision of an imitation that Sterling had written as a youth and published in his *Poetical Works*, 17–21. It was reprinted in the *American Museum* 4, no. iv (Oct., 1788):385.

2.

Whether he purposes to go;
Thro' *Apalachian* rocks and snow.
Cannadean-forests, *Funda's* frost,
Or bleak *Ontario's* barbarous coast;
   Or visits *Niagara's Fall*:
With soul, not liable to fear,
He sees tremendous dangers near;
Smiling, he sees; superior to them all.

In the third stanza, Sterling says that no evil can surprise the "Heav'n-protected man." While the poet was slowly walking through Ogle's "pleasing lawns," suddenly "A *Buffalo* of monstrous size" rushed forth:

4.

Such never drank *Ohio's* floods,
Or bellow'd in *Virginian*-woods:
Such and so fierce did ne'er advance
'Gainst *Spanish Don* with daring lance;
   Such ne'er in *Hole* of *Hockley** bled.
Yet *me* unarm'd the savage saw,
With fear and reverential awe,
Spurning the ground, he came, he gaz'd, he fled.
   *Notorious for Bull baiting.

Sterling claims that he is protected by virtue, and would be even in the arctic regions: "on *Hudson's* dreary shore, / Where icy mountains, bursting, roar; / Where Hyperborean tempests blow." He concludes that the man of virtue is safe in any situation, even amidst "the hissing brood." The imitation contains six octaves of iambic tetrameter. The structure of the eight-line stanza (consisting of three couplets, the third of which is within an envelope), rhyming *aabbc dd c*, implies that there will be a progress through line five, then an interruption or qualification in lines six and seven, and a conclusion in line eight. In only two of the six stanzas (nos. 2 and 6) does the meaning reinforce the stanzaic structure.

On the basis of these *American Magazine* poems (not all of which were attributed to him), Sterling has been remembered for expressing nascent nationalism, for celebrating Richardson and Pope, and for introducing sentimentalism into American literature. Earlier literary historians have thought "On the Invention of Printing" his best poem, but "A Pastoral" seems more interesting for several reasons, including its important American literary nationalism and its use of the *translatio studii* motif. Fortunately, he continued writing, and his last poems are more successful.

"Verses occasioned by the Success of the British Arms in the Year 1759" appeared on the front page of the *Maryland Gazette* for January 3, 1760. Although the poem is anonymous and undated, the place of publication, style, and content (especially praise for Governor Sharpe and the insinuation that the Maryland legislators have been deficient in supporting the war, ll. 177–80) all suggest Sterling's authorship.[69] The opening asks whether "echoing Joys" shall resound throughout the land, and "the muse alone forbear to sing" (ll. 1–8). The next two verse paragraphs (ll. 9–20) enumerate the English victories in America during the past year ("Louisburg reduc'd and Quebec subdu'd") and praise General Amherst. Then Sterling recalls the English who have died in the war, especially the heroic General Wolfe, who is compared to famous Romans who perished defending "Native Rights," and urges Wolfe as an example for the future (ll. 29–46).

The body of the poem (ll. 47–174) portrays a single planter's progress in clearing, planting, and harvesting as representative of the way of life of the American farmer and of the progress of American civilization. This is similar to Crèvecoeur's later technique in his sketch "Andrew the Hebridean," *Letters from an American Farmer* (London, 1782).

A pulsating movement between life and death, joy and sorrow, progress and destruction is found throughout this section as well as throughout the entire poem (e. g., the successes of Amherst and death of Wolfe). Sterling opens his description of a planter's progress with remarks on his future safety:

> Big with the Prospects which before us rise,
> And future Harvests waving in our Eyes
> We view with silent Glee, the Chearful Swain,
> In safety smiling o'er his Teeming Grain;
> Nor fears the Harvest lost, or furtive Foe,
> Nor shelters more from War's destructive Blow.
> His bellowing Kine, concealed with prudent Care

[69] Compare the description of corn in its husk ("Wrapt up in State...to Eastern Kings...Hid from the Public," ll. 164–66) to the description of manuscript books in "On the Invention of Letters" ("Shut up, like eastern kings, from public day," l. 116).

While Armies ravag'd and the Foe was near,
At large, they roam again their native Woods,
Feed their own Fields and drink their usual Floods;
Pure and serene they run, as they ran before,
No more polluted now with human Gore.
(ll. 47–58)

After a verse paragraph describing the lambs and cattle feeding in peace, Sterling chronicles the process of conquering the frontier:

The *Planter* there amidst his swarthy Slaves,
Proscribes the Ground where yet the Forest waves;
The Slaves obedient to their Lord's Decree,
The keen edg'd Ax apply to ev'ry Tree;
Redoubl'd Blows thro' all the Wood resound,
Redoubled Blows the neighboring Woods rebound;
The Forest nods and trembles at the Sound,
And cracking, rattling tumbles to the Ground.
The Trees now prostrate, all their Glories fade,
Their branching Honours, once a grateful Shade,
Laid low on Earth, a dreary Thicket gloom
No more to rise, and ne'er again to bloom.
The Parent Birds forsake their downy Nests,
Their Cares all flutt'ring in their little Breasts,
Pearch on the neighb'ring Trees, or wing the Skies,
Bemoan their helpless Young, in doleful Cries.
But cease, my Muse, act a more gen'rous Part,
Nor wound, with plaintive Tales, the tender Heart;
Perhaps too soon, thy mournful Lays may flow,
And weep some Friend in elegiack Woe,
Or if thy Wings, with Satyr fledg'd, shall rise
Some fool or Knave or Hypocrite chastise;
But here, 'tis thine to touch the pleasing String,
And grateful Strains in chearful Notes to sing.
(ll. 67–90)

Although both Cook and Lewis had earlier lamented the passing of the wilderness, Sterling is more sentimental than any previous American poet. His emotions concerning the sacredness of the wilderness may not be as strong as Lewis's, but he deliberately tries to rouse the "tender Heart's" sympathies. Like James Fenimore Cooper over seventy-five years later, Sterling fastens on the chopping down of trees as the symbolic death of the wilderness.

Slaves pile up the wood and burn it; then the land is planted and the crops grow. After the planter becomes "Free and contented in his own Estate" (l. 106), his recreations (racing, hunting, and fishing) are portrayed:

The Race-Horse here invites him to the Course,
Elate with Hopes, he meditates the Purse;
Now a Hunter, he seeks the adjacent Woods,
A Fowler now, he haunts the neighb'ring Floods;
There, Fish of various Kinds afford Delight,
Amuse his Hours, and feast his Appetite.
(ll. 109–14)

The poet lists the planter's diet: meats from domestic and wild animals
and birds, various fruits, and his usual drink—apple cider (ll. 115–28).
The cultivation of tobacco ("Source of his wealth, first Object of
his Cares") is described, as well as the attacks on the plant by the
"Budworm" and "Hornworm." After comparing the planter's feeling
for his destroyed tobacco to a shepherd's grief over the devour-
ing of his sheep by wolves (ll. 145–50), Sterling passes on to the
curing, packing, and shipping of tobacco:

But Foes repell'd, all noxious Insects gone,
And the ripe Plant to full Perfection grown,
Now leaves the Field, and from inclement Skies
To the hospitable Roof's Protection flies;
Whence, cur'd, and neatly packt and priz'd with Care,
Attending Ships receive their freighted Fare,
And wafted by these to *Britannia's* Shore.
Adds to the Masters Wealth, increasing Store.
(ll. 151–58)

Sterling next writes a lush description of corn:

See the Maize in extended Rows arise,
Shoot out a Thousand Silks of various Dyes,
It's flower'd Tassils waving in the Wind,
And wanton Blades in am'rous Sports entwin'd,
The Grain in silken Foliages conceal'd,
Wrapt up in State, disdains to be reveal'd:
So Eastern Kings, in lazy Pride enthron'd,
Hid from the Public, beam their Glories round.
(ll. 159–66)

He concludes the planter's story with the thought that "Indians no
more their Savage War shall wage," and that the farmer may now
tend his crops in peace because "Amherst's Care each helpless Briton
shields" (l. 176).

The three final verse paragraphs (ll. 175–210) again compliment the
war's leaders and apologize for the poet's inability to do them justice.
Were he an Addison or a Pope, he could rise to the occasion, but his
muse is "Confin'd to Woods, and us'd to rural Scenes, / She dares not
rise in such exalted Strains." "Verses Occasioned by the Success of the

British Arms in the Year 1759," written in Sterling's usual heroic couplets, has a cyclic structure. It opens with a survey of the military actions of the past year (ll. 1–46); the body contains a generalized, chronological progress-piece describing the planter's life (which is telescoped within the course of a year): clearing the ground, planting the crops, portraying the usual recreation and diet, and harvesting the crops (with special descriptions of the most important Maryland produce, tobacco and corn); the ending returns to the theme of the opening and shows how the military secures the planter's efforts. The subject of the poem is not really the history of the military conquests of 1759, but the thoughts occasioned by those conquests and by the ending of the war: the progress of English civilization in America. Sterling's thesis, admirably reinforced by a pulsating pattern within a cyclic structure, is that the joys and progress of life are repeatedly undercut by misery and destruction. The examples from past history and from ever-present natural cycles reinforce the implied theme. Nevertheless, the poet stresses the bounty and fertility of America and seems to hope that war, poverty, destruction, and death will not always reappear.

After the Hallam Company performed in Chestertown (where Sterling lived), Kent County, in January, 1760, it moved on to Annapolis late in February, and Sterling evidently accompanied the actors. At the opening of the theater in Annapolis, a special "Prologue" and "Epilogue" were recited. Jonas Green wrote up the opening night in his *Gazette* for March 6, 1760:

> Monday last [March 3] the THEATRE in this City was Open'd, when the Tragedy of the ORPHAN, and LETHE (A Dramatic Satire) were perform'd, in the Presence of his Excellency the Governor, to a polite and numerous Audience, who all express'd a general Satisfaction. The principal Characters, both in the Play and Entertainment, were perform'd with great Justice, and the Applause which attended the whole Representation, did less Honour to the Abilities of the Actors than to the Taste of their Auditors. For the Amusement and Emolument of such of our Readers as were not present, we here insert the *Prologue* and *Epilogue*, both written by a Gentleman in this Province, whose poetical Works have render'd him justly Admir'd by all Encouragers of the Liberal Arts.

Green's "Gentleman" could hardly have been anyone other than James Sterling, Maryland's best-known contemporary poet.[70]

---

[70] Verbal echoes from Sterling's earlier poetry (e. g., compare "Maria's Land" in l. 5 above to "Maria's Shores" in *An Epistle to . . . Dobbs*, 1:28), the senti-

The "Prologue," like Sterling's earlier "A Pastoral," is a progress-piece on the future glory of America:

PROLOGUE, *spoken by Mr.* Douglass.

Lo! to new Worlds th'advent'rous Muse conveys
The moral Wisdom of dramatic Lays!
She bears thro' Ocean Phoebus' high Command,
And tunes his Lyre in fair *Maria's* Land;
O'ertakes his Sun, Communicates his Fires,
And rising Bards in Western Climes inspires!
See! Genius wakes, dispels the former Gloom,
And sheds Light's Blaze, deriv'd from *Greece* and *Rome*!
With polish'd Arts wild Passions to controul;
To warm the Breast, and humanize the Soul!
By magic Sounds to vary Hopes and Fears;
Or make each Eye dissolve in virtuous Tears!
'Til sympathizing Youths in Anguish melt,
And Virgins sigh for Woes, before unfelt!
Here, as we speak, each heart-struck Patriot glows
With real Rage to crush Britannia's Foes!
To quell bold Tyrants, and support the Laws,
Or, like brave *WOLFE*, bleed in his Country's Cause!
Europe no more, sole Arbitress, shall sit,
Or boast the proud Monopoly of Wit;
Her *youngest Daughter* here with filial Claim,
Asserts her Portion of Maternal Fame!
Let no nice Sparks despise our humble Scenes,
Half-buskin'd Monarchs, and itin'rant Queens!
Triflers! who boast, they once in Tragic Fury
Heard *Garrick* thund'ring on the Stage of Drury!
Or view'd, exulting, o'er each gay Machine,
The Feats of Covent-Garden's Harlequin!
Athens from such beginnings, mean and low!
Saw Thespis' Cart a wond'rous Structure grow;
Saw Theatres aspire, and with surprize,
Ghosts, Gods, and Daemons, or descend or rise!
To Taste, from Censure, draw no rash Pretence;
But think Good-Nature the sure Test of Sense!
As *England's* Sons, attend to Reason's strains;
And prove *her* Blood flows richly in your Veins;
Be what *we* Act, the Heroes of our Parts;
And feel, that *Britons* here have Roman Hearts!

Here, as in several earlier poems, literary nationalism and the *translatio* motif are Sterling's major themes. The "Epilogue, spoken by

mentality of ll. 13–15, and the characteristic Sterling themes—all also suggest his authorship.

Mrs. Douglass," comments upon the efficaciousness of the play's moral. The advertisement for *The Provoked Husband* in the *Maryland Gazette* for March 13 noted that "By particular Desire, Mr. Douglass will speak the Prologue which was spoken at the Opening of the Theatre."

On the same day, March 13, 1760, Sterling's last published poem appeared in the *Pennsylvania Gazette*. It was reprinted in the *New York Gazette*, April 14, 1760, and in the *Boston Gazette*, May 26, 1760. Dated "Kent, in Maryland, November 18, 1759," the poem is prefaced with this editorial comment:

> *Being a Production of this Country, and containing a sufficient Share of that Energy of Expression, Dignity of Sentiment, and Glow of Spirit, which characterize all the Performances of the reverend and worthy Author of the Epitaph on Lord* Howe *(Published in a late* American *Magazine) from whose Hand they come, it is hoped that, even now, after all that has been already published on this Subject, they will not be unacceptable to your Readers.*

The body of Sterling's "*Panegyrical* VERSES *on the Death of General* WOLFE" is an imaginative creation of Amherst's speech on learning of General Wolfe's death. After setting the scene (ll. 1–12), Sterling has Amherst address the conquering British army:

> 'Victorious Bands! no more indulge your Grief;
> 'With noble Envy view your bleeding Chief!
> 'He bleeds, a Race of Warriors to supply,
> 'Instructed thus to conquer, thus to die;
> ' 'Gainst Earth's proud Thrones, in impious League combin'd,
> 'To vindicate their Country, and Mankind;
> 'The Sons of Fraud and Murder to explore
> 'Thro' Nature's Bars, impervious now no more;
> 'Thro' Ice-bound Seas their Thunders to convey,
> 'Or burst, thro' sailing Isles, their dreadful Way;
> 'Thro' fomeful Rocks, that rise in Cloud-top'd Spires,
> 'Thro' Storms, and Cataracts of floating Fires;
> 'Where quakes the strong ribb'd Frigate to the Blast;
> 'Where groans the Shrowd, and reels the shudd'ring Mast;
> 'Where Winds 'gainst Winds, in boist'rous Combat blow;
> 'All Hurricanes above, and Whirlpools all below.
>
> (ll. 13–28)

Amherst continues the catalogue of heroic actions that Wolfe's death will inspire (ll. 29–40), which will give "new themes to a fourth Epic Muse" (l. 42), and then predicts the effects of his death on the other generals, as well as on the army. Amherst closes his speech with a picture of Wolfe's spirit rising to "Fame's golden Gate" (l. 82). Sterling concludes the poem with a compliment to Amherst and a prediction of the future greatness of America:

> But *Britain*, zealous for her AMHERST, pays
> To living Worth its unclaim'd Right of Praise.
> She bids her Champion wield her Sov'reign Sword,
> Till West obeys an universal Lord.
> While a new World, to GEORGE's Empire won;
> Disowns a Bound, and tires th'unsetting Sun.
> (ll. 91–96)

Sterling's last published poem, like so many of his earlier works, is a public, occasional poem, praising a famous man. In heroic couplets, the elegy consists of an imagined speech within a framework.

Two years later, the *Maryland Gazette* for March 11, 1762, published an essay signed "Philo-patris," dated "Kent County, March 1, 1762." In sermon form, the article urges landed gentlemen to engage in trade. "Philo-patris" (who was, as I have earlier argued, James Sterling) points out that there is a "common and false Distinction . . . between the landed and the trading Interests." Trade, he says, is good for the country and benefits everyone:

> As Agriculture, on the one Hand, is so universally allow'd to be the essential Foundation, and Support of the trading Interest; so, on the other, it seems only Necessary to make appear, that Trade is the true and only Support of the landed Interest; and in Order to do this, I shall endeavor to prove,
> 1st. That a flourishing Commerce give full Employment to the People.
> 2dly. That it greatly increases the Number of Inhabitants.
> 3dly. That it raises the Prices of Commodities, and consequently the Rents and Value of Land.

The entire argument is well reasoned, and the second part states what Sterling evidently thought was the main motive for immigration to America:

> 2dly. Let us now enquire, if, in a political Sense, a flourishing foreign Commerce may justly be esteem'd the true Parent of People; and in this the Task seems no way arduous; for where ever that pleasing Object of the Poor, full Employment, is, thither will they most certainly migrate. Like Birds of Passage, they will explore every unknown Region to reach the Necessaries, and Conveniences of life.

Sterling attributes the barbarians' invasions of Europe to their poverty and sketches the effects of poverty on various peoples and countries throughout history.

Near the conclusion of the sermon, Sterling describes (as Crève-coeur did later) the American's progress from poverty to wealth:

> Since Commerce then is this grand Source of numberless Blessings to a state, how assiduously ought we to court the Embraces of a Mistress, who yields such constant and diffusive Happiness. From the benign Influence alone of her auspicious Smiles, with what Pleasure does the industrious Farmer contemplate the rising Value of his fruitful Acres; behold his little Cottage gradually metamorphos'd into a superb and elegant Building; his Gardens regularly laid out and decorated; his Stables filled with Horses of the noblest Blood; the Grandeur even of an Equipage; and a Train of obsequious Servants to attend his Nod. His Sons receive their Education in those wise and useful Institutions, Public Seminaries of Learning; travel for the Improvement of useful Knowledge; and oft return the best, and brightest Ornaments of their Country.

If "Philopatris" was not James Sterling, then another Kent County minister had similar interests and opinions and possessed, like Sterling, a sure pen. A reply to the article appeared in the *Maryland Gazette* for April 8, 1762: "A Countryman" asked that "Philopatris" "point out the ways and means of improving trade."

On Thursday, November 10, 1763, "after long enduring with the utmost Patience and Resignation, the excruciating Pain of the Stone in the Bladder, the Learned and Reverend Mr. James Sterling" died. His obituary and epitaph were sent to Jonas Green by "Euphranor," who had spent "many joyous Hours . . . in his Company."[71] After deprecating the general tendency to eulogize the dead, "Euphranor" grants that "the best of Men have their Foibles; yet at the same Time it ought to be observ'd, that Imperfections in Men of superior Merit, Parts, and Learning, as they are ever plac'd in a conspicuous Point of Light, are always more taken Notice of, than the same or worse Failings in those of an inferior Class." Then "Euphranor" claims that Maryland, by Sterling's death, has lost its best literary man:

> The Province of *Maryland* has lost a Great and Good Man, a most valuable Member of Society; and in spite of his Failings (for these no doubt he had) I am not afraid to add, that he was an Honour and Ornament to the sacred Cloth he wore, as well as to the Country he liv'd in; for I will venture to assert, without fear of being contradicted

---

[71] "Euphranor's" letter, dated Nov. 14, 1763, was published in the *Maryland Gazette* for Nov. 17. Although "Euphranor" was the pseudonym of the author of a mediocre essay on taste, *Maryland Gazette*, Aug. 26, 1746, the essayist need not be the same person as Sterling's eulogist.

by competent Judges, that his uncommon Abilities and extensive Learning, particularly in all the Branches of polite Literature, stand unrival'd in this Part of the World, and I doubt not but several of the elegant Performances he has favour'd the Public with, will be accounted an incontestable Proof of the Assertion.

Showing that he has adopted some of Sterling's own sentimentalism, "Euphranor" emphasizes Sterling's "feeling" heart, saying that the poet was "very easily melted down into Tenderness and Compassion for the Sufferings of his Fellow Creatures; and ready on all Occasions to relieve and assist them, as far as ever lay in his Power." Of Sterling as a minister, he writes: "He was no Bigot in Religion, yet active and zealous in discharging the Duties of his Function; greatly admir'd as a noble, elegant and pathetic Preacher by all who ever heard him; and in particular much esteem'd by his Parishoners, which alone is no small test of his merit." Finally, Sterling's friend says that since Sterling "was himself a very considerable Poet, 'tis a Pity methinks he shou'd drop into the Grave, without some little Notice at least from the Muse"; and so "Euphranor" writes an "Epitaph, on the late Rev. Mr. James Sterling":

> Stranger, who e'er thou art, one Moment stay,
> And take a useful Lesson in your Way.
> No tomb superb, or speaking Marble Bust
> Here courts your Eye,—this covers nought but dust;
> And yet this Dust (now tremble human Pride,
> And lay your gaudy Trappings all aside)
> This humble Dust, by Worms possest, contains,
> All of Great Sterling that on Earth remains.
> All that remains of Talents so sublime,
> As ne'er before adorn'd this Western Clime.
> Buried in Silence lies that rapt'rous Tongue,
> On which admiring Crowds have often hung;
> To hear God's comforts to a World dismay'd,
> With all the Charms of Eloquence, display'd:
> Or when with sweetest Notes he tun'd his Lay,
> Enraptur'd Souls with Pleasure dy'd away:
> But all the mortal Frame is now dissolv'd in Clay.
> His nobler Part has upwards wing'd it's flight,
> To where congenial Spirits dwell in Light:
> And thence, with Pity views vain Man, who must,
> With his whole Race, consume to Worms and Dust.

James Sterling is interesting partially for his use of the *translatio studii* idea, which, combined with the progress-piece, became a favorite genre of American poetry in the Revolutionary and Federalist periods. He used sentimentalism in American poetry at a time when this sensibility was appearing in English literature. Although most of his poetry is less than excellent, a few poems, notably "Verses Occasioned by the Success of the British Arms in the Year 1759," seem entirely successful, with structure reinforcing and complementing theme and with a satisfying complexity. Nevertheless, his best is not as good as the best by Richard Lewis, whose poems are better unified and more complex. Most of Sterling's poetry is public and occasional, and, to a degree, ephemeral. But he reflected contemporary and avant-garde vogues in competent poetry, and transformed his Irish literary nationalism into American literary nationalism. His career and poetry both belie the notion that there was a lag in early American literature.

THOMAS BACON

"SIGNIOR LARDINI"

The Reverend Thomas Bacon (1700?–68) published more titles than any other colonial Marylander. His numerous sermons on charity schools and the education of slaves went through several editions in Annapolis and London. As his great compilation *The Laws of Maryland* testifies, he was a meticulous and indefatigable worker. The proprietary party recognized him as a superior political writer. When Benjamin Franklin attacked Maryland's government in the London press, Bacon answered the charges. Dr. Alexander Hamilton and the Tuesday Club cherished Bacon—partly for his extraordinary musical ability. Bacon composed music and was judged the best violinist of colonial Maryland. As poet, letter-writer, composer, musician, political essayist, compiler of laws, and minister, Bacon importantly contributed to colonial Maryland's intellectual life.

Nothing is known of Thomas Bacon's parents, early life, or education; but his younger brother, Anthony Bacon, M. P., matriculated as a pensioner in Trinity College, Dublin, on April 10, 1735, and received his B.A. in the spring of 1739.[1] Thomas Bacon is usually said to be a native Manxman because of his familiarity and correspondence with persons living on the Isle of Man, but this correspondence

---

[1] George Dames Burtchaell and Thomas Ulick Sadleir, *Alumni Dublinensis* ..., ix and 30. Cf. Sir Louis B. Namier, "Anthony Bacon, M. P., and Eighteenth-Century Merchant," *Journal of Economics and Business History* 2 (1929–30): 20–70. Cf. n. 12 below.

contains no references to his family.[2] Since he had a much younger half-brother, William Bacon, who later came to Maryland, it seems unlikely that he could have repeatedly written to his friends on the Isle of Man without once mentioning his family—if they lived there. In the only biographical sketch of Bacon by a contemporary, the Reverend Jonathan Boucher wrote: "Mr. Thomas Bacon's first debut in life, appears to have been in the care and management of a depot, or bank, of coals in Dublin; to which he was appointed by his townsmen, the shipowners in Whitehaven."[3] Bacon was, evidently, a native of the Whitehaven area, Cumberland county. If the management of the Dublin depot was not connected with the Custom-House, Bacon must have left the depot before 1737. Bacon's *Book of Rates*,[4] a factual compilation of over five hundred pages, was "Ordered to be Published by the Chief Commissioners and Governors of His Majesty's Revenue of Ireland." The title page reveals that the author is "Thomas Bacon, of the Custom-House, Dublin." Boucher's biographical sketch also notes that while Bacon managed a depot, he met "a smart widow, who kept a coffee-house, whom he married." The coffee-house became "Bacon's coffee-house, in Essex Street," but its former name, like his wife's, is unknown.

According to the novelist Samuel Richardson, Bacon "had been concerned with the Press as a Corrector," and in November 1741, he "proposed to set up a public paper . . . and to take up his freedom of the Company of Stationers in Dublin."[5] When Bacon journeyed to London prior to starting his newspaper (probably to set up an exchange of correspondence and newspapers, and to buy books), he visited the most famous bookseller of the time, Thomas Osborne, of

---

[2] The Callister Papers. Letter Books and correspondence of Henry Callister, in the Maryland Diocesan Society Library, deposited in the Maryland Historical Society, Baltimore. A microfilm of these manuscripts is in the library of the University of California, Berkeley.

[3] William Hutchinson, *History of the County of Cumberland* (Carlisle, England, 1794) 2:41n. The Sketch of Bacon is merely signed "Biographia Cumb.," but the *Gentleman's Magazine*, "A Short Account of the Late Mr. Boucher," 74 (1804):591–93, reveals that Boucher wrote the sketches marked "Biographia Cumbriensis" (592) for Hutchinson. I am indebted to Mr. Daniel Hay, Borough Librarian of Whitehaven, for attempting to locate information concerning the Bacon family for me.

[4] The contemporary binder's title of Thomas Bacon, *A Compleat System of the Revenue of Ireland . . .* (Dublin, 1737). Copy at the Library Company of Philadelphia.

[5] Samuel Richardson, *The History of Sir Charles Grandison*, 1st ed. (London, 1754), 7:441.

Gray's Inn. Osborne took him to see Richardson, whose *Pamela* was enjoying such amazing popularity. Richardson, "then knowing not any other Irish Bookseller, or Printer and being about to publish his Third and Fourth Volumes of *Pamela*, was induced to enter into agreement with him, and to furnish him with the sheets as they came from his Press, in order to his reprinting them in Dublin." But by the time the sheets were sent, George Faulkner (another Irish printer) had stolen copies and published a surreptitious edition. "In resentment of such base treatment," Richardson sent Bacon 250 copies of "the genuine Edition."[6] Bacon continuously advertised the third and fourth volumes of *Pamela* in the *Dublin Mercury*, from January 23 to April 20, 1742.

Thomas Bacon had begun publishing the *Dublin Mercury*, a biweekly newspaper, on Saturday, January 23, 1741/2.[7] The first issue reveals that he was a considerable bookseller, for he had "lately imported a large Quantity of Books in most Languages and Faculties, among which are many of the best Editions of the most celebrated Authors, which were purchased out of several Libraries lately sold in London." He auctioned a number of libraries (printed catalogues were given away "gratis"), including those of Captain Richard Miller, the Reverend Mr. Rich, the Reverend Michael Hartlib, and the Reverend Thomas Bullen.[8] A comparison of Bacon's *Dublin Mercury* with other Dublin newspapers of the same time shows that Bacon's was more literary. He published nineteen poems including three by Gay, in the seventy-one issues of the *Dublin Mercury*. His *Dublin Mercury* imprint was: "Dublin: Printed by Thomas Bacon, Printer and Bookseller, at Bacon's Coffee-House in Essex-Street, where Advertisements are taken in for this Paper, and all Manner of Printing work done at reasonable Rates." In the second issue (January 26, 1741/2), Bacon claimed that he had "settled the best Correspondence" and would be "supplied with the greatest Variety of" newspapers and letters, and "is thereby enabled to furnish the freshest and most material Advices to the Publick."

[6] Ibid. Cf. William M. Sale, Jr., "*Sir Charles Grandison* and the Dublin Pirates," *Yale University Library Gazette* 7 (1932–33):80–86.

[7] I have used a microfilm of the *Dublin Mercury* kindly furnished me by the British Museum. Their holdings are nos. 1–71; Jan. 23–Sept. 25, 1742. Wanting are nos. 29, 30, 41, 44, 45. Nos. 1, 9, 10, 21, 26, 38–40, 43, 49, 50, 54, and 58 are imperfect, each wanting pp. 1 and 2.

[8] These catalogues are mentioned in the *Dublin Mercury* for Apr. 20 and May 18, 1742, and in the *Dublin Gazette* for Nov. 27, 1742, and Feb. 1, 1742/3.

In printing notices of charity working-schools and musical events, Bacon probably gratified his own interests. The puff for "The Messiah, Mr. Handell's Sacred Oratorio, which in the Opinion of the best judges, far surpasses anything of that Nature, which has been performed in this or any other Kingdom" (No. 23, April 10, 1742) was followed up in the *Mercury* for April 17, by high praise for the performance: "Words are wanting to express the most exquisite Delight it afforded to the admiring crowded Audience. The sublime, the grand, and the tender, adapted to the most elevated, majestic, and moving Words."[9] Bacon's religious concerns were probably responsible for the following unusual note on the weather:

> The mild refreshing Rains we have had these few Days past, which were so greatly wanting, must fill every Heart with Joy at the pleasing Prospect of a plenteous Season, and the utmost Gratitude to the most benign Creator of all Things, whose bounteous Hand pours forth Blessings according to the Measure of his own Goodness, and not acording to our Demerits.[10]

On Monday, September 27, 1742, Bacon received permission to print the official newspaper of Ireland, the *Dublin Gazette*, and the first issue under his editorship appeared on Tuesday, September 28, 1742. Bacon published it through the issue for July 12, 1743, when, without notice or explanation, the newspaper ceased. Over a month later, August 23, 1743, Augustus Long began publishing the *Dublin Gazette*.

During the period while Bacon printed newspapers and managed the coffee-house in Essex Street, he also sold books; auctioned boats, libraries, and merchandise; and printed books and catalogues. He was not exempt from the printers' quarrels of the day. He agreed with two other Dublin printers John Smith and George Ewing to publish a translation of the Abbé Prevost's *Dean of Coleraine*. It appeared in eleven numbers, beginning in the *Dublin Mercury*, Tuesday, September 7, 1742, and continuing in the *Dublin Gazette* until November 16, 1742. In September Edward Exshaw published a broadside (reprinted in the *Dublin News Letter* for September 11, 1742) claiming that it was unfair for Bacon et al. to print the *Dean of Coleraine*, since he had intended to do so. In the *Dublin Mercury* for September 14, 1742,

---

[9] As this is also printed in the *Dublin Gazette* for Apr. 17, 1742, Bacon probably did not write it.
[10] *Dublin Mercury*, May 8, 1742.

John Wheeler (whom Exshaw had first asked to do a translation of *Coleraine*) appealed to *"Mr. Exshaw's tender Conscience*, whether he has not us'd me worse than he pretends he has been by the above Gentleman?"* Thomas Bacon sided with Wheeler and condemned Exshaw in his paper for September 17. Bacon said that Smith, Ewing, and he had announced their intention to publish the translation in the *Dublin Mercury*, August 28, 1742, and that according to the custom among Irish printers no one should then have attempted to bring out the book. However, Exshaw tried to get one into print before them, the result being an inaccurate and sloppy production. Bacon devoted the last page of this issue of the newspaper to printing in parallel columns the original French of Abbé Prevost's *Dean of Coleraine*, Exshaw's faulty version, and that published by Smith, Ewing, and Bacon. Edward Exshaw answered this charge in the *Dublin News Letter* for October 5, 1742, and Bacon wrote another signed reply in the *Dublin Gazette* for October 9. He also advertised in this issue of the *Gazette* a pamphlet, *A large Collection of Gross Errors, Blunders, Mistakes, &c. extracted from the Translation (erroneously so-called) of the Dean of Coleraine Published by Edward Exshaw and Company*. Since Exshaw had guaranteed that any one who purchased his edition of the *Dean of Coleraine* could have his money back if he showed that the translation was not exact, the projected pamphlet was embarrassing.[11]

When Bacon abandoned his publishing career in July, 1743, he began studying for the ministry under Thomas Wilson, bishop of Sodor and Man, probably with the intention of going to Maryland, where his brother Anthony had been succeeding in business since his graduation from Trinity College in 1739.[12] Although he did not leave for Maryland until the summer of 1745, he must have been planning for some time to emigrate, for on July 28, 1744, Henry Callister, a Manxman living in Oxford, Maryland, wrote to his brother Ewan:

[11] It was advertised in the *Dublin Gazette*, Oct. 9–Nov. 13, 1742, as "Now preparing for the Press, and speedily will be published," and in the *Dublin Gazette* for Tuesday, Nov. 16, as "On Monday the 29th Inst. will be published." Perhaps the pamphlet was not published.

[12] Possibly, the Anthony Bacon who graduated from Trinity in 1739 is not the brother of Thomas Bacon. Callister's letter of July 28, 1744, records that Anthony Bacon had already been a merchant in Maryland and was now a merchant in London. Probably, however, Namier (see n. 1 above) is correct. There are scattered references to the business concerns of Anthony Bacon in the *Maryland Gazette*: see May 31, 1753; July 29, 1762, app.; Apr. 5, Sept. 6, and Nov. 22, 1764.

This Mr. Bacon you speak of I suppose is Brother to Mr. Anthony Bacon who kept a store on this River and is now a Merchant in London, for I heard that one Bacon a Brother of his in Dublin who kept ~~a Coffee-House there and~~ [line drawn through this clause by Callister in MS] who wrote a Book of ~~Rates and was a Brother to Mr. A. Bacon~~ [in MS] was expected into this Country after getting orders in London to be inducted Parson of our Parish and that he had another brother in Dublin who kept a Coffee house [the last clause was added by Callister between the sentences].[13]

Reverend Jonathan Boucher, writing fifty years later, attributed Bacon's emigration to financial causes, but Boucher invalidates his testimony by saying that Bacon became a minister in Maryland: "Not succeeding in Dublin, Mr. Bacon was encouraged and assisted by his brother to try his fortune in Maryland; whither he soon after went; and there, entering into holy orders, obtained, first . . . ."[14] Actually, Bishop Wilson ordained Bacon a deacon on September 23, 1744, at Kirk Michael "by permission of the Bp of London, for a missionary," and ordained him a priest on March 10, 1745.[15]

Bacon left the Isle of Man shortly after June 18, 1745, bound for America.[16] He probably arrived in Maryland in August or September. He had been there for at least several weeks when Callister wrote to William Tear on November 5, 1745, that Bacon had "given us some sermons which have got the better of most of the Audience." Callister characterized him as "a very agreeable Companion, and a sober and learned Man." Bacon brought his wife and his son, John ("Jacky") with him. Bacon and Callister became friends, and not the least of their common interests was music. Callister wrote that he "should have pass'd for a tip-top Musician if the Rev'd Mr. Bacon had not come." Callister added, "His performance on the Violin and Violon-

[13] Callister Letter Book, Maryland Diocesan Society Library, Maryland Historical Society. Since it has been claimed on the strength of this letter that Bacon's younger half-brother William kept the coffeehouse in Dublin, the actual draft of the letter seems worth noting. Callister evidently had Thomas Bacon in mind but was uncertain of the facts.

[14] Hutchinson, 2:41n.

[15] Thomas Wilson, *Sacra Privata* (Oxford and London, 1854), 388. His certificates of ordination as deacon and priest are at St. Peter's; the latter is printed in Samuel A. Harrison and Oswald Tilghman, *History of Talbot County, Maryland* (Baltimore, 1915), 1:278.

[16] Bacon delivered a letter from Ewan Callister, of the Isle of Man, to Henry Callister bearing that date. Henry Callister to Ewan Callister, Nov. 12, 1745, Callister Papers, 48.

cello have afforded us much delight . . . . I have a pretty set of Musick and he has still a better."[17]

By November 12, 1745, Bacon had been "received Curate of this Parish," (St. Peter's, Talbot County, Maryland), replacing that "Brute of a parson," Nathaniel Whittaker.[18] The governor of Maryland, Thomas Bladen, gave him a letter of induction as rector of St. Peter's on March 31, 1746.[19] Nearly a year after Bacon came to Maryland, Callister wrote that he was "the worthiest Clergyman I ever knew, not excepting the Bishop Thomas Wilson, Bishop of Sodor and Man, he is a ~~strong friend of~~ [crossed out in MS] Vindicator of T. S. M. how ~~can he help it~~ [in MS] and a potent advocate for him."[20] In September, 1746, Bacon was living in Oxford, Maryland, "next door but one to" Callister's house.[21] But by August, 1747, he had moved to Dover, Maryland. He had become "a very considerable Man here and in great Esteem with every Man from the Governor to the Parish Clarke." Callister wrote, "I am very happy in his conversation and friendship and so is every one that is acquainted with him." Evidently Callister and Bacon had played concerts together and Bacon had composed several pieces: "I have sent you enclosed a Couple of his Minuets which are excellent." According to Callister, Bacon had "innumerable fine things."[22] Fifty years later, Jonathan Boucher wrote of his musical talent: "he was thought particularly to shine as a musician. He was an exquisite performer; and several pieces of music, of his composing (under the humorous signature Signior Lardini) are still preserved and much esteemed in Maryland." On January 28, 1746/7, Bacon sent Callister "St——pson's Compendium . . . which you will find easy and at the same time, full enough for any young Student in Composition," and requested that Callister send him the "Book of Songs."[23]

[17] Callister to Tear, Nov. 5, 1745, Callister Papers, 47.
[18] Ibid.; Harrison and Tilghman (hereafter cited as Harrison), 1:276–77 n. 5, identify the "brute" as Whitaker. The *Maryland Gazette* for June 16, 1747, reported that "Mrs. S. C. of Patapsco" was fined one penny for publicly whipping the "R——d Mr. N[athanie]l W[hittake]r with a Hickory Switch, it being imagined by the court that he well deserved it."
[19] Printed in Harrison, 1:278. Most accounts give the date as Mar. 3.
[20] Callister to William Henderson, Aug. 21, 1746. Callister Papers, 67. Harrison explains that T. S. M. is an abbreviation for Thomas, Sodor, and Man (Bishop Wilson).
[21] Callister to "Dear Brother," Sept. 21, 1746, Callister Papers, 72.
[22] Callister to William Tear, Aug. 23, 1747, Callister Papers, 100.
[23] Hutchinson, 2:41. "Signior Lardini" was Dr. Alexander Hamilton's facetious

Callister wrote to his brother Ewan, August 23, 1747, that last March, Mrs. Bacon "with tears of gratitude" told of the Bacons' obligation to Ewan, and that Bacon toasted him. Callister added that the minister now had "a very considerable income." Dover was a little-frequented area, and Bacon wrote Callister, "Make your Way now and then thro the Shrubbs and Bushes to get at us for a while and I promise that we'll have a new high Road prepared for opening a more convenient Communication with you next Year at the farthest." But despite the difficulty of getting to Bacon's house, he was not to be ignored. He sent this note to Callister on January 22, 1749:

> This is to Summon you and Mrs. Callister to attend, according to Promise, at my House-Warming on Wednesday next.—Should be glad Mr. and Mrs. Emerson wou'd bear you Company.... His Excellency of Oxford will be here with the facetious and merry Magistrate Captain. Fail not to obey this Summons as you will answer the cont[rary?] at your Peril.[24]

In 1749, Bacon published *Two Sermons, Preached to a Congregation of Black Slaves* ... (London, 1749). Here, he reveals that he exhorted the slaves whenever opportunity offered: "at their *Funerals* (several of which I attended)—and to such small Congregations as their *Marriages* have brought together, as well as at my own House, on Sunday, and other Evenings, when those in the neighbourhood come in."[25] Throughout his ministerial career, Bacon attempted to educate the poor. To this end, he devised a scheme for a charity working school (one of Bishop Wilson's characteristic enterprises) and succeeded in setting up the school by 1752. In the *Maryland Gazette* for September 19, 1750, he published "A General Plan or Scheme, for Setting up and Supporting a charity school in the Parish of St. Peter's in Talbot County, for the Maintenance and Education of Orphans and other poor Children."

To educate the slaves, their masters' permission was necessary; and to do a good job, the masters had to teach them. Therefore, Bacon next brought out *Four Sermons, upon the great and indispensable Duty of all Christian Masters and Mistresses to bring up their Negro*

---

name for Bacon. "History of the Tuesday Club," MSS, Evergreen House, Johns Hopkins University Library. Callister Papers, 53.

[24] Callister to Ewan Callister, Aug. 23, 1747; Bacon to Callister, May 3, 1748; Callister Papers, 118. "His Excellency of Oxford" was Robert Morris (see n. 32 below). "The merry magistrate Captain was certainly Capt. Thomas Porter." Harrison, 1:287.

[25] Thomas Bacon, *Two Sermons* ... (London, 1749), 9.

Slaves in the Knowledge and Fear of God (London, 1750). These sermons were published by the Society for the Propagation of the Gospel in Foreign Parts (SPG). Bacon corresponded with the secretary of the SPG, received pamphlets for distribution in Maryland,[26] and complained of the state of religion in the new world:

> Religion among us seems to wear the face of the Country; part moderately cultivated, the greater part wild and savage. Where diligent conscientious Pastors are seated, there improvement is to be seen, in proportion to their time and labours. Where others are fixed all things appear with a Desart aspect or over-running with an useless growth of Weeds and brush, sprung up since the decease of the last laborious husbandman.

According to Bacon, deism was rampant in the colony; Matthew Tindal's *Christianity as Old as the Creation* (London, 1730) could be found in "most Houses where any body reads." Since few of the common planters could understand Tindal, the situation could be worse. Bacon reported that most of the attacks on religion and on the clergy used ridicule "as best suited to their capacities and most taking with the Vulgar." The inspiration for ridicule came mainly from John Trenchard and Thomas Gordon's *Independent Whig* (London, 1720–21), "a Book every where to be met with." But Lord Shaftesbury's method of ridicule "would be of little force" if it were not for the "irregularities of the clergy."[27] The SPG also published Bacon's *Six Sermons, on the several Duties of Masters, Mistresses, Slaves, . . .* (London, 1751).

By 1751, Bacon's plan to open a charity working school was well advanced. On Sunday, October 14, 1750, he preached *A Sermon, at the Parish Church of St. Peter's, in Talbot County, Maryland . . . for the benefit of a charity working school to be set up in the said parish . . .* (London, 1751), which was sold for the school at the comparatively expensive price of one shilling. Bacon's report of progress and list of subscribers appeared in the *Maryland Gazette* for June 12, 1751. To gain support for his scheme in Virginia, he sent the proposal

---

[26] Harrison notes (1:280 n. 9) that he has in his possession one of the 200 copies of "Mr. West Littleton's Discourses in defence of Christianity" given out by Bacon. His copy is inscribed "A Present from the Society for promoting the Gospel in Foreign parts to Mr. Robt. Lloyd, by the hands of the Rev'd Thomas Bacon."

[27] William Stevens Perry, *Historical Collections Relating to the American Colonial Church* (Hartford, Conn., 1885), 4:324–26. Reprinted in Harrison, 1:281–82.

to John Blair (deputy auditor-general of Virginia from 1728 to 1771 and twice acting governor), who received it on July 11, 1751. The next day, Blair wrote Bacon his approval and showed the proposal to Commissary William Dawson. On July 14, Bacon arrived in Williamsburg, preaching in the morning on "My Yoke is Easie," and in the evening on "There is a time for all Purposes." On the sixteenth, Bacon dined with John Blair, who noted "We had fine musick." After dinner with Dr. Gilmore and Bacon on July 17, Blair commented in his diary that the violin (presumably played by Bacon), was "fine" and that Mr. Pettitt danced well. Bacon preached twice on July 21 and on the next day "took his leave of us this day with my thanks and good wishes." His charity working school was puffed in the *Virginia Gazette*, July 25, 1751.[28]

When Bacon returned to Virginia in October, 1751, he inserted a notice in the *Virginia Gazette*, October 24, acknowledging contributions received for the charity school. On the evening of October 27 he preached at Williamsburg; and on November 6 he dined with the council, John Blair speaking to Colonels Corbin and Grymes about the charity school for him.[29] Bacon put his musical abilities to work for the charity school; a "concert of Music in the College Hall Williamsburg, for the benefit of the School" raised 23½ pistoles. He published a list of contributors in the *Maryland Gazette*, June 11, 1752; shortly thereafter, the school was ready to open. On August 23, 1752, Bacon preached *A Sermon . . . at the Parish Church of St. Peter . . . on opening a Charity Working School*; and in October, 1752, he held a concert at Upper Marlborough, Prince Georges County, for the project. Plans for a house (dormitory?) sufficient to accommodate twenty pupils were begun in 1752, but it was "not completed and delivered over by the contractors to the Trustees until 1755."[30] Dr. Thomas Wilson's letter to Bacon, dated January 10, 1754, reveals that the scheme was well regarded in England:

> As for the School you will find the noble Present of 100 Guineas by Lord Baltimore, besides 20 £ from himself, and 5 £ from his Lady and 5 £ from Mr. Calvert annually, so you see by God's good Blessing, the Design flourishes beyond what you ever thought, go on

[28] Lyon G. Tyler, ed., "Diary of John Blair," *William and Mary Quarterly*, 1st ser. 7 (1898–99):142. The *Virginia Gazette* puff was reprinted in the *Boston Gazette*, Sept. 3, 1751.

[29] Ibid., 147–48.

[30] *Maryland Gazette*, Apr. 12, 1752, and Harrison, 2:488.

briskly, get the House finisht, enlarge your Views, fear Nothing! The reason I did not print and publish the Accounts that are to be annexed to your Sermon, was this. I thought they wou'd come out with much more Eclat and Figure, when the House was near finished; and when we cou'd tell the World, that Lord Baltimore was a Patron of it. Furnish me therefore with everything necessary for a proper Appendix to your last Sermon; we must not multiply things of this kind for the printing of such long Accounts are very expensive, and it had better be done when the School House is near finished. —in the mean Time you may publish how the Design is going on, in your Paper.—Nothing will please more on this Side the Water, than pushing on the school, and making it a great thing.

By May, 1755, the building was finished, and Bacon requested the trustees to meet "next Saturday" between eleven and twelve "to receive the House from the Builder, to agree with a Master and House Keeper and to Settle the Children."[31]

Since coming to Maryland, Bacon had been active in church and political affairs, but had not neglected his social life. He was elected an honorary member of Dr. Alexander Hamilton's Tuesday Club on November 26, 1745, at Sederunt (meeting) 25. Thereafter he was a frequent and welcome guest, often playing the violin for the members, and he composed a number of elaborate musical pieces (which were carefully transcribed by Hamilton into the "Records" and "History") for the Tuesday Club anniversary odes. Bacon attended a meeting on February 24, 1746/7; and on May 26, 1747, he and Robert Morris entertained the club with music, Bacon playing a "viol a gambo or six-stringed bass." On April 26, 1748, the club requested Hamilton to write Bacon "and some other honorary members to invite them to the anniversary." On March 14, 1748/9, just before Anthony Bacon's return to England, the London merchant attended the Tuesday Club with his brother, who "entertained the Society with some excellent pieces of music on the violin." The Reverend John Gordon, on May 16, 1749, reported that he, Bacon, and Robert Morris had formed the Eastern Shore Triumvirate, an affiliate of the Tuesday Club. On September 26, 1749, a letter from Gordon was read in the club which told of the festivities at a meeting of the Triumvirate. At the fifth aniversary of the club, May 15, 1750, "after Supper, the Musicians Con Stromenti of the club, played the anniversary music,

31 Maryland Diocesan Society Library. Bacon sent this extract to Callister, who carefully preserved it. Dr. Thomas Wilson was the bishop's son. Also, Bacon to Callister, May 13, 1755, Callister Papers, 208.

323

with two violins and a Bass, and met with great approbation, the piece consisting of an overture, air for his honor [Charles Cole], minuet, and Pastorale, composed by Mr. Bacon, otherwise Signior Lardini."

Bacon visited the Tuesday Club on September 18, 1750, when he tried to drum up support for the charity school; that night John Charlotte, Charles Cole's servant whom Jonas Green celebrated in a facetious poem, presented a poem "Humbly Inscribed" to Thomas Bacon, "musician of the club." Bacon attended the sixth anniversary meeting, May 14, 1751, when his music for the anniversary ode was performed. Two days later, May 16, Bacon was present when the Eastern Shore Triumvirate's poem was read aloud in the club; John Bacon, Thomas Bacon's son (who had been appointed squire of the Eastern Shore Triumvirate), was elected an honorary member. Bacon came to meetings three times in 1752: June 16, October 10 and 26 (the last two times with his son). In 1753, he attended on June 26 and July 10. John Bacon on September 24, 1754, asked for and received the Tuesday Club's commission to serve against the French at the Ohio. And Thomas Bacon's last recorded attendance at the Tuesday Club was on December 16, 1754.[32]

On March 18, 1751, Bacon wrote to his influential brother, Anthony, opposing the ordination of a Maryland schoolmaster, Thomas Johnston. Bacon had served as a visitor of the school in Talbot County where Johnston taught and knew his habits: he was ignorant, contentious, and intemperate. Nevertheless, Johnston was ordained and returned as a clergyman to Maryland.[33] In Annapolis, Bacon attended Masonic meetings as well as the Tuesday Club. The Freemasons requested him to preach for the meeting on June 25, 1753. The society, pleased with the sermon, published it at its expense.[34] Bacon's was the

---

[32] Dr. Alexander Hamilton, "Records of the Tuesday Club," under the dates cited. MSS, Maryland Historical Society. Dr. Alexander Hamilton, "The History of the Tuesday Club," 2:397. The Reverend John Gordon, while minister of St. Ann's, Annapolis, had been a founder of the Tuesday Club. Robert Morris (d. 1750) employed Henry Callister and was the father of the "Financier of the American Revolution." Bacon probably wrote the obituary of Morris which appeared in the *Maryland Gazette*, July 18, 1750, as well as the inscription for his tomb. See Charles Henry Hart, ed., "Robert Morris of Oxford, Md.," 45–52. Morris's epitaph is on p. 48. Henry Callister, at Morris's request, read aloud Plato's *Phaedo* to the dying planter. Ibid., 48. Dr. Alexander Hamilton wrote a "Eulogium" on Morris which is in the "Records" for the meeting of Sept. 18, 1750.

[33] Fulham Palace Papers, 21:188–89; William Wilson Manross, ed., *Fulham Papers*, 301.

[34] The unique extant copy of Bacon's sermon is preserved in Masonic Hall,

third Masonic sermon printed in colonial Maryland, following the Reverend William Brogden's of December 27, 1749, and the Reverend John Gordon's of June 25, 1750. In early September, 1753, Bacon returned to Annapolis to preach a funeral sermon for his friend, a founding member of the Tuesday Club, alderman of Annapolis, and judge of the Provincial Court, Captain Robert Gordon, who died September 9, 1753, age seventy-seven.[35]

Evidence of Bacon's role in Maryland politics first appears in his relations with his clerical brethren in 1753. Bacon was friendly to the proprietary interests. So were most of the clergymen, but many lacked Bacon's moderation. Maryland had an established church, and the leaders of the proprietary party had the good sense to realize that a large proportion of the people resented supporting it. A number of the clergy were too hot-headed and arrogant to realize that their position was precarious. An even more important consideration in the controversy that developed was that if the clergymen brought their complaints before the governor, they would be acknowledging the proprietor, rather than the church, as their source of authority.

After Bacon was elected clerk of a meeting of Maryland's parochial clergy, held on Wednesday and Thursday, August 22–23, 1753, he read Lord Baltimore's letter to him, dated London, September 14, 1752, thanking him for his congratulations on acceding to the title. He also read a reply he had drawn up in the name of the "subscribing Parochial clergy of Maryland," but the letter was objected to by the meeting because Lord Baltimore's letter had been "directed only to a private person, [and] cou'd not be taken Notice of in a public way." However, the letter that a "Baltimore Bard," the Reverend Thomas Chase of St. Paul's, Baltimore County, submitted in its place was also thought improper. At length, the clergy decided to accept Bacon's letter, as modified by the Reverends William Brogden, Charles Lake, and Thomas Cradock.[36]

Grand Lodge of Massachusetts, Boston. I am indebted to Mrs. Muriel D. Taylor, Librarian, who kindly allowed me to examine it.

[35] *Maryland Gazette*, Sept. 13, 1753.

[36] Brogden and Cradock have already been mentioned. The Reverend Charles Lake (d. 1764) was the "Clergyman of Maryland" who advertised in the *Maryland Gazette* for Nov. 14, 21, 28 and Dec. 5, 1752, his "Proposals for Printing by Subscription, in Two Volumes, Octavo, "*FLORILEGIA SACRA: Or Christian* . . . ." The author is revealed in Hamilton's minutes of the Tuesday Club meeting for Nov. 20, 1750. Thomas Bacon, "Proceedings of the Parochial Clergy," 257–73.

On Thursday, August 23, 1753, an address to Governor Horatio Sharpe by Bacon and James Sterling congratulating him on his appointment was read, "examined and debated, Paragraph by Paragraph," and approved. Bacon also drew up a remonstrance by the clergy against giving an appointment to "a certain Person [Reverend Matthias Harris], in holy Orders, lately arrived in this Province, [who] labours under a most vile and scandalous Report . . . till he shall fully clear up his Innocency." The clergy decided to put off protesting against "the dangerous Encroachments of Popery" until the meeting on the "second Tuesday after the assembly sits."

Bacon found that the governor and "some friends of the Government" feared the results of the meeting to be held in October, so he dissuaded a number of his friends from attending it. "But upon farther Consideration, I told his Excellency that, with his Leave, I wou'd be upon the Spot; as well to prevent Mischief, if in my Power, as to give him timely Notice of what was a doing, that he might take proper Measures."[37] Thomas Jennings, "in the Conference Chamber at a ball given by the Governor," chided Bacon about the meeting of the clergy, "which was overheard and reported with sufficient Aggravations" (p. 365). This became a *cause célèbre* among the clergy who sided with the popular party.

On Saturday, October 6, the Reverend Thomas Chase and the Reverend Thomas Cradock (Hamilton's "Baltimore Bards") came to Annapolis and reported that the following day an unusual and significant sermon would be delivered. That Sunday, Cradock preached on the "absolute Necessity of an Ecclesiastical Jurisdiction over the Clergy" in Maryland and recommended "the same to the Consideration of the Legislature." Bacon arrived in Annapolis on October 9, was visited "immediately upon my Arrival" by Chase and Cradock, and later by the Reverends James McGill, William Brogden, Isaac Campbell, and Theophilus Swift. "These met all together at my Lodging at Middleton's, but I engaged my self purposely with Mr. Alexander Malcolme at another Place, being willing to learn something of their Schemes, and endeavour to form a small Party before I cam to any Conference with them" (p. 366).

The next morning, the tenth, Bacon went to see the governor and then joined the clergy at Middleton's, the tavern where Bacon was

[37] Thomas Bacon, "An Account of what passed at a Meeting of the Clergy at Annapolis in October 1753, with other Matters relating thereto," *Maryland Historical Magazine* 2 (1908):364–84.

staying. They "intended some opposition to the Inspection Law" (p. 366) but were effectively thwarted by Bacon and his party. Bacon recorded the following argument with the fiery Reverend Thomas Chase:

Before we parted, Mr. Chase, with an Air of Authority, demanded of me, Sir, did not Mr. Jennings speak to you in the State House about Meetings of the Clergy?
A. He did.
Q. Did he not brow-beat you, and use you ill?
A. You never heard me say so, and I shou'd be glad to know your Author. Neither am I quite so tame as to take a Browbeating or Ill usage from any one without becoming Notice.
Q. Well, sir: But did not Mr. Jennings talk warmly to you? Was he not very angry at Meetings of the Clergy? and did he not say he wou'd lay them by the Heels, or send them a packing to their own Parishes if he were Governor?
A. Mr. Jennings expressed his dislike of Meetings of the Clergy, unless by legal authority. But I don't think him capable of treating any one, much less such a Body of Men as the clergy with so much ill Manners as you express.
Q. And pray, Sir, what were his Objections to Meetings of the Clergy? What Reasons did he give you for his Dislike of them?
A. His Dislike was founded upon the ill Use that men assembled together without any Authority might make of a supposed Power they might assume to themselves when they proceeded in a formal Way by Votes and Resolutions as we had done in our former Meeting. But he shou'd have no Objections to a regular Meeting under a proper Authority, such as that of a Commissary, in Case the Proprietary shou'd approve of one: As he explained himself to me when I waited on him the next Morning.
Q. So then I find that Gentleman treated you in such Language, that you thought it incumbent on you to call on him next morning for an Explanation.
A. The Room was so crowded that I declined talking with Mr. Jennings there, and told him I wou'd wait on him in the morning, which I did accordingly, having from my first particular Acquaintance with him, lived upon such Terms of Friendship, that I cou'd have free Access to him at any convenient Time without Ceremony.
(pp. 367–68)

The main business of the clergy's meeting was to draw up the charge that Catholicism and various Protestant dissenting sects were growing in the colony, and that abuses of the established religion must be halted. Bacon "found, from Chase's calling for Things in Order, that he was the Man behind the scenes who managed the Wires, and some others present were little more than Poppets played about by him in different Attitudes" (p. 368). The Reverend James McGill read a paper containing "Seventeen Quere's which filled three sides of a Sheet of Paper, composed of all the Articles relating to Popery and Jacobitism which had been agitated in the Committee of Agrievances, and drawn up in the very Stile and Spirit of Dr. Carol." After Bacon defeated a number of the charges brought by Chase, the meeting agreed on seven. Bacon wanted to submit the complaint to the governor, and Chase, to the Committee of Aggrievances of the Lower House.

Chase argued that they ought to give their complaints to the committee because if they did not, they would be thought afraid. Bacon, backing up his argument with reference to the Bible and to Buckingham's popular play, *The Rehearsal*, replied:

> That St. Paul had taught us this distinction by saying All things are lawful to me, but all things are not expedient; and had shewn that Expediency is to be prefer'd to an indiscriminate Assertion of Right, when our doing things, in themselves allowable, may be the Occasion of Offence. That to infer the necessity and expediency of Actions from our Right of Exerting, them, wou'd lead us into endless Absurdities; And to do things, merely to shew we were not afraid of doing them, without any other cogent Reason, was too much of a Piece with Drawcansir in the Play, who excuses his insulting two Kings by saying
>
> All this I do because I dare.
>
> (p. 372)

On October 11, the argument between the two opposing groups of clergy became more intense. Bacon, to shift the members' attention away from strictly party lines, proposed an "Address to the Proprietary for establishing a legal Ecclesiastical Jurisdiction for restraining the Irregularities of our own Body, and taking away that Reproach which did more real Injury to the Cause of our holy Religion than all the Attempts of Papists, separatists, and Infidels put together." Chase's temper got the better of him and he told Bacon that he had done "very ill in speaking of Matters transacting among us to the Governor, or any one out of doors" (p. 381). Bacon replied that he had not looked upon their meeting as a court of inquisition and that obviously Chase had talked with members of the Committee of Aggrievances, raising their hopes. Then Bacon became angry and warned Chase:

> I had told him, the Evening before, I was not of a Temper to bear a Reprimand I was not conscious of having deserved, and now must

take the Liberty of giving him an Instance of it, by letting him know he took too much upon him, and he had done very ill, in presuming to reprimand me without any Authority from my Brethren, to whom I was willing to submit my Cause, and beg their Pardon if they judged me guilty of any Indecency. That to have shewn less Heat and more Candour in his Proceedings wou'd have better suited his Character as a Clergyman: and that whatever Ends of Party or Popularity he had in View, I was neither to be persuaded against Reason, nor Browbeaten into a Resolution of joining in them. (p. 381)

Finally, Chase got the signature of Hugh Deans, Thomas Cradock, William Brogden, and James McGill and carried his petition to the Committee of Aggrievances. Bacon, with one more signature than Chase could attain (Alexander Malcolm, Walter Chalmers, Theophilus Swift, Isaac Campbell, and Samuel Claggett) took his to the governor. Bacon "got a most satisfactory answer in every point" from the governor; Chase's report was "thrown out in the Gross by the Majority" (p. 382) in the Lower House.

Bacon is best remembered for his monumental production *The Laws of Maryland* (Annapolis, 1765), which was "the most important of the legal publications of the Province of Maryland, . . . and a specimen of typography which was not exceeded in dignity and beauty by any production of an American colonial press."[38] The first intimation that he planned to compile the laws of Maryland is found in his satiric attack of March 16, 1752, on two persons who had suggested that they might compile the laws. Bacon, writing under the pseudonym "Charles Payne," addressed to Henry Callister a Hudibrastic poem entitled "A Letter. Originally wrote Three Thousand Years Ago."[39] The first forty-two lines reflect pastoral conventions as well as Bacon's typical interests: reading, gardening, music, and dancing. He invites Callister to visit:

> The fairy Queen, with Magic Train,
> Too, waits upon you once again;

[38] Lawrence C. Wroth, *A History of Printing in Colonial Maryland, 1686–1776* (Baltimore, 1922), 95.

[39] Callister Papers, 189–92. The format of Bacon's poem is explained by Jonas Green's editorial in the Mar. 28, 1750, issue of the *Maryland Gazette*, where Green wrote that he was going to entertain his readers "with some musty Records from venerable antiquity, which perhaps may suit their Humor and please them, as People are commonly very attentive to a detail of Occurences that happened Several Thousand Years ago." Green's editorial prefaces the widely reprinted story "Pulgah to his daughter Shual," which first appeared in the *Universal Spectator*, July 3, 1731, no. 143.

And says She'll Dance, or Slow, or Quick
As you shall move your Fiddle Stick.
(ll. 18–21)

Then he begins the primary subject of the poem. Lines 43–53 satirically describe "Dr. B——rr——w" [Barrow?] who had said that he could reduce the laws into a compendium "if the Legislature thought proper."[40] Lines 54–104 castigate "Doctor K——llm——n" [Killman?][41] who

> practises, or says he practises Physic intirely on Mechanic Principles, and insists that the whole Faculty of Physic at Home, are all Blockheads who don't proceed upon the Same, there being as he asserts no Certainty in any other Theory or Practise, But that from this Rationale he is always certain of the operation of his Medicines before he Administers; 'tis not therefore to be imagin'd, But he'll as easily Reduce the Practice of the Law to this same Mechanical Certainty, which he has already render'd so perspicously Perfect in the Science of Physic.[42]

Bacon, who perhaps recalled Ebenezer Cook's similar satire in *The Sot-Weed Factor* of "an ambidexter Quack, / Who learnedly had got the knack / Of giving Glisters, making Pills, / Of filling Bonds, and forging Wills," says that Killman will compile the laws as he practices medicine:

He'll prove the Use of the Inspection
's Like a venereal Injection:
He'll Show the Levy's like a Blister,
And that the Law may want a Glyster:
He'll cleanse it of Its foul Proceedings,
By Purges and repeated Bleedings:
He'll Fumigate th'Assembly's Acts,
And Show the Nature of the Tracts,
When they're compiled in Abstracts:
Explain their Meaning and Invention
By Hamastatical Invention.
(ll. 63–73)

The last twelve lines of the poem bid Callister good-bye and remind him to write. Bacon's style and subject (the ridicule of false learning) are typically eighteenth-century Scriblerian.

Thomas Bacon's friend Jonas Green was probably attempting to create a favorable public attitude for Bacon's projected edition when

[40] Bacon's note to l. 43.
[41] Rhymes with *Tilghman*.
[42] Bacon's note to l. 54.

Green published, October 11, 1753, the New York governor's speech on the lack of a published body of laws and commented in an editorial note: "There is not, perhaps, a Province, or Colony, in all his Majesty's Dominions, where the Laws of the Province, or Colony, so much want Revising, as in Maryland (where not a compleat Body is to be purchased at any Price)." On December 10, 1753, Bacon petitioned the Talbot County Court for permission to use the printed collection of laws deposited there, in compiling "a complete abridgment of all the laws in force in this Province . . . in the same manner as he formerly abridged the Laws of the Revenue in Ireland."[43]

After 1753, the economic situation on the Eastern Shore worsened, and Bacon's energies were directed toward compiling the laws; consequently, the St. Peter's charity school suffered. Robert Morris, one of the original trustees and no doubt the wealthiest, had died; Callister was slowly going bankrupt.[44] Therefore, it is not surprising that on January 19, 1760, Calvert asked Governor Sharpe about Lord Baltimore's annual contribution to the "school at St. Peter's Parish in Talbot County late Benefice of Mr. Bacon."[45] Sharpe, May 23, 1760, replied:

> for want of a sufficient Number of Subscribers (the accidental Donations that were expected falling short) the Scheme could not be carried into Execution; There was a House built for the purpose and a master nominated but the Expence of Building have exhausted the Funds I think within two or three years after my Arrival in the Province there was no money left to maintain the Boys or pay the Master, and as other Gentlemen from that time declined paying their annual Subscriptions Your Lordship's Agent likewise declined paying any more money.[46]

Calvert's letter of March 21, 1763, instructs Sharpe to ask Bacon to account for the £100 that Dr. Wilson sent him for St. Peter's charity school. Wilson meant to make trouble for Bacon if the account was not forthcoming, and the archbishop, who is "concerned in all Charities to America," advised Bacon to make the accounting.[47] On December 28, 1763, Sharpe replied to Calvert that he had told Bacon

[43] Harrison, 1:288.
[44] Lawrence C. Wroth has given a short account of the decline of the Maryland tobacco trade at this time in "A Maryland Merchant and His Friends in 1750," *Maryland Historical Magazine* 6 (1911):213-40.
[45] *Archives of Maryland*, 31:528.
[46] Ibid., 9:415.
[47] Ibid., 31:541. The archbishop may be advising Wilson to press Bacon; Calvert's meaning is not entirely clear.

what was expected, whereupon Bacon "promised me that a proper and satisfactory account should be sent to the Doctor." Either Sharpe knew an aspect of Bacon that escaped everyone else, or he did not like him, for he commented, "nevertheless I question either the Doctor's Threats or any other measure will obtain it, as Mr. Bacon has now nothing farther to ask."[48] Over six months later, Dr. Wilson again wrote to Calvert, who sent the letter on to Sharpe. On August 22, 1764, Sharpe replied: "Tho I wrote some Weeks ago to the Reverend Mr. Bacon concerning Dr. Wilson's Complaint against him I have not yet received any answer."[49] Since the matter is not mentioned again in the existing records, and since Dr. Wilson later brought out another edition of Bacon's sermons, it seems probable that Bacon satisfactorily accounted for the funds.

Bacon's charitable and educational concerns did not end with the failure of St. Peter's charitable school. Under Commissary Thomas Dawson of Virginia, a convention of clergy met at the College of William and Mary, October 30–31, 1754, setting up a fund for the relief of widows and orphans of clergy, to which Bacon subscribed.[50] At a meeting on February 5, 1761, the associates of Doctor Bray decided to open two schools in Maryland under Bacon's directions. Perhaps Bacon took this opportunity to revive St. Peter's. He wrote, July 14, 1761, to the Vestry of All Saints Parish, proposing to open a school at Frederick, where he now had his living.[51] At the same time, he asked whether an "itinerant Master or two in this Parish upon the Plan of the Welsh Circulating School might not be of signal Advantage to Numbers of Poor Planters and Farmers and their children." To promote harmony between the English and the Germans in the back-country around Frederick, he questioned "whether a school to be settled in this Town, wherein all Dutch children should be taught to read and write English gratis" might not help. On November 26, 1763, he was named one of the visitors for the public school in Frederick County.[52]

[48] Ibid., 14:128.

[49] Ibid., 165, 176–77.

[50] Fulham Palace Papers, XIII, 178. William Wilson Manross, ed., *Fulham Papers*, 220.

[51] Edgar Legare Pennington, *Thomas Bray's Associates and their Work Among Negroes* (Worcester, Mass., 1939), 60. The letter is printed in the *Maryland Historical Magazine* 6 (1911):271–72.

[52] *Archives of Maryland*, 58:517.

The 1750s were eventful years—if sometimes only too sadly so—in the personal life of Thomas Bacon. On the last day of the meeting of the clergy, when he and Chase quarreled, October 11, 1753, he wrote to Callister that he knew nothing of the Newton fair, or would probably have gone. Dr. Alexander Hamilton, he reported, was so taken up in electioneering now, and, after the election next Wednesday ("as is hoped by his Friends"), would be "so employed in the Great Business of the Province" that they can not expect to see Hamilton's "sober Phyz" until after the assembly breaks up. As usual, he sent Callister news of his garden: "My Tuberoses are too green to take up, and two of them just on the point of flowering for a second Time,—When taken up I will save a flowering one for you.—White Everlastings are all perished with me, and I must trust to Virginia for a revival of them among us."[53] James Dickinson and Bacon evidently lent one another a helping hand with their gardens. When Dickinson went away, he took up his "Stock of the Iris:" "They may not be perhaps taken sufficient care of as Mr. Bacon too will be from Home all this Week."

On January 28, 1755, Bacon wrote Callister and requested that he and his wife come over next Saturday night "to assist at the demolishing a Sirloin" and to spend the evening in "Music, chat, Cards." Bacon asked Callister to bring his "dancing Pumps" and to tell Hanmer and Brereton that they too were "desired and expected." Although Bacon's wife was well when he wrote Callister on May 12, she soon became ill and died. About the same time, Rachel Beck, a mulatto, accused him of rape. He brought a suit of libel against her in the August court, 1755. Unable to pay the £100 fine after being found guilty, she was committed to jail.[54]

In the spring of 1756, Bacon's only son was killed in action. Like his father, "Jacky" Bacon was an honorary member of the Tuesday Club. He had been appointed Champion of the Eastern Shore Triumvirate and had appeared at the meeting of the Tuesday Club on September 24, 1754, at Jonas Green's house, when he "applied to his honor the President for a Commission from under the Great Seal, to serve under his honor and the Club, against the French at the Ohio." Hamilton then wrote that "Sir John Gabble" (Hamilton's facetious name for

---

[53] Miscellaneous Manuscript Collection, Historical Society of Pennsylvania.
[54] Dickinson to Callister, June 30, 1755, Callister Papers, 206, 211. Harrison, 1:279.

John Bacon) was "not only Champion to the Eastern Shore Triumvirate but second Lieutenant to the Independent Maryland foot Company, now on their March against the French at the Ohio."[55] John Bacon probably wrote "A Recruiting Song, for the Maryland Independent Company, By an Officer of the Company," which appeared in the *Maryland Gazette* for September 19, 1754, and was reprinted in the *Scots Magazine* for March, 1755.[56] On Monday, September 30, 1754, Lieutenant John Bacon marched from Annapolis with a party of soldiers. Six months later, the *Maryland Gazette* for April 8, 1756, reported that Lieutenant John Bacon had been killed and scalped about five miles from Cumberland Fort. In a letter to Callister of April 13, 1755, Thomas Bacon wrote that he had seen the "shocking paragraph . . . on Sunday last relating to my son," but that David Robinson says that "Jacky" is still living. The *Gazette* of April 15 reported that his clothes and scalp had been found. On Easter Monday Bacon wrote Callister that he was "much obliged for your kind Communication of Circumstances relating to the melancholy loss of my Son."[57]

Bacon signed a collective testimony from a number of Maryland clergymen for a candidate for ordination, Philip Walker, on October 15, and wrote a personal testimonial for him on November 3, 1755.[58] A typical letter to Callister, April 3, 1756, is full of news of musical activities and of Bacon's duties as minister:

> By the firing of the Guns I expect your Ship is arrived. I wish you Joy. You'll not forget that Mr. Hanson expects the Musical Society at his House on Monday. Coll Chamberlaine I hope has Notice, and that Business will not prevent your attendance.—We shall want what Music you and he have with the Tenor Fiddle which please to bring up with you. And Monsr de L'Amour [Charles Love] must not fail.— If you have any News it will be acceptable to the Bearer, tho' I shall not see it till my Return from the Chapel tomorrow Evening, being obliged to baptise a Sick Child this Afternoon at the upper End of the Parish where I am just setting out.[59]

[55] Dr. Alexander Hamilton. "The History of the Tuesday Club," 3:415–16. MSS, Evergreen House, Johns Hopkins University Library.

[56] *The Scots Magazine* 17 (Mar., 1755):139–40.

[57] Callister Papers, 207 and 216.

[58] Fulham Palace Papers, XXI, 210–13, 214–15. William Wilson Manross, ed., *Fulham Papers*, 301.

[59] Bacon to Callister, Apr. 3, 1756, Callister Papers, 215. "Monsr de L'Amour" is Charles Love, who had appeared as a musician with the Hallam Company in Maryland in 1752. He advertised in the *New York Mercury* for July 2, 1753, that he taught the violin, hautboy, bassoon, French horn, and flute. He gave a

On October 26, 1756, Bacon wrote to Callister about "the most delightful concert America can afford":

> We had on Friday and Saturday last at Coll Lloyd's the most delightful Concert America can afford. My Honourable the B[ass?] Fiddle being accompanied on the Harpsichord by the famous Signor Palma who really is a thorough Master on that Instrument and his Execution surprizing.—He returns this Week to the Colonel's from Annapolis of which I am to have Notice, and am directed by the Colonel to request your Company on the Occasion.—Signor Palma, the best natured Man of a Top hand I ever met with has promised me one Evening at Jimmy Dickinsons, where I shall also expect your Attendance. My Man brings down the Tenor Fiddle.[60]

Over a year after the death of his second wife, Bacon married Elizabeth Bozman Belchier, daughter of Colonel Thomas Bozman of Oxford Neck, and then needed innumerable household items: "*When a man's married*—You know the old Song.—I have so many wants I did not think on before."[61] But Bacon rashly married without publishing the banns or getting special permission from the governor. For this he was fined 5,000 pounds of tobacco. Sharpe asked Calvert to remit his share of the tobacco. Because Bacon had previously, on December 10, 1755, married his present wife, Elizabeth Bozman, to a reprobate clergyman (the Reverend John Belchier)[62] without "Pub-

---

concert in New York, which was advertised in the *Mercury* for Jan. 21, 1754. At the Tuesday Club in early July, 1755, he played the "Quakers' Sermon," and Callister refers to him as present in Philadelphia in June, 1759. Callister Papers, 310.

[60] Callister Papers, 259a. Signior Juan Palma (John di Palma) was a professional musician, living, at this time, in Philadelphia. He gave voice lessons and conducted music at public ceremonies. See Provost William Smith's account of the Philadelphia College's production of Mallet's masque *Alfred* in the *Gentlemen's Magazine* 27 (Apr., 1757):178–79. Advertisements for Palma's Philadelphia concerts of Jan. 25 and Mar. 25, 1757, are found in the *Pennsylvania Gazette* of Jan. 20 and the *Pennsylvania Journal*, Mar. 25, 1757. Four of Palma's compositions were recorded in a manuscript book of songs by Francis Hopkinson; see Oscar G. T. Sonneck, *Francis Hopkinson and James Lyon* (New York, 1967), 33. On Feb. 13, 1750, Dickinson attended the Tuesday Club as a "Stranger," when he relayed the respects of Bacon, Morris, and Gordon to the club. He was voted an honorary member on this date and was elected a member of the Eastern Shore Triumvirate on Sept. 18, 1750, in place of Robert Morris, deceased.

[61] Ethan Allen, "Rev. Thomas Bacon 1745–1768, incumbent of St. Peter's Talbot Co., and All Saints, Frederick Co., Maryland," [*American Quarterly*] *Church Review* 17 (1865): 430–51. And Callister Papers, 259a.

[62] Harrison, 1:293–95, gives a full account of Elizabeth Bozman's previous marriage.

lication and Certificate," further charges were brought against him. These, however, were not prosecuted. Bacon's letter to Callister, March 17, 1757, shows him depressed and in poor financial condition —and sick of abridging laws: "The Laws are my only Employment and Amusement; yet they are a dry sort of Stuff and sometimes apt to stick in the Throat."[63]

Early in 1758 two Prince Georges County lawyers, Thomas Clark and George Scott, petitioned the legislature for "some Encouragement . . . towards the Publication" of a volume of the laws of Maryland. Bacon replied with his own petition for support. At this time, the legislature took no action on either petition. On June 1, 1758, James Bisset, a Baltimore lawyer, in the *Maryland Gazette* advertised proposals for an abridgment of the laws of Maryland. Bacon replied with an announcement, on June 22, that he was continuing work on "a Body of Laws together with an Abridgment . . . the Charter of the Province, and other useful matters." Bacon petitioned the legislature again for "encouragement" in compiling the laws; but the method of supervision, as well as the contents of the laws, became a matter for dispute between the proprietary and popular parties. The Lower House appointed ten members (five from the Upper and five from the Lower House) to supervise the preparation of the laws, but added that only three members of the committee (all from the Lower House!) were "To supervise and correct the Press." When the Upper House rejected these terms, the Lower House ordered the act published in the *Maryland Gazette*, where it appeared on October 30, 1758.[64] James Bisset advertised on January 4, 1759, that his *Abridgement* had received many subscriptions and would soon be published. It was brought out by Bradford's Philadelphia press and advertised in the *Maryland Gazette* for June 28, 1759, as "just published." The legislature finally did not subsidize the publication costs of Bacon's *Laws of Maryland*, which was financed by private subscriptions and public sales.[65]

Sometime toward the end of 1758, Bacon was appointed minister of

[63] Callister Papers, 275.

[64] Wroth's discussion of Bacon's various troubles with competitors, 98–105, has been supplemented by information contained in the subsequent publication of the *Archives of Maryland*, 55:lii, 414, 435, 461, 560, and 592. See especially the *Archives of Maryland*, vol. 56, where J. Hall Pleasants, the editor, recapitulates the story in his introduction, lxxi–lxxiii, lxxiv, and prints in the app. 514–15, the text of the act from the *Maryland Gazette* of Oct. 30, 1758.

[65] Wroth, 102–103, and 211–12.

All Saints, Frederick, the richest living in the Province. Although the last record of Bacon at St. Peter's, Talbot County, is for May 27, the Reverend Samuel Hunter, previous rector of All Saints, did not die until October, 1758. Bacon employed a curate, George Goldie, at £100 a year to help him serve the large parish. On February 15, 1762, Sharpe wrote to Frederick, Lord Baltimore, that Bacon had come to Annapolis in the beginning of the winter "in order to Collate or examine his manuscript Acts of Assembly with the Records" and was still there. Sharpe planned to "induct him in the usual form" when Bacon returned to Frederick County.[66]

In 1760 the Vestry of All Saints Parish, Frederick, petitioned the Assembly for new church buildings. After a few members of the legislature objected that "the large sum required" was "without the known consent of the inhabitants," Bacon obtained a large number of signatures for the petition. He wrote to Walter Dulany, "I can venture to affirm that there never was a more universal Concurrence and Harmony among so large a Body of People, so divided in Denominations, Sentiments, and Interests, than in the present case."[67] Although the citizens of Frederick County evidently liked Bacon, All Saints Parish was the largest Maryland parish, and there were attempts to divide it. A bill for the division of All Saints appeared in the legislature and was defeated. Bacon thought that it might be introduced again in 1760, and he wrote to Dulany against the measure: "The Truth is that the Petition sent down from their Honours with a Bill the last Session, was an old one drawn up immediately upon Mr. Hunter's death.—That tho' I believe such a Division might be agreeable to the People over the Mountains in general, yet cou'd they suppose that it wou'd take place before my Death, they wou'd in a large Body oppose the proposed Division unless my Life were secured in the Incumbency, by the Dividing Act." The act was not passed. Evidence of Bacon's involvement with the manifold interests of his Frederick County parishioners turns up in many places. Together with such frontiersmen as Thomas Cresap and Jonathan Hagar, the Reverend Thomas Bacon was to be a manager of a project to open

[66] Nelson Waite Rightmyer, *Maryland's Established Church*, 158 and 194. Sharpe to Calvert, June 4, 1759. *Archives of Maryland*, 9:343; 14:20. For the curate's name, see John Cary's letter to Walter Dulany, May 26, 1768, Dulany Papers, Maryland Historical Society; see also Allen, 449.
[67] Bacon to Dulany, Apr. 11, 1760, Dulany Papers, Maryland Historical Society.

the Potomac River to small craft "from Ft. Cumberland at Will's Creek, to the Great Falls."[68]

The authorship of *An Answer to the Queries on the Proprietary Government of Maryland* . . . ([London?], 1764) poses a problem that has not been positively solved and perhaps will never be. But the evidence indicates that the pamphlet was composed by Bacon, sent to London, revised by Cecilius Calvert (Lord Baltimore's cousin, and secretary in England for the province of Maryland), and published there.[69] The story begins with a series of queries by Benjamin Franklin published in the *London Chronicle* on September 19, 1758, attacking Maryland's proprietary government.[70] To these queries, no answer was made. But when *An Historical Review of the . . . Government of Pennsylvania* appeared in London in 1759, Lord Baltimore became concerned lest a similar work should appear about Maryland. Because sufficient materials did not exist in London to frame an answer, and because Lord Baltimore desired "to stand justifiable against Virulent Calumny," Cecilius Calvert suggested that a historical review of the policies of the Calverts be written in Maryland. "What do you think of the Rev. Mr. Bacon? he has a Capacity and acquired Abilities for the Compiling such Work in its fair Character and Nature." On January 19, 1760, Calvert sent a copy of *An Historical Review* "as a Sort of Method for Mr. Bacon . . . to delineate the History of Maryland."[71]

Bacon's letter to Walter Dulany of April 11, 1760, reveals that he was writing for the proprietary party, using materials furnished him by Dulany and others:

> The Subject of Ports has often engaged my thoughts,—I shall with much Pleasure engage in it at the proper Season, and wish I were better qualified for the Office assigned me by my Friends.—You will, from Time to Time, as Matter occurs, favour me with Hints: And my Business will be to connect and put them together as well as I am able.—It will be sufficient Honour to me to have the compiling of

[68] Bacon to Walter Dulany, Sept. 24, 1760. Dulany Papers, Maryland Historical Society. *Maryland Gazette*, Feb. 11, 1762.

[69] I follow the view of J. Hall Pleasants, editor of the *Archives of Maryland*, 59:xiv. *Calvert Papers*, no. 684, Maryland Historical Society, contains a draft of the *Answer*.

[70] Sharpe to Calvert, May 26, 1760, refers to "those scandalous queries that were some time ago published in the London Chronicle." *Calvert Papers* 9:418. See Leonard W. Labaree, et al., eds., *Papers of Benjamin Franklin*, 8:162–68.

[71] Calvert to Sharpe, Nov. 18, 1759. *Archives of Maryland*, 31:521.

much better Sentiments than my own; and I shall, in that case, like a Crabb Tree Stock, engrafted on by the skilful Gardner, make a flourish with Blossoms and Fruit which Nature never meant I shou'd bear.

Governor Sharpe, who had no love lost for Bacon, replied to Cecilius Calvert on May 26, 1760; in short, the idea horrified him. He argued that a history would take a long time to prepare, that the compiler would have to live in Annapolis while he prepared it, and that if Bacon was "to leave his Parish . . . on such an Account, there would be such an Out Cry against him as you can scarcely imagine." His enemies and the patriot party would shortly learn what he was doing and would "stick at nothing that might render him odious and infamous." Echoed throughout the province would be the cry, "A Clergyman taken from the Parishioners by whom he is supported and who by Law are obliged to support him to Vindicate an ill Administration!" The patriots would accuse Lord Baltimore and the lieutenant governor of a "Catalogue of Vices." "These Considerations having made me decline Communicating Your Proposal to Mr. Bacon."

Sharpe said that as soon as he could, he would send "a continued Narrative of the Assembly'd Proceedings" since the beginning of the present war, "which I think will be sufficient to convince impartial Judges that whatever were" the "Professions and Pretences" of the patriot party, "their Study from the Beginning hath been by all means to avoid granting supplies for his Majesty's Service and to increase their own Power." Then Sharpe proposes the method used in *An Answer* . . . : "What think you of Subjoining to the Queries the inclosed Answers?"[72]

In the London *Public Ledger* of November 17, 1763, there appeared another series of queries attacking the position of the proprietary party of Maryland. The queries were expanded and amplified in [Stephen Bordley], *Remarks upon a Message, sent by the Upper to the Lower House of Assembly of Maryland, 1762 . . . . By a Friend to Maryland. Printed in the year MDCCLXIV.*[73] In reply to these charges came the *Answer*. It is probable that Bacon wrote out the charges, commented on them, and refuted them, quoting extensively

[72] Ibid., 9:418.
[73] Although the editors of *Papers of Benjamin Franklin*, 11:108 n. 8, say that this pamphlet "has been variously attributed to Thomas Ringgold, Edward Tilghman, and James Tilghman," it has in fact been decisively attributed to Stephen Bordley by J. Hall Pleasants; see *Archives of Maryland*, 59:lxx; the *Remarks upon a Message* is reprinted in the app., 372–408 .

from the Assembly's sessions. The major evidence for attributing the *Answer* to Bacon (with revisions by Calvert) is not because Lord Baltimore and Cecilius Calvert earlier wanted him to do so, but because Daniel Dulany wrote to Calvert on September 10, 1764: "It was said that an Answer was preparing to the *Remarks* with the Assistance of Mr. Bacon. He is an ingenious Man, and well acquainted with the springs of our Political Disputes, and I think that, by recurring to former Proceedings, a great Deal will be found done to his Hands." [74] Perhaps Dulany was wrong—but few, if any, men were more knowledgeable about the Maryland political scene than he. Bacon probably wrote the reply and sent it to Calvert, who revised it and had it printed in London.

The *Laws of Maryland* was virtually completed by July 24, 1762, when Bacon appeared before two justices of the provincial court and

> produced Six Manuscript Books or Volumes in Folio, marked No. 1, No. 2, No. 3, No. 4, No. 5, and No. 6, containing a Transcript of the Acts of Assembly of this Province, now in Force or Use from the Year 1637, to the Year 1762, ... as the same have been collected into one Body by the aforesaid Thomas Bacon; and made Oath on the Holy Evangels of Almighty God, That they had carefully and diligently Examined and Compared all the several Acts contained in the said Transcript, ... with the Original Acts which Passed the Great Seal of this Province, where such Originals were extant, or to be found in the Secretary's Office of this Province; and, where the Originals of any of the said acts cou'd not be found, with the Records of the same, as they stand Recorded in the Secretary's Office aforesaid. And that the said several Acts contained in the said six Volumes or Transcript, and by them so Signed as aforesaid, are true Copies of the Original Acts, or Records respectively, with which the same have been by them Compared and Examined as aforesaid, to the best of their Knowledge, Skill and Belief. [75]

This oath was signed by Bacon, Reverdy Ghiselin, John Brice, and George Steuart. Although the printing of the huge book was not completed until July, 1766, [76] Jonas Green puffed *The Laws of Maryland* in the *Maryland Gazette* for August 21, 1765: "The Work is

---

[74] *Calvert Papers*, 2:233. See also [J. Hall Pleasants and James W. Foster, eds.,] "State of the Province of Maryland in 1758," *Maryland Historical Magazine* 33 (1938):228–47, which reprints, 229–33, both Franklin's "Queries" from the *London Chronicle*, Sept. 19, 1758, and, 233–47, Governor Horatio Sharpe's manuscript "Answers to the Queries" from Portfolio 2, item no. 7, Maryland Hall of Records.

[75] Quoted in Wroth, 106.

[76] Wroth, 109.

esteemed a Masterly Performance—it has been long wanted—long looked for—and, doubtless, will be always admired and preserved as a collection of a very entertaining and useful Knowledge, necessary for the Inhabitants of this Country to be possessed of—by them to be handed down to their Posterity."

Like Richard Lewis and Jonas Green, Bacon was evidently interested in science. When Henry Callister sold his microscope and apparatus to Governor Sharpe, he also sent "Adams' Micrographia illustrated,[77] which will be necessary to his Excellency for some time, to explain the use of the several microscopes and parts in the box." Although the book belongs to "my good friend" Bacon, the governor "need not be in a hurry to return it to Mr. Bacon; who, not having the Machine, can have no use for the book."[78] In November, 1764, Bacon evidently visited the Eastern Shore, for Callister mentioned to a correspondent from the Isle of Man, whose letter he had received just two or three days before, that he had shown it to Bacon, who "express'd much satisfaction in being so honourably mention'd." Callister could not promise "to send you at this time any of Mr. Bacon's musick, but I shall send you some the next Opportunity, I expect; If the ship stays a day or two longer I may send you one or two things."[79]

Not long before his death, Bacon again contributed to Maryland's political propaganda. His version of the biblical story of Balaam and the Ass, addressed to "My Dear Fellow Planters and Country-men," seems never to have been printed—perhaps because its moderation was unacceptable to the colonists of 1767. Bacon's persona is a country farmer who "never attempted to write before, & having no more than a common Country Education cannot be suposed to write like others." Writing about the colonies' relation to Britain, he tries to win the sympathy of his audience by praising the popular anti-Stamp Act writers: "The Author of the Considerations [Daniel Dulany] struck at the very Foundation of the Stamp-Act, and the Farmer [John Dickinson] hath excellently seconded that first-Rate Champion in the Struggle for Constitutional Liberty." Bacon claims that all he can do is to echo their sentiments and "bring them to a Level with common Understandings." But in fact, he conservatively argues that "the In-

[77] An edition of George Adams, *Micrographia Illustrata*, 1st ed. (London, 1746).
[78] Callister to John Seagar, Nov. 15, 1764, Callister Papers, 694.
[79] Callister to William Tear, Nov. 20, 1764, Callister Papers, 78.

terests of *Great Britain* and her *American* Colonies are reciprocal, and cannot be separated in any Measure whatsoever, without proportionable Prejudice to both." The essay concludes by warning the English politicians not to treat the Americans too severely. Since this manuscript is evidently a draft, it may never have been completed for publication.[80]

On July 27, 1767, Sharpe wrote to Frederick, Lord Baltimore, that Bacon was "now advanced in years and declining."[81] Later that summer Bacon went to Warm Springs, Virginia, to escape the flux then prevalent in Frederick. On May 8, 1768, the Reverend Bennet Allen wrote Governor Sharpe that Bacon was dangerously ill.[82] Ten days later, May 18, 1768, at a meeting of the American Philosophical Society in Philadelphia, the "Rev. Mr. Bacon of Maryland" was elected a member.[83] John Cary's letter to Walter Dulany, dated "Frederick Town, Thursday, 15 minutes after 3 o'clock in the morning 26th May 1768" begins, "Our worthy, our good, and sincere friend, The Revd Mr. Bacon is now no more; he departed this life about ten minutes ago, Sincerely lamented by all honest men here."[84]

Thomas Bacon is a good example of an eighteenth-century American man of letters. Born and educated "at home" (i. e., Great Britain), widely traveled and well read, he was a versatile man of wide interests. His correspondence with Henry Callister—on gardening, fairs, friends, music, dancing,—provides a good glimpse of the varied cultural life of colonial America. His many literary productions (including fables, political essays, journalism, letters, private poems, and sermons), his musical compositions (several are extant) and performances, and his interest in the law—all testify to the ability of a man who (without the literary genius of Richard Lewis or Dr. Alexander Hamilton) made an important contribution to the cultural life of his time.

[80] Manuscript Department, Maryland Historical Society.
[81] *Archives of Maryland*, 14:410.
[82] Bacon to Walter Dulany, July 30, 1767. Dulany Papers, Maryland Historical Society, and *Archives of Maryland*, 14:494.
[83] This information was kindly given me by Dr. Whitfield J. Bell, Jr., Librarian of the American Philosophical Society.
[84] Dulany Papers, Maryland Historical Society. Obituaries appeared in the *Maryland Gazette*, June 9, 1768; the *Pennsylvania Chronicle*, June 13; and in Rind's *Virginia Gazette*, June 23.

APPENDIX

THE IDENTITY OF GEORGE ALSOP

No previous investigator has ascertained any biographical facts concerning Alsop, and my surmises may be wrong. A few facts emerge from Alsop's *A Character of the Province of Maryland*: he was twenty-eight when his picture was engraved; he was a zealous Anglican and a fervent Royalist; he had some education and considerable literary ability; he had served two years at a "Handicraft" apprenticeship in London; he knew surgeons-hall in London and the burial customs of Westminster; he was a bond servant in Maryland; his brother (whose first name began with a "P") was serving an apprenticeship at "Joyner's Hall' while Alsop was in Maryland; his parents were alive in 1658–63; and he had a literary friend named William Boghurst.[1] Several inferences may be made from these facts. George Alsop was born about 1637 or 1638; he was probably from London or a suburb; and his parents were not people of means.

First, I should dispose of the obvious red herring. Two sermons were published by a George Alsop in Restoration England. *An Orthodox Plea for the Sanctuary of God, Common Service, White Robe of the House, Being writ for the good of all . . . by G. A. Sometime of Oxford, of St. Johns* (London, 1669) was written by a George Alsop who was admitted sizar at twenty years of age to St. John's, Cambridge, on June 28, 1645. He was the son of Francis Alsop, a

---

[1] Certain other facts may be adduced from *A Character of the Province of Maryland*, but these are irrelevant here, as I have not found them useful in determining Alsop's identity.

tailor of Darley, Derbs; and he took the B. A. in 1647 or 1648.[2] Since *An Orthodox Plea* is dedicated to Henry King, bishop of Chichester (1592–1669), the author is probably the same George Alsop whom Bishop King ordained a deacon in 1666 or 1667 and a priest in 1669. Since the Maryland George Alsop evidently had not attended college and since he was born about 1637 or 1638, he cannot be this George Alsop.[3] *A Sermon Preached at Sea Before the Honourable Sir Robert Robinson, Knight, Principal Commander of His Majestie's Squadron of Ships, now riding at Spitt-Head, November the 24th, 1678 . . . By George Alsop, M. A. Chaplain to Sir Robert Robinson* (London, 1679)[4] is by a George Alsop with a Master's degree—probably the same Alsop who wrote *An Orthodox Plea*. Therefore, the only other known Restoration publications by George Alsop were by a different individual.

The Maryland Calverts and many of their connections were from Westminster, a London suburb.[5] A check of the published Westminster parish registers revealed that a George Alsop was born there to Peter (a tailor) and Rose Alsop on June 19, 1636. The date disagrees by approximately one year with the age given below his portrait ("Anno Do: 1666, Aetatis Suae 28"), and this difference remains unresolved. But if the parents of this George Alsop were living in 1658–63, and if he had a younger brother whose name began with a "P" (very probably "Peter," since a Peter Alsop became a member of the Joiner's Company later), then we could have our man. The will of Peter Alsop (1672) of Westminster (St. Martin-in-the-Fields), Middlesex, provided just this information. The will refers to Peter's wife Rose and to his sons George and Peter Alsop. Therefore, the George Alsop who was born in Westminster on June 19, 1636, is probably—though not positively—the Maryland author.

Furthermore, the *Calendar of State Papers* reveals that a George Alsop, who evidently had no college degree, began a ministerial ca-

---

[2] John and John A. Venn, *Alumni Catabrigienses*, pt. 1, vol. 1 (Cambridge, 1922), 24.

[3] "P. B.," *Notes and Queries*, 1st ser. 8 (Dec. 17, 1853):585.

[4] Samuel Pepys and Sir Robert Robinson corresponded about this sermon. See Joseph Robson Tanner, *A Descriptive Catalogue of the Naval Manuscripts in the Pepysian Library at Magdalen College, Cambridge* (n. p., 1903), 207–208. A biographical sketch of Captain Robert Robinson may be found in John Charnock, *Biographia Navalis* (London, 1794), 1:62–64.

[5] See Mrs. Russel Hastings, "Calvert and Darnell Gleanings from English Wills," *Maryland Historical Magazine* 21 (1926):303–29. All other references are contained in the chapter on Alsop.

reer about 1666. A letter provides the key information that the father of this George Alsop was named Peter. (This minister cannot be the college graduate who published two sermons, for his father's name was Francis.) The area where this George Alsop began his career was near Westminster. In addition, the only literary man of the Restoration named William Boghurst had a number of connections with this area.

Although the evidence is certainly not conclusive, it is more than probable that our Maryland author was born in Westminster in 1636 and became a minister when he returned to England, and that he lived until sometime after 1673.[6]

[6] Because of the literary artistry of Alsop's *Character*, I have even wondered whether there ever existed an indentured servant named George Alsop, and I have suspected that Lord Baltimore paid some man of letters to write the tract; but the reference to a little-known Maryland planter (Thomas Stockett) as Alsop's master, the earliest recorded usage of certain American words (e. g., *Monack* for woodchuck), the fact that a George Alsop witnessed the patent recording Stockett's purchase of Bourne, and Alsop's knowledgeable discussion of the Susquehanna Indians all testify to Alsop's authorship.

BBREVIATIONS

USED IN THE BIBLIOGRAPHICAL NOTES

(Location symbols are those used in the various National Union Catalogs.)

Baer   Elizabeth Baer, *Seventeenth Century Maryland: A Bibliography*. Baltimore, 1949.

Church   George Watson Cole, *A Catalogue of Books Relating to . . . America, forming a part of the library of E. D. Church*. 5 vols. New York, 1907.

Clark   Thomas D. Clark, *Travels in the Old South: A Bibliography*. 2 vols. Norman, Okla., 1956–60.

DAB   Allen Johnson and Dumas Malone, eds., *Dictionary of American Biography*. 22 vols. New York, 1928–58.

Davis   Richard Beale Davis, *American Literature through Bryant*. New York, 1969.

DNB   Sir Leslie Stephen and Sir Sidney Lee, eds., *Dictionary of National Biography*. 22 vols. London, 1908–1909.

Evans   Charles Evans, *American Bibliography: A Chronological Dictionary* [of American imprints through 1800]. 14 vols. Chicago, 1903–59.

Guerra   Francisco Guerra, *American Medical Bibliography, 1639–1783*. New York, 1962.

Lemay   J. A. Leo Lemay, *A Calendar of American Poetry in the Colonial Newspapers and Magazines and in the Major English Magazines Through 1765*. Worcester, Mass., 1972.

NI   Clifford K. Shipton and James E. Mooney, *National In-*

dex of American Imprints Through 1800: The Short-Title Evans. 2 vols. [Worcester, Mass.], 1969.

Rubin   Louis D. Rubin, Jr., *A Bibliographical Guide to the Study of Southern Literature*. Baton Rouge, 1969.

Sabin   Joseph Sabin, Wilberforce Eames, and R. W. G. Vail, *A Dictionary of Books Relating to America*. 29 vols. New York, 1868–1936.

STC   A. W. Pollard and G. R. Redgrave, *A Short-Title Catalogue of Books Printed in England, Scotland, & Ireland And of English Books Printed Abroad 1475–1640*. London, 1926.

Vail   Robert W. G. Vail, *The Voice of the Old Frontier*. Philadelphia, 1949.

Wegelin   Oscar Wegelin, *Early American Poetry . . . 1650–1799*. New York, 1930.

Wing   Donald Wing, *Short-Title Catalogue of Books Printed in England, Scotland, Ireland, Wales, and British America . . . 1641–1700*. 3 vols. New York, 1945.

Wroth   Lawrence C. Wroth, *A History of Printing in Colonial Maryland, 1686–1776*. Baltimore, 1922.

BIBLIOGRAPHICAL NOTES

ANDREW WHITE

CHECKLIST OF PUBLICATIONS RELATING TO AMERICA

1. *A Declaration of the Lord Baltemore's Plantation in Mary-land.* London, 1633.
Baer 20. Sabin 103351. Vail 85A.

A facsimile of the unique extant copy, edited by Lawrence C. Wroth, was published in a limited edition of 100 copies in Baltimore, 1929.

White sent a Latin version of the *Declaration* to the general of the Jesuit order in Rome. This document, entitled "Declaratio Coloniae Domini Baronis de Baltamoro in Terra Marie prope Virginiam: qua ingenium, natura et conditio Regionis, et Multiplices Ejus Utilitates Ac Divitiae Describuntur," was discovered in Rome about 1832 by William McSherry, who made a manuscript copy which he brought back to America. Nathan C. Brooks translated this copy into English in 1844 and 1845 and read it at the Maryland Historical Society. The translation was printed under the title "A Report of The Colony of the Lord Baron of Baltimore, in Maryland" in Peter Force, comp., *Collection of Historical Tracts*, 4, no. 12 (Washington, D. C., 1846), [3]-7; and a small number of Force's pamphlets, which bore the title *A Relation of the Colony of the Lord Baron of Baltimore ...*, were reissued the following year with the seal of the Maryland Historical Society (Baltimore, 1847). The first printing of the Latin text was in the [Woodstock College, Maryland] *Woodstock Letters* 1 (1872): 12-24, with a new English translation. The Latin text was again printed, and now with a new, facing English translation [by J. Holmes Converse] in Edwin A. Dalrymple, ed., *Relatio Itineris in Maryland-*

iam, Maryland Historical Society *Fund Publication, No.* 7 (Baltimore, 1874), 44–53. The best text (Latin only) was transcribed from the original in Rome and published by Thomas A. Hughes, *History of the Society of Jesus in North America*, 4 vols.: 2 vols. of text and 2 vols. of documents (London and New York, 1907–10), *Documents* 1:145–49.

2. *A Relation of the successful beginnings of the Lord Baltimore's Plantation in Maryland*. London, 1634.
   Baer 21. Clark 176. Sabin 69291. Vail 86.

   This was reprinted by Brantz Mayer, ed., in John D. G. Shea's *Early Southern Tracts*, no. 1 (New York, 1865), but without the last four pages (containing the conditions of plantation). It also appeared in *Historical Magazine*, 9, no. 10 (Oct., 1865), 293–98, and in *Old South Leaflets*, 7 (1906), no. 170. No reprinting is complete or accurate.
   Another version of the 1634 *Successful Beginnings* was written in Latin and sent to the general of the Jesuit order. McSherry also copied this (see above); and Brooks's translation appeared in Force's *Collection*, 4, no. 12, [8]–24, and was reissued by the Maryland Historical Society (Baltimore, 1847). The Latin text was first published, with a new English translation, in the *Woodstock Letters* 1 (1872):71–80, 145–55. McSherry's Latin text with a new translation [by Converse] appeared in Dalrymple's *Relatio Itineris in Marylandiam*, 10–43. The best text (Latin only) appears in Hughes, *Documents* 1:94–107.
   A different English version of the 1634 *Successful Beginnings* was enclosed in a letter, dated May 30, 1634, from Leonard Calvert to Sir Richard Lechford (hence often cited as the "Lechford" version). This is now in the Maryland Historical Society and was first printed in *The Calvert Papers*, 3 vols., Maryland Historical Society *Fund Publication, Nos. 28, 34*, and *35* (Baltimore, 1889–99), 3:26–45, ed. by Clayton Colman Hall, with annotations by Thomas Hughes. It was again published in Clayton Colman Hall's *Narratives of Early Maryland, 1633–1684* (New York, 1910; reprint, New York, 1959), 25–45.

3. *A Relation of Maryland*. London, 1635.
   Baer 22. Church 432. Clark 175. Sabin 45314. STC 17571.
   Vail 88.

   This was reprinted by Francis L. Hawks in New York, 1865; a large paper edition added Brantz Mayer, "Memorandum on the Charter of Maryland," 75–78, and the text of the charter, 79–103; at least the supplement to the large paper edition must have been printed later than 1865, for Mayer dated his memorandum "Baltimore, Md., 25th October, 1866." It also appears in Clayton Colman Hall's *Narratives*, 63–112; and a facsimile edition of *A Relation of Maryland* has been published (Ann Arbor, 1966) in the March of America facsimile series, no. 22.

4. "Objections Answered Touching Mariland," in *A Moderate and Safe Expedient* . . . . London, 1646. 9–16.
Baer 27. Sabin 49802. Vail 106. Wing M2322.

"Objections" was reprinted in Bradley Tyler Johnson, *The Foundation of Maryland* . . . , Maryland Historical Society *Fund Publication, No. 18* (Baltimore, 1883), 24–30; and in Hughes, *Documents* 1:10–15.

BIBLIOGRAPHY, BIOGRAPHY, AND CRITICISM

The standard bibliography for Andrew White's American publications is Elizabeth Baer's *Seventeenth Century Maryland; A Bibliography* (Baltimore, 1949). Lawrence C. Wroth, "The Maryland Colonization Tracts, 1632–1646," in *Essays Offered to Herbert Putnam* . . . (New Haven, 1929), 539–55, discussed these tracts, but no one previously has realized that White must have written most of the 1635 *Relation* and probably composed "Objections Answered Touching Maryland" (part of *A Moderate and Safe Expedient*). Lathrop C. Harper first pointed out that the latter was a Maryland pamphlet: "A Maryland Tract of 1646," *Bibliographical Essays; a Tribute to Wilberforce Eames* (Cambridge, Mass., 1924), 143–48. After the bibliographical works by Wroth and Baer had appeared, it was established that White's *Declaration* (rather than a separate printing of *The Charter of Maryland*) was actually the first Maryland promotion tract: John Cook Wyllie, "The First Maryland Tract: A Reconsideration of the Date of Printing of the Maryland Charter," in *Essays Honoring Lawrence C. Wroth* (Portland, Me., 1951), 475–83. The standard Jesuit bibliography, Carlos Sommervogel's edition of Augustine de Backer, *Bibliothèque de la Compaynie de Jésus*, vol. 8 (Brussels, 1898), cols. 1091–93, lists White's writings, including his early religious works. There is a brief checklist of the most important scholarship in Rubin, 350; and two bibliographies list the more recent (and mainly ephemeral) writings: John Tracy Ellis, *A Guide to American Catholic History* (Milwaukee, 1959), and Edward R. Vollmar, *The Catholic Church in America, an Historical Bibliography* (New York, 1963).

White's important letter of February 20, 1637/8, was printed in *The Calvert Papers*, 1, Maryland Historical Society *Fund Publication, No. 28* (Baltimore, 1889):201–11. Bernard C. Steiner, "Father White's Report to Lord Baltimore," *American Catholic Historical*

Researches, n.s. 7 (Jan., 1911):21–23, merely summarizes the letter (this note is simply reprinted from Steiner's *Beginnings of Maryland*, Johns Hopkins University *Studies in Historical and Political Sciences*, vol. 21, nos. 8–10 [Baltimore, 1903], 97–98). The best edition of Andrew White's various reports to the general of the Jesuit order, as well as the best edition of the annual letters of the Maryland Mission, is found in Hughes, *History of the Society of Jesus*. The original manuscripts are now available on microfilm in the United States: for an account of the great microfilm collection of Jesuit records, see John F. Bannon, "The St. Louis University Collection of Jesuitica Americana," *Hispanic American Historical Review* 37 (1957):82–88.

Hughes, *Documents* 1:128, also prints the letter of John Bollandus, dated March 1, 1647/8, which states that White compiled a dictionary and a grammar of the Indian language and translated a catechism into it. This information seems first to have appeared in Phillippe Alegambe's edition (cited below) of the *Bibliotheca Scriptorvm Societatis Iesv* (1643). Additional weight was given to the statement that White had compiled these works when Father William McSherry found White's "Relatio Itineris" in the Jesuit archives at Rome about 1832 and reported that a manuscript Indian catechism was with it. McSherry promised a copy to John D. G. Shea but said he was prevented from copying it because "in the troubles in Italy the valuable papers were boxed up and stored for safety." John Dawson Gilmary Shea, *History of the Catholic Missions among the Indian Tribes of the United States, 1529–1854* (New York, 1855), 494. See also Shea's *The Catholic Church in Colonial Days . . . 1521–1763* (New York, 1886), pp. 41n and 65n; this is vol. 1 of Shea's *History of the Catholic Church in the United States*. Bernard Ulysses Campbell, "Sketch of the Early Missions in Maryland," *U. S. Catholic Magazine* 11 (1848):529–35, 580–85, esp. 585, also was told that McSherry had found an Indian catechism with White's "Relatio Itineris." A search conducted in the middle of the nineteenth century failed to find the catechism (see *Historical Magazine* 2 [1858]:239); Thomas A. Hughes was unable to find it in the early twentieth century; and Francis X. Curran, "The Mystery of Andrew White," *Woodstock Letters* 85 (1956):377, reported that he could shed no light on the manuscript.

The best bibliographical guide to White's religious publications is Sommervogel's edition of *Bibliothèque* (cited above). For his education, see Edwin H. Burton and Thomas L. Williams, eds., *The Douay College Diaries, 1598–1654*, 3 vols. (London, 1911); Thomas Francis Knox, ed., *The First and Second Diaries of the English College, Douay* (London, 1878); and Edwin Henson, ed., *Registers of the English College at Valladolid 1589–1862* (London, 1930).

The first scholarly article on White was written by Bernard Ulysses Campbell, using the materials found in the Jesuit archives by Mc-Sherry: "Biographical Sketch of Father Andrew White and his companions, the first Missionaries of Maryland, with an historical account of the first ten years' Mission," *Metropolitan Catholic Almanac and Laity's Directory* [i. e., *Sadliers' Catholic Directory, Almanac and Ordo*] *for 1841* (Baltimore, [1840]), 43–68. Campbell also published a "Sketch of the Early Missions in Maryland" (cited above). Richard H. Clarke, on the bicentennial of White's death, wrote a sketch in the *Metropolitan Magazine* 4 (1856):73–84; and J. A. Doonan inaugurated the first volume of the *Woodstock Letters* with "An Historical Sketch of Father Andrew White, S. J., The Apostle of Maryland," 1 (1872):1–11. The two major sources for White's biography are Hughes (cited above) and Foley. Foley is poorly organized and contradictory—but indispensable: Henry J. Foley, *Records of the English Province of the Society of Jesus*, 7 vols. in 8 (London, 1875–83). Edmund Bedingfield, *The Life of Margaret Mostyn* (London, 1878), 53 and 152, provides a glimpse of the older White.

Brief sketches of White are available in all the standard biographical dictionaries. Thompson Cooper in the *DNB*; Edward I. Devitt in the old (1912) *Catholic Encyclopedia*; Richard J. Purcell in the *DAB*; and F. G. McManamin in the *New Catholic Encyclopedia* (1967). Several older sketches are cursory or inaccurate: Joseph Gillow, *A Literary and Biographical History . . . of the English Catholics from 1534*, vol. 5 (London, 1885); [Andrew A. Lambing], "Very Rev. Andrew White, S. J., the Apostle of Maryland," *American Catholic Historical Researches* 3 (1886):13–20; George Oliver, *Collections Towards Illustrating the biography of the Scotch, English, and Irish Members* (London, 1845); and Richard H. Tierney, "Father Andrew White, S. J., and the Indians," U. S. Catholic Historical Society *Historical Records and Studies* 15 (1921):89–103. The old, but still valuable, general history of Maryland is always worth consulting: John Thomas Scharf, *History of Maryland*, 3 vols. (Baltimore, 1879). G. T. Morse, "Ark and the Dove, Ancestral Ships of Maryland; with an abstract of Father White's narrative of the voyage from England to Maryland, 1633–1634," American Antiquarian Society *Proceedings* 49(1939):102–20, adds nothing new.

Edwin Warfield Beitzell has recently written an article and a book which contain valuable information: "Father Andrew White, S. J., the Apostle of Maryland," St. Mary's Historical Society *Chronicles* 4 (Dec., 1956): 81–90; and especially *The Jesuit Missions of St. Mary's County, Maryland* (Baltimore, 1960). Francis X. Curran, in "The Mystery of Andrew White," *Woodstock Letters* 85 (1956): 375–80, discusses several of the cruxes of White's biography. Of special interest is Mathias Tanner, *Societas Jesu Apostolorum Imitatrix sive gesta praeclara* (Prague, 1694), 803, which contains a woodcut showing Andrew White baptizing the emperor Chitomachon. Some other seventeenth-century books which mention White are John Gee, *The Foot Out of the Snare* (London, 1624), penultimate page; Henry More, *Historia Missionis Anglicanae Societatis Jesu* . . . (Avdomari [Saint-Omer, France], 1660), 390–91; [John Keynes], *Florus Anglo-Bavaricus* . . . (Leodii [Lüttich, Belgium], 1685), 55–57; and Phillippe Alegambe, ed., Pedro de Ribadeneira, *Bibliotheca Scriptorvm Societatis Iesv* (Antverpiae [Antwerp], 1643), 32.

The earliest critical mention of White is in Moses Coit Tyler, *A History of American Literature, 1607–1765* (Ithaca, 1949; first printing, 1878), 53. Montrose J. Moses included a short discussion in *The Literature of the South* (New York, 1910), 37–39; and Kenneth B. Murdock, in Arthur Hobson Quinn, ed., *The Literature of the American People* (New York, 1951), 23–24, provides a brief characterization.

JOHN HAMMOND

CHECKLIST OF PUBLICATIONS

1. *Hammond Versus Heamans, Or, An Answer to an Audacious Pamphlet, Published By . . . Roger Heamans . . . By John Hammond.* London, [1655].
Baer 40. Church 537. Clark 94. Wing H619.
Reprinted in the *Maryland Historical Magazine* 4 (1909):236–51, and in the Massachusetts Historical Society's *Photostat Americana Series*, no. 24 (Boston, 1920).

2. *Leah and Rachel, or, the Two Fruitful Sisters Virginia, and Mary-land . . . By John Hammond.* London, 1656.
Baer 46. Church 548. Clark 95. Sabin 30102. Vail 137A. Wing H620.

Reprinted in Peter Force, *Tracts* 3, no. 14 (Washington, D. C., 1844), and in Clayton Colman Hall's *Narratives*, 277–308. Excerpts have appeared in many anthologies of American literature.

BIBLIOGRAPHY, BIOGRAPHY, AND CRITICISM

Elizabeth Baer's *Seventeenth Century Maryland* is excellent. There is a brief checklist of the scholarship in Rubin, p. 345.

Harry Wright Newman, *Anne Arundel Gentry* (Baltimore, 1933), 189, claims that John Hammond is the brother of the Reverend Henry Hammond and a son of Dr. John Hammond, physician to Henry, Prince of Wales; but full evidence is not cited. G. C. Moore Smith, "Temple and Hammond Families," *Notes and Queries* 151 (Oct. 2 and Dec. 25, 1926):237–39 and 452–53, provides notes on Dr. John Hammond's descendants—none of whom was named John. See Smith's edition of *The Letters of Dorothy Osborne to William Temple* (Oxford, 1928), 323, for a genealogical chart of Dr. John Hammond's family. *The National Cyclopaedia of American Biography* 10 (New York, 1909), 45, following information provided in "Some Colonial Families: Hammond and Cromwell of Maryland," *American Historical Register*, no. 9 (1895):867–73, confuses the author John Hammond (d. 1663) with Major General John Hammond (d. 1707). A few records of John Hammond may be found in *The Calvert Papers* 1:48; Herbert Read McIlwaine, ed., *Journal of the House of Burgesses of Virginia, 1619–1658/9* (Richmond, 1915), 84; in Bernard C. Steiner, *Maryland Under the Commonwealth,* Johns Hopkins University Studies in Historical and Political Science, ser. 29, no. 1 (Baltimore, 1911), 151–53; see 84–101 for "The Maryland Civil War, 1654"; and in the *Archives of Maryland*, 10, 41, and 49. John Hammond's inventory is in Testamentary Proceedings 1D, ff. 97–98, Maryland Hall of Records, Annapolis. Records of Hammond's land grants are located in Gust Skordas, ed., *The Early Settlers of Maryland: An Index to Names of Immigrants Compiled from Records of Land Patents, 1633–1680* (Baltimore, 1968), 205. B. Bernard Browne, "The Battle of the Severn," *Maryland Historical Magazine* 14 (1919): 154–71, recounts the key battle which resulted in Hammond's fleeing

Maryland. Some source material is printed in Thomas Birch, ed., *A Collection of the State Papers of John Thurloe*, 5 (London, 1742): 482–86. And a recent discussion is Manfred Jonas, "The Claiborne-Calvert Controversy: An Episode in the Colonization of North America," *Jahrbuch für Amerikastudien* 11 (1966):241–50. Two articles by Edwin W. Beitzell shed incidental light on Hammond: "William Bretton of Newtown Neck, St. Mary's County," *Maryland Historical Magazine* 50 (1955):24–33, and "Newtown Hundred," ibid. 51 (1956):125–39.

The earliest critical notice is in Moses Coit Tyler, *History of American Literature*, 53–57. The evaluation by Montrose J. Moses, *Literature of the South*, 39–41, is not as good. Jarvis M. Morse, *American Beginnings* (Washington, D. C., 1952), 130–32, only summarizes. Three recent characterizations of Hammond are Louis B. Wright, in Robert E. Spiller et al., eds., *The Literary History of the United States* (New York, 1948), 41–42; Kenneth B. Murdock, in Arthur Hobson Quinn, ed., *Literature of the American People*, 23; and Jay Broadus Hubbell, *The South in American Literature, 1607–1900* (Durham, 1954), 22–23.

GEORGE ALSOP

PUBLICATION

A Character of the Province of Mary-Land . . . By George Alsop London, 1666.
Baer 60. Clark 29. Church 594. Sabin 963. Vail 153. Wing A2901.

There are four modern editions, though none is absolutely accurate or thoroughly annotated: (1) John D. Gilmary Shea's edition appeared as William Gowans's *Bibliotheca Americana*, no. 5 (New York, 1869); (2) The Maryland Historical Society reissued Gowans's edition as its *Fund Publication, No. 15* (Baltimore, 1880); (3) the best reprint was edited by Newton D. Mereness (Cleveland, 1902); and (4) Clayton Colman Hall included an expurgated text in his *Narratives*, 335–87.

A doctoral dissertation just completed at the Pennsylvania State University contains the best text and annotations yet prepared of Alsop's tract: Harry H. Kunesch, Jr., ed., "George Alsop's *A Character of the Province of Maryland: A Critical Edition*" (Ann Arbor, University Microfilms, Inc., 1970; in *Dissertation Abstracts*, 31 [1971]: 4775–A).

BIBLIOGRAPHY, BIOGRAPHY, AND CRITICISM

Elizabeth Baer's *Seventeenth Century Maryland* gives a thorough bibliographical account of Alsop's *Character*. There is a brief checklist of the scholarship in Rubin, 337.

No previous biographical sketch is worth consulting. Ernest Sutherland Bates, in the *DAB*, 1:227–28, gives no information. The will of Peter Alsop, tailor, of St. Martin-in-the-Fields, Westminster, may be found in the Prerogative Court of Canterbury, under the year 1672 (Eure), folio 117. Additional information concerning Peter and Rose Alsop, the parents of George Alsop, may be found in the Public Record Office, Chancery Proceedings, Bridges' Division, bundle 380, no. 1: see Great Britain, Public Record Office, *Lists and Indexes, No. 39: Index of Chancery Proceedings Bridges' Division, 1613–1714*, vol. 1, A–C (London, 1913), 32. (I have not had an opportunity to follow up this lead.) Alsop's baptism is printed in J. V. Kitto, comp., *The Register of St. Martin-in-the-Fields, London, 1619–1636* (London, 1936), 127. For "P. A." (Peter Alsop, brother of George), see Henry Laverock Phillips, *Annals of the worshipful company of Joiners of the City of London* (London, 1915), 105. For a few later glimpses of Alsop as an Anglican minister, see Public Record Office, S.P. 29/255, no. 238; S.P. 29/256, no. 56; S.P. 29/277, no. 14; and S.P. 29/450, no. 127. The gist of these documents is published in Public Record Office, *Calendar of State Papers, Domestic Series, October 1668 to December 1669* (London, 1894), 201, 213; and ibid., *Calendar of State Papers, Domestic Series, 1670* (London, 1895), 314, 733.

The best evaluation is still Moses Coit Tyler, *History of American Literature*, 57–61. Montrose J. Moses, *Literature of the South* (New York, 1919), 41–44, follows Tyler's lead. There are brief characterizations in Robert E. Spiller et al., eds., *Literary History of the United States*, 42–43; Arthur Hobson Quinn, ed., *Literature of the American People*, 24–25; and Jay Broadus Hubbell, *The South in American Literature*, 61–62.

EBENEZER COOK

CHECKLIST OF PUBLICATIONS

1. *The Sot-Weed Factor: or, A Voyage to Maryland . . . By Eben. Cook, Gent.* London, 1708.
   Clark 67. Sabin 16234. Wegelin 88.

Modern editions began with the reprint prepared by Brantz Mayer for Shea's *Early Southern Tracts*. Bernard C. Steiner, ed., *Early Maryland Poetry*, Maryland Historical Society *Fund Publication, No. 36* (Baltimore, 1900), 11–31, also reprinted *The Sot-Weed Factor*. In the twentieth century, the poem has often been anthologized.

Lawrence C. Wroth, *The Maryland Muse by Ebenezer Cooke: A Facsimile, with an Introduction* (Worcester, Mass., 1935), 20–26, pointed out that a second edition of *The Sot-Weed Factor* was probably printed in Annapolis about 1728 (drafts for a preface to the second edition exist, and the 1731 edition has the notation "*The Third Edition*"), but no copy of this edition is extant. Edward H. Cohen, "The 'Second Edition' of The Sot-weed Factor," *American Literature* 42 (1970):289–303, also presents the evidence for a second edition.

2. *Mors Omnibus Communis. An ELOGY on the Death of Thomas Bordley, Esq. . . . By Ebenezer Cook, Poet-Laureat, of Maryland.* Annapolis, [1726 or 1727?].
    Evans 39843. NI 185.

    The unique copy of this broadside elegy is in the John Carter Brown Library. Lawrence C. Wroth briefly discusses it in *The John Carter Brown Library Annual Report 1952–1953* (Providence, 1953), 51–54. It is printed in facsimile in Parke-Bernet Catalogue No. 1385, *Important Americana . . . Sale Nov. 25, 1952* (New York, 1952), 32. An excerpt appeared in Elizabeth Bordley Gibson, *Biographical Sketches of the Bordley Family of Maryland* (Philadelphia, 1865), 20. It is reprinted with a brief discussion in Edward H. Cohen, "The Elegies of Ebenezer Cooke," *Early American Literature* 4, no. 2 (1969), 49–72, esp. 51–52 and 62–63.

3. "An Elegy on the Death of the Honourable Nicholas Lowe," signed "E. Cooke, Laureat," appeared in the *Maryland Gazette*, no. 67, December 24, 1728.
    Lemay 99.

    It is reprinted in Bernard C. Steiner, ed., *Early Maryland Poetry*, 53–54; and in Cohen (see no. 2 above), 64–65, with a discussion, 53–55.

4. *Sotweed Redivivus: Or the Planters Looking-Glass . . . By E. C. Gent.* Annapolis, 1730.
    Evans 3266. Wegelin 89. Wroth 60. NI 185.

    Reprinted in Steiner (see no. 3 above), 33–52.

5. *The Maryland Muse. Containing I. The History of Colonel Nathaniel Bacon's Rebellion in Virginia. Done into Hudibrastick Verse, from an old MS. II. The Sotweed Factor . . . By E. Cooke, Gent.* Annapolis, 1731.
    Evans 3407. Wegelin 90. Wroth 70. NI 185.

Printed in facsimile, with an informative and wide-ranging introduction, by Lawrence C. Wroth, *Maryland Muse By Ebenezer Cooke*, reprinted from the American Antiquarian Society *Proceedings* 44 (1934):267–335.

6. "A Poem. In Memory of the Honourable Benedict Leonard Calvert" exists in a manuscript folio notebook (call no. △ E₃V4), 13–14, at the U. S. Naval Academy Library, Annapolis.

Walter B. Norris, "Some Recently Found Poems on the Calverts," *Maryland Historical Magazine* 32 (1937), 127–28, first printed the elegy and attributed it to Cook. Because all the other non-student poems in this notebook are by Lewis and because Richard Lewis said that he had written "Lays" on the death of B. L. Calvert, I suggested an attribution to Lewis in "Richard Lewis and Augustan American Poetry," *PMLA* 83 (1968):94, but Cohen's arguments (see no. 2 above), 57–60, are convincing.

The poem is printed in Norris, 127–28, and, with a better text, in Cohen, 67–68.

7. "An Elegy on the death of the Honourable *William Lock*, Esq. ... 1732. By Ebenezer Cook, Poet Laureate."

This elegy is found in an undated and unsigned letter addressed to "Mr. Gowan" (presumably William Gowans, 1803–70) in the Bozman-Kerr Papers, Manuscript Division, Library of Congress.

It has been published in the *Maryland Historical Magazine* 14 (1919):172–73, and, in a better text, in Cohen (see no. 2 above), 66–67.

Although Cohen says, p. 56, that the transcription is in the hand of John Leeds Bozman, it is more probably in the hand of John Leeds Kerr (Bozman's nephew), for Bozman died before Gowans became active. The letter is prefaced with this note: "The following is a copy of a Manuscript in my possession. I do not pretend to offer it as claiming a place among the Reliques of Ancient English Poetry, or coeval with Percy's Ballads or the Song of Chevy-Chase; but comparatively considering the date of our primitive Settlements in this Country, it must be allowed to bear some marks of Antiquity, and may therefore perhaps afford amusement to the *Amateurs* of the *petit Histoire* of Maryland." Perhaps Kerr never sent the letter: I have not been able to find any nineteenth-century printing of the poem.

BIBLIOGRAPHY, BIOGRAPHY, AND CRITICISM

For the Maryland imprints, Lawrence C. Wroth, *A History of Printing in Colonial Maryland 1686–1776* (Baltimore, 1922), is the best guide. A recent checklist of Cook's poetry is John E. Van Domelen, "Ebenezer Cook," *Bulletin of Bibliography* 24 (1963–66):94. Perhaps the best list of separate publications is in *The National Union*

Catalog: Pre-1956 Imprints, 121 ([London], Mansell, 1970):181. A brief list of recent scholarship is in Rubin, 340–41; and the most recent guide is Davis, 51.

The best biographical sketch is Lawrence C. Wroth's "Ebenezer Cooke" in the *DAB*, 11:189–90, which is based on Wroth's full investigation (cited in no. 5 above). An early attempt to give a biographical account was made by Bernard C. Steiner in *Early Maryland Poetry*, 7–9. Hester Dorsey Richardson, *Side-Lights on Maryland History*, 1 (Baltimore, 1913), 243–45, contributed a few facts; and Elias Jones, *Revised History of Dorchester County, Maryland* (Baltimore, 1925), 279–90, attempted a genealogy of the Cook(e) family. Wroth gathered together nearly all the extant evidence and supplied full sources for his biographical facts. Edward H. Cohen (see no. 2 above) restates Wroth's information and conveniently gathers the elegies. A few additional unimportant notices of Cook's activities are in the Maryland Hall of Records, Annapolis. John Fox, a Virginia poet, mentions Cook's activities in a letter to Thomas Bordley, Bordley MSS, Maryland Historical Society.

For Cook's treatment of his sources in "The History of Colonel Nathaniel Bacon's Rebellion in Virginia" (no. 5 above), see Wroth's facsimile; Jay B. Hubbell, "John and Ann Cotton of Queen's Creek, Va.," *American Literature* 10 (1938):179–201; and Bertha Monica Stearns, "The Literary Treatment of Bacon's Rebellion in Virginia," *Virginia Magazine of History and Biography* 52 (1944):168–71. St. George Leakin Sioussat, in *Economics and Politics in Maryland 1720–1750* ... (Baltimore, 1903), brilliantly discusses the poems within the contexts of the economic history of the early eighteenth century.

The earliest critical notice is in Edward Duffield Neill, *Terra Mariae; or, Threads of Maryland Colonial History* (Philadelphia, 1867), 200. Moses Coit Tyler, *History of American Literature*, 483–88, is good on the *Sot-Weed Factor*. Montrose J. Moses, *Literature of the South* (New York, 1919), 46–49, is more appreciative than evaluative. James Talbot Pole, "Ebenezer Cooke and the Maryland Muse," *American Literature* 3 (1931):296–302, is based on his M. A. thesis done at Columbia in 1931: "Ebenezer Cooke: *The Sot-Weed Factor*, An Edition." Richmond Pugh Bond, *English Burlesque Poetry 1700–1750* (Cambridge, Mass., 1932), 259–60, summarizes the poem. Brief characterizations have appered in Robert E. Spiller et al., eds., *Literary History of the United States*, 50–51; Arthur Hobson Quinn, ed.,

Literature of the American People, 55; and in Jay Broadus Hubbell, *The South in American Literature*, 63–65.

WILLIAM PARKS

BIBLIOGRAPHY

Parks may not have written for his newspapers and other publications, but he probably did. The standard account of his American newspapers is Clarence S. Brigham, *History and Bibliography of American Newspapers, 1680–1820*, 1 (Worcester, Mass., 1947): 218–19. A list of his Maryland imprints may be found in Lawrence C. Wroth, *History of Printing in Colonial Maryland*; and a more complete list, including his Virginia imprints, is contained in Wroth's *William Parks, Printer and Journalist of England and Colonial America* (Richmond, 1926). In the latter work, Wroth adds considerably to the list of imprints found in Clayton Torrence, *A Trial Bibliography of Colonial Virginia*, 2 vols. (Richmond, 1908–10). Wroth's list has been supplemented by William Henry Castles, Jr., "The *Virginia Gazette*, 1736–1766: Its Editors, Editorial Policies and Literary Content," *Dissertation Abstracts*, 33:3350–51 (Tennessee). All earlier bibliographies have omitted his Welsh printing: see William Rowlands, *Cambrian Bibliography*, D. Silvan Evans, ed. (Llanidloes, Wales, 1869), 327–28.

BIOGRAPHY AND CRITICISM

The earliest biographical notice was by Isaiah Thomas, *History of Printing in America*, 2nd ed., 1 (New York, 1874):320–21, 332–34. Lawrence C. Wroth, *William Parks, Printer and Journalist*, is an excellent biography, superseding all earlier accounts, including Wroth's own *History of Printing in Colonial Maryland*. The *DAB* sketch, by Wroth, is also excellent. Wroth published the will of William Parks in the *William and Mary Quarterly*, 2nd ser. 2 (1922):92–96. Leola V. Walker has recently adduced evidence of Parks's positions in the city government of Williamsburg: "Officials in the City Government of Colonial Williamsburg," *Virginia Magazine of History and Biography* 75 (1967):35–51, esp. 47.

There are a number of studies of William Parks's newspapers. An early but valuable account is Elizabeth Christine Cook, *Literary In-*

fluences in Colonial Newspapers, 1704–1750 (New York, 1912), 150–73. On the influence of Parks's *Maryland Gazette,* see Alfred Owen Aldridge, "Benjamin Franklin and the *Maryland Gazette,*" *Maryland Historical Magazine* 44 (1949): 177–89. Nicholas Joost disagreed with Aldridge concerning Parks's deism, and he published " 'Plain-Dealer' and *Free Thinker*: A Revaluation," *American Literature* 23 (1951): 31–37. Joost added a further note in "William Parks, Benjamin Franklin, and a Problem in Colonial Deism," *Mid-America,* n.s. 23 (1952): 3–13. For studies of Parks's *Virginia Gazette,* see Robert M. Myers, "The Old Dominion Looks to London: A Study of the English Literary Influences upon *The Virginia Gazette,* 1736–1766," *Virginia Magazine of History and Biography* 54 (1946): 195–217. A more recent survey, which supplements but does not supersede Myers is that of William H. Castles, Jr. (cited above). A study of the Monitor essay series is George H. and Judith C. Gibson, "The Influence of the *Tatler* and the *Spectator* on the 'Monitor,' " *Furman Studies* issue of the *Furman University Bulletin* 14, no. 1 (Nov., 1966): 12–23.

Some minor aspects of Parks's career are examined in Rutherfoord Goodwin, "The Williamsburg Paper Mill of William Parks, the Printer," *Papers of the Bibliographical Society of America* 31 (1937): 21–24 (a revised and expanded version was published separately at Lexington, Va., in 1939); August Klapper, *The Printer in Eighteenth-Century Williamsburg* (Williamsburg, 1955); and C. Clement Samford and John M. Hemphill II, *Bookbinding in Colonial Virginia* (Williamsburg, 1966). A convenient summary of Parks's publishing activities may be found in Douglas C. McMurtrie, *A History of Printing in the United States* . . . Vol. II, *Middle and South Atlantic States* (New York, 1936), 109–14, 278–84.

There is a brief account of Parks in Jay Broadus Hubbell, *The South in American Literature,* and a popular account by David Morgan, "William Parks—He Made Thoughts Live in Ink," *Virginia Cavalcade* 4 (Winter, 1954): 38–42.

RICHARD LEWIS

Checklist of Publications

1. *The Mouse-Trap, or the Battle of the Cambrians and Mice. A Poem. Translated into English, By R. Lewis.* Annapolis, 1727. Evans 3038. NI 362A. Sabin 32487. Wroth 43.

The only reprint is in Bernard C. Steiner, *Early Maryland Poetry*, 57–102.

2. An untitled, undated, anonymous poem, published in the Philadelphia *American Weekly Mercury*, no. 495, July 3, 1729, p. 3, col. 1–2.

   The 43-line poem is prefaced by the editorial statement, "We have receiv'd the following Lines out of the Country from an unknown Hand, Occasioned by some of our late Publications."

   Reasons for tentatively attributing this poem to Lewis are discussed in the text. Lemay 122.

3. "To Mr. Samuel Hastings, (Ship-wright of Philadelphia) on his launching the Maryland-Merchant, a large Ship built by him at Annapolis" was published in the Annapolis *Maryland Gazette*, Dec. 30, 1729. (No copy of this issue is extant.)

   This anonymous, undated poem was first attributed to Lewis by Alfred Owen Aldridge, "Benjamin Franklin and the *Maryland Gazette*," 186–89. The poem was reprinted in the *Pennsylvania Gazette*, Jan. 13, 1729/30, pp. 1–2, citing "From the Maryland Gazette, Decemb. 30." Lemay 129. It was also reprinted in the *American Weekly Mercury*, Jan. 14, 1729/30, pp. 3–4. Lemay 130.

4. "A Journey from Patapsco to Annapolis" was probably first published in the *Maryland Gazette*.

   Although the earliest printings of the poem contain no attribution, the author's name appeared in the reprinting cited as item *e* below. In addition to the following printings, the poem has been anthologized (in whole or in part) several times in the twentieth century.
   a. *Pennsylvania Gazette*, May 20, 1731. Lemay 184.
   b. *New York Gazette*, June 21, 1731 (slightly abridged). Lemay 187.
   c. London, *Weekly Register*, Jan 1, 1731/2. Lemay 198. This is a revised version of item *a* above. All subsequent eighteenth-century printings are from this version.
   d. London, *Gentleman's Magazine* 2 (Mar., 1732):669–71. Lemay 215.
   e. London, *Weekly Register*, Apr. 7, 1733. Lemay 252A. This printing first identifies the author: "By Mr. R. Lewis."
   f. London, Eustace Budgell's *Bee* 1 (Apr. 14, 1733):393–404: "by Mr. Lewis," Lemay 254.
   g. London, *London Magazine* 2 (Apr. 1733):204–207: "By Mr. R. Lewis." Lemay 258.
   h. Philadelphia, *American Museum* 9 (Jan.–June, 1791): 9–16. Reprinted from item *d* above.
   i. Baltimore, *The Metropolitan, A Monthly Magazine* 4 (Apr., 1856):188–90. This printing is supposedly from a partly illegible

manuscript; the poem is attributed to a Father John Lewis, S. J., and entitled "The Rev. Father Lewis—His Journey from Patapsco to Annapolis, April 4th, 1750."

j. Edward Duffield Neill, *Terra Maria: or, Threads of Maryland Colonial History* (Philadelphia, 1867), app., 239–52. Reprinted from item *d* above.

k. Percy H. Boynton, ed., *American Poetry* (New York, 1918), 24–29. Reprinted from item *d* above.

5. "An Account of the same Aurora Borealis," *Philosophical Transactions of the Royal Society of London* 37 (1731–32):69–70.

This is excerpted from Lewis's letter to Peter Collinson, dated Dec. 10, 1730.

6. "Food for Criticks."

It seems probable that this poem was printed in the *Maryland Gazette* before the end of May, 1731.

Reasons for tentatively attributing this anonymous poem to Lewis are discussed in the text.

This poem was printed, untitled, in the *New England Weekly Journal*, June 28, 1731, where it has local reference to Boston, Cambridge, etc. Lemay 188. It also appeared under the title "Food for Criticks" in the *Pennsylvania Gazette*, July 17, 1732, where it contains local references to Philadelphia, Pennsylvania, etc. Lemay 232. Long excerpts from the *New England Weekly Journal* version were printed by Evert A. Duyckinck and George L. Duyckinck, *Cyclopaedia of American Literature*, ed. M. Laird Simons, 1 (Philadelphia, 1875): 77–78.

7. *A Rhapsody*. Annapolis, 1732.

Evans 39995. NI 424A. Wegelin 241. Wroth 77.

This folio sheet, printed on both sides, is dated at the end, "March 1, 1731–2." George Sherburn, in Percy H. Boynton, ed., *American Poetry*, 601, who knew of only the *Gentleman's Magazine* reprinting of the poem, wrote, "This poem is almost certainly by Lewis." Wegelin and Wroth both unhesitatingly attribute it to him; and C. Lennart Carlson, "Richard Lewis and the Reception of his Work in England," *American Literature* 9 (1937–38):312 n. 34, wrote: "Although there is no conclusive external evidence to show that this poem is by Lewis, the attitude of the author, his pious resignation and implicit trust in God's care, as well as the style of his work, its imagery and descriptive touches, all suggest that he must be the author."

The poem was reprinted in the *Maryland Gazette*, Feb. 9, 1732/3 (Lemay 244); and in *Gentleman's Magazine* 4 (July, 1734):385 (Lemay 321).

8. "To John Ross Esqr, Clerk of the Council" exists in a manuscript folio notebook (entitled "Verses to the memory of his Excell'y

Benedict L. Calvert, Late Governor of Maryland Who died at Sea, June —— 1732"–call no. △ E3 V4) at the U. S. Naval Academy Library, Annapolis.

A manuscript note on the flyleaf says "Purchased in 1849 from Miss Eliza Maynadier from the library of the late Col. Maynaider of Annapolis." The poem, found on pp. 1–2, is dated at the end "Annapolis May 10, 1732."

Although Lewis's name is not signed to this poem, the reference to it in his "Verses, to the Memory of His Excelly Benedict Leonard Calvert . . ." (see no. 10 below) definitely attributes the poem to Lewis. "To John Ross" has been printed by Walter B. Norris, "Some Recently Found Poems on the Calverts," 118–20.

9.   "Congratulatory Verses, wrote at the arrival of our Honorable Proprietary" appeared in the *Pennsylvania Gazette*, Aug. 21, 1732.
Lemay 234.

Reasons for tentatively attributing this anonymous undated poem to Lewis are given in the text.

10.   "Verses.   To the Memory of His Excelly Benedict Leonard Calvert; Late Governor of the Province of Maryland . . ." exists in the manuscript folio notebook (see no. 8 above), pp. 5–12, at the U. S. Naval Academy Library, Annapolis.

The poem is signed at the end "Richd Lewis." This is the only poem in the notebook that has an attribution. It was printed by Norris (see no. 8 above), pp. 121–27.

11.   "A Letter from Mr. Richard Lewis, at Annapolis in Maryland, to Mr. Collinson, F. R. S. containing the Account of a remarkable Generation of Insects; of an Earthquake; and of an Explosion in the Air," *Philosophical Transactions of the Royal Society of London* 38 (1733–34):119–21. Lewis's letter to Peter Collinson is dated Oct. 27, 1732.

12.   *Carmen Seculare, for the Year M, DCC, XXXII . . . . To the Right Honourable Charles, . . . Lord Baron of Baltimore* [Annapolis, 1732].
Evans 39994.   NI 424A.   Wroth 76.

This folio pamphlet is dated Nov. 25, 1732. Although the original publication was anonymous, the contemporary reprinting settles the question of authorship. *Carmen Seculare* was reprinted in the London *Gentleman's Magazine* 3 (Apr., May, 1733):209–10, and 264. Lemay 257 and 259. On p. 209, the editor notes, "By Mr. Lewis, Author of the beautiful Poem inserted in our 4th Number, entitled, a Journey from Patapsco To Annapolis." It was reprinted (from the *Gentleman's Magazine*) in the Philadelphia *American Museum* 4, no. 5 (Nov., 1789):413–16; and again reprinted (in a garbled version) from the *Gentleman's Magazine* in the *U. S. Catholic Historical Magazine* 1 (Jan., 1887):54–59.

13. "Upon Prince Madoc's Expedition to the Country now called America, in the 12ᵗʰ Century. Humbly inscrib'd to the worthy Society of Ancient Britons, meeting at Philadelphia, March the 1st, 1733-4," was published in the *American Weekly Mercury*, Feb. 26, 1733/4.
Lemay 290.

> The poem is dated Jun. 29. 1733–4, but "Jun." obviously is a typographical slip for "Jan." The poem is signed with the pseudonym "Philo Cambrensis." I have given in the text my reasons for attributing the poem to Lewis.

14. "An Elegy on the much lamented Death of the Honourable Charles Calvert, Esq; formerly Governour in Chief of the Province of Maryland; and at the time of his Decease, Commissary-General, Judge of the Admiralty, Surveyor-General of the Western Shore, and President of the Council, Who departed this Life, February 2, 1733-4."
Lemay 294.

> This anonymous poem appeared in the *Maryland Gazette*, Mar. 15, 1733/4, 1–2. The unique copy of this issue of the *Maryland Gazette*, pp. 1–2 only, is in the manuscript notebook at the U. S. Naval Academy Library that contains several of Lewis's poems. Carlson (see no. 7 above), p. 314, first attributed this poem to Lewis, and I agree. The poem was reprinted by Norris (see no. 8 above), pp. 128–34, without attribution.

15. "Proposals . . . For founding An Academy at Annapolis for the Education of the Youth of this Province."

> This anonymous, undated manuscript was printed in the *Archives of Maryland* 38:456–61, by Bernard C. Steiner, who suggested an attribution to Lewis.

BIBLIOGRAPHY, BIOGRAPHY, AND CRITICISM

There is a brief list of the scholarship in Rubin, p. 241; and Davis, p. 54, provides a guide.

The most inclusive previous treatment is my "Richard Lewis and Augustan American Poetry," 80–101. The above chapter revises, corrects, and enlarges this article. In that article, p. 90, following George Sherburn (see no. 7 above), p. 601, I suggested that Lewis wrote "To the Right Hon. Lord Baltimore" (a poem that appeared in the *Gentleman's Magazine* 7 [Dec., 1737]:761); but this brief (32 lines) poem does him no credit, and it is probably by Thomas Brerewood, Jr. (1694?–1747), brother-in-law of Lord Baltimore. See Mrs. Russel Hastings, "Calvert and Darnell Gleanings from English Wills," *Maryland Historical Magazine* 22 (1927):342n.

There was a brief inquiry concerning Lewis by "B. W." in the *Historical Magazine* 4 (1860):152–53, but modern scholarship on Lewis began with Bernard C. Steiner's reprinting the *Muscipula or the Mouse Trap* in his *Early Maryland Poetry*. Mr. Steiner admitted in his "Introduction," p. 9, that he knew "nothing" of Lewis at that time. Eight years later, however, in Steiner's "Benedict Leonard Calvert, Esq. Governor of the Province of Maryland, 1727–1731," *Maryland Historical Magazine* 3 (1908):191–227, 283–342, esp. 340, Steiner had turned up the key letter from Calvert to Hearne that reveals all we yet know about the early life of Lewis. Steiner followed this up with "Richard Lewis," *Maryland Historical Magazine* 5 (1910):71–72, a brief discussion of Lewis's contributions to the *Philosophical Transactions of the Royal Society of London*. Steiner's last piece dealing in part with Lewis was "Early Classical Scholars of Maryland," *The Classical Weekly* 14, no. 24 (May 2, 1921), 185–90.

George Sherburn wrote an excellent note on Lewis in *American Poetry*, ed. Percy H. Boynton (New York, 1918), 600–602. Sherburn traced most of the English printing history of "A Journey from Patapsco to Annapolis" and he described several of the influences (including James Thomson) on Lewis. Lawrence C. Wroth added some information in *History of Printing in Colonial Maryland*, 65. Edward Holdsworth's Latin *Muscipula* and its various English translations (including that by Lewis) were discussed by Richmond Pugh Bond, *English Burlesque Poetry*, 215–23. "A Journey from Patapsco to Annapolis" was hailed by Robert A. Aubin, *Topographical Poetry in XVIII-Century England* (New York, 1936), 245–47, as the "first American journey-poem." Walter B. Norris first called attention to the existence and importance of the manuscript notebook (see no. 8) in "Some Recently Found Poems on the Calverts," 112–35. Unfortunately, Norris's texts are inaccurate. At the same time, C. Lennart Carlson, "Richard Lewis and the Reception of his Work in England," 301–16, published an account of the English printings of "A Journey from Patapsco to Annapolis," and added a few biographical facts. Carlson also included a discussion of "A Journey" in *The First Magazine: a History of the Gentleman's Magazine* (Providence, 1938), 189–92. Alfred Owen Aldridge, "Benjamin Franklin and the *Maryland Gazette*," 177–89, first noted the publication of "A Journey" in the *Pennsylvania Gazette*, suggested (pp. 186–89) that "To Mr. Samuel Hastings" was by Lewis, and called attention to the elegy and epitaph on Lewis.

JONAS GREEN

PUBLICATIONS

Green frequently wrote news notes and editorial comments in his newspaper, the *Maryland Gazette*, from 1745 to his death in 1767. To mention particular items from this wealth of material would be invidious, but I will list three pieces, which I believe are his: an apologia, May 3, 1753; a poem entitled "Memorandum for a Scene-Hauling in Severn River, near a delightful spring at the foot of Constitution Hill," Aug. 22, 1754 (reprinted in the *Maryland Historical Magazine* 52 [1957]:251); and the punning essay "Properties of a Gardiner," June 15, 1758. In addition to the many notes printed in the *Maryland Gazette*, Green wrote a large number of poems as the poet laureate of the Annapolis Tuesday Club. Dr. Alexander Hamilton copied out these poems in his "Record of the Tuesday Club" at the Maryland Historical Society and also in the "History of the Tuesday Club" at the Johns Hopkins University Library.

BIBLIOGRAPHY, BIOGRAPHY, AND CRITICISM

For an account of Green and a bibliography of his press, see Lawrence C. Wroth, *History of Printing in Colonial Maryland*. Douglas C. McMurtrie, in *History of Printing in the United States*, 114–17, provides a summary of Green's printing career, with excellent bibliographical notes on prior scholarship, 423–26. The standard bibliography of Green's *Maryland Gazette* is in Clarence S. Brigham, *History and Bibliography of American Newspapers* 1:219–22.

The earliest account of Green is in Isaiah Thomas, *History of Printing in America*, 1:321; 2:155–56. The *DAB* sketch is by Victor H. Paltsits. Minor corrections of the account in Wroth were made by William C. Kiessel, "The Green Family, A Dynasty of Printers,"

New England Historical and Genealogical Register 104 (1950):81–
93. Dr. Alexander Hamilton described Green at length in his "History
of the Tuesday Club," 1:345–46, and ch. 1 of bk. 6 is a facetious account (burlesquing the genre of hero-worship) "Of the witty sayings, apothigms and jests of Jonathan Grog Esqr [i. e., Jonas Green],
and other ingenious men"; and Benjamin Mifflin visited Green on his
tour of Maryland in 1762: see Victor Hugo Paltsits, ed., "Journal of
Benjamin Mifflin on a Tour from Philadelphia to Delaware and Maryland," *Bulletin of the New York Public Library* 39 (1935):432. Hamilton left several wash drawings of Jonas Green in his "Record of the
Tuesday Club" and in his "History of the Tuesday Club." Those in
the "Record" are listed in Anna Wells Rutledge, "Portraits in Varied
Media in the Collections of the Maryland Historical Society," *Maryland Historical Magazine* 41 (1946):295–96. And Charles Willson
Peale painted a miniature of Jonas Green: Charles C. Sellers, *Portraits
and Miniatures by Charles Willson Peale* (Philadelphia, 1952).

The first sustained discussion of Green's *Maryland Gazette* was
Elizabeth Christian Cook, *Literary Influences in Colonial Newspapers*, 173–78. Martha C. Howard has also indicated Green's indebtedness to the English periodical tradition in "The *Maryland Gazette*:
An American Imitation of the *Tatler* and the *Spectator*," *Maryland
Historical Magazine* 29 (1934):295–98. An account of Green's policies may be found in David C. Skaggs, "Editorial Policies of the
Maryland Gazette, 1765–1783," ibid. 59 (1964):341–49, which includes his successors. And for an annotated edition of the evaluation of
a contemporary, see my "Hamilton's Literary History of the *Maryland Gazette*," *William and Mary Quarterly*, 3rd ser. 23 (1966):273–
85.

On Green's Annapolis friends and milieu, see Charles A. Barker,
The Background of the Revolution in Maryland (New Haven, 1940);
Joseph Towne Wheeler, "Reading and Other Recreations of Marylanders, 1700–1766," *Maryland Historical Magazine* 37 (1943):37–55;
and Aubrey C. Land, *The Dulanys of Maryland* (Baltimore, 1955).

DR. ALEXANDER HAMILTON
CHECKLIST OF PUBLICATIONS

1. *Specimen medicum inaugurale, de morbis ossium ipsam substantiam afficientibus, ex causis internis oriundis.* Edinburgh, 1737.
   Guerra, p. 769.

2. A satire, signed "Theophilus Polypharmacus" on a poem ("The Baltimore Belles" by the Reverends Thomas Chase and Thomas Cradock) in the (Annapolis) *Maryland Gazette*, Feb. 4, 1745/6.

3. A mock advertisement (on the Reverend Thomas Chase), signed "Jehoiakim Jerkum" in the (Annapolis) *Maryland Gazette*, Mar. 18, 1745/6.

4. A satirical essay ("What News?") on American manners in the (Annapolis) *Maryland Gazette*, Jan. 7, 1746.

5. An evaluation of the American writings for Jonas Green's newspaper, signed "Don Francisco de Quevedo Villegas," in the (Annapolis) *Maryland Gazette*, June 29, 1748.
   Reprinted, with an introduction and notes, in my "Hamilton's Literary History of the *Maryland Gazette*," 273–85.

6. "A Discourse Delivered from the Chair in the Lodge-Room at Annapolis, by the Right Worshipful the Master of the Brethren of the Ancient and Honorable Society of Free and Accepted Masons," in John Gordon, *Brotherly Love Explained and Enforc'd* (Annapolis, 1750), 23–27.
   E40541. NI 316. Wroth 141.

7. *A Defense of Dr. Thomson's Discourse on the Preparation of the Body for the Small Pox.* Philadelphia, 1751.
   Evans 6689. Guerra A-243. NI 335.

8. "The Tuesday Club of Annapolis," *Maryland Historical Magazine* 1 (1906):59–65.
   This is the third chapter of the tenth book of Hamilton's "History of the Tuesday Club," which is now located at the Johns Hopkins University Library.

9. *Hamilton's Itinerarium: being a narrative of a Journey from Annapolis, Maryland, through Delaware, Pennsylvania, New York, New Jersey, Connecticut, Rhode Island, Massachusetts and New Hampshire, from May to September, 1744.* Ed. Albert Bushnell Hart. St. Louis, 1907.
   Clark 93.
   A recent and more thoroughly annotated edition is *Gentleman's Progress: The Itinerarium of Dr. Alexander Hamilton 1744*, ed. Carl Bridenbaugh (Chapel Hill, 1948).

BIBLIOGRAPHY, BIOGRAPHY, AND CRITICISM

A checklist of the scholarship is in Rubin, 344–45; and a brief bibliography is in Davis, 52.

For Hamilton's family and education, see George Hamilton, *A History of the House of Hamilton* (Edinburgh, 1933); Hew Scott, *Fasti Ecclisiae Scoticanae; the succession of ministers in the Church of Scotland from the Reformation* . . . (Edinburgh, 1915–50), has accounts of his father, two brothers, and two brothers-in-law, all of whom were ministers; and *List of the Graduates in Medicine in the University of Edinburgh from 1705 to 1866* (Edinburgh, 1867).

A brief biographical sketch of Hamilton by Hester Dorsey Richardson is in the *DAB*, but Carl Bridenbaugh's introduction to his edition of Hamilton's *Itinerarium*, pp. xi-xxxii, is fuller—though both are faulty in some details.

A number of articles deal directly and indirectly with the Tuesday Club. For Benjamin Franklin's visit to the club, see Robert R. Hare, "Electro Vitrifrico in Annapolis: Mr. Franklin Visits the Tuesday Club," *Maryland Historical Magazine* 58 (1963):62–66. For the insulting exchange between Hamilton and a supercilious colonial physician, see my "Franklin's 'Dr. Spence': The Reverend Archibald Spencer (1698?–1760), M. D.," ibid. 59 (1964):199–216. The earliest account of any length was the Reverend John G. Morris, "The Tuesday Club," *American Historical Record* 2 (1873):149–55. Walter B. Norris, in *Annapolis: Its Colonial and Naval History* (New York, 1925), 61–66, gives a brief sketch of the club, as do most of the histories of Maryland and of Annapolis. Dr. Sarah Elizabeth Freeman has written of Hamilton's various designs and medals of the club in "The Tuesday Club Medal," *The Numismatist* 57 (1945):1313–22. Hamilton's facetious wash drawings in "The Record of the Tuesday Club" are catalogued by Anna Wells Rutledge, "Portraits in Varied Media," 282–326. The same authority has discussed his drawings (including those in "A History of the Tuesday Club") in "A Humorous Artist in Colonial Maryland," *American Collector* 16 (Feb., 1947): 8–9, 14–15.

Hamilton's manuscripts are in the Huntington Library (the manuscript of the "Itinerarium"); the Library of Congress ("Record of the Tuesday Club, Vol. II"); the Maryland Historical Society ("Record of the Tuesday Club, Vol. I"; correspondence to and from Hamilton in the Dulany Papers; and two fragments of manuscript volumes, also in the Dulany Papers: (1) the last four leaves of the Preface to the "Record of the Tuesday Club," and (2) pp. 503–64 of the "History of the Tuesday Club"); and the Johns Hopkins University ("Annapolis, Md. Tuesday Club Record Book," being the minutes taken in and shortly after the club meetings; and the three volumes of "The History of the Ancient and Honourable Tuesday Club," which contains in vol. 3, pp. 465–700, a portion of an earlier draft of the "History").

Brief evaluations of Hamilton's *Itinerarium* may be found in the *Cambridge History of American Literature* 1 (New York, 1917): 11–13; in Jay Broadus Hubbell, *The South in American Literature*, 67–69; and in Arthur Hobson Quinn, ed., *Literature of the American People*, 103–105.

JAMES STERLING

Checklist of Publications

Publications Before Immigration to America

1. *The Rival Generals. A Tragedy as it was Acted at the Theatre-Royal, in Dublin: by his Majesty's Servants. By J. Sterling. A. B. Dublin: Printed by J. Carson, for Pat. Dugan, on Cork-Hill, Bookseller, MDCCXXII.*

    La Tourette Stockwell, *Dublin Theatres and Theatre Customs 1637–1820* (Kingsport, Tenn., 1938), 322 n. 58, locates a copy at Trinity College, Dublin. I have not been able to examine a copy, but Daniel Hipwell, "The Rev. James Sterling," *Notes and Queries*, 8th ser. 9 (1896):195–96, and the British Museum *Catalogue*, vol. 229, col. 727, distinguish between two Dublin editions of this year: one is octavo, one is twelvemo.

    No. 6011 in Carl J. Stratman, *Bibliography of English Printed Tragedy, 1565–1900* (Carbondale, Ill., 1966).

2. *The Rival Generals . . . . Dublin: J. Carson, 1722.*
    Copy: British Museum (see note to no. 1 above).
    Stratman 6010.

3. *The Rival Generals: A Tragedy. As it was Acted at the Theatre-Royal in Dublin, By his Majesty's Servants. By J. Sterling, A. B. London: Printed for A. Bettesworth, at the Red Lion in Pater-Noster-Row. 1722. Price 1s. 6d.*
    Copies: DLC, DFO, PU; and British Museum *Catalogue*, vol. 229, col. 727.
    Stratman 6009.

4. [Sterling has three poems, pp. 261, 245, 401, in Matthew Concanen], *Miscellaneous Poems, original and translated, By Several Hands. Viz. Dean Swift, Mr. Parnel, Mr. Delany, Mr. Brown, Mr. Ward, Mr. Sterling, Mr. Concanen, and Others. Published by Mr. Concanen. London: Printed for J. Peele, at Locke's-Head in Pater-noster-Row. MDCCXXIV.*

Arthur E. Case, *A Bibliography of English Poetical Miscellanies, 1521–1750* (Oxford, 1935), no. 332.

5. *The Prologue to the Parricide spoke by Mrs. Sterling the Author's Wife.* [Dublin, 1726?]

Stockwell, 322 n. 63, located a copy in the Gilbert Collection, Charleville Mall Library, Dublin.

6. *A Poem on the Art of Printing.* [Dublin], 1728.

This broadside contains two poems: Sterling's 54-line piece begins, "Say, Cadmus, by what Ray Divine inspir'd"; the other poem, by Constantia Grierson, begins "Hail Sacred Art! thou Gift of Heaven, design'd." The broadside is reproduced in E. R. McClintock Dix. "An Early Eighteenth-Century Broadside on Printing," *Royal Irish Academy Proceedings* 27 (1908–1909): 401–403. David F. Foxon, in a letter dated Mar. 14, 1967, kindly informed me that there are two other editions of this broadside at the British Museum (cf. British Museum *Catalogue*, vol. 92, cols. 321–22). Sterling's and Grierson's poems were also reprinted in the Philadelphia *American Weekly Mercury*, Dec. 24, 1728; and Sterling's piece (slightly revised) was included in *The Poetical Works of the Rev. James Sterling* (Dublin, 1734), 118–21; see no. 9 below.
See also American Publications, no. 6 below.

7. *The Loves of Hero and Leander from the Greek of Musaeus. By Mr. Sterling. To which are added, some New Translations from various Greek Authors, viz. Anacreon, Sappho, Julian, Theocritus, Bion, Moschus-Homer. By* [George Ogle], *Esq; Dublin: Printed by Andrew Crooke, Printer to the King's most Excellent Majesty at the King's Arms in Copper-Alley, 1728.* Copies: CSmH (top of title page mission), MH.

8. *The Loves of Hero and Leander. From the Greek of Musaeus. By Mr. Sterling. To which are added some new translations from various Greek authors, viz. Anacreon, Sappho, Julian, Theocritus, Bion, Moschus, and Homer. By another hand. London: J. Walthoe, 1728.* Copies: IU; British Museum *Catalogue*, vol. 167, col. 512.

9. [Sterling has four poems, pp. 62–65, in Matthew Concanen], *The Flower-Piece: A Collection of Miscellany Poems. By Several Hands. London, J. Walthoe . . . & H. Walthoe, 1731.*

    Arthur E. Case, *Bibliography of English Poetical Miscellanies*, no. 367.

10. *The Poetical Works of the Rev. James Sterling, Vol. I. Dublin: Printed by and for George Faulkner, in Essex-street, M, DCC, XXX, IV.*
    Copies: CLU-C, DFO, Bodleian.
    Stratman 6007.

    Only vol. 1 was published.

11. *The Parricide. A Tragedy. As it is Acted at the Theater in Good-man's Fields. By Mr. Sterling. London: Printed for John Walthoe, over-against the Royal-Exchange, in Cornhill. MDCCXXXVI. Price 1s. 6d.*
    Copies: CSmH, DLC, DFO, PU.
    Stratman 6008.

    Since Sterling's wife retired from the stage early in 1732, no. 5 above proves that *The Parricide* was written and acted considerably earlier than 1736.

12. ["The Loves of Hero and Leander. From the Greek of Musaeus. By Mr. Sterling. Museum ante omnes. Printed for J. Walthoe. Price one shilling."]

    This advertisement is at the end of the text of *The Parricide* (see no. 11 above): Lawrence C. Wroth, "James Sterling: Poet, Priest, and Prophet of Empire," American Antiquarian Society *Proceedings* 41 (1931):12 [of which an offprint is conveniently available], has specu-lated that it may be a printing of about 1735. It may also be no. 8 above.

13. "A new Prologue (wrote by Mr. Sterling) to the Conscious Lovers, which was acted in Goodman's Fields, in Honour of the Royal Wedding."
    London Magazine 5 (May, 1736):269.
    Lemay 407.

14. *A Friend in Need is a Friend in Deed, or, A Project, at this Critical Junction, to gain the Nation a hundred thousand Pounds per An-num from the Dutch: by an Irish Whale Fishery, Inscrib'd to Arthur Dobbs, Esq. Dublin, 1737.*
    Copy: RPJCB.
    This is attributed to Sterling in the John Carter Brown Library

catalogue. Since the attribution evidently depends on the similarity of this poem and *An Epistle to . . . Arthur Dobbs* (American Publications, no. 11 below), the authorship is questionable.

15. *An Ode on the Times, address'd to   the hope of Britain. London, Printed for R. Doddesley, at Tully's Head in Pall-Mall and Sold at the Pamphlet Shops* [1738].

This is entered in Stationers Register Feb. 28, 1738, to Thomas Gardner. It was previously printed in no. 10 above, *The Poetical Works of the Rev. James Sterling* (Dublin, 1734), 1–9.

There are numerous copies of this poem which (so far as I know) only David F. Foxon (in private correspondence, dated Mar. 6, 1967) has also attributed to Sterling.

Of most interest in the foregoing list is no. 10, the *Poetical Works*. In addition to reprinting *The Rival Generals* and *The Loves of Hero and Leander*, this volume includes six prologues or epilogues, five occasional poems, three political pieces, two ballads, two elegies, two translations, two *vers de société*, two poems on Swift, one imitation of Horace, one paraphrase of the Bible, one *ut pictura poesis*, one poem on printing, and several epigrams. These poetic genres are the same ones that Sterling used in America.

American Publications

1. "The Sixteenth Ode of Horace's Second Book, imitated and inscribed to His Excellency Samuel Ogle, Esq." appeared in the (Annapolis) *Maryland Gazette*, Mar. 31, 1747, p. 1. Lemay 827, 830.

This anonymous, undated poem was reprinted in the (Philadelphia) *Pennsylvania Gazette*, Apr. 23, 1747. I attribute it to Sterling because of its close similarity to no. 18 below.

2. "An Epithalamium . . . on the late Marriage of the Honourable Benedict Calvert, Esq.; with the agreeable young Lady, of your City, his Kinswoman" appeared in the (Annapolis) *Maryland Gazette*, May 18, 1748, dated "Kent County, April 29, 1748." Lemay 881.

The dateline, plus the content and style, suggests Sterling's authorship.

3. *An Epistle to the Hon. Arthur Dobbs, Esq.; In Europe From a Clergyman in America.* Dublin, MDCCLII.

Sabin 91330 incorrectly lists this as the second edition. Copies are at the Library of Congress and the Wisconsin Historical Society. In "To the Public" (sig A^v), Sterling says he is conscious that "some lines are defective in Diction, and some Sentiments are too warmly express'd." He explains that these faults "escaped his Notice chiefly on

Account of the ill State of Health he was in by a change of climate."
He adds that "very few copies [are] now printed," and that he will
amend the faults if the book should "merit a second edition." The
London edition, however, has practically no changes (see no. 4
below).

4. *An Epistle to the Hon. Arthur Dobbs, Esq.; in Europe from a
   Clergyman in America.* London, 1752.
   Sabin 91330.
   Copies are at the John Carter Brown Library and the Huntington
   Library. This is a reprinting of no. 3 above. Despite the misleading
   "To the Public" in the Dublin edition (omitted in this edition), these
   two printings differ only in the following:

		Dublin	*London*
Canto I.	181:	they	thy
	641:	statues	statutes
Canto II.			note to l. 240 misnumbered "235."
	314:	cape	cope
			note to l. 508 misnumbered "507."
Canto III.	33:	Lightemanant	Light emanant

   The poem was reviewed in the *Monthly Review* 6 (1752):237, and
   listed in the "Monthly Catalogue for March and April," *London
   Magazine* 20 (1752):195.

5. *A Sermon, preached before his Excellency the Governor of
   Maryland, and both Houses of Assembly at Annapolis, Decem-
   ber 13, 1754. By James Sterling.* Annapolis, 1755.
   Evans 7574. NI 804. Sabin 91331. Wroth 186.
   No. 6 below is a reprint.

6. *Zeal against the Enemies of our Country Pathetically Recommended: In a remarkable Sermon . . . By James Sterling.* London,
   1755.
   Sabin 91332.   See Wroth 186.
   A reprint of no. 5 above, but omitting the opening prayer.

7. "A Poem, Occasioned by his Majesty's most gracious Benevolence
   to his British Colonies in America, lately invaded by the French"
   was first published in the (Annapolis) *Maryland Gazette*, Dec.
   12, 1754.
   Lemay 1233, 1234, 1236, 1241, 1242.
   It was reprinted in the *Pennsylvania Gazette*, Jan. 14, 1755; the
   Pennsylvania Journal, Jan. 14, 1755; the *New York Gazette*, Feb. 3,
   1755; and the *Boston Gazette*, Feb. 11, 1755. Although the poem is undated and unsigned, I attribute it to Sterling because of its plea for

colonial union (which echoes Sterling's *Sermon*, nos. 5 and 6 above) and because of the reference in lines 84–85 to conversation and friendship with Horatio Sharpe, Maryland's governor.

8. An essay signed "Philopatris" urging Marylanders to fit out privateers. *Maryland Gazette*, Aug. 12, 1756.

   This essay, with an accompanying extract from a sermon preached on Aug. 1 on the same topic, is probably by Sterling, since the pseudonym is used later (see no. 23 below) by a Kent County writer, and since the citizens of Chestertown (Sterling's home) were at this time preparing a privateer.

9. "A Poem. On the Inventions of Letters and The Art of Printing: Addrest to Mr. Richardson in London . . ." appeared in the (Philadelphia) *American Magazine or Monthly Chronicle* 1 (Mar., 1758): 281–90.
   Lemay 1426.

   Dated "Kent County, Maryland, December 15, 1757," the poem is a revised and enlarged version of the work (Publications Before Immigration to America, no. 6 above) that Sterling originally wrote in 1728 for the Dublin Stationers Company.

   Albert H. Smyth, *The Philadelphia Magazines and their Contributors, 1741–1850* (Philadelphia, 1892), 37, attributed it to Sterling on the strength of a contemporary manuscript notation in the British Museum copy of the *American Magazine*. Lyon Norman Richardson, *A History of Early American Magazines, 1741–1789* (New York, 1931), 119–20, and Lawrence C. Wroth, "James Sterling," 36, concur. Wroth pointed out that the poem is ascribed to Sterling in a manuscript note in the Library of Congress copy of the *American Magazine*.

10. "The Patriot, A Poem" appeared in the *American Magazine or Monthly Chronicle* 1 (Apr., 1758):332–35.
    Lemay 1434.

    Although the poem is neither dated nor signed, it was attributed to Sterling by Richardson (see no. 8 above), p. 121, and by Wroth (see no. 8 above), p. 36, because of content and style; and I agree.

11. "The Dame of Cyprus" was published in the *American Magazine or Monthly Chronicle* 1 (Apr., 1758):335.
    Lemay 1435.

    This anonymous, undated poem has not previously been attributed to Sterling, but it appears in the *American Magazine* between two other poems by him (no. 10 above and no. 12 below), and it is in style and subject typical of Sterling.

12. An untitled epigram, beginning "Leda's twin-sons, when they together shin'd," was published in the *American Magazine or Monthly Chronicle* 1 (Apr., 1758):335–36. Lemay 1436.

Dated "Kent in Maryland," this charming *vers de société* in Latin and English is attributed to Sterling on the basis of the dateline.

13. "A Pastoral. To his Excellency George Thomas..." appeared in the *American Magazine or Monthly Chronicle* 1 (May, 1758):390–97. Lemay 1441.

This anonymous, undated poem is attributed to Sterling by Smyth (see no. 8 above), p. 37, Richardson (see no. 8 above), p. 120, and Wroth (see no. 8 above), p. 36, on the basis of contemporary manuscript annotations in the British Museum and Library of Congress copies of the *American Magazine*. Written in 1744 on the death of Alexander Pope, the poem is prefaced by letters from the author and Provost William Smith. The first half of the poem is reprinted in Kenneth Silverman, ed., *Colonial American Poetry* (New York, 1968), 328–31.

14. "The Royal Comet" appeared in the *American Magazine or Monthly Chronicle* 1 (Aug., 1758):550–52. Lemay 1472.

Dated "Kent in Maryland, July 14th, 1758," the poem has been attributed to Sterling by Richardson (see no. 8 above), p. 121, on the basis of an annotation in the Library of Congress copy, and by Wroth (see no. 8 above), p. 37, because of the dateline.

15. "Epitaph on the Late Lord Howe" was published in the *American Magazine or Monthly Chronicle* 1 (Sept., 1758):604–605. Lemay 1484.

Dated "Kent in Maryland, August 14th, 1758," the poem was reprinted in the *Maryland Gazette*, Nov. 16, 1758; the *New Hampshire Gazette*, Mar. 2, 1759; and the *New York Gazette*, Mar. 19, 1759. It has been attributed to Sterling by Smyth (see no. 8 above), p. 39, by Richardson (see no. 8 above), p. 119, and by Wroth (see no. 8 above), p. 37. The prefatory note contains biographical information identifying Sterling as the author.

16. "Elogium" was published in the *American Magazine or Monthly Chronicle* 1 (Sept., 1758):609. Lemay 1487.

Dated "E Comitatu Cantii in Mariae Provincia," this poem has been attributed to Sterling by Wroth (see no. 8 above), p. 37. Richardson (see no. 8 above), p. 118 n. 83, however, attributed the poem to John Beveridge; but in the opinion of Leo M. Kaiser, "John Beveridge: Latin Poet of Two Worlds," *Classical Journal* 58 (1963):224 n. 1, the poem is not by Beveridge. Because of the dateline, I concur with Wroth.

17. "Apollinis Querla, Sive Epigramma" appeared in the *American Magazine or Monthly Chronicle* 1 (Oct., 1758):642.
Lemay 1506.

It is reprinted in John Beveridge, *Epistolae Familiares* (Philadelphia, 1765), 46–47, where it is attributed to "Authore Rev. Ja. Sterlino."

18. "The 22d Ode of the first Book of Horace imitated; and inscribed to the Lady of his late Excellency Samuel Ogle, Esquire" appeared in the *American Magazine or Monthly Chronicle* 1 (Oct., 1758):642–43.
Lemay 1507.

Dated "Kent in Maryland, October 25th, 1758," this imitation was reprinted in the *American Museum* 4, no. iv (Oct., 1788), 385. Richardson (see no. 8 above), p. 121, attributed it to Sterling on the basis of a contemporary manuscript notation in the Library of Congress copy of the *American Magazine*; and Wroth (see no. 8 above), p. 37, ascribed it to him because of the dateline. It is a revision of a poem that Sterling previously published in *The Poetical Works of the Rev. James Sterling* (Dublin, 1734), 17–21. Reprinted in Silverman (see no. 13 above), pp. 331–33.

19. "Verses Occasioned by the Success of the British Arms in the Year 1759" was published in the *Maryland Gazette*, Jan. 3, 1760.
Lemay 1695.

Style, content, and place of publication suggest an attribution to Sterling. Reprinted in Silverman (see no. 13 above), pp. 339–44.

20. "Prologue, spoken by Mr. Douglass" was published in the *Maryland Gazette*, Mar. 6, 1760.
Lemay 1732.

Jonas Green, editor of the *Maryland Gazette*, said that the author was "a Gentleman in this Province, whose poetical Works have render'd him justly Admir'd by all Encouragers of the Liberal Arts." I attribute it to Sterling because of the style, content, and Green's remarks. The poem has been reprinted several times since George O. Seilhamer included it in his *History of the American Theatre Before the Revolution* 1 (Philadelphia, 1888):116. Reprinted in Silverman (see no. 13 above), pp. 345–46.

21. "Epilogue, spoken by Mrs. Douglass" was published with no. 20 above in the *Maryland Gazette*, Mar. 6, 1760.

   Lemay 1733.

   For the attribution, see no. 20 above. It has been reprinted several times since its appearance in Seilhamer, vol. 1, pp. 116–17.

22. "Panegyrical Verses on the Death of General Wolfe" appeared in the *Pennsylvania Gazette*, Mar. 13, 1760.

   Lemay 1734.

   Dated "Kent, in Maryland, November 8, 1759," it was reprinted in the *New York Gazette*, Apr. 14, 1760, and the *Boston Gazette*, May 26, 1760. The prefatory note indirectly identifies the author: "Being a Production of this Country, and containing a sufficient Share of that Energy of Expression, Dignity of Sentiment, and Glow of Spirit which characterize all the Performances of the reverend and worthy Author of the Epitaph on Lord Howe [no. 15 above] (published in a late *American Magazine*) from whose Hand they come. . . ."

23. An essay (evidently part of a sermon) signed "Philo-patris" and dated "Kent County, March 1, 1762" on the relation between trade and agriculture. *Maryland Gazette*, Mar. 11, 1762.

   See no. 8 above. The subject, dateline, and form suggest Sterling's authorship.

Bibliography, Biography, and Criticism

For Sterling's English plays, Carl J. Stratman, *Bibliography of English Printed Tragedy*, is excellent. The only previous attempt to list Sterling's American poetry is Lawrence C. Wroth's monograph "James Sterling," 25–76. Rubin, 295, lists the most recent scholarship; and Davis, 57, gives a bibliography.

The histories of drama usually contain information on Sterling. Of the older histories John Genest, *Some Account of the English Stage from 1660–1830* (Bath, 1832), is still useful. Allardyce Nicoll's survey, *A History of English Drama, 1660–1900*, vol. 2 (Cambridge, 1952), contains a brief characterization. For the history of Sterling's plays on the London stage, see Emmett L. Avery, *The London Stage, 1660–1800: A Calendar . . . Part 2: 1700–1729* (Carbondale, Ill., 1960); and Arthur H. Scouten, *The London Stage, 1660–1800; A Calendar . . . Part 3: 1729–1747* (Carbondale, Ill., 1961). Probably the best portrait of Sterling and the Irish stage of his day is La Tourette Stockwell, *Dublin Theatres and Theatre Customs*. Recently, William Smith

Clark has contributed two studies which add to our knowledge of the Irish theater of the period: *The Irish Stage in the Country Towns, 1720 to 1800* (Oxford, 1965) and *The Early Irish Stage: The Beginnings to 1720* (Oxford, 1955).

Modern biographical study of Sterling began with W. Sparrow Simpson's request for information in *Notes and Queries*, 8th ser. 9 (1896):23–24. W. A. Henderson's reply, ibid., 196, merely quoted David E. Baker et al., *Biographica Dramatica* (London, 1812), and added a note on the production history of *The Parracide*. Daniel Hipwell's reply, *Notes and Queries*, 8th ser. 9 (1896):195–96, gave a brief bibliography. W. J. Lawrence, in *Notes and Queries*, 10th ser. 3 (1905):385–86, gave a budget of information on Sterling's first wife; and Lorton Wilson, ibid., 13th ser. 1 (1923):13–14, presented a genealogy of the poet. Annette Townsend, *The Auchmuty Family of Scotland and America* (New York, 1932), explains Sterling's relationship with Robert Auchmuty. And George Dames Burtchaell and Thomas Ulick Sadleir, *Alumni Dublinenses* ... (Dublin, 1935), supply the little information known of Sterling's education.

Three works provide nearly all the known facts concerning Sterling's ministerial career: Gerald Fothergill, *A List of Emigrant Ministers to America, 1690–1811* (London, 1904); Nelson Waite Rightmyer, *Maryland's Established Church* (Baltimore, 1956); and William Wilson Manross, ed., *The Fulham Papers in the Lambeth Palace Library* (Oxford, 1965). Although Rufus Wilmot Griswold only knew Sterling as an "anonymous writer of Kent, In Maryland," he wrote an appreciation of Sterling's poetry in the *American Magazine* and quoted excerpts from it: *The Poets and Poetry of America* (New York, 1874), 24 (first published in 1842). The earliest identification of American poetry by James Sterling was made by Albert H. Smyth in *Philadelphia Magazines*. Later, Lyon N. Richardson added to this list in *History of Early American Magazines*; and at the same time, Wroth published his masterful monograph.

Several works contribute to an understanding of Sterling's mercantile concerns. Wroth is the best authority. The basic facts are in Great Britain, Board of Trade, *Journal of the Commissioners for Trade and Plantations from January 1749–50 to December 1753* (London, 1932). An early discussion of the Labrador proposal is in Edwin Swift Balch, "Arctic Expeditions Sent from the American Colonies," *Pennsylvania Magazine of History and Biography* 31 (1907):421. More recent is Bertha Solis-Cohen, "Philadelphia's Expedition to Labrador," *Pennsylvania History* 19 (1952):148–62; Leonard Woods Labaree et al., eds., *The Papers of Benjamin Franklin*, 4 (New Haven, 1962); and Percy G. Adams, "The Case of Swaine Versus Drage: An Eighteenth Century Publishing Mystery Solved," *Essays in History and Literature Presented by Fellows of the Newberry Library to Stanley Pargellis* (Chicago, 1965), 157–68. Thomas Seccombe's biographical sketch of Sterling in the *DNB* is not as full as Lawrence C. Wroth's more recent *DAB* account. Biographical sources are available at the Maryland Hall of Records, Annapolis, and some have been published in the *Archives of Maryland*, cited in the footnotes to the text. A long obituary and an epitaph of Sterling by "Euphranor" appeared in the *Maryland Gazette*, Nov. 17, 1763.

Although Smyth, Richardson, and Wroth all have some critical judgments of Sterling, there has appeared so far only one discerning evaluation: Kenneth Silverman, in his anthology *Colonial American Poetry*, 6–7, which also contains the only modern reprintings from his poetry, 328–33, 339–46.

THOMAS BACON

CHECKLIST OF PUBLICATIONS

Separate Titles

1. *A Compleat System of the Revenue of Ireland, in Its Several Branches of Import, Export, and Inland Duties . . . By Thomas Bacon, of the Custom-house, Dublin.* Dublin: R. Reilly, 1737.

2. *Two Sermons, Preached to a Congregation of Black Slaves, at the Parish Church of S. P., in the Province of Maryland, by an American Pastor.* London: John Oliver, 1749. Sabin 2687.

    For a reprint, see no. 11 below.

3. *Four Sermons, Upon the Great and Indispensible Duty of All Christian Masters and Mistresses to Bring Up Their Negro Slaves in the Knowledge and Fear of God . . . By the Rev. Thomas Bacon . . . .* London: John Oliver, 1750. Sabin 2685.

4. *A Sermon Preached at the Parish Church of St. Peter's, in Talbot County, Maryland: On Sunday the 14th of October, 1750 for the*

Benefit of a Charity Working School to be Set Up in the Said Parish, Etc. London: John Oliver, 1751.

5. *Six Sermons on the Several Duties of Masters, Mistresses, Slaves, Etc.* London: John Oliver, 1751.
Sabin 2685.

6. [*A Sermon Preached at the Parish Church of St. Peter, in Talbot County, Maryland: On Sunday the 23d of August, 1752, on Opening a Charity Working School, Etc.* London: John Oliver, 1753?].
   No copy known. Title found in no. 12 below.
   Cecelius Calvert wrote to Bacon, Jan. 5, 1754, "He [Frederick, Lord Baltimore] thanks you for your obliging Dedication & Edifyed Sermon, Preached on the occasion at St. Peters Parish the 23d of August 1752." From Baltimore's reply, it seems unlikely to me that the reference could have been to anything but a separate printed sermon, dedicated to Baltimore, with the above title.

7. [*Four Sermons, Preached at the Paris Church of St. Peter, in Talbot County, in the Province of Maryland, . . . Viz. Two Sermons to Black Slaves, and Two Sermons for the Benefit of a Charity Working-School, in the Above Parish, for the Maintenance and Education of Orphans and Poor Children, and Negroes.* London: John Oliver, 1753].
   No copy known. No. 12 below is evidently a reprint. Further evidence for the existence of this volume is that it was once in the Maryland Diocesan Society Library, and although the volume cannot now be located, the catalogue card (in the Peabody Library, Baltimore, in 1965) has the above title.

8. *A Sermon, Preached at Annapolis, in Maryland, Before a Society of Free and Accepted Masons . . . June 25, 1753.* Annapolis: Jonas Green, 1753.
Wroth 163.

9. [Thomas Bacon and Cecilius Calvert]. *An Answer to the Queries on the Proprietary Government of Maryland, Inserted in the Public Ledger. Also an Answer to Remarks Upon a Message Sent by the Lower House of Assembly of Maryland, 1762. Published in 1763. Containing a Defence of the Lord-Proprietor From the Calumnies and Misrepresentations of the Remarker; and Also a Vindication of the Upper House, in Their Conduct Relative to a*

Supply Bill for his Majesty's Service. By a Friend to Maryland. [London: ?], 1764.
Sabin 45069. Wroth 248.

The authors are determined by *Archives of Maryland*, 59:lxxi-lxxxii; see also *Archives of Maryland* 9:417–18.

10. *Laws of Maryland At Large* . . . . Annapolis: Jonas Green, 1765 [for 1766].
Evans 10049. Sabin 2684. Wroth 254.

11. *Two Sermons, Preached to a Congregation of Slaves, at the Parish Church of S. P. in Maryland. By An American Pastor.* London, 1782.

A reprint of no. 2 above.

12. *Four Sermons, Preached at the Parish Church of St. Peter, in Talbot County, in the Province of Maryland, . . . Viz. Two Sermons to Black Slaves, and Two Sermons for the Benefit of a Charity Working-School, in the Above Parish, for the Maintenance and Education of Orphans and Poor Children, and Negroes.* London, Printed by J. Oliver, 1753. Reprinted at Bath, by R. Cruttwell, 1783.

13. *Sermons Addressed to Masters and Servants, and Published in the Year 1743, by the Rev. Thomas Bacon . . . Now Republished With Other Tracts and Dialogues on the Same Subject, and Recommended to All Masters and Mistresses to be Used in Their Families. By The Rev. William Meade.* Winchester, Va.: John Heiskell, Printer, [1813].
Sabin 2686.

14. *Writings of the Rev. Thomas Bacon.* London: Religious Tract Society, n.d.

15. *Writings of the Rev. Thomas Bacon.* Philadelphia: Presbyterian Board Publication, 1843.

16. *Tract, Addressed to Masters and Mistresses, on the Subject of the Religious Instruction of Their Slaves* [n.p., n.d.].

*Work Attributed to Bacon on
Doubtful Authority*

General Abridgment of Cases in Equity Argued and Adjudged in the High Court of Chancery, Etc., Vol. 1. London, 1732.

This is ascribed to "Mr. Bacon, a gentleman of Ireland" by the Hartwell Catalogue. It has also been ascribed to "Mr. Pooley": Sweet & Maxwell's *Legal Bibliography*, 2:109–10.

Works Perhaps Never Completed or Printed

1. *A General Treatise of Naval Trade and Commerce. As Founded on the Laws and Statutes of This Realm. In Two Volumes . . . With an Appendix, by Thomas Bacon. Setting Forth the Material Points Wherein the Laws Relating to the Revenue of Ireland Differ From Those in Force in Great Britain.* Vol. 1. Dublin: Thomas Bacon, 1742.

   No copy found.
   Probably only the appendix was to be composed by Bacon. According to the advertisements in his newspapers, the first volume was published in Aug., 1742 (*Dublin Mercury*, no. 59. Aug. 14, 1742). This volume was advertised in the *Dublin Mercury* and *Dublin Gazette* through *Dublin Gazette* no. 1610, Jan. 25, 1743. If vol. 2 were never published, Bacon's appendix probably does not exist. Sweet & Maxwell's *Legal Bibliography*, 2:164, lists London editions 1738–39, 1740 and 1753.

2. *A Large Collection of Gross Errors, Blunders, Mistakes &C. &C Extracted from the Translation (Erroneously So Called) of the Dean of Coleraine Published by Edward Exshaw and Company.* Dublin: Thomas Bacon, 1742.

   No copy found.
   This was advertised in the *Dublin Gazette*, nos. 1577–1587, as "Now preparing for the Press, and speedily will be published." In the *Dublin Gazette*, no. 1588, for Tuesday, Nov. 16, it was advertised as "On Monday the 29th Inst. will be published." No further advertisements appeared. It seems unlikely that it was printed.

Newspapers Published by Bacon

1. The *Dublin Mercury*, nos. 1–71. Jan. 23 to Sept. 25, 1742. British Museum holdings: Wanting nos. 29, 30, 41, 44, 45. Nos. 1, 9, 10, 21, 26, 38–40, 43, 49, 50, 54, and 58 are imperfect, wanting pp. 1 and 2.
   Munter 136. [R. L. Munter, *A Hand List of Irish Newspapers, 1685–1750* (London, 1960)].

2. The *Dublin Gazette*, nos. 1 [for no. 1574]–1658. September 28, 1742–July 12, 1743.
   Copy: British Museum.
   Munter 137.

Published Manuscript

"Proceedings of the Parochial Clergy," *Maryland Historical Magazine* 3 (1908):257–73.

BIBLIOGRAPHY, BIOGRAPHY, AND CRITICISM

There is a general account of Bacon, a detailed story of his compiling the *Laws of Maryland*, and an excellent bibliography of his Maryland imprints in Lawrence C. Wroth, *History of Printing in Colonial Maryland*. The best list of his publications is in *The National Union Catalog: Pre-1956 Imprints*, 29:532–33. There is a brief checklist of the scholarship in Rubin, p. 337, and a brief bibliography in Davis, p. 49.

The best biography is Ethan Allen's "Rev. Thomas Bacon 1745–1768, incumbent of St. Peter's Talbot Co., and All Saints, Frederick Co., Maryland" [*American Quarterly*] *Church Review* 17 (1865): 430–51. Allen's sketch in William B. Sprague, *Annals of the American Pulpit* 5 (New York, 1859):117–21, is a condensation of this article. The *DAB* sketch by Harris Elwood Starr adds no information. An interesting biographical note by a young contemporary of Bacon, the Reverend Jonathan Boucher, is in William Hutchinson, *History of the County of Cumberland* (Carlisle, England, 1794), 2:41n. The major sources for Bacon's ministerial career are Nelson Waite Rightmyer, *Maryland's Established Church*; William Wilson Manross, ed., *Fulham Papers*; and Ethan Allen's article, cited above.

Bacon's own newspapers (cited above) provide the best information concerning his activities in Whitehaven and Dublin. His dealings with Samuel Richardson and his relationship with the other Dublin printers are mentioned by William M. Sale, Jr., "*Sir Charles Grandison* and the Dublin Pirates," *Yale University Library Gazette* 7 (1932–33):80–86. Information about Bacon's millionaire brother Anthony may be found in Louis B. Namier, "Anthony Bacon, M.P., an Eighteenth-Century Merchant," *Journal of Economics and Business History* 2 (1929–30):20–70. Namier ignores American sources.

For Bacon's friends and early career in Maryland, see Samuel A. Harrison and Oswald Tilghman, *History of Talbot County, Maryland*, 2 vols. (Baltimore, 1915). Bacon's friendship with Henry Callister (whose voluminous papers in the collections of the Maryland Diocesan Society Library are deposited at the Maryland Historical Society) is a major subject of Lawrence C. Wroth's "A Maryland

Merchant and His Friends in 1750," *Maryland Historical Magazine* 6 (1911):213–40. Dr. Alexander Hamilton characterizes Bacon under the mock-name of "Signior Lardini" in his "The History of the Tuesday Club," MS, the Johns Hopkins University Library, and chronicles his visits to the club in "The Record of the Tuesday Club," MS, Maryland Historical Society. Bacon's intellectual interests are, in part, the subject of two articles by Joseph Towne Wheeler: "Reading Interests of Maryland Planters and Merchants, 1700–1776," *Maryland Historical Magazine* 37 (1942):26–41; and "Reading Interests of the Professional Classes in Colonial Maryland, 1700–1776," ibid., 36 (1941):184–201. On his political publications, see J. Hall Pleasants, in the *Archives of Maryland*, 59:lxxi-lxxxii. There is no criticism.

INDEX

Bennett, Richard, 37, 188
Berkeley, Gov. William, 101–108
Beveridge, John, 300
Bisset, James, 336
Bladen, Thomas, 319
Blair, John, 322
Blount, Richard, 11
Bogherst, William, 53, 343
Bond, Dr. Phineas, 226, 241
Bond, Dr. Thomas, 226
Bordley, John Beale, 246, 247, 250
Bordley, Stephen, 191, 232, 245, 246, 247, 339
Bordley, Thomas; brings Parks to America, 74; and Cook, 81, 93, 94, 112
Boston, 74, 117, 188, 194, 218, 219, 220, 223, 224
Boucher, Rev. Jonathan, 189, 201 n, 255, 314, 318, 319
Bozman, Col. Thomas, 335
Bradford, Andrew, 112, 194, 195
Bray, Rev. Thomas, 6, 332
Brent, Col. Giles, 104
Brereton, 333
Brett, Dr. John, 226
Brice, John, 340
Brogden, Rev. William, 191, 208, 239, 325, 326, 329
Brooke, Father John (alias Ferdinand Poulton), 24
Brotherly Love Explained, 239
Buchanan, Lloyd, 288
Buckskin (the word), 187, 221–22
Buffalo, 187, 301, 302
Bullen, John, 245, 246, 247, 252
Bullen, Thomas, 315
Burlesque, 5, 59, 74, 77, 91, 190, 211; defined by Lewis, 129–30
Byfield, W., 180–81

"C" (probably Henry Callister), 210
Cadwalader, Dr. Thomas, 226, 227
Callister, Ewan, 317, 320
Callister, Henry, 189, 193, 210, 264, 317, 318, 319, 320, 329, 330, 331, 333, 334, 335, 341, 342
Calvert, Gov. Benedict Leonard (d. 1732), and Lewis, 126, 127–28, 129, 160–64, 165, 170, 267
Calvert, Cecil, second baron Baltimore (d. 1675), 4, 5, 6, 8, 11, 12, 13, 14, 16, 17, 24, 28, 29, 31, 32, 33, 34, 36, 37, 51, 64, 168

Calvert, Cecilius, 322, 331, 335, 338, 339, 340
Calvert, Gov. Charles (d. 1734), 126, 129, 162, 188, 267; elegy on, 176–79
Calvert, Charles, fifth baron Baltimore (d. 1751), 74, 93, 121, 165, 247. *See also* Lewis, Richard, *Carmen Seculare*
Calvert, Elizabeth, 267, 269
Calvert, Frederick, sixth baron Baltimore (d. 1771), 274; and Thomas Bacon, 322, 325, 331, 338, 339, 340, 342
Calvert, George, first baron Baltimore, 8, 10, 11
Calvert, Leonard, 15, 17, 19, 20, 21, 23, 24, 27, 28, 32
Calvert, Philip, 43
Campbell, Isaac, 326, 329
Canada, 25, 285
Canadian, 300
Canary Isles, 13
Cape Breton, 287
Carroll, Charles, 123, 245, 328
Carter, Charles, 125
Cartesian philosophy, 147, 148
Carthegena, 287
Cary, John, 342
Casson, Henry, 288
Catalogue, 19, 55; of rivers, 133, 137 n, 165; of nature, 150, 154. *See also* Promotion tract
Catholics, 28, 29, 30, 31, 32, 57, 66, 85, 193, 227, 276, 287, 327; prejudice against, 29–31, 287; satirized, 85. *See also* French and Indian war; White, Andrew
"Cato," 211
Catskill Mountains, 226
Cecil county, 93
Celebrations, occasions of, 173. *See also* St. David's Day, St. Patrick's Day
Cervantes, 104, 222
Chamberlaine, Col. Samuel, 189, 334
Character types. *See* American character
Charles I (king of England), 29, 49
Charles II (king of England), 32, 105
Charleston, 190
The Charter of Maryland, 112
Chase, Richard, 200
Chase, Rev. Thomas, 190, 191, 193, 197, 200, 229, 230, 325–29, 333
Chesapeake area, 106

English (*cont.*)
merchants swindled by Americans, 57–58, 78, 90; merchants usurious, 106
Enlightenment, 293
Essay series, 114; "Busy-Body," 131; "The Monitor," 115; "P. P.," 120; "The Plain-Dealer," 115–18; "Virginia Centinel," 209
"Eumolpus," 237
Evins, Ellinor, 50, 65
Evolution, 226
Ewing, George, 316, 317
Exshaw, Edward, 316, 317
"Th'Extinguisher" (Jacob Henderson), 121

Fall, Henry, 245
Farrell, Hubert, 105, 108
Faulkner, George, 315
Federalist period, 312
Feke, Robert, 223
Fendall, Josias, 43
F. H. C. Society, 254
Fitzhugh, William, 250, 254, 288
Fleet, Henry, 5, 17, 18, 21
Flint, Mary, 194
Florida, 13
Folk: anecdote, 75, 78, 228; song, iv, 90–91; story of bear sucking paws, 85; story of Americans cheating English, 57–58, 78, 90; story of greenhorn's encounter with Indians, 84
Forester, Rev. George W., 281
Francis, Tench, 188
Franklin, Benjamin, 75, 188, 192; and William Parks, 117, 118; and Richard Lewis, 131, 147, 148, 181, 182; and Jonas Green, 194, 198, 212; and Dr. Alexander Hamilton, 234, 236, 237, 252; and James Sterling, 270, 272, 273; and Thomas Bacon, 313, 338
—*Autobiography*, 20, 117, 181; "Craven Street Gazette," 212; *Nature ... of a Paper Currency*, 131; "The Speech of Miss Polly Baker," 198. *See also* Newspapers cited, *Pennsylvania Gazette*
Frederick, king of Prussia, 299
Freedom and Love, 239
"a Freeholder," 237, 238
Freemasons, 188, 239–40; sermons, 208, 324–25

French and Indian war: in Green's *Maryland Gazette*, 209; and John Bacon, 324, 333–34; James Sterling on, 281–82, 282–87, 292, 294, 299–300, 308–309
Frontier, 50, 77, 187, 221–22; barbarism of, xi, 64. *See also* Wilderness
Frontiersman, 337; development as hero, 176. *See also Buckskin*
Fuller, William, 34
Fust, Johann, 293
"Future Glory of America." *See* Translatio theme

Galloway, John, 191
Galloway, Samuel, 191
Gassaway, John, 245
George I, 279, 282
Georgia, 276
Gerard, Father John, 9
Ghiselin, Reverdy, 340
Gifford, Henry, 260
Gilmore, Dr. George, 322
Glorious Revolution, 6, 287
Golden Age. *See* Primitivism
Goldesburgh, Elizabeth, 68
Goldesburgh, Thomas, 68
Goldie, Rev. George, 337
Golding, Master, 18
Gooch, Sir William, 122, 199, 236
Gordon, Rev. John, 191, 193, 202, 208, 233, 239, 245, 246, 247, 248, 250, 252, 323, 325
Gordon, Robert, 191, 245, 252, 325
Gordon, Thomas, 321
Grantham, Capt. Thomas, 106, 107
Granville, George, 277
Great Awakening: Hamilton and, 226–27, 228; Sterling and, 262–63, 264
Great Chain of Being, 58, 226, 278
Greece, 132, 135, 152, 154, 284, 291
Green, Frederick, 201
Green, John, 195
Green, Jonas (1712–1767), 125, 189, 190, 191, 192, *193–212*
—biography: birth, 194; parents, 194; to Philadelphia, 194; marriage, 195; to Annapolis, 195; children, 195, 201; finances, 195, 196, 198, 200, 209; scientific interests, 197–98; lawsuit, 200; religion, 198, 208, 209; civic affairs, 209, 211; printing career, 193–202, 208–11; and *Maryland Gazette*, 196–

"Philalethes," 118
"Philanthropos" (Jacob Henderson), 238
"Phil-Eleutherus," 197
"Philo-Muses" (Dr. Adam Thomson), 197
"Philo P. P. P." (Jonas Green), 206
Philosophical Transactions, 137, 166, 293
"Philotypographus" (Dr. Alexander Hamilton), 238, 239, 288, 309
Phoenicians, 85, 99
Picts, 83
Piedmont plateau, 73, 187
Pine, John, 137
Piper, Michael, 74
"A Planter," 236
Planter's lot described, 303–306
Plowden, Edmund, 26
Political writing: 120–22, 198, 199–200, 211, 235, 237–38; Thomas Bordley's, 112; Daniel Dulany's, 121–22; Thomas Bacon's, 338–40, 341–42
Politics, 74, 216, 244–45, 246; anarchy of colonial, 285; Bacon's role in, 325–29, 338–39, 341–42; printing comes to Maryland because of, 112; Hamilton's role in, 216, 244–45
Population: of Maryland, 73, 74, 187; of colonies, 287; of England, 30, 58, 60
Poulton, Ferdinand. *See* Brooke, Father John
Preston, Richard, 37
Prevost d'Exiles, Antoine François, 316, 317
Price, Rev. Roger, 261
Price, William, 44, 45
Primitivism, 54, 225, 246–47, 276. *See also* America, as Eden
Prince, Thomas, 194
Printing: exactness of, demanded, 267; poems on, 123, 288–93. *See also* Green, Jonas; Parks, William
Pritchard, John, 197
Privateers, 288
Progress-piece, 191; Lewis's use of, 134–35, 136, 168; Sterling's use of, 280, 291, 292–93, 307, 311
Promotion tract, x; purpose and audience, 6; influence on creation of American character, 6–7; catalogues in, 13, 19, 55; devices of, 19, 20, 65;

Promotion tract (*cont.*) organization of, 53 n; Indians and, 21, 62; letters and, 19, 20, 65
—Andrew White's, 4–5, 8, 11–24, 27, 28–29; John Hammond's, 5, 28, 38–42, 46–47; George Alsop's, 5, 48, 51–67, 68–69
—anti-promotion tract, 74, 75, 76; "New England Ballad" as, 90–91; and "New England's Annoyances," 91; and *Sot-Weed Factor*, 90–92
Psychology, Lockean, 147
Pufendorf, Samuel, 122
Puritans, 5, 26, 28, 32, 33, 34, 35, 36, 44, 49, 62, 69

"Quaker Sermon," 189
Quakers, 58, 68, 69; in *Sot-Weed Factor*, 88, 89, 91; satirized, 220
Quevedo Villegas, Don Francisco de, 222, 233–37, 239

Rabelais, 222
Randolph, John, 123
Razolini, Onorio, 218
Reade, Capt. John, 4
Reading, Thomas, 74
Reason, idea of, attacked, 147; praised, 292; and religion, 264
"A Recruiting Song, for the Maryland Independent Company," 334
Religion, 66; and promotion tracts, 28–31; of Maryland, characterized, 321; of Dr. Alexander Hamilton, 226–27, 238; toleration, 34, 169; Presbyterians, 66, 79, 217, 226. *See also* Catholics; *Clergy of Maryland*; Deism; Great Awakening; Puritans
Remarks upon a Message, sent by the Upper to the Lower House, 339
Retreat. *See* Wilderness, as retreat
Rich, Rev., 315
Richard, James, 200
Richardson, Joseph, 211
Richison, Thomas, 189
Rider, John, 113
Ridgely, Nicholas, 120
Rights of Englishmen, 284
Roanoke, 23
Robertson, Mary, 213
Robinson, David, 334
Rogers, William, 191, 246, 251, 252
Romans, 303

Men of Letters in Colonial Maryland was set manually on the Linotype and printed letterpress at Heritage Printers, Inc., Charlotte, North Carolina, bound at Kingsport Press, Inc., Kingsport, Tennessee.

The book was designed in Janson type by Jim Billingsley; the calligraphic initials were handlettered. The paper on which the book is printed bears the watermark of the S. D. Warren Company and was developed for an effective life of at least three hundred years.

THE UNIVERSITY OF TENNESSEE PRESS
Knoxville